The *Odyssey* Re-Formed

The *Odyssey* Re-Formed

Frederick Ahl and

Hanna M. Roisman

Cornell University Press

ITHACA AND LONDON

First published 1996 by Cornell University Press.

The paper in this book meets the minimum requirements of the American National Standard for Information Sciences—Permanence of Paper for Printed Library Materials, ANSI Z39.48-1984.

Library of Congress Cataloging-in-Publication Data

Ahl, Frederick
The Odyssey re-formed / Frederick Ahl and Hanna M. Roisman.
p. cm.
Includes bibliographical references (p.) and index.
ISBN 0-8014-3221-9 (cloth : alk. paper). — ISBN 0-8014-8335-2 (paper : alk. paper)
1. Homer. Odyssey. 2. Odysseus (Greek mythology) in literature.
3. Epic poetry, Greek—History and criticism. I. Roisman, Hanna. II. Title.
PA4167.A37 1996
883'.01—dc20 96-53

FOR

NANCY SOKOL

AND IN MEMORY OF

DAVID KELLER

CONTENTS

PREFACE

This book came into being because two critics, beginning from different suppositions and working along different lines, found themselves reaching similar conclusions about the *Odyssey* and therefore decided to write together, rather than separately. After almost four years of collaboration, argument, and compromise, which yielded a work neither of us could have produced alone, it was no longer possible to determine who had come up with a particular idea or who had developed it first. There is a little of both of us in every sentence. While we have separately drawn on our previously published work, a comparison of the ideas shows how we have tempered and reshaped each other's thinking. We also became progressively more aware as we worked of how our approaches to the *Odyssey* had been conditioned both by our divergent, general cultural upbringings and by our specific scholarly backgrounds.

Influenced also by our constant need to teach the *Odyssey* in English translation as well as in the original, we have written with an eye for the general reader, whose knowledge of Homer is not based on a reading of the original Greek. Of course there are moments when a key word or phrase cannot be satisfactorily rendered by an English word or expression, or when a wordplay would require a substantial departure from the conventionally "literal" sense if we were to reproduce it in English. In such cases we cite the Greek text in transliterated form to make our point clearer. The translations, which are no more than quite literal and unliterary renditions of the Greek, are our own and are based on Thomas W. Allen's Oxford Classical Text (second edition, 1917).

We discuss the *Odyssey* more or less book by book—though we treat some passages in more detail than others, focusing particularly on instances in which the narrator or an internal speaker seems to be contradicting something stated authoritatively as fact elsewhere in the epic, for our central concern is with what we would describe as Homeric rhetoric. Nonetheless, we made a conscious decision to stay within the vocabulary of conventional critical discourse and to avoid, wherever possible, the technical diction of rhetoric or deconstruction.

Advice and suggestions have flowed from many friends, colleagues, and, above all, students in our classes over the years. In attempting to answer students' questions we have been led into many new areas of thought and interpretation.

We owe an especial debt of gratitude to Bernhard Kendler of Cornell University Press and to the anonymous reader of the manuscript when it was under consideration. Without Bernie's encouragement the manuscript might never have seen the light of day. The Press's anonymous reader saved us from some serious errors and helped us hone many an argument. Marian Rogers has put the manuscript neatly in shape, and colleagues from across the country offered advice at various stages of our work. We would also like to thank Colby College for giving us the opportunity to work together at critical moments; John Coleman of Cornell University for making his office available to us during the summers; Judith Ginsburg, David Mankin, Piero Pucci, Beatrice Gershenson Rosenberg, and Nancy Sokol of Cornell University for their help and encouragement; Joel J. Farber of Franklin and Marshall College; Rosemary Donnelly of the Athens Centre; our current and former students at Colby, Cornell, Penn State, Tel Aviv, and Vassar, especially Sharon Ace, Christopher H. Roosevelt, and Zila Rozenblitt; and, above all, Yossi, Elad, and Shalev Roisman and Mary, Kate, and Sid Ahl, who had to put up with us as we struggled to get the book together.

FREDERICK AHL and HANNA M. ROISMAN

Ithaca, New York, and Waterville, Maine

INTRODUCTION

The *Odyssey* is probably the best known and generally loved work in ancient Greek literature. Although usually read in translation, it is better served by translators than most ancient "classics," and, with the exception of its constant and vital wordplay, most of its elements survive remarkably well in the skilled verse renditions of Robert Fitzgerald, Richmond Lattimore, and Allen Mandelbaum, to name only the most popular poetic versions available. The reader who wishes to explore the deeper poetic resonances of the *Odyssey*, however, faces a daunting task. The mass of critical scholarship is so enormous and so often addressed exclusively to the professional scholar that it is hard to know where to begin. The temptation is either to give up altogether or to take refuge in some slim volume which reassures us, in layman's language, of the work's simplicity and that shapes it into terms and thoughts comfortable to our own cultural sensibilities. That is why there are, essentially, two different *Odysseys* to be found in modern discussion: the complex and much disputed *Odyssey* of the scholar, which lies largely out of reach of the general reader, and the straightforward tale of the "ideal Greek hero" commonly presented in the brief overviews offered in high school and undergraduate courses.

A sophisticated grasp of the *Odyssey* is nonetheless within reach of readers who do not know ancient Greek, provided they engage some issues which intrigue and puzzle scholars. Greekless readers may even be able to perceive themes in the text that elude scholars, since they are free of the subtle constraints of dogma and schools of interpretation that channel and direct scholarly inquiry. Our aim is to help such readers come to terms with the *Odyssey*. We cannot, of course, summarize all problems or all theories about the *Odyssey* and Homer that have arisen during the last two centuries, though in the notes we try to direct adventurous readers to several contested issues. Nor can we comment on the entire *Odyssey*, or even most of the scholarly literature, since every line of the *Odyssey* has been the subject of academic contention over years and centuries.

We see the *Odyssey* as a work created by an artistic imagination, a poem which is not just open to critical and interpretative readings but demands them. Hence the bulk of this book is, in fact, a detailed reading of the epic itself. Our reading is founded upon two methodological assumptions. First, we assume that the manipulative power of language is central to the construction and art of the *Odyssey*. Our second assumption is that the Homeric muse presupposes the existence of a broad pool of mythic material known to the ancient audience from bardic and other traditions which she could modify or even displace with her new formulation. These two assumptions are interlocked. The first prompts us to a rhetorical reading of the *Odyssey* along the lines of ancient practice, which preferred artful and oblique expression, figured speech, to plain and blunt statements. This rhetorical reading exposes the narrative strategies which allow us to detect the dialectical tension between the competing versions of the mythical material that we hypothesize in our second assumption.

We are, then, reading for the inexplicit rather than for the explicit—or, to put it another way, we are reading for the rhetorical and poetic Homer rather than for the scholar's Homer. Our hope is that we can escape the conventional positivist demand for the explicit—for "facts," for "logical consistency." The categories of fact and logical consistency contain what are generally agreed to be the "straightforward" statements made in a text, which are then accepted as true and reliable indications of authorial meaning and intent. Any contradictions that arise among such statements are usually accounted for by the postulation of diverse accretions in an oral tradition, imprecise rhapsodic redaction, and so forth. Yet if we listen to the Homeric muse and the characters in their dramatic interactions, we quickly see that what persuades is more important than what is factual (and thus, in a modern sense, "true"). Or, to state it differently: poetic truth, as Homer's Alcinous recognizes, is not at all the same thing as fact. Once we have taken this step, we can begin to perceive and to enjoy the complex strategic thrust of the narrative, which is far richer than conventional, nonrhetorical readings admit, and find evidence of a breathtaking and inimitable artistic imagination.

Similarly, our assumption that the Homeric muse selects and innovates within a large force field of mythic traditions enables us to avoid the scholarly stalemate that results from accepting the theory that the *Odyssey* is an oral composition insofar as it ratifies positivist readings and, at the same time, from rejecting (or ignoring) the historical consequences of the oral theory, namely, that the bards must have been manipulating and selecting from numerous, regionally varied, and often conflicting traditions. Once we allow ourselves to follow the various voices of the poem (i.e., the narrative muse and interacting characters) as they inform, entertain, challenge, and persuade, we are much freer to react critically to what they say and to follow their rhetorical maneuvers wherever they lead. In our reading there are no ultimately "authoritative" voices or statements, only artful constructions and appeals whose status as "truth" depends upon the decision of the listeners, internal or external to the *Odyssey*. Careful listening discloses competing rhetorical truths (rather than scholarly inconsistencies) that are evoked by allusion to other parts of the epic or of its traditional mythic matrix. Far from being a rational rhapsodic arrangement of a canonical tradition, the *Odyssey* is, then, a creative (even radically innovative) work, challenging and paradoxical.

Having outlined what we would attempt to do, we must now explain how we believe the critical stalemate that impelled us to undertake this study came about.

The Beginning of Modern Criticism

Modern classical scholarship begins with an assault on Homer. Most studies of Homer are a mixture of wild assumptions and extreme caution. Beginning with Charles Perrault, François d'Aubignac, and, above all, F. A. Wolf, attention focused on what were taken to be inconsistencies and contradictions in the texts of the *Iliad* and the *Odyssey*. The conclusion was that the epics were really collections of shorter works of different poets sutured together by rhapsodes.[1] There was, of course, no conclusive evidence, and there were those who disagreed, none more eloquently and economically than H. J. Rose. Rose, ironically enough in retrospect, blames the success of the "separatists" on literary critics, with their "microscopic hunting of minute inconsistencies and flaws in logic."[2] Nowadays "unitarians" who call themselves literary critics would probably blame "philologists."

Separatism enjoyed less success in Britain and the United States than in Germany and France until the late 1920s when Milman Parry advanced, in French, and in Paris, his "oral" theory of Homeric composition and insisted that the *Iliad* and the *Odyssey* should not be treated as "literary" epics.[3] English-speaking scholars then began to react with more enthusiasm. The timing was right. The "oral" theory was born in the days when even the excavator of Cnossus, Arthur Evans, was convinced that Greek speakers were not well established in Greece until around 1000 B.C.E. Recollections in Greek literature of the Bronze Age, of the Trojan War, and of the Mycenaean and Minoan civilizations that archaeology had dramatically brought to light must, then, have carried over from non-Greek civilizations. The theory of Homeric oral composition admirably suited the data as interpreted at the time, and parallels drawn from Yugoslav oral poetry were ethnically and geographically almost perfect. At the time the Greeks were generally thought to have entered the Balkan peninsula from the mountains to the north. And it was known from Greek and Roman sources that the Celts, who had once occupied central Europe, continued to preserve their bardic traditions orally long after writing was available to them. The pieces all fitted.[4]

Some scholars, however, notably B. L. Ullman, disagreed. Ullman contended that the Greeks must have learned alphabetic writing from the Phoenicians as soon as (or even before) they arrived. He thought the forms of the earliest known Greek inscriptions most closely corresponded to Phoenician scripts of the thirteenth century B.C.E. But most classicists followed Rhys Carpenter in preferring a date closer to that of the earliest Greek alphabetic inscriptions: around the beginning of the eighth century B.C.E.[5] Then, in the 1950s, Michael Ventris and John Chadwick deciphered tablets found chiefly in Pylos, Mycenae, and Cnossus, written in a script scholars called Linear B, some of which were dated to as early as the sixteenth century B.C.E.[6] This script proved to be Greek, and to contain names and grammatical forms strongly evocative of the Homeric poems.

These discoveries made it clear that the Greeks had been in the Mediterranean area for a millennium, maybe more, before the date scholars had generally surmised, and that at least some major centers had developed a means of writing Greek. Yet Homeric scholars were not ready to abandon the "oral" theory of the transmission of the *Iliad* and the *Odyssey*, even though holding to it meant they had to turn a blind eye to certain differences between the Homeric epics and their modern parallels. The language and forms of the Homeric poems more closely resembled what was now known to be everyday use between 1400 and 1200 B.C.E. than what could be reconstructed as everyday use in any area of the Greek-speaking world between 775 and 500 B.C.E. In short, the oralists were postulating that an illiterate society maintained not only detailed memories of towns and peoples that had long since ceased to exist, but that it did so in an archaic form of language remarkably faithful to Bronze Age usage and magnificently rich in vocabulary, imagery, and style. In the parallels adduced from modern oral traditions, emanating from cultures reinforced by long centuries of at least liturgical literacy, the poetry is, by and large, in the contemporary vernacular of the singers, rustic in style, and discontinuous in theme.

Greek heroic, hexameter poetry maintains at least the residue of the forms and conventions of Homeric diction from the *Iliad* to Nonnus's *Dionysiaca* in the sixth century C.E. Epic usage demanded archaism, formulaic utterances, and repetitions. Thus the presence of constantly reused epithets and phrases, also imitated by Latin epicists, need not indicate that the earliest surviving works of that tradition, the *Iliad* and the *Odyssey*, were any more "oral" than, say, the *Aeneid* or Apollonius's *Argonautica*, once it is granted that writing was available. There is little doubt that the written conventions and transmission of epic, together with the practice of public recitations of the *Iliad* and the *Odyssey* (not to mention their use as texts in schools) enabled epic language and diction to survive and remain familiar long after it ceased to resemble the vernacular in any part of the Greek-speaking world.[7] Education in the Greek world was, from our earliest knowledge of it, inextricably intertwined with the Homeric poems, to the annoyance of Plato and, later, the Christians, and defending Homer's place in the curriculum was high on the agenda of the last pagan emperor of Rome, Julian, in the fourth century C.E.

In theory, of course, the Homeric poems could have been written down in the Linear B script of the Greek Bronze Age. But many scholars thought Linear B (which was used for writing on clay) was unsuited to the writing of poetry. G. S. Kirk comments that the Greeks of the second millennium B.C.E. "still lacked a script suitable for literature; the Linear B syllabary was evidently confined to basic documentary uses, whereas cuneiform and hieroglyphs had long been used for historical, religious, and even purely artistic literature."[8] It would be fairer to say that there is no epigraphic *evidence* that poetic texts were recorded in Linear B, since other commentators observed how unsuited Linear B is for writing on the very medium upon which it was written—clay. It is better suited to writing with ink on leaves or papyrus.

Here we see the conflicting conclusions drawn from two different arguments from silence. Kirk's contention that Linear B is not suitable for writing literature assumes that only the kinds of alphabetic scripts used in the Western world are really adequate to that end. Yet if people could write in a system without vowels (which had to be adduced by the reader), as did the Phoenicians, it could be argued that equally satisfactory results could be achieved by people writing with a syllabic writing system (such as Linear B) that required the reader to suppress superfluous vowels. Notable poetic literatures, such as those of China and Japan, were produced by peoples writing in scripts which offer difficulties that make Egyptian hieroglyphs or Linear B seem masterpieces of economic design.

The arguments about Greek illiteracy (or the unwieldiness of Linear B) could not so readily be used against alphabetic writing, if it were available around 1100 B.C.E. Rhys Carpenter's late date for the transmission of the alphabet, therefore, assumed great importance as a tenet for the advocates of the "oral" Homer. The latest examples of Linear B belong to around 1200 B.C.E. If the alphabet was not introduced until, say, 800, the

Greeks were illiterate for three or four centuries. Therefore, scholars contended, transmission of the epics had to be oral. To cite Charles Beye: "Since no system of writing is known to have survived the collapse of the Mycenaean culture, it is necessary to assume the oral, not written transmission of this material."[9] This is not quite correct. Unless the Cypriots reinvented the linear script ex nihilo, their syllabary, which was used for writing Greek until at least the third century B.C.E., is precisely such a survival. The Cypriot syllabary is an obvious "relative" of Linear B. At least ten of its symbols are virtually identical to those of Linear B in form and value. And it was used alongside the Greek alphabet in Cyprus for around five hundred years *after* the latest date suggested for the introduction of the Greek alphabet.

The consensus among Greek epigraphers remains that the earliest Greek alphabetic writing dates to around 775 B.C.E., and most place its introduction to Greece about a generation before the earliest extant examples. Such a cautious dating may be wrong. But, given the accepted criteria of proof, namely, the presence of tangible evidence for alphabetic writing in Greek, there is currently no acceptable means of *demonstrating* that such a dating is wrong, until archaeologists unearth inscriptions of an indisputably earlier date. In the unlikely event such a discovery is made, the introduction of the alphabet will be reassigned to a generation before the most conservatively late dating of the new evidence. Many classicists would probably echo Rhys Carpenter's contention: "I hold it unthinkable that it [the alphabet] should have lingered for any considerable lapse of time among this intensely active people."[10] The problem with Carpenter's idealized and active Greeks, however, is that they spent a surprising number of centuries trading with people who used alphabetic writing before it occurred to them to adapt it for their own use at such lightning speed and over such a wide geographic area.

True, experts on Canaanite alphabetic writing insist, as Ullman did, that, given the development of the Canaanite scripts, it makes sense to postulate a transmission of the alphabet from Phoenicians to Greeks *at least* two hundred, and perhaps even six hundred, years earlier.[11] But this supposition is not popular with classicists. If archaeological evidence some day establishes that the Greeks used alphabetic writing much earlier, classicists who favor a late dating will have erred only as to the time of its introduction, not as to its use at a given moment. They would be respectably wrong. Semiticists can afford to be bolder, since their reputations and research do not depend on whether the Greeks adapted the Phoenician alphabet in the Bronze Age or the Iron Age.

Peter James has recently rethought a theory that offers another, neglected, and less "respectable," way out of the dilemma. Following in the footsteps of Cecil Torr and Jens Lieblein and, more apologetically but more definitively, of Immanuel Velikovsky, he denies the existence of what scholars have come to call the Dark Ages of Greece following the fall of the Bronze Age civilizations of Mycenae and Cnossus.[12] Whatever the virtues or drawbacks of James's theory may be—and this is not the place nor are we the people to comment on them—they do not materially affect the issue of continued literacy among the Greeks, which, in our judgment, is as adequately demonstrated as can be expected by the continued existence of the Cypriot syllabary bridging whatever period of time may have elapsed between the fall of Mycenae and the introduction of alphabetic writing among the Greeks. Michael Ventris's declaration, which was deservedly questioned, that he made no use of the Cypriot syllabary in the early phases of his decipherment of Linear B should not be taken, even if believed, to mean that there is no direct connection between the two syllabic systems of writing. James is probably right, however, in his assessment of why those who denied the existence of the "Dark Ages" of illiteracy were ignored or, in Velikovsky's case, mocked: "Torr went against the grain of contemporary trends. . . . Velikovsky was too much of an outsider. . . . Academic inertia and the convenience of following long established traditions have discouraged any serious challenge to the accepted chronology." Advocates of the "oral" Homer enjoy a secure position because the scholarly consensus, by and large, favors their position and because there is not (and probably cannot ever be) hard evidence that their beliefs are either correct or incorrect. Adam Parry observed: "That the poems themselves, as we have them, were in fact composed in the process of improvising recitation has not been proven, and probably cannot now be proved."[13] The oral composition theory is so entrenched that it is hard to write about the epics without either assuming its validity, as does Gregory Nagy in his influential study *The Best of the Achaeans,* or disputing it on, more or less, its own ground, as Barry Powell does in his more recent *Homer and the Origin of the Greek Alphabet.*[14] In *The Cambridge History of Classical Literature,* often the first resort for many English-speaking readers, the "orality" of Homer is presented as beyond question: "This orality of Homer is of prime importance not only as a factor in the transmission and survival of his work but also in determining its true quality. It is imperative to understand about the *Iliad* and *Odyssey* that they were composed wholly or substantially without the aid of writing, by a poet or poets who were effectively illiterate, and for audiences that could not (or at least for literary purposes did not) read."[15] Similarly, Nagy observes of the *Iliad* and *Odyssey:* "We see at work here an inherited medium where the composition can be simultaneous with performance—or at least where composition becomes a reality only in performance."[16]

The problem is that we "see" or "hear" this "oral" Homer only in the mind's eye of scholarly hypothesis and imagination. It would be fairer to say that the Homeric epics have some features in common with the oral epic and bardic traditions that anthropologists have transcribed from more recent cultures than to insist on their literal orality. The *Iliad* and *Odyssey* were remarkably fixed written texts from the moment that their presence first became evident around three thousand years ago, until scholars decided that they might have originated in oral tradition. In this respect they are quite unlike, say, the Byzantine epic *Digenis Akritas*, which survives in different recensions (and in Bulgarian as well as Greek). Ruth Finnegan's observation is salutory here: it is not possible to draw a clear line between oral and written literature (especially in the case of Homer), since "oral" literature does not usually reach the hands of scholars until it has taken written form.[17]

In antiquity, most written poetry was also performed and was therefore arguably more committed to engaging a live, plural, listening audience than an isolated and silent reader. A middle road is taken by scholars like R. D. Dawe in his translation and commentary on the *Odyssey*. Dawe assumes there are both oral and written elements in the work before us: "By the time the reader has worked his way through the commentary in this book, he is likely to have reached the conclusion that at any rate some of the episodes in the poem owe their shape and substance to written composition: the scissors and paste are still detectable. But in other places we may find an imprecision or blurring of themes which smacks of something more extempore." Following this path, he aims "to bring the reader into the closest possible contact with what—according to our present texts—Homer actually said; not what a rational man might suppose he must have meant, and not with what we might wish he had said; but with what he did say."[18]

Critics are often happy to assume that neither the *Iliad* nor the *Odyssey* is "literary," since such an assumption liberates them from the obligation to produce cogent literary *interpretations* of either epic. Literary criticism has been regarded with great suspicion and as an inexact and unscientific pursuit since the time of Plato (at least). Socrates in *Protagoras* 347E rejects "the discussion of the meaning of texts from the poets, 'whom it is impossible to interrogate about what they were saying.'" Since Socrates equates "the meaning of a text with the intention of its author," he rejects such interpretation because "some say the poet meant one thing, some say he meant another thing, and they go on talking about something they have no power to verify."[19] M. C. Stokes notes that literary criticism is "an activity the Platonic Socrates held in this dialogue (347A–348A) and elsewhere to be of little importance."[20] But, increasingly, scholars are breaking free. Parry's theory of the "oral" origins and transmission of Homeric epic encouraged us to approach the *Iliad* and the *Odyssey* not as the products of a master poetic craftsman but as a patchwork, with evident sutures, of different and sometimes conflicting oral traditions. It has, as Michael Lynn-George remarks, given the notion of the "naive" *Iliad* and *Odyssey* popular a century or so ago, a new lease on life. Both the oral and the naive Homer are rooted in the assumption that the poems cannot be consciously and rhetorically complex, a verbal tapestry, with contradictions and paradoxes an integral part of its design: its woof and warp, its contrasting colors.

The complexity of the *Odyssey*, for the scholar who espouses the "oral" theory, arises because a number of simple traditions are combined, not because the complexity was born of an artistic imagination. The epic is a patchwork of (simple) independent traditions assembled by someone (or some group) who, through either artistic carelessness or scholarly meticulousness, failed to disguise the seams in the work. Whoever put the whole work together is, then, aptly named a rhapsode, a "stitcher of song."

The reasons subtending scholarly belief in the oral nature of Homeric epic have little or nothing to do with the facts, such as they are, that we have at our disposal. Lynn-George states the matter this way:

> All [Milman] Parry's work took shape within the horizon of a world whose cardinal points had been charted by Matthew Arnold. For this critic concerned with the *translation* of Homer, the epics were conceived as the great utopia of transparency: Homeric poetry possessed "the pure lines of an Ionian horizon, the liquid clearness of an Ionian sky." Within this context of unequivocal purity, transparency and translatability, Arnold promulgated those four cardinal truths—"directness," "simplicity," "rapidity" and "nobility"—which were to acquire canonical status in Homeric scholarship. Parry's theory of orality was to be marked by a constant return to and reworking of these principles.[21]

Where a word, phrase, passage, or entire work is susceptible of more than one meaning, an effort is usually made to select among the possibilities to determine the *single* meaning deemed most appropriate. Since the most honored level of scholarship among classicists has been, necessarily, the establishment of authoritative texts, it is hardly surprising that the criteria of textual criticism have passed over into literary criticism of ancient authors. We can be sure that only one of the various alternative readings offered by manuscripts or editors can be correct. Therefore we tend to assume, by extension, that only one resonance of a particular word or phrase is "intended" in a given context. The resonance selected will usually be that which reinforces what we take to be the most straightforward, the most *explicit* interpretation of the text.

Some critics who think differently have despaired. "The modern era," R. Palmer argues concerning classical scholarship, "is something like the 'golden age of literalism.'" Similarly, Maija Väisänen notes that minimalist interpretation, the intentionality of what is taken as explicit, still remains, for some, an article of faith.[22] That it should be so is odd at the end of a century when D. H. Kahnweiler sponsored such cubist artists as Picasso because, Pierre Assouline observes, "he wanted the painting to be more faithful, more precise, more exact than a photographic reproduction."[23]

But much progress is being made. Michael Nagler, Norman Austin, Seth Schein, and Richard Martin have achieved remarkable success in combining the "oral" Homer with a high level of poetic criticism.[24]

The Explicit and the Implicit

Preference for directness and simplicity of diction owes something to the widespread belief that there exists a special relationship between simplicity and truth—that "the one" is more likely to be true than "the many." The ideal of simplicity pervades our artistic as well as our intellectual and religious concepts and often defines scholarly goals in terms of a search for *Struktur und Einheit.* For many, simplicity is the essence of the classical itself: a style of art, literature, and thought that seeks and defines an ideal in clear, straightforward terms and forms. The classical artist is giving us clear models he approves and wants us to approve. Ambiguity, ever subversive of the straightforward and sincere, cannot be part of his repertoire unless he expressly tells us that it is. The results of this mode of thought are frequently odd. One complaint leveled against the "oral" Homer by some critics was that it "deterred the reader from taking Homer's expression at its face value."[25] Paolo Vivante recognized that the "oral" theory had replaced poetic complexity with other scholarly complexities. He did not want either. Although the scales are tipping toward a more penetrating literary approach to the epics, the problem remains that scholars find it difficult to pursue literary analysis without maintaining that Homer is one person, not a "committee" of bards.[26] Such an approach, however, amounts to a declaration of scholarly war on those convinced that the *Iliad* and the *Odyssey* are "oral."

There seemed no convenient way out until the deconstructionists, as foes of authorial intentionality, reunified Homer and stayed clear of oralist wrath by talking of text rather than of poet, thereby allowing us to examine the text's poetic implications quite apart from presuppositions about what the poet (or poets) may or may not have intended. The text is an entity regardless of how it was assembled. Deconstructionists, in fact, are following, however unconsciously, a Stoic approach to criticism "that would seem explicitly to sanction the idea that the reader, not the text, determines the field of reference, and hence the scope of the meaning."[27]

What neither Stoics nor deconstructionists (because of their reluctance to discuss intent) take sufficiently into account is the extent to which, and the methods by which, poets actively deconstruct their audiences or readers: that poets who produce works for performance often compose dialectically, in full awareness that meaning is never complete until the written or spoken words are heard or read.

The beauty of a deconstructive approach to Homer is that scholars who employ it can both have their cake and eat it. Piero Pucci comments:

> It is therefore with polemic intent and with a specific strategy in mind that in this book I speak of Homeric "writing." I use this expression to refer to the original mode of composition and performance of the lays that developed diachronically in the *Iliad* and the *Odyssey*. In this way I intend to provoke a rethinking on the nature of Homeric oral poetry as a phenomenon as technically complex and literarily sophisticated as written poetry. This intent and this strategy, however, do not imply a denial or a neglect of the specific oral features of Homeric poetry. . . . Today we read it as a book, but at one time it was a song, a lay. Yet even as a song it was a kind of "writing," because it was always a *technically* complex form of orality.[28]

Pucci adopts a stance totally opposite to Vivante's. He maintains the poetic complexity of the *Iliad* and the *Odyssey*, despite conceding their orality, by contending that all complex "oral" works (of which he offers only the *Iliad* and the *Odyssey* as examples) are, in a sense, "written." In effect, the word "text" becomes, for the deconstructionist, a substitute for "poet(s)," "poem," and the meanings found in them by the scholar. It allows the scholar to read the text as a written and fixed unity without challenging the prevailing consensus that it is oral and discontinuous. In a similar fashion, A. Ford, who tries to recreate a sense of Homer's view of poetry, treats the epic as a text that can and should be analyzed as it now stands.[29]

In the last twenty years or so, scholars have become more skeptical about the contribution of oral theory to the understanding and appreciation of Homer. Some years ago J. Clay took a bold stand: "I consider the problem of composition secondary to the problem of interpretation, although I am not so naive as to ignore the fact that the latter has implications for the former."[30] B. C. Fenik remarked that "the ruling theory of the day (oral poetry) explains only half" the issues.[31] J. Griffin, in his work on characterization, death, and pathos, among other themes, suggests that we should not give ourselves over completely to the oral theory, but that we should, rather, try to approach both the *Iliad* and the *Odyssey* "in a manner not wholly different from the way in which the Greeks themselves approached them." Unlike Dawe, Griffin seeks help in understanding Homer in the mass of Greek commentaries on Homer, combining his study with Eastern sources, like the Old Testament, that must have influenced both Homer and Hesiod.[32] His work allows for psychological explanations as well as for symbolism, of which hard-core oral theory cannot approve.

A Rhetorical Reading

Although we incline more toward a "literary" than an "oral" Homer, we do not, frankly, consider that casting our votes one way or the other will fundamentally alter our view of the text of the *Odyssey*. On the contrary, we agree with Clay that the whole matter of "orality" has assumed an exaggerated position in Homeric scholarship and that it has masked, sometimes diverted, but never changed the more fundamental debate about the degree of intellectual and rhetorical complexity of the epic itself. In this sense we also basically agree with the deconstructionist critics, such as Pucci and Ford. And our reading of the *Odyssey* will follow the text quite closely from book to book.

Deconstruction has more in common with the methodology of ancient intellectualism than do the majority of scholarly models, which are dominated by the impetus to translate poetry into historical, sociological, or archaeological structures—that is, into a data base of explicit and self-contained statements. Like Stoic criticism, deconstruction is reluctant to draw conclusions about the artist once its examination is advanced and moving toward interpretations and conclusions. Deconstruction is, however, so cautious of the pitfalls in assessing artistic intent and design that it credits its own eyes too much for reading and the artist too little for producing the text. Artistic design is inseparable from artistic intent, and we are reluctant to credit the scholar for what we suspect the poet has produced.

Deconstruction does not, however, go to the allegorizing extremes of ancient philosophers whose readings of the epics often generated wholly unrecognizable recreations of their originals. As Robert Lamberton comments in connection with Plato *Republic* 2. "We know relatively little of methods of interpreting literary texts in antiquity. . . . Nevertheless, it seems clear . . . that, by Plato's time, the whole of the *Iliad* and *Odyssey* had been interpreted allegorically, and there is no doubt that explication of texts as well as myths formed part of the sophists' curriculum in the fifth century."[33] It would be a mistake, however, to assume that all or even most readers of Homer in antiquity were reading allegorically.

Scholiasts, like modern commentators, had their own reasons for approaching the texts as they did—to make at least the surface, the explicit level, of the poems accessible to an audience sufficiently distanced in time, culture, and language to require prompting and help with fundamentals. Philosophers, such as Plato, were in direct competition with Homer. Unable to obliterate the *Iliad* and *Odyssey*, other than under the censorship of the ideal state, they attempted to expropriate them for their own purposes. And in the days of Julian and the Neoplatonists, when the intellectual battle with Christianity was at a critical stage, they were only too happy to enroll Homer (suitably allegorized) to aid their cause.

Yet in between these extremes of scholiastic clarification of the explicit (but forgotten), on the one hand, and of the philosophical retooling of Homer to make him serve one's own ideology, on the other, there were the rhetoricians. They saw in Homer examples of the most refined figured usage and skilled argument. No texts are so frequently cited among the Greek rhetoricians, major and minor, as the Homeric. The ancient rhetoricians saw that the manipulative power of language is central to the construction and art of the *Odyssey*. And we would concur. Yet these rhetoricians are the "lost" literary critics of antiquity. We forget how much they base their arguments on the practice of poetry even when they are directing their readers toward expertise in oratory and prose.

Since the Homeric poems were the basis of Greek education for centuries, it made sense to teach rhetoric from texts already familiar to student as well as to teacher. But there is more to it than this. Precisely because the rhetoricians were teaching and examining the structure of argument, they had less investment than the scholiast, for example, in oversimplifying, and virtually no interest or investment in converting the works as a whole into a kind of philosophical theology. And our approach to Homer takes at least part of its cue from them.

It would help our evaluation of the various innuendoes and allusions Odysseus uses in addressing his inner audiences, and, ultimately, our evaluation of Homeric discourse more generally, if we consider to what extent Greek rhetoricians and poets engaged in, or even respected, the kind of forthright expression scholars generally admire. Was explicitness as crucial to their understanding of a work of art as it is to the interpretations favored by the modern classical scholar? Certainly Greek writers of classical and Hellenistic times were keenly aware that *parrhēsia* ("the right to say everything," "sincerity," "blunt expression") in the expression of opinions on religious, moral, or political issues is dangerous not only in tyrannical regimes, but in democracy too. The writer is generally safer to adopt some form of rhetorical "figured" speech. Further, Plutarch warns in *The Flatterer* 66E–74E, that blunt, outright expression of our thoughts is not only more dangerous than "figured" speech, but usually less effective, even among friends. Recognizing this, ancient rhetoricians devoted much time and energy to what they called "figured problems": how to express oneself safely, tactfully, and effectively in every imaginable situation.[34]

Ancient poets and critics had little use for forthright expression. Outspoken bluntness fails, says Aristotle, because the blunt speaker does not frighten us as much as the oblique speaker. The people we fear, he observes in *Rhetoric* 1382B, are "not those among our victims, enemies, or adversaries who say everything forthrightly [*parrhēsiastikoi*], but those who are gentle, ironic, up to everything. Since you cannot see when they are close, you can never see when they are far away." *Parrhēsia*, "saying everything" bluntly, does not make the speaker formidable. And "formidable speaking," *deinotēs*, was a major style of oratory in antiquity, as Demetrius points out in the fifth section of his *On Style*.[35] The chief feature of *deinotēs* is its compactness (*On Style* 240–45). It relies on the listener to adduce details omitted altogether by the text (or the speaker). The modern reader, however, is not accustomed to such an implicit, allusive style of writing. We find picturesque, explicit description, which conjures fairly well delineated images before the mind's eye, more to our taste than the noncommittal and ambiguous shapes provided by the ancient writer. That is, perhaps, why *emphasis*—as we use the term—carries the opposite meaning to the one it carried among critics in antiquity: covert allusion.

Homer's muse, for example, gives us an elaborate description of how Apollo comes down among the Greek ships with his rattling arrows on his shoulder to bring a plague on the encampment, how he starts by killing the mules and the dogs before moving on to the soldiers. The entire description of the plague itself, however, does not extend to even one full hexameter line:

> And the pyres of the dead burn unceasingly. (*Iliad* 1.52)

When the German writer G. E. Lessing, in his famous work *Laocoön*, discusses the fundamental differences between the art of the painter and that of the poet, he says of "the painting of the plague": "What do we see on the artist's canvas? Dead bodies, burning funeral pyres, the dying busy with the dead." None of this, he notes, is in the Homeric picture. All the Homeric muse says is that the funeral pyres burn constantly.[36] Everyone in the audience is left to reproduce their own mental image of the dying camp. The dying can be old or young, free men or prisoners, male or female, relatives or strangers. The text is unrestrictive and brief. In this forceful style, the readers or listeners must do some work themselves, they must participate in the creative process exactly as the deconstructionist surmises. *Deinotēs* involves asking questions of one's listeners without revealing one's own position on the issue, driving them to perplexity by what amounts to cross-examination (*On Style* 279). The writer, then, does not simply dole out answers. He engages us in dialectic, forces *us* to supply answers to questions he asks.

The contrast between modern and ancient approaches is of the utmost importance. When we emphasize something, we proclaim it to our readers, leaving no doubt that we want its presence noted and remembered. The ancient writer does the opposite. In the Homeric passage cited above, of course, the details we are called upon to supply can come from a common background of experience that ancient readers could supply from plagues in their own lifetimes. But sometimes we are prompted to supply much more precise and specific information. In *On Style* 288, for instance, Demetrius cites a passage from Plato's *Phaedo* (59 C) in which he says the philosopher wishes to reproach two friends of Socrates, Aristippus and Cleombrotus, for not visiting Socrates in prison before his execution. Plato does not attack them openly (*diarrhēdēn*), Demetrius notes, for this would be to commit himself to reproaching them. Instead he has Phaedo ask who was with Socrates. Phaedo enumerates those present. Cleombrotus and Aristippus are missing from the list. When asked whether Aristippus and Cleombrotus were there, Phaedo answers: "No, they were in Aegina." Everything, Demetrius concludes, comes through (*emphainetai*) in the expression "They were in Aegina." The point is to achieve reproach without committing oneself to an outright statement of reproach: "The effect is more forceful because it is achieved by letting the fact *speak for itself* rather than having the speaker make the point himself" (288; our italics). For modern readers the facts do not speak at all. We look for the explicit statement of the situation and for authorial evaluation of the acts and those who committed them. Plato does not "emphasize" (in our sense) the issue about Aristippus and Cleombrotus. The reader must find the points for himself and suppose the judgment he passes is his own, not one suggested by the writer. Unfortunately, since we expect something to be said clearly and obviously, we often presume, as do some editors of the *Phaedo*, that what is not "emphasized" in our way is not "emphasized" in anyone's way—or even being said.

Here is the risk the writer takes when he employs figured speech. It is a risk that would not have been nearly so great in antiquity as it is today, as we will see shortly from what Quintilian says. But modern scholars tend to overlook or ignore such innuendo.

Figured speech (*schēma, eschēmatismenos logos*) is the art of making statements from which one stands back. The speaker does not commit himself explicitly to any view, since the critical links in thought must be established by the reader or listener. The text, in short, is incomplete until the audience completes the meaning. Quintilian comments:

> Bordering on—if not actually identical with—this figure [*emphasis*] is one which we use a great deal nowadays. For now I must come to that kind of figure which is both extremely frequent in occurrence and particularly eagerly awaited. In it we want something other than what we actually say to be understood by exciting some suspicion to that effect. It is not the opposite of what we say, as in irony, but something which lurks there for the reader to discover. (*Instructing the Orator* 9.2.65)

We should particularly note Quintilian's observation that such figured usage is frequent and that it resembles *emphasis.*

Let us suppose for a moment that Quintilian and Demetrius are right: that figured speech of this kind was common in antiquity, and that it was, as Demetrius suggests, widely used in the Homeric poems. If the reader or listener is expected to participate in the act of artistic creation, we do not have to assume that tensions, even contradictions, between two statements in a work are necessarily caused by authorial inattention. Homer's muse need not have been nodding simply because the text does not conform to our expectations. Scholars have been slow to examine the Homeric poems in the light of ancient figured usage not only because of their reluctance to abandon the ingrained habit of thinking that "meaning" resides in the explicit but also because of the hypothesis that the *Iliad* and the *Odyssey* are, essentially, transcribed "oral" poems with obvious sutures patching over the different strata of composition. Such contradictions as are suggested by an explicit reading, then, are adduced as further "evidence" of the oral nature of these epics. In Latin epic there is a similar escape hatch for the critic of the *Aeneid* or the *Pharsalia.* Both works were left unrevised when their poets died. Thus any "contradictions" yielded by an explicit reading can be explained away as things the poets would have emended if they had had the opportunity.

Accepting the Consequences of Orality

Whether we accept or dispute the "oral" theory of the transmission of the Homeric poems, most would agree that the Homeric epics were based on a rich and varied mythic tradition (or, some would suggest, folk tradition) and were not, therefore, works of fiction created in a vacuum. Yet, though we may suspect that stories about, say, Odysseus found in the fragments of what are known as the Cyclic epics derive from originals of comparable antiquity to the *Odyssey,* discussion of these versions rarely emerges from the footnotes into the analysis of the Homeric texts themselves. Why? First, there is no clear way of knowing their date. We may either assume that these other fragmentary epics draw on mythic material of approximately the same antiquity as the *Odyssey*, or assume that they are conscious variants or modifications of the *Odyssey*. Most critics, in practice if not always in theory, assume the latter. For the sake of argument, we will generally assume the former, as does Laura Slatkin, who maintains: "The *Iliad* and the *Odyssey* interpret the mythological material they inherit. . . . They select not only from among different myths—combining those chosen into a narrative within which certain central concerns illustrated by the myths are allowed full development—but also from among different variants and aspects of a single myth."[37] We claim this not because we have evidence to hand that others lack, but because it is worthwhile, when evidence is lacking, to test all available hypotheses when examining a problem. The common assumption, generally unquestioned, has no more evidence to support itself than has ours and isolates the *Odyssey* from other Greek poetry—as if it were a work of fiction rather than the product of a tradition.

If the *Iliad* and *Odyssey* are "oral" poems from a rich and varied bardic tradition, the fact that they are also in their *written* form, arguably, the earliest surviving works of Greek literature becomes, if anything, less important. Yet scholars are reluctant to use variants of Iliadic and Odyssean myth derived from "later" writers as a basic tool for interpreting the Homeric epics, since there is no solid *written* proof that a given, specific variant was actually available to the Homeric poet or poets. A variant of the Odysseus myth found in Hesiod, Stesichorus, or the Cyclic epics, for instance, is not eagerly seized upon and used to enrich our sense of the mythic storehouse from which "Homer" is drawing and to which he is alluding. On the contrary, it is generally ignored, dismissed, or certainly excluded from the fabric of Homeric interpretation because it *might* be the invention, the fiction, of the later poet (if indeed the poet is later) rather than a traditional variant available to but not used, or obviously alluded to, by "Homer." The temptation is to look not for an excuse to deploy the critical material to maximum effect, but to minimalize its significance.

Granted, the problem of what is fiction based on myth and what is "traditional" myth is often impossible to resolve even within the Homeric poems. Any answer given must, like so many hypotheses and theories pertaining to early Greek literature, be based on an argument from profound silence. Yet if we assume that the various non-Homeric traditions pertaining to Odysseus, for example, are *fictions* developed from (or composed in rivalry to) Homeric material and invented by later poets, then Homer is left in a hermetically and hermeneutically sealed vacuum. Indeed, reluctance to acknowledge that later variants drew from the same (or at least a similar) pool of tradition as that from which Homer drew weakens the claim that the Homeric epic is itself myth rather than fiction. But if we assume that there existed, in whatever form (oral or written), variants in the story of Odysseus that are of comparable antiquity to those found in the *Odyssey*—if we accept, that is, the mythic nature of the discourse—then these variants deserve careful consideration.

Scholarly methodology here is not very consistent. While we are suspicious that what appear to be variations on Homeric themes in later writers are not really a valid part of the contemporary Homeric tradition, we are, ironically, no less suspicious of the mythic nature of passages in Homer that are themselves uncorroborated by later literary use. If Homer presents a story found nowhere else in antiquity, we often call it a fiction or invention rather than a mythic variant. In a recent comment on *Odyssey* 7.324, for example, J. B. Hainsworth suggests that Alcinous's story about how the Phaeacians took Rhadamanthus to visit Tityus in Euboea is an "invention" of Homer's. His reason for such an assumption is that no later writer refers to any such tradition.[38]

Part of the difficulty resides in our reluctance to distinguish between the narrative muses of the *Iliad* and *Odyssey* and the internal characters who may have some rhetorical reason for modifying a traditional story as they narrate it. A case in point is Achilles' statement to Priam in *Iliad* 24.611 that the children of Niobe were left unburied *because Zeus had turned the people into stone.* Malcolm Willcock, who italicizes the words we have also italicized here, describes the clause as "another bland invention of the poet."[39] If this story, then, is a fiction, it is presented as a rhetorical fiction framed by Achilles (rather than the Homeric muse) to adapt a myth to his persuasive needs at the time of speaking. If Willcock is right, we should remind ourselves that all myth is subject to fictionalizing when renarrated for a specific rhetorical purpose. And a great deal of "Homeric" myth occurs in contexts where an internal narrator tailors a myth that he appears to assume is familiar to internal (and perhaps also external) audiences to make it more compatible with the thrust of his argument at the time. It is, then, unwise to assume that a myth found in Homer is necessarily represented in its hypothetically "original" form, since the internal narrators often have reason to inflect tradition to suit their own rhetorical goals. Similarly, either the Muse herself (or the internal narrator) may be well aware that she (he) is modifying, subverting, or even omitting the most familiar version of the myth.

Critics ancient and modern have felt most comfortable in assuming that Homer is "traditional" only when later writers corroborate what he says, and later writers are only traditional when they repeat Homer. Such reasoning is circular and self-defeating: such symmetrical corroboration could more easily be the product of copying and imitation by later writers than of independent treatment of the same source. Surely the reverse assumption is more likely to be correct: that the richness and persistence of often widely divergent variants validates the notion of a large pool of myth available to "Homer." If we argue the "mythic" nature of the *Odyssey* narrative yet avoid attributing to "Homer" knowledge of a tradition not explicitly acknowledged, we treat the epics as if they emerged ex nihilo, as fictions, in defiance of the logic of our own assumptions.

Horizons would expand if we at least took Hesiod into more generous account, since he is the only generally accepted rival of "Homer" for the distinction of being the earliest surviving Greek poet. If we concede the hypothesis of M. L. West and others, in fact Hesiod predates Homer. Hesiod, West contends, "may not have known the *Iliad* and *Odyssey* that we know (my own belief is that they were composed later than his poems), but he was certainly familiar with epic poetry about Troy and other subjects."[40] The notion offers interesting possibilities, since Hesiod often produces details that supplement or differ from what we know in the Homeric poems. West's hypothesis allows, in theory, a glimpse of mythic versions that might predate Homer, at least in written form.

It is hard, then, not to be disappointed when West declares Hesiod's observation that Circe bore Odysseus children "new and fanciful" and describes Hesiod's comment that Odysseus fathers Nausithous and Nausinous with Calypso as "building on the *Odyssey*."[41] He is suggesting now that the *Theogony* is *later* than the *Odyssey*. These statements may be a holdover from West's earlier edition of the *Theogony* (which contains no suggestion that Hesiod might precede the written Homer). If not, he is only toying with us in suggesting that Hesiod was earlier.

West's idea that Hesiod did not "know" Homer echoes the scholiast's gloss on Agrius at *Theogony* 1013: "Homer does not know these people, Agrius and Latinus."[42] What Homer does not say, Homer does not know. Similarly, James Frazer, commenting on the mention of Telegonus in Apollodorus's *Epitome* (7.16), states: "Telegonus is unknown to Homer, who mentions no offspring of Ulysses by the enchantress Circe."[43] Aristotle is generally more cautious in this regard, talking of Homer's decision to exclude or include rather than of any lack of knowledge of other elements. In *Poetics* 1459 A he suggests that Homer excerpted for his *Iliad* only one part of the myth of the fall of Troy and then took bits and pieces from elsewhere to complete the desired end product. Aristotle saw Homer as a conscious artist shaping his work to give it unity, to make it "one." "In composing the *Odyssey*, he did not develop everything that had happened to Odysseus, as for example his being wounded on Mt. Parnassus or his pretended madness when the army was being levied . . . but he built the *Odyssey* around a single core of action, *praxin*, as we would call it and likewise the *Iliad*" (*Poetics* 1451A).[44]

West, then, goes well beyond either Aristotle or the scholiast when he says that the sons of Odysseus, mentioned above, are "new and fanciful."

He implies not that "Homer" decided not to use them, or did not know of them, but that Hesiod invented them. Thus they are *not* traditional (and thus not available to the poetic tradition, whether oral or not) because they are not mentioned by Homer. His procedure seems arbitrary, in light of his own expressed belief that Homer was later than Hesiod. And he has no trouble elsewhere accepting that a great deal of Hesiod that differs from what is found in the Homeric tradition is nonetheless traditional and of great antiquity.

The scholiast, by contrast, does not dispute the traditional nature of what Hesiod says about Agrius and Latinus. Rather he observes: "Nevertheless they do live in the inner parts of the islands; the Latins occupy Italy and the Etruscan territory where Circe lived. The islands are said to be the Electrides (Amber) Islands."

Odd details from other sources may have a pedigree as venerable as anything Homeric and may shed light on the Homeric. The scholiast on Apollonius Rhodius *Argonautica* 4.816 says Thetis used to throw the children she bore to Peleus into a cauldron of water to discover whether they were mortal. If they proved mortal, she killed them. Peleus, annoyed that she had killed so many of their children, prevented her from throwing Achilles into the pot. This variant of the better-known story in which Thetis is the protective mother dipping Achilles in the waters of the Styx to ensure his immortality, needless to say, gives us a far less agreeable picture of Thetis. Yet there is no means of knowing which version of this folkloric motif has claim to greater antiquity unless we make the purely mechanical decision to assign priority on the basis of the date at which the version first appears. We prefer, on the whole, to assume that the Iliadic muse may have been familiar with this as well as other mythical variants when she chose to sculpt Thetis as an ever-mourning mother who cannot accept her son's mortality and laments him even while he is still alive.

Adam Parry saw some aspects of the critical problem to which we allude. Milman Parry and many of his successors, he argues, "made the unreasonable assumption of a sort of monolithic tradition, a tradition allowing only those forms of expression that we actually find in the [Homeric] poems."[45] The elder Parry was taking what we have called a minimalist position: keeping the data base as restricted as possible to the absolutely explicit (ironically enough in support of a theory that has no basis whatever in the explicit). Such inflexibility is hard to understand in scholars who believe the Homeric epics were patched together and transmitted orally. Indeed, the basis of the Homeric oral theory is that there *must* have existed conflicting traditions from which a rhapsode could assemble his own, individual song. And the most fruitful product of the "oral" theory has been the identification of those areas of conflict that had, previously, often passed unnoticed or unremarked. Adam Parry comments: "The tradition must actually have been far more complex and far more flexible. It certainly was if the evidence of Serbocroatian poetry offers any useful analogy. The *Iliad* and the *Odyssey* that we have, with their splendid coincidence of meaning and form, were the result of generations of selections from the fluid tradition, and of the long years over which Homer himself perfected his songs."[46]

Oral tradition, in short, assumes it is dealing with variants on "set" themes in set phraseology, and there is no reason to preclude Hesiod from contact with it because fewer scholars think of Hesiod's epics as "oral."

West's rejection of Hesiod's mention of Odysseus's children by Circe and Calypso as "new and fanciful" goes even farther than Hainsworth's observation that Alcinous's tale of Rhadamanthus and Tityus is an invention. There is a rich tradition about Odysseus's children by Circe and Calypso. It is not an isolated *hapax mythoumenon*, a one-of-a-kind mythic variant. West's comment seems designed to isolate Hesiod's reference to Odysseus's other children from "tradition," to minimize the possibility that "Homer," for example, was singing for an audience that might have known of Agrius or Telegonus. If Agrius and other extra sons of Odysseus are *fictions* of an individual poet at a given time, they can be omitted as part of the data base of mythic variants available to Homer even by a scholar who thinks that Hesiod predates Homer.

If there is anything in the concept of "oral tradition," it must posit some interaction between what the poet is singing and what the audience already knows or thinks it knows. The reciters, then, were presumably not only themselves well aware of mythic variants but performed for audiences well versed in multiple, varied mythic narratives. Reciters, by focusing on one version rather than another, are not necessarily "rejecting" other versions out of hand. The concept of "rejecting" alternative readings is more appropriate to scholarly than to poetic discourse, to history than to myth, to textual rather than to literary criticism. It makes little sense when applied to the relationship between poet-reciter and audience in the "oral" poetry of a pre-literate society precisely because myth is not fiction, even though it can be fictionalized. Further, Greek poetic tradition retained a strongly oral base for centuries after writing became widespread, as we can see not only in tragedy but in Pausanias, who often preserves local traditions of fairly obvious antiquity, but isolated from the mainstream of literary tradition. It was the *literary* tradition, not the oral tradition, that narrowed over generations as it came into the hands of scholars and was subsumed into the schoolroom, and edited into a canon.

Some subsequent variants, of course, simply *must* be later fictions. In Sophocles' *Oedipus Tyrannus* for instance, the (previously unattested) plague afflicting Thebes at the time of Oedipus's investigation of Laius's death most plausibly owes its first appearance in the Oedipus myth to the poet's reaction to the great plagues at Athens in 430 and 427 B.C.E. Sophocles, like the other surviving tragedians, is very careful to make his plays (i.e., his reworkings of traditional myth) speak to contemporary circumstances in some kind of oblique way. Playwrights are, further, ready to invent supplementary characters to add to a myth. Other subsequent mythic variants, though clearly old, are of no particular importance in the literary tradition: they are simply different spellings or forms of names that make no special difference to the general shape of the tale in its canonical form. The Homeric muse, for example, calls Oedipus's wife Epicaste while almost all other versions call her Jocasta. But there is nothing to suggest they were two separate persons from two distinct traditions. The case of the Homeric Zethus and the more common Tereus is much the same; similarly, Pandareus and Pandion.

But certain mythic traditions and characters have an arguably independent pedigree in that they appear in several different authors in different times and places even if they do not occur in the Homeric texts. Thus Odysseus's non-Homeric son by Circe, Telegonus, is unlikely to be simply a variant of Telemachus. The pedigrees and traditions associated with each are distinct, for all the resemblance in their names.

If a poet alters or edits a commonly known tradition, there will be those in the audience who are aware that he is doing so. Myth is, in antiquity, what audiences, what cultures as a whole, "know," and poets could hardly expect their audiences to suppress this knowledge. On the contrary, one can argue that audiences of epic *expected* to hear variants or "inflections" of what they "knew," as the audiences of Greek tragedy did at a later date. While most Greek tragedy draws its themes from a canon of heroic themes, the artistry of Aeschylus or Euripides lies in making their versions of well-known tales, such as that of Orestes' vengeance, different from all others yet also recognizably the same. As Telemachus remarks in *Odyssey* 1.352, people always enjoy the newest, the most recent, version best.

Unfortunately, we are not in the habit of reading classical epic, either Greek or Latin, in such a way. Modern scholars know, for example, that numerous variants in the Aeneas tradition were current among (and published by) Vergil's contemporaries or immediate scholarly and literary predecessors. But the dominant interpretative practice is to assume that Vergil (and his contemporary readers) are suppressing rather than alluding to variant traditions. Aeneas, for instance, appears in ancient art assisting Paris's abduction of Helen from Sparta—a tradition drawn from the *Cypria*, one of the so-called Cyclic epics, dating to before 550 B.C.E.[47] The chief ancient authority for Aeneas's negotiations with the Greeks is a contemporary of Vergil's who lived and taught at Rome: Dionysius of Halicarnassus. Dionysius, in *Roman Antiquities* 1.46–48, summarizes earlier writers, particularly the fifth-century Hellanicus of Mytilene. According to Dionysius, Hellanicus related that Aeneas abandoned Troy after Neoptolemus captured the acropolis, taking with him "his father, his ancestral gods, his wife, and his children, and the most valuable people and possessions" (46.4); he then negotiated to leave the Troad after surrendering all the fortresses (47.4–5). Sophocles in his *Laocoon* had Aeneas move to Mt. Ida before Troy's capture (48.2). Menecrates said Aeneas, after Achilles' funeral, quarreled with Paris, overthrew Priam, and became "one of the Achaeans," betraying the city to them (48.3–4). It was "a literary tradition which . . . had its roots in the pre-Vergilian literary tradition."[48] "Virgil's account of Aeneas's motivation does in passing answer very carefully the charges made by the hero's detractors, which it is clear enough that Virgil must have known," observes N. Horsfall in reference to *Aeneid* 2.[49] He is correct in all but two points. First and obviously, the narrative is in Aeneas's voice, not in Vergil's authorial voice. Second, if Vergil's Aeneas is responding to other traditions, then both hero and author know their audiences will be aware of those variants. The same situation might well have applied to Homer's muse and the *Odyssey*.

In the opening lines of the *Odyssey*, a voice, usually identified with that of the poet, instructs the Muse to tell of a man who saw many cities and suffered much as he tried, successfully, to save his own life and, in vain, to save the lives of his men, who, fools that they were, brought destruction upon themselves by eating the cattle of Helios, the Sun (1.1–10).[50] The impression one gets from this mandate to compose is that the voice, or perhaps we should say the persona, giving the order has in mind a notion of the general shape of the tale to be told. The Odysseus envisaged in the request is not at all responsible for the deaths of his crew members, whose folly in eating forbidden food, not any rashness or negligence on his part, is the cause of their demise.

As the Muse spins her story, however, and especially as she recounts what Odysseus tells the Phaeacians about his travels, it becomes clear that only a tiny fraction of his crew actually died as a result of eating the cattle of Helios. Odysseus claims that he set out from Troy with twelve ships. But only one of these was left by the time he reached Thrinacia, where the fateful cattle were kept. And—though he does not posit precise figures—that ship seems already to have been shorthanded by at least six men. Even if we were to grant him an entire complement of hands for this last vessel, only between 8 and 9 percent of his crew perished as specified in the instructions given to the Muse. Of the remainder, as we shall see, a considerable number perished as a direct result of Odysseus's rash or negligent actions.

The Odysseus envisaged in the formula prescribed to the Muse is a much less culpable figure than the one who emerges in the Muse's account, represented as Odysseus's own apologia. It would be entirely possible, if arguably less dramatically interesting, to conceive of an *Odyssey* in which Odysseus does lose all his crew, at one fell swoop, as the result of a single act of disobedience on their part. That is not what we get. Yet it is possible that the voice issuing instructions to the Muse thought that such an innocent Odysseus is precisely what the "audience" expected. Does that demanding voice, then, ask the Muse to reiterate what it takes to be the vulgate of Odysseus's return journey?

Although we would be the first to admit that there is no means of answering this question, we are asking our own readers to follow us for a short while and see what happens if we answer yes and move on from there. We have postulated, in our own infinitesimal way, something akin to a thought theorem in the full knowledge that the assumptions we make may well be flawed, for we have attempted to deduce from the text and from other sources a sense of precisely that irretrievable audience of the unknown days when the *Odyssey* was new and could still surprise those who heard it. That is why we say that the Odyssean muse does not provide what the demanding voice calls for, and why we will go on to postulate that substantial parts of Odysseus's narrative of his experiences in *Odyssey* 9–12 are fictional, and thus "new" rather than mythic, even though the fictions are built upon archetypal mythic substructures. Those other traditions of Odysseus's return that are not simply derived from the *Odyssey*—such as the tales of his sons by Calypso and Circe (on which we will comment further)—take no interest whatever in the fate of his crew. It is possible, then, that the prefatory ten lines of the *Odyssey* are alerting us to one aspect of the most common opinion about Odysseus's return up to the point at which the *Odyssey* is formulated. And there is nothing in the text itself to lead the reader to suspect that the epic will undermine that tradition of Odysseus's total innocence in the matter of his crew's annihilation until book 9.

On the other hand, scrutiny of Odysseus's own narrative in *Odyssey* 9–12 does suggest that the voice asking the Muse to recite the familiar story with an innocent Odysseus is not the only voice that could have made the request. There are traces, we will suggest, of an Odysseus even more culpable than the Homeric Odysseus admits to being for the destruction of his crew, a tradition that we will discuss in Chapter 4. The Homeric muse and her Odysseus, then, may be generating an account that falls somewhere between total innocence and total responsibility. The problem is that, until recently, modern scholars have inclined to be apologists for Odysseus, even to read the *Odyssey* as if the ten-line preamble actually defined what occurs during the body of the narrative. Criticism of the *Odyssey*, though not dominated by a Stoic or Pauline urge to represent the

Homeric Odysseus as the "ideal man," still tends to justify his behavior even when he himself makes no attempt to excuse it. The assumption is made that the proem outlines what actually happens later in the poem and that the Muse wants to exonerate Odysseus from any blame for the death of his own men and to present him in a more favorable light than that which might have prevailed in previous tradition.[51] Although Hellenists are more open to the darker side of Odysseus than Latinists are to the darker side of the Aeneas which subtends the *Aeneid*, the reflex to defend Odysseus's honor remains strong.

The divergence between what is demanded of someone and what is given in response to that demand is not peculiar to the preamble. We shall see this again and again in the body of the epic, most notably in the contrast between what Alcinous asks Odysseus to explain and what Odysseus actually explains. The voice that demands a narrative often has expectations at odds with what the narrator is ready to supply, even if that narrator begins, as does Apollonius's Polyxo in her response to Hypsipyle in *Argonautica* 1.667–707, with an assurance of agreement and compliance. Once you ask someone to tell you something, you cede, until the narrator you have empowered is silenced, your right to control or shape what is said.

The Odyssean muse shows us this process at work not only in the larger issues of moral responsibility but in such smaller details as how the nature of an order changes as it is passed down a chain of command. Calypso, for instance, when speaking to Odysseus at 5.160–70, gives him the impression that it is *her* decision to let him leave, even though the Muse assures us that Calypso is reluctantly passing on (in an edited version) the commands she has received (in an edited version) from Hermes, who is himself reluctantly reporting the commands of Zeus, which were in turn prompted by a complaint registered by Athena (1.81–87; 5.31–42, 97–115). Calypso expropriates and represents as an act made of her own free will a decision she has been forced to make.

In sum, we take it for granted that Homer was the "most many voiced," the *polyphōnotatos*, of the poets, as Dionysius of Halicarnassus describes him (*On Literary Composition* 16). Simplicity, we feel, is, in antiquity, not something inherent in a work of art, but an illusion that results from the most complex, precise, and careful planning, as in the architecture of the Parthenon. Classical art is simple only to the extent that it is a finite attempt to refract and convey some sense of either the complexities of the world around us or the ideas and concepts that have their fullest perfection only in mathematics and the mind. And art is finite only in terms of its physical boundaries. A text or painting may well be *designed* to generate an infinite nexus of suggestions rather than to provide a finite "message": to raise questions rather than to deliver answers. True, much art involves the creation of what will look like an order and symmetry hard to find in nature. Yet what often animates great art is that it is so structured as either to exist in defiance of the order it seems to define or to be potentially subversive of that order.[52]

When we see the possibility that the *Odyssey* presents a narrative that may differ from what the audience "knows," we will first seek indications that "Homer" has subsumed or incorporated a variety of mythic versions into his narrative, or that he might be playing his version *against* what he anticipates that his audience knows rather than resort to saying that he did not know, or is rejecting, a different version. As often as not, classical poets find ways of incorporating multiple variants within a single narrative, thereby generating a dialectical tension between themselves and their audiences. They are, in short, deliberately creating an unwritten work that is differently inscribed in the mind of each listener or reader: the very thing deconstructionsts call the text itself.

[1]

Rival Homecomings

As the *Odyssey* opens, the poet asks the Muse, the daughter of Zeus, to sing in him the man who suffered much, saw much, and experienced much in the attempt to save his own life and the lives of his comrades after the sack of Troy (*Odyssey* 1.1–10). He invites the Muse to commence with events leading up to the destruction of Odysseus's crew for their consumption of the cattle of the Sun. Once the appeal is completed, the Muse's voice takes over, we are invited to believe. The poet, who appears to know the story he is prompting the Muse to recite through him, vanishes from view and does not intervene again.[1] The Muse does not take her mandate very literally. She begins not as the poet suggests, but with Odysseus on Calypso's island—after his crew has already perished. And, as we have noted, most of Odysseus's men die well before they have an opportunity to eat the cattle of the Sun.

Activating the narrative of Odysseus's homecoming, as the Muse represents it, is a matter of crucial timing: the decision can be taken among the banqueting gods with some guarantee of success only because Poseidon, who would object, is banqueting elsewhere—among the Ethiopians (1.11–26). The Muse instantly establishes that Odysseus's return is the final return, the last homecoming of a survivor of the Trojan War (1.11–15). For his part, however, Zeus is thinking ahead to the long-term consequences of the return of Agamemnon, the commander in chief. Agamemnon, murdered by his wife's lover, Aegisthus, has just been avenged by his son, Orestes (1.26–43). Zeus, that is to say, is already preoccupied with the deeds of the next generation. Odysseus threatens to fall between the cracks of the narrative, marooned for eternity on the island of Calypso, "Concealer," lost to, and in, time. The goddess Athena, Odysseus's protector, expresses precisely this fear to Zeus and adds that Odysseus may himself be beguiled and forget his desire to return (56–57). That, at least, is how the Muse represents the matter. But, as she does, she upstages the revenge myth of the next generation by setting it in her narrative before, rather than after, Odysseus's return.

Odysseus's seven-year stay with Calypso could indicate, as such stays often do in Celtic myth, not a specific length of time but removal from time. The Irish hero Bran, for instance, returns from his travels to discover that no one knows who he is, though they have ancient stories about him.[2] The Homeric muse may herself be "rescuing" Odysseus from a similar never-never land to which other tradition (including Hesiod) assigns him, in which he fathers, among others, Nausithous and Teledamus upon Calypso and Telegonus upon Circe, and in which his return occurs at a rather later date.[3] After all, Telegonus and Nausithous would be at least ten years younger than Telemachus. If Telegonus and other sons such as Euryalus, who are mentioned in various traditions, are to arrive in Ithaca in search of their father at around the same time as Odysseus returns home from Troy, then the twenty-year absence of the hero postulated in the *Odyssey* is not nearly long enough. The Homeric Athena is acting in a Hesiodic manner: arranging and rationalizing a confused and disparate tradition, giving, indeed establishing, a kind of "historical" sequence to bring Odysseus back to Ithaca closer to the end of the Trojan War.

The return of Agamemnon, leader of the Greeks, and its consequences in the next generation, then, become the narrative warp upon which the return of Odysseus is woven. Agamemnon is subsumed into and subordinated to the narrative substructure of the *Odyssey*. The process of making one's rivals one's footnotes has begun. In fact, Agamemnon, or rather his ghost, appears at two convenient junctures later in the *Odyssey* to comment on events (11.405–61; 24.106–19, 192–202).

Athena, the Muse tells us, puts Odysseus back in Zeus's mind by means of a sound play which links Odysseus's name not only to its resonances of pain (*odynē*), but, perhaps, to Zeus's own name.[4] It thus becomes harder for Zeus to think about himself without also thinking about Odysseus. The ploy pays off. When Zeus responds to Athena, he places his own self, *egō*, "I," in between Odysseus's name and the adjective *theioio*, "divine," which qualifies (and adds divine color to) that name (1.65). Not only is there now something of Odysseus in Zeus, but something of Zeus in Odysseus. In the Muse's narrative, then, Athena (born, as Hesiod *Theogony* 886–91 would have it, from Zeus's head after his ingestion of Metis, "Thought") insinuates Odysseus into the mind of Zeus and takes control of the situation, ensuring the dispatch of Hermes to Calypso to secure Odysseus's release, and herself going to Ithaca to dispatch Telemachus to Sparta in search not of his father, but of some narrative of his father's return, his *nostos* (1.81–95).[5] Her dispositions are important. Had she gone to Calypso's island and Hermes to Ithaca, we would move closer to other traditions, often described as sub-Homeric, where Hermes travels to Ithaca and becomes Penelope's lover and father of the goat god, Pan.[6] Athena is controlling the switch points to guide her train onto totally different, even possibly newly laid tracks. Zeus is given no chance to object.

As the poet has invited the Muse into his head to tell the story, the Muse describes Athena putting the story into the head of Zeus and authorizing her own intervention in the narrative. The connection between the act of returning and the presence of thought is nicely made by Douglas Frame in his discussion of the relationship between the Greek words *nostos* (return) and *nous* or *noos* (thought).[7] As he points out, Odysseus's companions lost their *nostos* because of their lack of *nous*. And Odysseus will not be able to return until the thought of his return is again in Zeus's mind. "It is very significant," Frame adds, "that *noos* is associated with a 'return from death.'"[8] There are those in Ithaca who consider Odysseus dead because he is lost to their own and others' perception. Zeus, the devourer of *mētis*, "thought," must again concern himself with the hero who is himself full of *mētis*, as his epithet *polymētis* implies.

Control of narrative and of events is now firmly in the hands of the divine and feminine: the Muse, Athena, and Calypso. Little wonder Samuel Butler thought that the poet of the *Odyssey* must be a woman. Once Athena, according to the Muse, sets events in motion, she quickly moves to become a participant in, rather than the narrator of, what she has begun. In fact, the distinction we often make between narrator and participant is systematically blurred in the opening of the *Odyssey*. *Odyssey* 1 is Athena's book, as the Muse narrates it. Thus, appropriately enough, her name is the last word of *Odyssey* 1.[9] Aside from the narrative Muse, no one other than the now-distant poet deserves the honor more.

Athena, as the Muse narrates the story, goes to Ithaca and is introduced, albeit disguised as a male mortal, into the human scene, where she meets Telemachus, gives him a fictional narrative of her assumed identity as Mentes, and then orders him, in effect, to leave this part of the epic (1.179–212, 279–97). Athena thus prompts Telemachus to search for a narrative on his own. While he is away, he picks up a few gifts, makes friends with Peisistratus, son of Nestor, king of Pylos, and is an audience for the narratives of Helen and Menelaus, whose ruptured marriage caused the war from which Odysseus has failed to return. But Telemachus achieves hardly anything that he set out to find. Athena's action in sending him away does not protect him or Penelope from potential dangers at home. Penelope, courted by 108 suitors, is left more vulnerable to their attentions. And it is easier for the suitors to plot to dispose of Telemachus discreetly (and anonymously) while he is away, instead of doing so in his home, thereby alienating Penelope.

The Muse, however, may have other considerations. Most obviously, Telemachus's absence provides a narrative pretext for incorporating two other stories of return into the substrate of her own narrative: those of Nestor and Menelaus. But there is more. If we note how persistent is the motif of a son of Odysseus searching for his father throughout the variants of the "return of Odysseus" theme in later writers, matters become more complicated. Euryalus, Odysseus's son by Euippe, daughter of the king of Thesprotia, comes to Ithaca in search of Odysseus, as does Telegonus, his son by Circe. The first is killed by Odysseus; the second kills Odysseus.[10] Granted our assumption that these versions may have been in the mythic "pool" available to Homeric audiences, the listener hearing the *Odyssey* for the first time has no reason to suppose that the quest by a son of Odysseus for his lost father would necessarily culminate in recognition and mutual acknowledgment. Nor would it yet be evident that Telemachus was Odysseus's only son.

When Athena mentions Orestes, already in Zeus's mind and famous for avenging Agamemnon and killing his mother's lover, she invites Telemachus to rival his epic contemporary with deeds of his own (1.298–300). There is an uncomfortable undertow in this allusion to that divinely approved mythic paradigm: Orestes had to avenge the murder of his father (killed on his return from Troy) when he himself returned from what amounted to exile. The parallel is further enriched when Telemachus, while away, strikes up a friendship with Peisistratus of *Pylos,* and the two youths travel together, much as Orestes, in most versions of his myth, traveled with his faithful companion, *Pyla*des. When Telemachus and Peisistratus arrive at Menelaus's palace in Sparta, the king's daughter is marrying not Orestes (her promised husband in most traditions) but Achilles' son Neoptolemus, and Menelaus seems nervous that Telemachus, who does not immediately introduce himself, may be Orestes. But more on this matter later. Suffice it to say for now that as the *Odyssey* opens there is some reason to suspect that the Muse is innovating and, perhaps, attempting to codify her version against the backdrop of competing variants.

Once Athena has put Odysseus in Telemachus's mind, as in Zeus's, she metamorphoses into a bird and vanishes from the scene (1.320–23). Telemachus joins the suitors and the musical program in progress. The minstrel Phemius is singing (what else?) the return of the Achaeans from Troy, made miserable by the very goddess who has just departed (1.325–28). But scarcely has Phemius begun when Penelope sweeps into the room and orders him to play a different song; the tale of the return is too melancholy and painful for her to bear (1.329–44), perhaps because it would not include Odysseus's return. The details of Phemius's song are not specified, and speculation as to its nature is pointless, though the ancient scholiast suggests Phemius is telling a false story about Odysseus's death, and some modern scholars accept this notion.[11] Since the Muse is already singing the song of Odysseus's return, Penelope's desire to silence songs of return is surely ironic. Its thread must be completed before the hero can get back to Ithaca, before it is a complete *nostos*, a complete song of return. In fact, as Telemachus will discover on reaching Sparta in his quest for news of Odysseus, part of Odysseus's return is already known—though not, it appears, in his home. Telemachus and Penelope seem not to know (and perhaps it is just as well) what Menelaus knows: that Odysseus is marooned in space and time (for Menelaus holds no high hopes that Odysseus will escape) in Calypso's land. Penelope's reluctance to hear songs of return does not help her keep apace of the latest tales. She seems intent on stopping a narrative of which she is about to become a part, a narrative progressing both externally with the Muse and internally with Phemius toward Odysseus's return to Ithaca.

Penelope's intervention in this delaying capacity is not altogether surprising. She has a talent for procrastination, for unweaving what she has woven. And weaving is a common metaphor for song and narrative in the *Odyssey*. Because Penelope puts the suitors off by weaving her father-in-law's death shroud, there is something about her which is not only reminiscent of the Moirai, or Fates, who spin the threads of people's lives, but of the rhapsode, the poet, who reweaves the threads of traditional tales. Penelope has been, for three years, almost as much the controller of time as Calypso, who holds Odysseus in suspended existence. Why only three years? Are these the years in which Telemachus has come of age?[12] As Odysseus has several years unaccounted for on Calypso's island, several years in Penelope's life are similarly isolated from the narrative and unaccounted for.

Shrewdly, the Muse presents Penelope's three-year strategy of the loom through the perceptions and words of one of her suitors, Antinous, who reports that she is masterfully deceitful and untruthful. She put a large loom (*megas histos*) in her hall, so that, she said, "I can weave the shroud and not let my work go for nothing" (2.98). Greeks of later years would certainly have found some ironic humor here, since the expression "to work the loom of Penelope" was proverbial for an exercise in futility. There may be a little wicked irony in Antinous's words too. Penelope is famous in myth as the waiting wife, faithful—or otherwise. Odysseus's return will end that phase of her existence and her fame rivaling that of famous women of the past, such as Tyro, Alcmena, and Mycena (whoever she was)—a fame, Antinous concedes, she has won by her actions (2.115–28). Comparison of Penelope with Tyro and Alcmena is not entirely what a faithful wife might appreciate, since both women are famous for being tricked by gods into sexual relationships: Tyro with Poseidon, whom she mistakenly thought was the river Enipeus; Alcmena with Zeus (unwittingly in some traditions) while her husband was away fighting.[13]

A passage later in the epic adds force to the mention here of Tyro, Alcmena, and Mycena. Odysseus claims to have met Tyro and Alcmena among the spirits of the dead in his catalogue of famous (in some cases notorious) women (11.235–47, 266–68). But this is as close as the Muse comes to conceding infidelity on Penelope's part. She passes over in silence all Penelope's activities in any but three or four of the nineteen years Odysseus was away. There are strong traditions elsewhere that Penelope was seduced by Antinous, sent away by Odysseus, and that she went to Mantinea in Arcadia, where she bore the god Pan to Hermes.[14] It is thus at least of passing interest that the Muse has Antinous, Penelope's seducer in other traditions, make sarcastic allusions to Penelope's fame as a waiting wife while the Muse maintains her chastity.

The *histos*, the loom, is Penelope's protection and security when all else fails her. Similarly, the security of Odysseus's *histos*, his ship's mast, is his salvation as he travels. The words "loom" and "mast," different in English, are identical in Greek. Odysseus is tied to his *histos* as he hears the Sirens' song. It saves him from drowning during a storm as he leaves Calypso's island.[15] As the ship's mast symbolizes what enables both vessel and sailor to move, so women (or goddesses) working at the loom are the picture of fixity and immobility: domestic tranquillity, or the illusion of it.[16]

Telemachus, in contrast to Penelope, has every reason to want the narrative to continue and takes his mother to task for stopping the song of returns. His rebuke takes the form of an order that she return to her room and weave, leaving narrative (*mythos*) to men, and especially to himself in his capacity as master of the house (1.358–59). Although Penelope's attempt to stop Phemius seems unsuccessful, the bard's narrative of the return is, in effect, brought to a halt. The suitors lust for Penelope, dispute with Telemachus, then dance. Phemius, it seems, does not return to his tales of homecoming at this point. He is prevented from usurping, with his own narrative, the Muse's narrative rights. It is her story, not his, and she (as narrator and controller) allows Penelope to succeed, by default, in silencing the song of Odysseus's return until book 5. At that later point the Muse herself, not Phemius, spins the yarn.

When Telemachus travels to Pylos, his questions about Odysseus mostly result in a series of miniature homecoming tales pertaining to Nestor, Menelaus, Agamemnon, and an aside or two about Idomeneus, Diomedes, and others. Further, the tale of Orestes' vengeance—the latest, and, presumably, most popular, song—threatens to upstage the others by assimilating Telemachus to its pattern. As Odysseus's son leaves Pylos, he has with him a faithful, friendly, and rather more worldly wise young companion, Peisistratus, to enjoy the improbable chariot ride over the mountains to Sparta much as Orestes, in most traditions, has Pylades as his usually more savvy companion. The insistent allusions to Orestes and to other motifs of the house of Agamemnon heighten the apprehension in a newcomer's reading of the *Odyssey*. Telemachus's lot may, in some ways, parallel Orestes'. Thus the idea, once popular among scholars, of the thematic separateness of the Telemachus narrative seems, in retrospect, both puzzling and unnecessary.[17] The Muse, in reminding us of the potentially centrifugal forces of myth, readies us for her centripetal assumption of control. The problem is that the *Odyssey* is too familiar to scholars: we do not let ourselves get caught up in the intricacies of its possible (but unfulfilled) developments. It is precisely in the element of narrative suspense generated by the active search of Telemachus for Odysseus that the dramatic tension (in which the *Odyssey* arguably surpasses all other Greek and Roman epics) lies.

Three centers of interest have been established: one static (yet, paradoxically, seething) with Penelope and the suitors in Ithaca; one with Telemachus, now moving away from Ithaca; one with Odysseus (whom we have yet to meet), of uncertain location but about to move. The roads to bring about the convergence have been built, but remain separate, as roads do. But that does not mean they are not part of a planned system. Some artist somewhere in the process made them meet.

At the Court of Menelaus

In *Odyssey* 4, Telemachus and his companion Peisistratus arrive in Menelaus's Sparta in their quest for information about Odysseus. We share Telemachus's curiosity, since we have not yet "seen" Odysseus in the Muse's narrative. It is tempting to summarize what Menelaus and Helen tell Telemachus, then pass to book 5 and Odysseus himself.[18] Yet if we do so, we are assuming that the Muse introduces Helen and Menelaus primarily to provide information to (and a safe haven for) Telemachus. True, their narratives yield the first apparently "new" information about Odysseus. Yet these narratives are so evidently shaped by Helen's and Menelaus's own experiences with each other that they tell us more about them than about Odysseus. But we must not get ahead of ourselves. Let us return to the beginning of book 4.

When the Muse brings Telemachus and Peisistratus to the palace of Menelaus and Helen in Sparta, a double wedding celebration is in progress. Hermione, Menelaus's daughter by Helen, is being sent away to marry Achilles' son Neoptolemus, also known to tradition as Pyrrhus. This marriage in process provides a further reminder that we are moving into the next mythic generation. The second wedding is more curious. Megapenthes, Menelaus's otherwise unimportant son by an unnamed slave girl, is being married in Sparta to an equally mysterious woman brought from Sparta (which is odd, since Menelaus is *in* Sparta at the time). The bride is the unnamed daughter of Alector—a man Eustathius calls the son of Pelops and Hegesandra (herself the daughter of Amyclas and thus closely associated with Sparta's "twin" city, Amyclae).

The double marriage is a rather ironic comment on events in the royal household. Menelaus clearly did not live a celibate life before his marriage to Helen, if we presume Megapenthes is marrying at an age over, rather than under, twenty-one, as was usual for Greek males. If we assume Megapenthes is younger than twenty-one, then Menelaus did not go unconsoled during his years without Helen. That such a situation might have caused some comment in the world of the *Odyssey* we may perhaps discern later from comments about Eurycleia, with whom Laertes would have had an affair had it not been for fear of his wife.[19]

Helen is thus involved in double marriage preparations which place her presumably legitimate daughter Hermione on a par with the child of a "slave girl."[20] And her daughter's marriage was, in most mythic traditions, a troubled one. Neoptolemus, Hermione's groom, brought back Andromache, Hector's widow, from Troy as his concubine and was himself murdered, with Hermione's connivance, by Orestes, as we see in Euripides' *Andromache.* Orestes had been promised Hermione's hand, but either the marriage was denied by Menelaus (who favored Neoptolemus) or Hermione was taken away from Orestes after their marriage had taken place.[21]

If, as is generally contended, the Homeric muse does not know these "other" versions, we might well ask why she bothers to connect the arrival of Telemachus and Peisistratus with the wedding at all. She is as careful to keep the king's two young visitors away from the wedding festivities for Hermione and Megapenthes as is Menelaus himself. Yet Telemachus and Peisistratus are more central to the attentions of Helen and Menelaus than are the bridal parties. Menelaus remains with the two guests throughout their stay, neglecting the feast that is presumably going on. The only significant allusions he makes to weddings of any kind are a backhanded slap at Helen's relationship with Deïphobus (her second Trojan husband) and a description of bedding down in the vile-smelling concealment of sealskins "beside a sea beast," *para kētei,* in Proteus's cave (4.443). *Para kētei* may even suggest, given the marital context, some kind of play with the word *parakoitis* (bedmate) and conjures an image of sexual revulsion rather like that suggested in Patrick Fermor's description of the stench when the garments a Sarakatsani woman has worn all her life are finally removed on her death.[22]

Helen, Hermione's mother, is not at the feast either. She spends her time either in her upper chamber or with the newly arrived guests (4.120ff.). Throughout the episode, both king and queen behave as if entertaining Telemachus and Peisistratus were the only social and familial event of importance at the time. Only when Telemachus is about to leave does Megapenthes appear and help Menelaus carry gifts to Telemachus's chariot as the latter prepares to return to Ithaca (15.97–123). Since Hermione is being sent away to marry Neoptolemus, Achilles' son never appears at all.

The Muse's decision is prudent. The famous Neoptolemus, not to mention Hermione, would, if introduced, cast Telemachus into the shadows. Neoptolemus, besides, was the killer of Priam, the father of both of Helen's Trojan husbands, Paris and Deïphobus. Thus Menelaus's selection of Neoptolemus as Helen's son-in-law would perhaps have had a bitter aftertaste for Helen too. As it happens, then, Menelaus not only fails to introduce Telemachus and Peisistratus to the marriage parties; he accommodates Telemachus and Peisistratus not in his opulent palace, but on the porch. They are hardly made as comfortably welcome as Telemachus was by Nestor at Pylos. Things could have been worse, though. At least Menelaus does not accede to his servant's suggestion that he send them off to find accommodation elsewhere.[23] Yet he treats them very gingerly. He seems a little worried one of the newcomers may be Orestes, who Menelaus fears might blame him for Agamemnon's death and for neglecting his duties as an uncle. He avoids even the most oblique allusion to what, in Apollodorus, is his own broken promise that he would marry Hermione to Orestes. Telemachus's companion, similarly, might be Pylades. In later writers, Orestes is almost always represented as traveling with Pylades. Finally, quite apart from any thought of broken promises to Orestes, Menelaus may have some reason for worrying about the arrival of princely, youthful visitors as he prepares to send Hermione off to wed Neoptolemus. Helen herself had been kidnapped shortly after her marriage, an event neither she nor Menelaus has forgotten.

The failure to introduce formally and in an engaging episode the son of the hero of the *Iliad* to the son of the hero of the *Odyssey* is one of the Homeric muse's most maddening (and probably deliberate) omissions. She whets our appetite for the encounter only to let it slip by without overt comment. But what is particularly delicious, as the scene proceeds, is the potential confusion of Telemachus with the feared Orestes. The parallel between the two has been drawn insistently since the Muse took up the narrative in book 1. And even if she "does not know" about the marriage rivalry of Neoptolemus and Orestes, she does seem aware that Menelaus has some explaining to do about why he did not protect his brother Agamemnon, Orestes' father, from Aegisthus's murderous hand.

As Menelaus and his young visitors settle down to dinner, Telemachus, of course, knows who Menelaus is (4.49ff.). But when does Menelaus realize who his guests are? The Muse leaves us to detect this for ourselves. The princely status and age of Menelaus's visitors allow for several possibilities. At first, Menelaus addresses his visitors in the dual, as a pair, but as hospitality ritual (as presented in the *Odyssey*) and etiquette require, he does not ask the guest's identity until the guest has been bathed and has dined.[24] When he overhears Telemachus's whispered admiration for the Zeus-like wealth around him in the palace, he must notice that Telemachus addresses his companion as "son of Nestor" (4.71). Thus one visitor is identified.

"No mortal," Menelaus responds to Telemachus, "would compete with Zeus; . . . maybe there's a man who competes with me—but maybe not" (4.78, 80). Menelaus underscores his pride in his wealth, then appends a lament that his riches have come at a price: Agamemnon (Orestes' father) was murdered while he, Menelaus, made his fortune in Egypt (4.90–93). Yet though Menelaus ostentatiously blames himself for not being present to help his brother, he does not now explain why he did not, on returning from Egypt, avenge Agamemnon. When the mention of Agamemnon's name produces no reaction from his listeners, Menelaus drops the subject. Further explanation of his failure to avenge he postpones until the following day when his visitor's identity as Telemachus is firmly established. On that occasion Menelaus says Proteus, the Old Man of the Sea, had urged him to hasten home to catch Agamemnon's murderer, Aegisthus—unless Orestes had beaten him to it (4.543–47). Even then, Menelaus gives no sense of how long he was in Egypt, though he is clearly prompting the conclusion that he returned too late for vengeance: Orestes had already acted.

Menelaus goes on to allude, obliquely, to what he calls his personal pain: presumably the rape of Helen by Paris and the subsequent Trojan War—their fathers must have told them about it, he declares to the youths (4.93–95). This time the response might, understandably, be more mixed—though the Muse does not describe it. Peisistratus's father, Nestor, is never averse to storytelling, but Telemachus has no father around to tell him about the war. Narrowing his target, Menelaus adds a wish that he could have his lost friends back, especially Odysseus, who must be greatly missed by Penelope and Telemachus (4.97–112). This series of names *does* provoke a reaction: Telemachus weeps, though he tries to hide his tears (4.113–16). Nothing, we will note, has been said directly, as yet. But Menelaus now knows who his second guest is (4.116–19).

It is doubtful, in this instance, that the weeper is trying to win recognition from his interlocutor by means of his tears, as is certainly the case in *Odyssey* 8.487–554, where the listening Odysseus weeps and attempts to disguise his tears for the express purpose of conveying to the watchful observer that the narrative of Odysseus and Troy has a special poignancy for him. We may be tempted to assume it is the purest accident that Menelaus mentions only Odysseus, of all the Greek heroes from Troy, and that he goes on to name Odysseus's wife, Penelope, and his son, Telemachus. Some have even argued that Menelaus is stupid (as he sometimes is in Euripides). But, if we look ahead, we will see that Menelaus observes a few lines later how struck he was by the physical resemblance of Telemachus to Odysseus. We must allow for the possibility that Menelaus spoke as he did to test a hunch about his visitor's identity.

Appreciation of this scene is often spoiled by the scholarly assumption that meaning lies only in what is explicit and underscored. In the *Odyssey*, it is routine for acknowledgment of what is observed to be postponed, even withheld altogether.[25] As in real life, so in epic: when someone sees us and does not greet us, he is just as likely to be ignoring us as to have failed either to notice or to recognize us. In the *Odyssey*, recognition and communication in general are *normally* indirect, by innuendo, in disguise.

Ill-timed self-disclosure, even in triumph, can be dangerous, as Odysseus points out in his narrative of the Cyclops (9.500–542). Sometimes it is simply tactless, as it would be if Alcinous made it plain that he sees Nausicaa's eagerness to launder clothes for her brothers, who are of marriageable age, as a hint of her own readiness for marriage (6.66–67). When Menelaus does not acknowledge Telemachus's identity after the Muse tells us he knows it (4.116–19), his caution is understandable. Knowing *who* Telemachus is does not explain *why* he is present. Relatives of warriors in the Trojan War might resent the king whose wife could be considered its cause. Better to discover what is on Telemachus's mind before admitting you know who he is. So Menelaus bides his time. Withheld acknowledgment allows expressions of kindness about Odysseus and his son to appear uncalculated, and thus genuine. Penelope adopts a similar strategy later in the *Odyssey* with Odysseus. She almost certainly figures out who he is well before she actually acknowledges him; the test of the bow she proposes (and he accepts) is not so much to see if he is Odysseus, but whether Odysseus is the man he was twenty years ago.[26]

Menelaus is prevented from exploiting his rhetorical advantage because Helen enters (4.120–22). In contrast to the reticent Menelaus, she instantly declares the visitor *must* be Telemachus, since no one else could so closely resemble Odysseus. Menelaus concurs, giving details which show how carefully he has noted the youth's physical appearance; he now acknowledges he has recognized Odysseus's son (4.138–54). There is no reason to assume this is pretense on his part to avoid being outshone by Helen. Later developments show he is her match, rhetorically. And his signs of recognition are precise.

When mutual recognition and acknowledgment set the company to lamenting Odysseus and Peisistratus's brother, Antilochus (4.155–215), Helen drugs everyone's wine with a potion she obtained in Egypt from the wife of Thon. It prevents grief even if one sees one's kin killed before the city gate (4.219–34). Again we find a possible allusion to another tradition. Herodotus says Helen was stopped by Thonis and detained in Egypt by Proteus while en route to Troy with Paris until Menalaus claimed her *after the war.*[27] The drug administered, Helen narrates a story whose overt purpose and early statements show how great a man Odysseus is (4.235–50): he came into Troy before the city fell, disguised as a beggar; he even had himself flogged to make the effect authentic, and he fooled everyone in Troy—well, almost everyone.

At 4.250 the narrative changes direction: *pantes—egō de,* "everyone, but I . . . " Suddenly Odysseus is at Helen's mercy (4.250–64): she recognized him, despite his efforts to elude her; she bathed him; she swore not to (and did not) betray him, for she now longed to return home to Sparta, regretting the mad passion for Paris which had brought her to Troy in the first place, longing for her bedroom at home and her husband.

Helen's narrative, of course, foreshadows Odysseus's recognition by Eurycleia in *Odyssey* 19.335–507 and might fulfill the useful purpose of alerting Telemachus to Odysseus's skill at disguising himself as a beggar.[28] But it is self-serving, even if it is "true." And there is no means of telling whether it is true or not. Helen's story here sharply contrasts with that in Euripides *Hecuba* 239–48, where Hecuba appeals to Odysseus on the grounds that *she* saved his life when he came into Troy and was recognized by Helen. Helen told her (though only her) about her discovery, and Hecuba kept the secret when Odysseus begged her for his life. The Euripidean Odysseus concedes that this is what happened. The Homeric Odysseus makes no reference to the incident, but the Homeric Helen clearly states that she told no one. Her point is that though Odysseus was disguised, she, Helen, saw through it. We can credit the Homeric Helen's claimed powers of observation, for she recognized Telemachus immediately on seeing him. But she has now revealed to us that she was unable to restrain herself from declaring her recognition instantly. Could she really have kept Odysseus's identity secret if she had discovered him in Troy? Was she really ready to betray Troy and return to Greece with Menelaus? Even more to the point, why was Odysseus with her (if he really was), and what was it about him that she recognized and why? At the very least she is claiming a personal contact and companionship with Odysseus such as would have made him run the risk of detection and betrayal.

The Muse does not overlook our questions. When Helen comes out of her chamber to entertain Telemachus and Peisistratus she is compared to Artemis, the virgin goddess par excellence, who has no interest in men or marriage. The insertion of the theme of celibacy and chastity has an ironic effect (and warns us to be careful about taking even comparisons of Penelope to Artemis too literally). We might cite the similarly puzzling comparison of Dido and Aeneas to Diana and Apollo—just before they have their famous and almost certainly sexual rendezvous in the cave (*Aeneid* 4.498–504). Similes in the *Odyssey* are generally remarkable for their appropriate inappropriateness. Odysseus's tears on hearing tales of Troy are compared to those of a captive Trojan woman (8.522–30). Similarly, the comparison of Eumaeus's tears on welcoming Telemachus home to those of a man who has not seen his son for ten years has to be read against the fact that when Telemachus enters Eumaeus's hut, he is also seen, but not acknowledged, by his real father, Odysseus, who has not seen him for twice the length of time noted in the simile.

At first, Helen's drug and her narrative seem to work: Menelaus declares Helen's story marvelous. But then he appends a tale of his own, introduced by a line almost identical to that used by Helen to introduce her narrative of Odysseus (4.242 and 271), telling how Odysseus had saved the Greeks concealed in the wooden horse (4.265–89). The story is not overtly self-promoting. On the contrary, Menelaus narrates as an observer. Helen, he says, accompanied by Deïphobus, walked three times around the horse, hailing the Greek warriors by name, and imitating the voices of their wives. One warrior, Anticlus, would have cried aloud in response, and the Greeks would have been detected, had Odysseus not clamped his hand over the man's mouth and silenced him until Athena led Helen away. In his story, then, it is Odysseus who prevents Helen from betraying the Greeks: precisely the opposite point from the one she is attempting to establish.

We may wonder, at this stage, what has happened to the power of Helen's potion, since Menelaus's story is a total refutation of hers, not just an addition to heroic lore about Odysseus.[29] The chronological setting is subsequent to Helen's: the eve of the fall of Troy. Menelaus's allusions to Deïphobus, Helen's *second* Trojan husband, and to her treacherous behavior undermine Helen's claims that she came to regret leaving Menelaus for Paris and that her sympathies had reverted to her husband and home. Menelaus has not forgotten the pain.

Helen's Expulsion

Helen has blundered rhetorically by allowing her narrative to be undermined by her behavior, and by making her claims so blatantly that she invites refutation, and is refuted. Menelaus's counternarrative is successful (if not necessarily "true") and puts a chill on the evening. Although Telemachus tactfully ignores the undertones of the rhetorical duel, he observes to Menelaus, first, that Odysseus's iron heart did not save him from destruction and, second, that it is now time to sleep (4.290–95). Nor does he miss either the irrelevance or the nasty undertow of the couple's exchanges. He follows up Menelaus's narrative of Odysseus in the Trojan horse by suggesting that this tale only makes things worse, since Odysseus was obviously lost subsequently anyway (4.290–93). In other words, neither of their stories has any bearing on his quest. Perhaps to avoid further altercation, he suggests that it's time for bed, for sleep (4.294–95). This observation prompts Helen to leave the room and supervise the sleeping arrangements. She is relegated to housewifely duties. When the narrative resumes the next day, Helen is not present. Menelaus is free to launch into a protracted narrative of his own return from Troy and his own adventures in Egypt and encounter with Proteus. In this Menelean tale, Odysseus is purely incidental, and Helen is completely absent.

Yet Menelaus is careful not to be rude. Although he refutes Helen's account of her longing to return to Greece, he never outrightly calls her a liar. She, as daughter of Zeus, is his passport to Elysium. That is all he needs her for. Nor does Menelaus claim, in his own voice, that he is superior in divine blessings to Odysseus. He adopts the kind of approach which Demetrius praises as a special part of formidable speaking, *deinotēs*: "The effect is more powerful because it is achieved by letting the fact speak for itself rather than having the speaker make the point for himself" (*On Style* 288). Menelaus achieves an abusive, discrediting effect without actually using abuse, *loidoria*. He lets his narrative do the necessary work for him while he himself stands back and treats Helen with formal courtesy and speaks with huge admiration for Odysseus.[30] The force of what is communicated, as Demetrius notes of *deinotēs* (*On Style* 241), lies not in what is said, but in what people pass over in silence.

When conversation resumes the next day, and Menelaus tells of his own return from Troy, Helen does not seem to be present. If she is, she is silent. Menelaus is free to narrate in his terms, to make himself the narrator-hero. We might think, as does Herodotus 2.113–20, that Helen was not with him on his return. When he describes himself withdrawn from his men and walking the Egyptian beach deep in thought, he is alone (4.367). He mentions Helen only as he reports what the Old Man of the Sea, Proteus, told him. In Proteus's "revelations" (as reported by Menelaus), the most striking detail is how much more blessed Menelaus is than any other returning hero (4.491–592). Locrian Ajax is dead "among his long-oared ships." Agamemnon's troops return alive, but Agamemnon dies. Odysseus survives; his troops are lost. Menelaus, by contrast, survives with most of his forces intact. Odysseus, Menelaus's chief rival as "returned hero," is shown as alive, but miserable, stranded, and helpless, having neither crew nor ship, and essentially a captive of Calypso, "who keeps possession of [*ischei*] him" (4.557–58). There is no allusion to Calypso's hope of giving him immortality, a matter the goddess later raises with Hermes in *Odyssey* 5.135–36. Odysseus's prospects look bleak.

Proteus's version of Menelaus's future (as reported, of course, by Menelaus) is more promising. He will find bliss and eternal springtime in Elysium, not death in Argos, when his time comes. "You," Proteus says, "possess Helen [*echeis Helenēn*] and are son-in-law to Zeus" (4.569). The contrast with Odysseus is sharp: Telemachus's father is possessed by a goddess, whereas he, Menelaus, is possessor of the daughter of Zeus, and through her the certainty of immortality. There was, then, more than first met the eye when Menelaus, the previous evening, had rebuked Telemachus, albeit gently, for comparing his palace to Olympian Zeus's: "No mortal would compete with Zeus; . . . maybe there's a man who competes with me—but maybe not" (4.78, 80).

The wily king has crushed Helen's attempt to tell her story to her own narrative advantage by using her "superiority" to Odysseus as a means of advancing her own claims to fame and recognition. Menelaus has taken over the narrative, as he takes control of Proteus despite Proteus's constant metamorphoses, and makes it tell the story his way: how much more blessed he is than any returning hero, including Odysseus. And Helen is his key to ultimate status: a family connection with Zeus, and immortality, part of the godlike affluence of his palace. That is all she is.

The two competing tales about Odysseus in *Odyssey* 4 are weapons in a struggle for narrative rights between husband and wife, the outcome of which will determine Helen's image in subsequent tradition. Odysseus, however central to Telemachus's search, is as incidental to Menelaus as he is to Helen. He is the heroic corpse each struggles to expropriate in a battle of narratives that Menelaus seems to win.

Heroism in the *Odyssey* is to some degree determined by one's ability to seize and exploit the narrative initiative. Helen attempts and fails. Menelaus seems to succeed, momentarily, by crushing Helen yet using her, and by co-opting the inner narrative voice of Proteus to build his own boastful stature. But he has not persuaded Homer's muse to invert the *Odyssey* and make it the tale of Menelaus.[31] His riches, status, and now housebroken wife are not to be the stuff of Homer's epic. Indeed, Menelaus is robbed of the status he seeks even as he thinks he is winning it. Homer's muse is about to usher Odysseus into the center with her own authorial voice, and then to give Odysseus the second largest narrative voice after her own: four of the epic's twenty-four books. During that narrative Odysseus will attempt to advance his kind of heroism beyond Achilles' Iliadic glory. He will claim to have heard Achilles' lament that he would rather be a slave of the poorest man on earth than king of the dead. The heroic choice of the *Iliad* dissolves in the face of death. How remarkable, then, Odysseus must be to reject the chance of immortality with Calypso, since he knows what death is! But in alluding to Odysseus's rejection of unheroic immortality with Calypso (while consigning Menelaus to an even more bourgeois version of the same with Helen), the Muse reinserts Odysseus into the world of heroic homecomings and consigns Menelaus to the sidelines.

There will, presumably, be other rounds in this ongoing fight. When we are offered another glimpse of the Spartan king's rather strained marriage, Helen gains narrative revenge by offering a neat explanation of an omen which utterly baffles her husband. But by then the listener's attention is far removed from Menelaus and Helen's war of polite words.

[2]

Arrival at Scheria

In *Odyssey* 1–4, the Muse keeps us waiting for a direct glimpse of Odysseus through her narrative eyes. In doing so she is not necessarily just beginning *in mediis rebus* but taking into account traditions that may have delayed Odysseus's return even further, until his Circean and Euippean sons had grown up. The Muse has Athena tell Zeus and the other gods, and thus tell us, that Odysseus is still alive and deserves the right to return to the world of geographical Greeks from a place where he is detained against his will: the island of the nymph Calypso, the "Concealer." Menelaus, in his own voice, as the Muse reports it, adds confirmation of this rumor's existence among mortals too. The opening books make it clear that although Odysseus's household is gradually being ruined in his absence, he probably still has the power to restore the situation if he arrives in time. But Menelaus leaves no doubt that Odysseus, from what he has heard, is in a pitiable state. And this impression is confirmed in our first direct encounter with Odysseus in book 5.

Opening Views of Odysseus

It is significant that Odysseus is introduced *after* he has lost his crew and is on Calypso's island in a dispirited state. The Muse, through Athena, implies that he found the first seven years or so of the nymph's company quite entertaining. But the picture we get of him after Hermes has told Calypso she must release him is pathetic. He weeps all day on the seashore and climbs reluctantly into bed with the more eager Calypso at night. He is, in short, hardly a lively and certainly not a very fertile partner for the nymph, who seems more irritated by the idea that she should be ordered by Hermes to give up Odysseus than by his actual departure. There may be something more than meets the eye to Odysseus's comment about Calypso to Arete in 7.246–47. Odysseus declares that "no man intermingles with her [*OUde TIS autêi / misgetai*]." (We capitalize *OU TIS*, "No Man," since this is later Odysseus's assumed name when addressing the Cyclops Polyphemus.) There is usually, as we will see, an ambiguity in the meaning of the verb *misgetai* which indicates both social and sexual intercourse. Odysseus's desolation is complete as he broods on this island of aristocratic loneliness, inhabited only by himself, Calypso, and the household help. On the other hand, this is not quite so grim a scenario as scholars sometimes suggest, and far removed from the life-threatening existence among savages that Telemachus imagines him living. The sailor marooned on a pleasant island with a beautiful goddess who proposes to make him immortal has limited claims on our pity. And Odysseus—*OUTIS*, "No Man," certainly does have sexual relations with her.

Uniquely among the returning heroes from the Trojan War, Odysseus has lost all his men, all his ships, and all his treasure. Little surprise, then, that he should later, when pressed, adopt the persona of a Cretan, associated with Idomeneus, the only Greek warrior at Troy who returned with troops and ships intact. The only alleged survivors of Odysseus's crew that we encounter in ancient literature are Achaemenides, who has to await identification and transportation to safety in a Roman epic (*Aeneid* 3.586–654), and Macareus, who is added by Ovid (*Metamorphoses* 14.158–59).[1]

The Muse's narrative "reality" of Odysseus's dispiritedness contrasts sharply with the lionhearted husband Penelope remembers and whose return she is said to be awaiting (4.724, 814). It stands in even starker contrast to Odysseus's reputation, expressed in the opening lines of the *Odyssey*. There Odysseus is declared a man of many wiles and resources (*polytropon*). Despite the assurance of "Homer," once the Muse takes over the narrative, we sense that Odysseus would be lost to memory without the timely intercession of Athena. Given Odysseus's failure to bring any companions back alive, such loss from memory could, in theory, be kinder than the alternative: the infamy of being remembered as the only hero to return with nothing to show for his absence but increased age. Odysseus has, both in the *Odyssey* and elsewhere in ancient tradition, a remarkable talent for achieving loneliness and desolation by destroying the societies and peoples with whom he comes in contact. Even in *Odyssey* 24, mayhem and chaos would overwhelm Odysseus's much reduced household and the population of his island were it not for the intervention of Athena and other gods. Ithaca would be as desolate as Troy.

Only as Odysseus starts to build his ship to sail away from Calypso does the Muse present him in a positive and creative mood.[2] Loaded with supplies and gifts, he sets sail, with some success, for seventeen days, until he comes within view of Phaeacia (whose geographical location is hardly more intelligible than that of Calypso's island). At this point, the one god excluded from divine counsels about Odysseus's return, Poseidon, spots the hero while he himself is traveling back from the land of the Ethiopians. In instant and negative reaction, Poseidon stirs up a storm (which Odysseus mistakenly blames on Zeus). Odysseus's response to the storm is a famous lament: how much more blessed were those who died at Troy at the hands of the Achaeans. To die at sea is to die unheroically. Again, he cuts a pathetic, nonheroic figure as his vessel disintegrates beneath him, as he laments and is left clinging to the ship's *histos* (mast), as his wife Penelope relies on her *histos* (loom) to save her from the suitors. The *histos* is salvation for both.

Help for Odysseus from another goddess is at hand, however, the Muse explains, in the person of Ino, daughter of the Phoenician sailor Cadmus. Ino, also known as Leucothea, appears to Odysseus in the guise of a great shearwater (*aithyia*) and never identifies herself to him otherwise. She tells him to let go of his mast (even though the storm rages on) and instead to rely on the protection of a veil she offers him. At this point, Odysseus wisely refuses to do as she bids. All he sees is a shearwater, whose appearance would not have surprised him, since the bird is often associated with storms and shipwreck, though normally with impending storms, rather than with storms in progress.[3] Its arrival is usually an ill omen, because of its habit of diving beneath the waves—which led the Romans to call it *mergus*, a name derived, according to Varro (*Lingua Latina* 5.78), from the verb *mergere*, "dive" or, in some cases, "drown."[4] A talking shearwater, however, would be something of an anomaly, not only because most birds cannot talk, but because the shearwater was proverbially quiet—deaf and dumb, in fact, Aristophanes of Byzantium and the naturalist Dionysius suggest.[5] This may be the point that Glaucus of Nicopolis is making in *Greek Anthology* 7.285:

> Neither this earth nor the tiny weight of this stone, but the whole sea
> which you observe is the site of Erasippus's tomb.
> For he went down with his ship, so where in the world you'll find his bones
> only the shearwaters know and can inform you about.

Glaucus is surely pointing out that no *human* will ever know where Erasippus is buried because the only creatures that know are seabirds who cannot speak (and probably, following convention, cannot hear either). The shearwater's appearance, then, cannot have consoled Odysseus, whose greatest fear, just voiced, is of dying unobserved and unreported.

Possibly Odysseus momentarily thinks the shearwater is Athena in disguise, offering help, even though he later accuses her (wrongly) of not helping him (6.324–27; 13.318–19). The identification of Athena with the shearwater is natural enough if the tradition whereby Athena is known as *Athēnē Aithyia* or *Aithyia Korē* is of some antiquity.[6] If Odysseus assumes the talking shearwater is Athena—and the goddess does occasionally appear, or, rather, disappear, as a bird in the *Odyssey*—he would, of course, be wrong.[7] Yet by associating the shearwater with Ino rather than Athena, Homer's muse heightens the irony of the scene. Ino, in all writers who provide details of her myth, achieves immortality by plunging into the sea with her son Melicertes and drowning herself. Since the identity of the talking shearwater is known to the reader, but not to Odysseus, a certain humor, surely, accompanies our knowledge of who offers Odysseus help. Had Ino identified herself, it would have seemed doubly imprudent for Odysseus to give up his mast in favor of a suicide's veil.

An especially large Poseidonian wave, however, leaves Odysseus no alternative but to take up Ino's offer. Thus there might be, for an ancient reader versed in myth, a sense that Odysseus has suffered a kind of death which, like Ino's, translates him into immortality. Her veil still in his grasp, he washes ashore in Phaeacia three days later. There he collapses and falls into a deep sleep. On awakening, he throws the veil back into the water and sleeps again. Although he kisses the earth in gratitude, he is still far from optimism. "What will happen to me?" (5.465) he wonders, now fearing he will be killed by frost, morning dew, or wild animals.

The Muse lays emphasis on the double occurrence of sleep on the new island's shores. Indeed, all that follows in the *Odyssey* from the beginning of book 6 until the Phaeacians return Odysseus to Ithaca in book 13 is marked off by a parenthesis of sleep. Odysseus is asleep as he arrives in Phaeacia, thanks to the magical talisman supplied by the Phoenician Ino, and asleep as he arrives in Ithaca, thanks to the magical transportation supplied him by the Phaeacian Alcinous. Understandably, there is a fantastical, dreamlike quality about *Odyssey* 6–12—as well there should be, for Phaeacia is possibly the invention of the Odyssean muse. Indeed, Phaeacia occupies, in the narrative of Odysseus's return, the place that Thesprotia occupies in other, non-Odyssean, versions.[8]

Landfall in Phaeacia

The Phaeacian episode starts with Odysseus's arrival on the shore of Scheria, naked, tired, and disheveled after the wreck of his *schedia*, "ship."[9] He falls asleep under a pile of leaves beneath a half-wild and half-cultured olive tree. The detail matters not only because it underscores his relationship to Athena, whose special tree was the olive, but also because olives rarely grow without human agriculture. If this olive is half-wild, half-cultured, it marks land once cultivated but now allowed to grow wild, or land until recently wild but now cultivated. The ambiguity of this symbolism is wonderfully apt. Scheria's inhabitants, we soon learn, have been in residence for only a single generation—the length of time it takes an olive tree to be ready to produce fruit. Further, the flourishing of Phaeacia is brief. Its people will be permanently cut off from the rest of the world after Odysseus returns to Ithaca, because of Poseidon's anger at the Phaeacians for transporting him home.

Curiously enough, Homer's muse goes on to compare Odysseus, concealing himself beneath the olive leaves, to a firebrand that a farmer in an outlying farm (with no neighbors to ask for brands to rekindle his fire) hides beneath dark embers (5.488). This image adds to the effect of the half-wild, half-cultivated olive tree. It suggests that Odysseus might have an important role in bringing a new vitality to the land he visits—although, we should concede, fire has destructive as well as creative potential. That the Muse is conscious of the force of her fire imagery in this Phaeacian context is later reaffirmed when Odysseus stands as a suppliant in the hearth of the royal palace.

No less interesting is the Muse's remark, as the book ends, that Athena (goddess of the olive) has hidden (*amphikalypsas*) Odysseus in a veil of sleep. Her word of hiding contains a verbal echo of the name of Calypso, Odysseus's companion for seven years, and of the veil given him by Ino, which he has just returned to its owner. Alternatively, the nymph's name is a reminder of the obscurity in which his life has been veiled for the mythical seven years, much as the surviving followers of the Welsh hero Brân in the *Mabinogi* are suspended in time during their seven years of feasting at Harlech.[10]

In this context, where Odysseus, hunted by Poseidon and aided by Athena, is associated, at the edge of the salt sea, with an olive, one thinks of the famous olive next to the saltwater spring on the Acropolis at Athens in a place sacred to Erechtheus, symbolizing the claims of both Athena and Poseidon to the land. The resprouting of this olive after the Persian sack of the Acropolis signified Athens's rebirth from fire (Herodotus 8.55).[11] Perhaps Homer's muse has this Erechthean olive in mind as she narrates, for once Athena has Odysseus safely established in the Poseidonian land of Phaeacia, she leaves Scheria for Athens and the "well-built house of Erechtheus," which scholars take to be precisely that shrine of Erechtheus (later destroyed by the Persians) on the Athenian acropolis (7.80–81).[12]

The land at which Odysseus arrives belongs on no map of the ancient world, despite later poets' determination to identify it with Corcyra or Drepane.[13] Much futile effort has been expended from antiquity on, aided and abetted by ancient cities of Italy and Sicily seeking Greek investments, to give the Phaeacians and other improbable peoples in *Odyssey* 6–12 a real geographical home. If we become too concerned with the geographical identity of Phaeacia, we fall into the trap of assuming that its inhabitants have some marginally real existence.[14] Phaeacia, like the Laestrygonians' land, stands on the nebulous border between myth and fiction, rather than on the slightly less nebulous border between myth and history.[15]

Further, with consummate irony, the Muse announces that the Phaeacians have not been long in their present location. This is almost certainly true. She has probably just created them and put them there herself. In *Odyssey* 6.4–10 she notes that the Phaeacians were brought there by Nausithous, "Swift in Ships," whom Alcinous, king of the Phaeacians, later tells Odysseus is his father (8.564–65; cf. 7.62–63). The detail is intriguing in many ways, not least because in Hesiod (*Theogony* 1017–18) Odysseus is Nausithous's father and Calypso his mother. If the Muse anticipates an audience familiar with that other tradition, she is appropriating, the moment Odysseus arrives in Phaeacia from Calypso's land, the name of Odysseus's Hesiodic son by Calypso to serve as ancestor of the Phaeacians. In doing so, she not only disposes of the "error" in rival versions but accounts, with more than Ovidian legerdemain, for how it may have arisen.

Nausithous, the Muse continues, brought his people to Scheria, their present home, from their no less ungeographical original abode, Hypereia, "Beyondland," far across the sea. They emigrated, the Muse adds, "through fear of the Cyclopes, who were their superiors in strength." The listener familar with Hesiod and other Greek poets must have been more startled than we are by this casual allusion to the mythic fabricators of Zeus's thunderbolts (a subject to which we will return shortly). Indeed, the reference gives us the sense yet again that the Muse is calculatedly directing myth down new and unfamiliar paths. For now, however, let us confine ourselves to considering how this adjustment affects the rhetorical situation of Odysseus.

The Phaeacians' national tradition requires that they accept that Cyclopes exist and are formidable foes. Although we are not told explicitly that Odysseus knows, as he narrates his travels, that the Phaeacians emigrated through *fear* of the Cyclopes, he has certainly been informed by Alcinous and Athena that the Phaeacians are closely related to both Cyclopes and Giants (7.59, 205–6). Odysseus therefore takes rhetorical advantage of the Phaeacians' belief in the existence of the Cyclopes in claiming to have visited their original homeland and in pointing out that the Cyclopes' superiority to humans is limited to superior size and physical strength.[16]

Views of Scheria

Most of what we (and Odysseus) learn about the Phaeacians emanates from the Phaeacian king, Alcinous, his daughter, Nausicaa, or Athena—herself disguised as a young Phaeacian maiden. But other characters contribute as well to Odysseus's perception of the land in which he has arrived, and they have their own individual reasons for representing themselves and their land in the way they do. In fact, contradictions sometimes emerge between what these characters say about Phaeacia, and what we may infer from passing comments by the Homeric muse.

We shall explore the contradiction between the young princess's assertions about the peacefulness of the Phaeacians and local reports and comments which hint otherwise.[17] Readers often gloss over these contradictions, wanting to see in Odysseus's encounter with the Phaeacians another opportunity afforded—but "heroically" rejected by him—of staying in a peaceful society rather than returning home to battle with the suitors for his wife and property. Not all the Phaeacians want Odysseus to stay; and how each represents the land to him depends to some extent on what he or she thinks may prompt him to go or to remain. The Muse too sometimes raises doubts as to whether Phaeacia is as peaceful as Nausicaa suggests. Suffice it to say, in preface, that the Phaeacian narrative is a complex "cat-and-mouse" game between Odysseus and the Phaeacians and among various groups of Phaeacians.

We begin with the gods. They, Alcinous says, appear in Phaeacia undisguised (7.201–6). Even assuming this boast was once valid in the not particularly long Phaeacian past, such divine openness does not prevail during Odysseus's visit. Whenever the Muse tells us that gods are present, they are disguised. Athena disguises herself as a young girl while leading Odysseus to Alcinous's palace. The morning of Alcinous's first meeting with Odysseus, Athena assumes the likeness of Alcinous's herald as she goes through the city to convene an assembly (7.19–20; 8.7–15). Later, while marking the spot where a discus Odysseus hurled has fallen, Athena appears as a Phaeacian to tell Odysseus that no Phaeacian will match or surpass his throw (8.193–98). Nor is Athena the only god who appears in disguise. Poseidon, divine ancestor of the Phaeacians (and Alcinous's own grandfather), is undetected by his descendants when he waits in Scheria for the return of the ship which takes Odysseus home, and roots it to the seabed with a stroke of his hand (13.159–69).

Are these disguised gods something new, or is Alcinous, and with him Nausicaa, simply deluded (or lying) about their previous open appearances?[18] Is it that Odysseus brings the "real world" and its troubles with him to Phaeacia, where the gods did, in the past, appear undisguised?

Nausicaa

Nausicaa is the first Phaeacian to speak with Odysseus in *Odyssey* 6, the one who takes the most personal and friendly interest in him, and the first arguably fictional, rather than traditional, mythic character introduced into the epic. The Muse disarms skeptics in her audience by creating a gently humorous mise-en-scène as Odysseus moves out of his isolation in the world of divine myth into what threatens to become the more isolated world of fiction. Indeed, if Odysseus cuts a pathetic (and at least faintly comic) figure as he pines on Calypso's island, he cuts a comically absurd figure when he awakens, naked, to the sound of women's voices in the midst of a thicket near the beach in Phaeacia. The voices, he suspects, are those of nymphs–naturally enough, considering he is emerging from seven years of residence with one nymph with the help of another. But the reality is not so divine. The voices are those of girls taking a break from doing laundry in a nearby river, and playing ball.

Yet the scene is hardly one of mundane reality. The girls' leader, Nausicaa, is a princess, and it is strange, even in the democratically aristocratic world of Homeric princes, to find a king's daughter doing laundry. True, she is washing *special* garments—and this point, we will see, is important. The Muse has prepared us, if not Odysseus, for the meeting between naked hero and girls with a wagonload of men's washing. Nausicaa has persuaded her father that his sons need clean clothing because two are married and three are "strong young bachelors" of an age to get married. Though she has said nothing directly about her own marriage, Alcinous realizes she is covertly hinting at her own readiness for marriage. Nonetheless, as the Muse points out, Alcinous never indicates to Nausicaa that he has grasped her hidden agenda. Obliquity, ancient *emphasis*, prevails. The pretext that laundry needs to be done allows Nausicaa, with marriage on her mind, to venture out of the palace to the shore with her maids. The Muse, then, has created an opportunity for Odysseus to meet her, first of the Phaeacians, under circumstances that would be quite proper, were he not stark naked and in need of a good wash himself.

Odysseus, embarrassed by his nudity, goes to at least minimal lengths to conceal it by cutting off a leafy branch to ensure some propriety before emerging from his hiding place:

> So saying, the godlike Odysseus emerged from under the dense scrub after snapping off a leafy branch with his heavy hand to protect his genitals. (6.127–29)

Such an entrance is not in high heroic style, though there is no need to assume that Odysseus uses the branch to conceal a satyrlike interest in the young girls, as some critics infer.[19] A notable feature of Odysseus's behavior in Phaeacia is his *lack* of sexual response to female overtures. The effect becomes even more droll when the Muse goes on to compare the naked Odysseus to a lion:

> For he came like a lion, mountain-reared, trusting in his strength [*alki*], who strides forward, though beaten by rain and wind, his two eyes ablaze, and still makes his way among the cattle or sheep, or chases the less domesticated deer. His stomach urges him to try to find his way even into tightly built sheep pens. (6.130–34)

Interpreters of this simile comment on its simplicity, its absurdity, or both.[20] Few miss its playful tone.[21] One moment Odysseus defensively and coyly emerges from the bushes carrying a branch to protect rather than conceal) his private parts; the next, he is a threateningly aggressive male lion trusting his strength, not fearing for his masculinity.

The simile is, as Homeric similes usually are, appropriately inappropriate. The Muse reminds us obliquely of what an unprotected girl might normally expect when a naked male emerges from concealment in ancient Greek poetry. Such encounters on beaches or by wells are usually a prelude to the girl's discomfiture rather than the man's (or god's): to her rape or seduction, as in *Odyssey* 16, when Eumaeus's nurse is seduced by a Phoenician sailor when she, like Nausicaa, goes to wash clothes. If the girl is not alone, but accompanied by other girls, her companions usually have the prudence to escape and leave her to her doom.[22] The Muse makes the most of the paradoxical situation by using language which normally describes the sexual nature of the threat posed by a man to a woman:

> So Odysseus intended intercourse [*mixesthai*] with the pretty-haired girls, although he was nude. For the need came upon him. (6.135–36)

The verb *mixesthai* (from *mignymi*, "mix, mingle") carries suggestions of both social and sexual intercourse in Homer. Here the sexual element is indubitably, and ironically, present. Its use following the aggressive lion simile also activates that other sense of *mignymi*, frequent in the *Iliad*, indicating the press and confusion of fierce fighting which makes it impossible for an onlooker to distinguish among the contending warriors. And this is precisely the Muse's point now. What charges a dramatic situation are the multiple possibilities of its resolution imagined by participants and onlookers, not the single resolution finally achieved. And the language used must express that multiplicity in its own multivalence.

Such consciousness of the sexuality of the language and situation as is present seems to emanate from the woman rather than the man. When Nausicaa uses the verb *mignymi* she uses it in the sense of social intercourse, though with at least tentative sexual overtones, since marriage is on her mind.[23] "No man mingles [*epimisgetai*] with us," Nausicaa tells her maids, in Odysseus's hearing (6.205). Similarly, when Nausicaa explains to Odysseus that she cannot lead him to the city herself, she declares she too would censure any other girl who "despite her dear father and mother, while they are still alive, mingles with [*misgētai*] men before the day of her public marriage" (6.286–88). While the overt reference is to social intercourse, the mention of marriage triggers the innuendo of sexual intercourse. A similar play on the levels of meaning in "intercourse" occurs later, in the account of Calypso's island that Odysseus relates to Nausicaa's mother, Arete: "There is an isle, Ogygia, which lies far off in the sea. There dwells the pretty-haired daughter of Atlas, guileful Calypso, a dread goddess, and with her No One mingles either god or mortal [*OUde TIS autēi / misgetai*]. Yet fate brought only me, in my wretchedness, to her hearth" (7.244–49). Here Odysseus screens, by using this word of more formal social as well as sexual contact, what the Muse makes clear: the fundamentally sexual nature of his relationship with Calypso (5.225–27). A reader already familiar with Odysseus's disguise of himself as "No Man" (*Outis*), when he tricks the Cyclops Polyphemus, might well smile at his contrived and multiple ambiguity here. Odysseus did, after all, "mingle" with Calypso sexually as well as socially even if no other No Man did.

Scholars from the time of Eustathius onward are quick to suggest that when the verb *mixesthai* is used of Odysseus in 6.136 the reader should not see anything "improper" in it. Eustathius insists that we not understand the verb with the meaning it carries in a phrase like *migē philotēti kai eunēi*, "mingles in love and in bed," but rather as in *andrasi misgetai*, "mingles with men." But the Homeric audience did not have Eustathius's morally chastening notes to reassure them—and Eustathius's alternative phrasing is itself not without sexual innuendo when Nausicaa uses it at 6.288. Nor do Nausicaa's companions feel confident that the situation is sexually secure. They instantly (and, to judge by normal mythic experience, prudently) run away. Greek heroes rarely leave sexual opportunities unrealized.

More puzzling than her companions' departure is the fact that Nausicaa does *not* run away. The Muse has not told her what she has told us: that, all appearances and mythic topoi to the contrary, Nausicaa is not in imminent danger of rape. The Muse's explanation is that Athena put courage in the girl to make her stay. Odysseus, then, confronted by only one of the girls with whom he desired, despite his nudity, to have social intercourse (while they, presumably, fear the sexual), has an opportunity to clarify the nature of his need and makes a very sensible decision in a setting which still leaves itself open to misunderstanding. Conventional modes of supplication will not work in this obviously unconventional situation. While it is normal in Homeric epic to implore people's help by seizing their knees, such an approach to the isolated Nausicaa poses several delicate, perhaps indelicate, problems. A physical gesture of this kind would suggest that his intent is rape and would, Odysseus recognizes, provoke the girl's anger rather than her pity. Besides, he is naked, apart from his brandished branch. Supplication would necessitate his dropping that flimsy screen, thereby so exposing himself that his intentions might appear different from what the Muse declares them to be—though resolving the scholarly dispute as to whether his condition was satyric.

The humorous nature of Odysseus's dilemma here is suggestive, then, of poetic parody. It recalls Anacreon's famous lyric fragment describing his own discomfiture on a beach among Lesbian girls playing ball (frag. 13: 358 *PMG*). While the later date of the Anacreontic text may suggest that it is a parody of the Homeric, the presence of humorous, parodic elements in the Odyssean scene make it more likely that both poetic texts are variants of a topos where a man intrudes on a group of attractive, unsuspecting girls at play.[24] In Anacreon's poem the Lesbian girls reject the intruder because he is too old (and possibly too male) for their tastes. Homer's muse, if anything, takes the parody a step further than does Anacreon. Odysseus, unlike Anacreon's male intruder, is not sexually interested in the girls, however much the circumstantial evidence may suggest the opposite. On the contrary: Nausicaa, divinely inspired not to run away, has marriage on her mind and raises the subject of marriage with the brine-covered stranger in a matter of moments.

The misunderstanding and potential misunderstanding resulting from this first meeting of Nausicaa and Odysseus continue when their encounter becomes known to Nausicaa's parents, Alcinous and Arete. Alcinous, skilled, as we have seen, in reading between the lines of what Nausicaa says, could easily read (perhaps as she herself hopes he will) too much between the lines and assume Nausicaa has been a participant in the reenaction of a familiar mythic, waterside encounter between unguarded girl and male emerging from hiding. Further, Odysseus handles the situation with Nausicaa cautiously not only to protect her good name, but to avoid a misunderstanding such as might lead him into the Homeric equivalent of a shotgun wedding with the king's daughter. Little wonder he later refuses to let any of the Phaeacian maidens wash him.

Odysseus chooses to approach Nausicaa verbally rather than physically, and in such a way that she will realize he poses no dishonorable sexual threat to her. He wonders, rhetorically and aloud, if she is in fact a goddess, more specifically, the virginal Artemis (whom no sane mortal would dare attempt to assault). In fact, if by any chance the girls are really a goddess and her nymphs, his intrusion on their beach games (especially since they have discarded their veils) might be construed as an act of impiety such as brought Actaeon to a terrible death. Odysseus, therefore, takes it for granted that Nausicaa has no husband—he alludes to the pride that such a shoot (or sprout) must bring her father, mother, and brothers when she joins the dance. Although he adds that she is attractive and that her future husband is a blessed man, he instantly reverts to his vegetable analogy: comparing her to the young shoot of a *phoinix*, a palm tree. She is the most beautiful thing he has seen since he once saw the shoot of a young palm on Delos beside the altar of Apollo.

It is a strange compliment. Beautiful women are not often compared to trees of any species in poetry. Occasionally, of course, they may be metamorphosed into trees, as in Ovid's famous story of Daphne's metamorphosis into a laurel tree as she escapes Apollo's attempted rape. Odysseus is, in effect, telling Nausicaa she is safe from rape by converting her into a tree with his simile. It is probable that the text is here hinting at some matter which would have been clearer to an ancient Greek audience than it is to us. The famous palm tree which grew on Delos and which was linked with the cult of Apollo and Artemis was widely known throughout the Greek world and was of special importance to Ionian Greeks, including the Athenians, for whom it was the object of an annual religious pilgrimage.[25] Tradition held that before the birth of Artemis and Apollo, Delos was a wandering island. It proved to be the only resting place available to Artemis and Apollo's mother, Leto,[26] who was pursued by the relentless wrath of Hera. Fittingly, Leto, the heavenly wanderer, arrives on Delos, a wandering island that stops floating only when Artemis and Apollo are born upon it, beneath a palm tree.[27]

The symbolism of Delos and its palm as places of rest and regeneration for wanderers (and particularly for the seafaring Ionians) is well established and has a special appropriateness for the wandering Odysseus, who escapes in Phaeacia, however temporarily, the wrath of Poseidon among a wandering, seafaring people, whose own wandering will cease once they have returned Odysseus to Ithaca. Further, the word *phoinix* is just as ambiguous in Greek as is the verb *mignymi.* It indicates not only "palm tree" but also "Phoenician" and the mythical bird, the phoenix, which regenerates itself from the ashes. As Pliny points out, the palm and the phoenix have something in common. Of the various kinds of palms he mentions, one, he claims, dies and is reborn from itself: *intermori ac renasci ex seipsa*—an ability it shares with the avian *phoinix,* "who, it is thought, takes its name from this palm" (*Natural History* 13.42). In Egyptian, as in Greek, *phoinix* designates both the mythical sun bird, the phoenix, and the palm tree.[28] The *phoinix* bird comes to bury its father at the temple of the Sun in Heliopolis (Herodotus 2.73). Horapollo observes:

> When they want to denote a soul spending a lot of time there, they depict the *phoinix* bird because it lives longest of all creatures in the world; it denotes a great flood, because it is a symbol of the sun—which is greater than anything else in the universe. (1.34)

Curiously enough, Horapollo adds that the phoenix also signifies in hieroglyphs a man returning from a prolonged residence abroad (1.35).[29] In short, Odysseus may be communicating more to both Nausicaa and an ancient audience than is evident to the modern reader, even if only a few of the resonances we have suggested are at work here. But it is worth noting that when Odysseus leaves Nausicaa and enters the city to take his place as a suppliant in the ashes of the palace fireplace, there is something phoenixlike about his reemergence into a world of more human dimensions after his prolonged sojourn in Calypso's never-never land and the refurbishing of his identity among the arguably fictional Phaeacians.

While Odysseus, at least rhetorically, takes Nausicaa to be divine rather than human, the princess, in her reply, suggests no similar illusion on her part that the brine-drenched sailor before her is anything other than an "unfortunate wanderer" (6.206). Nonetheless, as she recalls her frightened attendants, she introduces herself as daughter of Alcinous, king of the Phaeacians, and offers him not only food and drink, but a bath at the hands of her attendants. Odysseus accepts the food but declines, through modest shame, he declares, to let the young women strip (*gymnousthai*) and bathe him. Quite what remains to be stripped from him other than the olive branch he holds is not entirely clear.[30]

After a more seemly bath and a divine make-over by Athena, the renewed Odysseus makes a different impression on Nausicaa. "The gods," she says, "must have willed it that this man mingle [*epimisgetai*] with the godlike Phaeacians" (6.241). The skeptical reader, of course, will want to deny that the "naive" Nausicaa is conscious of any such wordplay. If so, it is worth considering what she adds in 244–46, punning on the word *posis*, which means either "husband" or "drink":

> How I'd like to have a man like this living here and called my husband [*posin*] and that it would be his pleasure to remain here. Oh well, give our guest food and drink [*posin*].

As the princess and Odysseus prepare to make their way into the city, the hardly oblique hints Nausicaa has made to her handmaidens are now directed toward Odysseus. Although she permits Odysseus to follow her wagon as they proceed through the countryside, she suggests he make his own way into town once they are near the city, fearing malicious gossip, which she characterizes as follows:

> "Who's this following Nausicaa, this tall and handsome stranger? Where did she find him? You can bet he'll be her husband [*posis*]. Maybe it's some wandering man from a faraway people she's brought in from his

> ship. For there are certainly no other neighboring peoples. Maybe he's some god who's come down from heaven in answer to her prayers—and she's been praying for him a lot—and she'll possess him all her days. Perhaps it is just as well if she's gone off and found a husband [*posin*] elsewhere. She has nothing but scorn for the local Phaeacians, though many fine men here have courted her." That's what they'll say, and this is the slander I'd have to put up with. And I'd say the same about another girl who did the same thing and mingles [*misgētai*] with men, despite her dear father and mother, while yet they live, before the day of her public marriage. (6.276–88)

If we grant Odysseus an ability to read between the lines at least equal to Alcinous's, Nausicaa's hints do not escape him. She is quite firmly and obliquely declaring, in the guise of reporting gossip, that she is much courted but has no interest in a Phaeacian husband.

Doubtless, Nausicaa will have some explaining to do when she returns to the palace and her discovery of Odysseus becomes public knowledge. After all, her laundry trip has taken all day. She clearly travels a considerable distance from the city to wash the clothes. She gets up at sunrise (6.48), obtains and packs a mule cart, washes the clothes, bathes, and plays ball on the beach. Allowing her some time to discover Odysseus and prepare him for his introduction to Phaeacia, it still takes her until around sunset to get back even though she drives her mules at quite a pace (6.316–20). Little wonder that Alcinous is, as we shall see, suspicious about what may have occurred.

Since it is Nausicaa who provides Odysseus's first contact with the Phaeacians, and since she appears to decide, once he has been washed and spruced up, that he would make a nice husband, the picture of Phaeacia and her family that she presents Odysseus may be so tailored as to make the place as attractive as possible to him. We must therefore not assume that what she says about Phaeacia is objective information. Let us take a couple of examples. Nausicaa claims to Odysseus that the Phaeacians do not care for arrows and quivers, but only for masts and the oars of shapely ships (6.270–71). Yet in 7.8–11 the Muse says Nausicaa's maid, the imperially named Eurymedousa ("Wide-Ruling"), is from Apeire ("Boundlessland") and that, once upon a time (*pote*), Phaeacian ships brought her from there as a *geras* chosen for Alcinous.[31] The language is military. A *geras* is a gift or token of honor from the spoils of war. When the word is used of a person by "Homer," it indicates someone captured in war. Thus Phaeacia was once at war with a place named Apeire, which we take as "Boundlessland" and which others take to refer to some "mainland" or other.

A people who sail around taking prisoners in such a piratical way are hardly entirely peace-loving. In fact, if the Phaeacians engaged in such plundering, they recall the occasionally piratical Phoenicians who appear in Eumaeus's narrative of his own life story (15.403–84). Are we to infer that the Phaeacians changed their life-style at a certain point—perhaps shortly after their arrival in their present land—from that of a warring people to that of a people who have given up war and contention? Or should we argue that Nausicaa's remark means that the Phaeacians prefer naval operations to land operations, not that they prefer commerce to war? Nausicaa still knows about the standard weapons of war. If a change has occurred, it is very recent.

Whether the Phaeacians do or do not make a habit of war, they are certainly well protected against external attack. Nausicaa explains to Odysseus in 6.262–65 that a wall runs around the city, and the "gates," the entrance through the wall, are narrow, even though they need to haul the ships through them. In short, the Phaeacians are aware that they must be ready to defend themselves. It is odd, then, that Nausicaa uses the word *eisithmē*, "way in," instead of *pylai*, "gates" (and a means of keeping people out), to describe these passageways. Is it because the walls just had openings without doors, or because she, having grown up after the Phaeacians made the transition into life without war, has no adequate military terminology? Or is she simply lying? One of the last two possibilities seems most likely. For in *Odyssey* 8, one of Nausicaa's remarks suggests she is at least minimally conversant with the technical terminology of warfare and military negotiations. When she comes to bid farewell to Odysseus, she asks him to remember her in his native land "for to me first you owe the price for your life [*zōagria*]" (8.461–62). The word *zōagria* is found only once elsewhere in Homeric epic: at *Iliad* 18.407, where it denotes the ransom tendered by a defeated warrior to his captor. Perhaps Nausicaa had taken careful notes on Demodocus's recitations of heroic saga!

There are other residual traces of weaponry in curious contexts in Phaeacia. The Muse represents Odysseus as noticing that the town is surrounded by "walls, long and high and crowned with palisades [*skopelessin*], a wonder to behold" (7.44–45). This is the only occurrence of *skopelessin* in the *Odyssey*. It is used in the *Iliad* several times, to describe the palisade erected by the Greeks to defend their trench. Here it represents the palisade along the coping of the *teichea makra*, the "long walls," which, like the Themistoclean walls of ancient Athens, were designed for defense. And, despite Nausicaa's assurances of the Phaeacians' love of peace, Athena says nothing to Odysseus about the Phaeacians being peaceful or well intentioned. Nor does the king, Alcinous, dwell on the issue of Phaeacian peacefulness when he talks to Odysseus. No less remarkably, Euryalus, a young Phaeacian whose name is identical with that of Odysseus's son by Euippe in other traditions, offers Odysseus, as a gift of reconciliation, a sword, all of bronze with a hilt of silver and a scabbard of newly sawn ivory wrought about it (8.403–5). A weapon of war, housed in a recently made scabbard of imported (unless the Phaeacians had hitherto unobserved elephants) ivory is an ambiguous gift of reconciliation from a peaceful people, as Odysseus seems partly to acknowledge. In his speech of thanks, he expresses the hope that Euryalus may never miss the sword he has given (8.414–15).[32]

If the Phaeacians are living in idyllic peace, as Nausicaa suggests, they have not ruled out the possibility of being attacked. The city is well fortified, and, as we shall see, the Phaeacians are suspicious of strangers. It is also striking that Athena, disguised as a young girl, repeats faithfully to Odysseus advice the young Nausicaa also gives him: to approach first not the king but the queen, Arete, if he wishes to ensure his hopes for returning home. Nausicaa also adds that the Phaeacian men can be hostile to strangers they suspect have come from far away (6.274–84). The disguised Athena puts their xenophobia in even more explicit terms:

> Nor do they tolerate strangers or give a welcoming greeting to anyone
> who comes from another land. (7.32–33)

These warnings prompt Odysseus to appeal to Arete rather than to Alcinous and to take up the most humble position of a suppliant in the palace fireplace among the ashes—even though he has not been told that such self-abasement is necessary.[33] Similarly, in his supplication, he avoids mentioning Nausicaa, anxious, no doubt, for his own safety as well as for her reputation. His anxieties seem confirmed, for Arete makes no reply to his supplications at first—which is disturbing, since her name means "the one who is prayed to."[34] Athena and Nausicaa appear to have been wrong. Odysseus is left sitting in the hearth for some time after his presence is noted, until the "ship-detaining" Echeneus, an elderly Phaeacian, intercedes on Odysseus's behalf and has him raised, phoenixlike, from the ashes and seated next to the host, as the custom requires. His destiny is left in the hands of the king and his elders.

This token of acceptance does not extend to a desire to encourage Odysseus to stay in Phaeacia. On the contrary, Alcinous immediately addresses the Phaeacian leaders and counselors, in Odysseus's presence, on the topic of Odysseus's immediate dispatch home. Phaeacian hospitality, *xenia*, then, extends not much farther than getting rid of the *xenos* at the earliest opportunity.[35] On the other hand, a speedy return home is exactly what Odysseus appears to want. So there is a coincidence of interests between Alcinous and Odysseus on this matter. And Arete has not yet spoken. It is becoming clear that Nausicaa was not quite accurate in suggesting that her mother called the shots in the palace.

We should not mistake Arete's silence for disinterest in the stranger. It is, rather, a matter of tact. When Odysseus arrives, the hall is crowded with Phaeacian nobles. It is not an appropriate time to question him with regard to what she has noticed about him. Arete speaks only when the other guests have left and the dishes are cleared away. Thanks to Nausicaa, she already knows more about Odysseus than the men probably do. The Muse tells us (7.230–35) that Arete herself had woven the clothes this stranger is wearing. This piece of information raises several interesting issues, most notably the following. Did Nausicaa deliberately select from among her laundered clothes an item she knew her mother would recognize? And is that why she suggested that Odysseus make his appeal to Arete rather than Alcinous?[36] Was she, in effect, marking him by this gesture as a potential husband and sending him home for approval in a discreet and oblique manner? This possibility is enhanced if we accept Norman Austin's suggestion that it indicates that the Phaeacians practiced a custom still prevalent among Anatolian Greeks of washing all the family's clothes in preparation for a wedding.[37] The garments Nausicaa washes are not necessarily soiled, but the "best clothes," that is to say, the wedding clothes of her family. If this is the case in the *Odyssey*, as Austin suggests, then the epithet *sigaloenta*, "shining" (6.26), used to describe the clothes is not simply decorative, a relic of oral tradition void of special meaning in this context, but an adjective admirably appropriate to the scenario.[38] The "best clothes" must be laundered before the wedding. And Alcinous has not missed Nausicaa's hints about wanting to get married herself. Thus the princely dress, woven by Arete herself, and which Odysseus wears as he stands before her, probably marks him as a bridegroom designate.

While Odysseus thinks of himself as a suppliant, Nausicaa has clad him as a suitor. And it would surely be within the realm of reasonable expectation that a man the princess thus marks out would accept an offer of the noblest possible marriage, especially since he owes, at least partially, his salvation to that princess. Thus there may be an undertone of rebuke as well as regret in Nausicaa's parting words to Odysseus later when she reminds him that he owes her *zōagria*—the price for his life (8.461–62).

Nausicaa has a genius in approaching the right parent with the right request and the right information. In spite of her advice to Odysseus to propitiate her mother first, Nausicaa had begun her day with a request to her father. Instead of asking Arete if it would be all right to wash the clothes and then asking for a wagon and mules to transport them, Nausicaa asks Alcinous for the wagon and mules first, even though the task of doing the laundry might be more within the jurisdiction of the lady of the house. Her mother is not kept in the dark about her plans, of course. Indeed, Arete provides Nausicaa with the necessities for the trip: a picnic basket, snacks, and wine in a goatskin. She also gives her daughter soft olive oil for her bath (6.76–80).[39]

Skeptics will contend that since Athena also insists that Odysseus make his appeal to Arete, we may be attributing undue cunning to the princess. To insist on too precise a distinction between the promptings of the goddess and the impulses of the young princess, however, is to reduce Nausicaa's role to that of a cipher manipulated by Athena, for then we must argue a similarly mechanical explanation for her behavior at the beginning of *Odyssey* 6, where the Muse says it was Athena who made Nausicaa stay behind to meet Odysseus while the others fled. At no point does Athena affect either Nausicaa's or Odysseus's mind to pursue thoughts or actions alien to their natures, as scholars have generally recognized.

Arete

Arete's first words when she and Alcinous are left alone with their guest go directly to the heart of her puzzlement and dilemma. She knows Nausicaa went on a washing expedition that morning. She recognizes the clothes Odysseus is wearing. Their provenance and what that provenance signifies are clear. Her daughter has chosen a husband. Arete's question, then, is directed toward understanding the circumstances under which Nausicaa made that choice. Hence her blunt enquiry of Odysseus:

> Stranger: the first question I myself shall ask of you is this: who are you, where are you from? And: who gave you these clothes? I thought you said you'd got here as a wandering seafarer? (7.237–39)

A lot crowds into this first question. The enquiries as to who the stranger is and where he is from, for all their abruptness, pose no special problem, for they immediately give way to Arete's more obviously urgent desire for an explanation as to why Odysseus is so dressed. She does not even notice that Odysseus fails to answer the questions about his identity.

Odysseus's guarded strategy is, presumably, governed by his uncertainty as to his own situation. Let us assume he does not, at first, grasp that he is dressed in a special (wedding) garment that Arete herself wove, but thinks the focus of her question is on the incongruity of his shining clothes with the brief tale of suffering he has offered to this point. Arete has deduced from his story—although he has not specifically said this to be the case—that he has been roving the seas. He realizes he must now offer rather more detail or risk undermining his own credibility.

We have noted that Odysseus does not respond at all to the question of who he is or where he is from. He replies as if his life had begun on Calypso's island and offers little more than a carefully pared-down version of *Odyssey* 5 and 6, editing out (or veiling in ambiguity) all details about his sexual relationship with Calypso. He implies, in contradiction to what the Muse has told us, that he was miserable throughout his seven-year sojourn there and that the immortal clothing Calypso gave him was constantly wet with tears. In short, he continues not only to guard his identity, but to convey with tactful obliquity his unwillingness to be detained against his will in a relationship with a woman, even a goddess.

Odysseus's focus on the motif of his contacts with and opportunity to participate in the "formidable" Calypso's immortality seems quite deliberate. His abbreviated version of other experiences intensifies the effect that he has emerged from a world of divinities. Zeus, using a thunderbolt, had shipwrecked him on Calypso's island. He was released either because Zeus ordered Calypso to release him or (a cunningly less megalomaniacal explanation) because his host goddess changed her mind about keeping him. As he departed, Calypso gave him more immortal garments (to replace those dampened by seven years of weeping, perhaps), and then another god, Poseidon, shipwrecked him again. What the fate of his most recent immortal outfit was he does not say—understandably, he avoids telling the queen that it has (presumably) been washed away at sea and that he was naked when he met her daughter on the beach. He simply concludes the main part of his narrative by saying that after swimming ashore at Phaeacia, he was blanketed in sleep by an immortal night (rather than by immortal clothing).

Odysseus's caution intensifies as he prepares to introduce Nausicaa into his narrative. He mentions that he slept not only through the night, but until the sun, after noon, was beginning to move toward its setting. In other words, he was asleep for half the daylight hours when, at least in theory, Nausicaa might have encountered him. He also makes a special point of saying that he saw the girls when they were playing (that is, after they had finished washing the clothes and themselves) and that the princess was among them, fair as a goddess. Given the divine context for his life and troubles that he has established in the earlier part of his reply, such a compliment is both more and less than conventional flattery on the part of someone who claims to have spent the last seven years living with a goddess—and yearning to leave her.

Odysseus carefully steers his words into the rhetoric of the "older generation" talking of the young: the princess showed wisdom surprising for her age (the young are *always* thoughtless). Then he adds statements at odds with what the Muse told us in book 6: he asserts that Nausicaa first gave him food and wine, then bathed him, and finally presented him with clothing. In book 6, the nourishment followed the bathing rather than preceded it (since Odysseus was naked prior to his bath), and the bath was self-administered because Odysseus was ashamed of his nakedness.

The most obvious implication of Odysseus's reply is that Nausicaa has treated him as an honored guest. Yet, if we look closely, we observe that

Odysseus could be hinting that the clothing Nausicaa provided him, however glamorous, seemed, after more than seven years of wearing immortal clothes, not as special as it would to someone (even a queen) who had been (mostly) in human company for the same period. In other words: "If I'm missing something ritually significant about these clothes, ma'am, you'll have to excuse me." He caps this prudently pruned summary with a declaration that what he is saying is the truth. Such an avowal of truthfulness is not only unusual for Odysseus; it is also undermined (for the external audience, such as ourselves) by our knowledge that if the Muse has not been lying to us, Odysseus is now lying to Arete, or at least misleading her by judiciously editing his narrative.

Odysseus's modified version of his first encounter with Nausicaa elicits a condemnation of Nausicaa's conduct by Alcinous. She should have brought you here herself, he avers. In response, Odysseus adds that she wanted to do so but that he insisted on traveling separately. This statement flatly contradicts what the Muse assures us took place. If the Muse was telling the truth, he is not. Although it is scholarly convention to disregard lies when made for "gentlemanly" reasons—even Charles Beye refers to Odysseus, in this context, as "the perfect gentleman"—we will miss something of the Homeric point if we adopt such a cavalier attitude to Odysseus's lie here.[40] There is more self-protection than courtesy in it. He is making it clear that *he* was ashamed and afraid to accompany Nausicaa, rather than vice versa, worrying that Alcinous would be angry if he saw him and his daughter together.

Alcinous, we remember, is not insensitive to covert speech. He knows that marriage was on Nausicaa's mind that morning. Yet the man before him is making clear, first, that he does not see any special significance in the clothes Nausicaa gave him, and, second, that his sense of shame, not Nausicaa's, prompted him to come into town apart from her. Alcinous recognizes, we suspect, that Nausicaa has picked out this stranger as the man she wants to marry and packaged him as a bridegroom for his first appearance in the palace. But he clearly detects Odysseus's undertone of reluctance. Does this stranger wish to dampen another splendid costume for another seven years? The mythic topos of the man and the young girl on the lonely beach has been completely reversed: he is the object of the girl's sexual designs rather than she of his.

The possibility that Odysseus, who has made a point of stressing his rejection of offers of immortality from Calypso, might actually be interested in accepting Nausicaa's oblique proposal of marriage is safely remote. Thus Alcinous can and does offer him Nausicaa's hand and an appropriate property to live in without much fear that it will be accepted. In fact, he makes the offer quite abruptly in only three lines of his response. The gesture serves at least two purposes. First, it honors Odysseus;

second, it offsets any complaint Nausicaa might make that her father is placing obstacles between her and the man of her choice.

The offer made, Alcinous speedily makes it plain that no one among the Phaeacians (including, presumably, Nausicaa), will detain the stranger against his will. He returns, in much more detail, to a discussion (totaling twelve lines) of Odysseus's departure. But this reply contains some statements that must surely be unsettling to a man who has sailed from Ithaca to Troy and has made at least some progress on the return journey. If, as Alcinous claims, Euboea is regarded as the most distant of lands by the Phaeacian sailors, their navigational knowledge of the eastern Mediterranean and Aegean is remarkably limited. There is hardly a place on the Euboean coast from which some other landmass is not visible. Certainly no one traveling in a westerly direction across the Aegean could fail to notice Attica beyond Euboea. If we assume the Phaeacians are approaching from the west and Euboea is the limit of their navigational horizons, then they can hardly know much about Troy and the Trojan War.

Even more curiously, Alcinous mentions that the Phaeacians saw Euboea only when they were transporting Rhadamanthus to see Tityus, the son of Gaea, on a round-trip journey they accomplished in a single day. There is a paradox here. Their most distant voyage took them no more than half a day's rowing from Scheria, which means either that their notions of distance are foreshortened or that their ships, powered by Phaeacian hands, could travel at speeds somewhere between those of a hydrofoil and a jet. If the latter, it is odd that they had not noticed there was land beyond Euboea.

The suggestion that Tityus was a resident of Euboea and that the Phaeacians had transported the usually Cretan Rhadamanthus there to see him is as odd as Alcinous's suggestion that Euboea is the most distant of lands. Tityus usually belongs to a much older mythic generation. In most other allusions to him in Homer and Hesiod, this fabled giant had been safely pegged down in the underworld since the world was quite young. And the Phaeacians have been in the land where they currently reside only for a generation. The Phaeacians, then, or at least Alcinous himself, have different concepts of time as well as of distance. This should not surprise us. We have seen that Alcinous also has different notions of the divine, for he claims that the gods come openly among the Phaeacians when they are making their great sacrifices (7.201–5)—even though Athena is at that very moment making her way among them in disguise.

There are further problems. Why would a member of the royal family of seagoing Cretans need to travel in a Phaeacian ship to Euboea or anywhere else for that matter? It is hard to respond without writing an epic of one's own. To compound the puzzle, Odysseus later tells us that he saw both Tityus and Rhadamanthus in the land of the dead. Is Odysseus perhaps trying to hint that Alcinous was engaged in a little rhetorical fictionalizing by reaffirming a more common version of the myth? The quickest (and least plausible) way out of the dilemma is to argue that Alcinous has a different Euboea, a different Tityus, and a different Rhadamanthus in mind. But there is no reason to assume Odysseus would have interpreted these references any differently than we would. Thus the next question must be why Odysseus does not panic upon hearing this curious excursus. Even though Ithaca lies within the borders of the world Phaeacian navigators claim to know (presuming they are in the western, rather than the eastern Mediterranean), their odd notions of time and space should prompt a little unease about their navigational skills. The Muse, however, says Odysseus "expressed delight" at what he heard (7.329)—though his response is, for him, unusually brief. It takes the form of a prayer to Zeus that Alcinous may be able to accomplish what he proposes, rather than an unqualified expression of confidence. And the recompense Odysseus suggests is that Alcinous will gain glory by his action. In the Homeric context, of course, glory, *kleos*, is no small reward. And this reward is especially pertinent for Alcinous and the Phaeacians, since they seem to belong to a different (perhaps fictional) world which has no existence outside the fabric of the Homeric narrative.

Although Alcinous maintains, throughout, his confidence in the prowess of the thought-controlled Phaeacian ships and their ability to move safely to any destination (as, for example, at 8.558–63), Arete, when she speaks to Odysseus, offers a rather different picture of what might happen on a voyage home. She raises the possibility that Odysseus, though a *xenos*, might be robbed en route by the Phaeacian sailors (8.442–45). We might compare the problems she envisages with those Herodotus (1.23–24) recounts as afflicting the bard Arion on his voyage from Italy to Corinth. Yet while it is true that rulers cannot always predict with confidence how their own mariners will behave, Arete treats the possibility of such robbery, by her own sailors of her own *xenoi* on the high seas, as anything but remote.

Odysseus responds with some pique, when it is his turn to speak, suggesting that Alcinous might possibly mistreat a *xenos* (such as himself) in Scheria. At this point he argues, ostensibly in defense of Nausicaa, but no less in self-defense, that he refused Nausicaa's suggestion to come with her to the palace, since he feared Alcinous's heart would darken with anger on seeing such a sight (7.304–6). Odysseus has now grasped, if he had not grasped it earlier, that among the potentially "insolent Phaeacians" whom Nausicaa mentions is her own father (6.274).

In sum: although Alcinous indicates that the journey home will involve no perils for Odysseus, Arete indicates the opposite—even though earlier suggestions from both Nausicaa and Athena suggested she was the right person for Odysseus to approach if he wanted to secure his return to Ithaca. Why, then, does she foresee problems that elude Alcinous—problems which, in fact, do not materialize on the homeward journey once it is begun? To sketch a solution, we must first retrace a few steps.

Tactics of Delay

Athena, disguised as a young girl, agreed with Nausicaa in indicating to Odysseus that if Arete liked him, he could hope to see his native land again. The goddess also outlined the queen's genealogy and revealed that her eponymous name, her nickname based on the role she fulfills, is Arete, "She to Whom One Prays." This detail Nausicaa did not mention.[41]

Although some scholars attribute much to the power of Arete, wishing to see in Scheria a relic of matriarchal society, Athena is careful to suggest that Arete does not have autonomous power independent of the king: although she is greatly honored by Alcinous, it was Alcinous who made her his wife. In her status she is no different from other women who "hold their household in subjection to their husbands" (7.66–68).[42] Her power mostly resides in settling quarrels—mainly quarrels among women. She will act as intermediary for men only if she likes them (7.74–75). Arete's sphere of intervention is thus limited and concerns women.

In this respect Phaeacia is not so different from the society of other cities whose rulers we meet in the *Odyssey*. The lord of Pylos, Nestor, is a patriarch and sole ruler. His wife is mentioned by name and no more. In Sparta, Helen tries to take charge but is put in her place by Menelaus. Although Nausicaa tells Odysseus that Arete will decide about his return, and although he is very careful to supplicate her first, Arete says nothing. Like everything else in Phaeacia, she is puzzling, and her silence (given the meaning of her name as "the one who is prayed to") is threatening to Odysseus, since it leaves his prayer unanswered, at least for the moment.

One might expect Arete to make more use than she does of the alleged power she wields in the palace and among the people. All along, however, she subordinates herself to her husband and keeps a respectful distance from the feasting kings. Her withdrawal and reticence strongly suggest that Alcinous is the one in charge. In fact, the kings are astonished when the stranger, Odysseus, appearing among them in the palace suddenly and out of nowhere, first approaches Arete rather Alcinous. We have also noted that Arete, whether through tact or subordination to the counsels of men, makes no reply at first to Odysseus's supplication. Even though she recognizes Odysseus's clothes as her own work, she does not question how the garment came into his possession until all the guests have left (7.228–39). And when, after Odysseus's narrative of the famous women in the underworld, she finally speaks among and addresses the kingly leaders, Echeneus and Alcinous are quick to qualify what she says and suggests (11.342–53).

There is surely some significance in her timing of this public statement—and not only because it occurs in the "female" context of a catalogue of beautiful mythical heroines in the underworld. It occurs during a natural pause: Odysseus has brought his narrative to a stop, asking permission to retire for the night, and hoping his dispatch home will occur the following morning, as Alcinous has earlier implied. He is, in fact, obliquely providing the Phaeacians the opportunity to make good their promise and transport him home immediately—though he courteously says he is leaving the matter of his departure to the gods and to his Phaeacian audience. He is prepared to spend the night aboard the black ship with the crew, he declares, but if that cannot be, he will spend it in the palace (11.330–32). There can be no doubt among his Phaeacian audience that spending a further night at the palace is not his first choice.

After Odysseus has spoken, "they [the Phaeacian princes] were all hushed in silence" (11.333). We recall, perhaps, the hushed silence after Odysseus supplicated Arete upon arrival at the palace (7.154). But whereas Arete said nothing on that first occasion, she now speaks:

> Phaeacians, what do you think of this man, with regard to his appearance and stature, and the balanced spirit within him? Although he is my *xenos*, each one has a share in this honor; so don't be too hasty in sending him on his way, and don't be stingy with your gifts to a man who is in such need. For, thanks to the favor of the gods, you've many treasures stored in your halls. (11.336–41)

Arete does not specifically respond to Odysseus's oblique request to be sent home immediately. Rather, she makes requests of the Phaeacians whose fulfillment would *prevent* his immediate departure. Gathering such gifts will take time. Thus her concern for honoring her departing guest is also an excuse for delaying him. The ploy is much the same as that of Penelope, who, on Odysseus's return, hints that the suitors should go and bring her suitable gifts (18.276–80). Odysseus has not expressed any desire to accumulate more treasures. His concern is with immediate departure, as his declaration of readiness to leave for the ship right away indicates.

It is as perplexing to the reader as it probably is to Odysseus, who has faithfully followed Nausicaa's directives in making himself Arete's rather than Alcinous's suppliant, that the queen is not only failing to help his departure but, apparently, trying to postpone it. The possibility must be dawning on him that the marriage-minded Nausicaa's reasoning was the opposite of what it seemed to be. She knew Alcinous and the men, eager to remove foreign visitors, would prefer to send Odysseus away. If she wants the stranger for her husband, her best bet is her mother.

If we read evidence for a Phaeacian matriarchy behind Nausicaa's words, we are deceived by her rhetoric as Odysseus, finally, is not, for Arete is slapped back into her place. The savvy master of protocol, Echeneus, intervenes to note an impropriety in behavior at the royal court. It does not pertain directly to the treatment of the stranger, but to Arete's interference in the decision as to when and how to send the stranger home. Echeneus politely but firmly reinstates the power of decision where it "belongs." Arete, he notes, spoke, of course, after his own heart, but "it is on Alcinous's decision that the deed and the word depend" (11.346). Alcinous, though he insists that he, like Echeneus, has nothing against what has been said, so phrases his response as to leave it unclear whether it is his wife's words or Echeneus's that he does not object to.[43] Yet the gist of his response is opposition to his wife's statement. The decision "to send Odysseus home," he announces, "is reserved for all the men and, most of all, for me, since I am in power over the people" (11.352–53).

It will be evident to Odysseus now that Alcinous has reaffirmed his control of the situation. Things will be just as they were when Odysseus arrived at the palace and when the king promised that all the chiefs and other elders would arrange for his transport home (7.191–92). Alcinous declares that Odysseus will depart the next day, as Odysseus presumably hopes, since he did not really expect to leave that night. The journey will not be postponed, as Arete recommends and as Nausicaa probably desires.[44] Nor does Alcinous encourage the chiefs, at this point, to bring further gifts, as his wife suggests, in addition to those they have already provided. He insists that he himself will make all their gifts complete.[45]

For the moment, it looks as if Alcinous has won the rhetorical laurels. But only for the moment. The sly Odysseus instantly converts the difference of opinion between Arete and Alcinous to his own advantage, under the guise of showing courtesy to Arete and apparently offering a compromise. He agrees to spend up to a year in Phaeacia and to accept gifts (of his own choice) so he will cut a better figure in his homeland on his return (11.355–61). The time limit he sets effectively rules out any fear Alcinous may have that the issue of marriage with Nausicaa will be raised again, and the increased treasure is the price to be paid.

Little wonder that Alcinous's reply has a touch of acid sarcasm:

> As we look at you, Odysseus, in no way do we think of you as a dissembler and a thief, such as the black earth breeds scattered far and wide, men that fashion lies out of what no man can even see. For there is upon you a beauty shaped by words and within you a noble mind. (11.363–67)

Alcinous takes up the matter of Odysseus's appearance, which, as we will see, becomes an issue of some importance among the Phaeacians. But he puts his visitor and his appearance in the context of liars and dissemblers.[46] Curiously enough, scholars have tended to read these famous words as if they were simply—and only—Alcinous's general and skeptical reaction to Odysseus's narrative of strange monsters and strange places, rather than Alcinous's acerbic response to the more immediate context: Odysseus's triumphant piece of bargaining. Perhaps there is more than a touch of truth in the observation made by the Phaeacian merchant Euryalus, that Odysseus looks more like a businessman than an athlete (8.159–64). The cost of *xenia* has just risen sharply.

To complicate matters for Alcinous, if he now grants Odysseus his request, he will appear to be yielding to the overt agenda of Arete, who may be delaying Odysseus's departure in order to nurture the hopes of an eventual marriage, though she has made no explicit remark to that effect. The best Alcinous can do is to follow up his polite nastiness to Odysseus with a request that he continue his narrative of travels that very night. If the piper must be paid, he must make music. But the man who pays the piper has the right to specify the tune. To deflate Odysseus's shrewd capitalization on Arete's suggestions, Alcinous touches on what seems to him, and to us, the most sensitive point of Odysseus's adventures he has heard so far: that Odysseus, for all his boasting, has said nothing about those who sailed with him to Troy. In his necromancy up to this point, Odysseus focuses on the heroes and heroines from earlier mythic generations. Now Alcinous wants to know what happened to those who followed him to and died at Troy.

Although most editors take 11.371–72 to mean "those who traveled with you to Troy [that is, the Greek expedition in general] and met their fate there," no doubt to allow the statement to accord with what Odysseus actually does, such a translation does not take full account either of the sense of "following" in the Greek *heponto* (which editors render as "traveled with") or of the double use of the Greek *hama* (which they render "with" rather than "together with" or "at the same time as"). The text itself is referring to Odysseus's own particular sailing companions in his own ships from the Ionian islands. Odysseus faces a difficulty if he is to oblige Alcinous here, since no one from Odysseus's squadron, aside from himself, earned any particular distinction at Troy so far as we can tell from the *Iliad.* And there is no mention of any of them dying.

Traveling back *from* Troy, however, proved lethal to his squadron. They all died, and in ignominious ways if we take to heart Odysseus's tearful remark in book 5 about how much better it would have been to die at Troy than to drown in the sea (5.306–10). His comrades drowned, were slaughtered, or were eaten as they followed him from Troy. There is not much Odysseus can say (without resorting to possibly detectable fiction) about their heroic deaths at Troy. That, presumably, is why Odysseus, in response, goes on to talk of his meetings with a small collection of "standard" Iliadic heroes, not all of whom died in glorious combat at Troy. Agamemnon was murdered by his wife and her lover on his return; Ajax committed suicide; Achilles, killed by Paris, proves to be a most unhappy ghost until Odysseus consoles him with the deeds of his son Neoptolemus.

Eventually, of course, Odysseus finishes his narrative and is given conveyance home. Nausicaa herself, in a touching meeting, concedes defeat but makes her claim to fame, desiring to be remembered as the girl who saved the hero. The Muse, of course, by telling us this, obliges her. Alcinous, now that time and many verses have passed, can give Odysseus the extra treasure he demands without appearing to be yielding ground to Arete and without enormous cost to himself. Each of his chiefs must contribute a tripod and a caldron; but, to make that burden lighter, they can recoup their costs from a tax to be imposed on the people (13.13–15).

When Odysseus finally leaves Phaeacia, then, the nobles are marginally poorer, Nausicaa lacks the husband she wanted, Alcinous is in trouble with Arete, and the people are not only worse off economically (thanks to the newly authorized taxes) but cut off from further maritime trade by Poseidon's vengeful blockade of their harbor with the fossilization of the ship that conveyed Odysseus. Odysseus, on the other hand, arrives home safe, sound, and rich, ready to spread terror and death among those who have occupied his home. If, however, we admit the possiblity that the Homeric muse has herself created Phaeacia, that it is her fiction, and that she has substituted Phaeacia for the point of his return to Ithaca found in other traditions—Thesprotia—an even more complex rhetorical scenario begins to emerge. Just as the Muse has passed over the problematic sons elsewhere attributed to his relationships with Circe and Calypso, omitting Telegonus altogether and converting Nausithous into the ancestor of the Phaeacians, so she has substituted Alcinous and his court for the Thesprotian kingdom and, most significantly, substituted Nausicaa for Euippe, the king's daughter whom Odysseus seduces and who becomes the mother of his son Euryalus. The *Odyssey* provides, then, no Telegonus to kill Odysseus, and no Euryalus for him to kill. The only faint recollection of his unfortunate Thesprotian son by Euippe, in this construction, is the young Phaeacian Euryalus who gives Odysseus his sword—which Odysseus prays he will never regret having surrendered.

The disastrous sexual relationship with the Thesprotian king's daughter is thus metamorphosed into a rather touching portrait of a young girl's desire to marry a reluctant hero who discreetly, politely, but unwaveringly refuses to succumb to any temptation. When Odysseus departs, the reader may feel, if anything, a certain disappointment that nothing comes of his relationship to Nausicaa. But there is little for the most Cato-like critic to find fault with. The Homeric Odysseus has sexual relationships only with goddesses, not with human women, and at their instigation, not at his. The Homeric muse has refurbished the more lustful Odysseus of other traditions with such rhetorical sophistication that she will later be able to relegate the entire Thesprotian episode to the status of a secondary falsehood in the context of a Cretan lie.

[3]

Friction in Phaeacia

From time to time, a certain tension arises in the interchanges between Alcinous and Odysseus. It manifests itself early in Alcinous's and Odysseus's relationship, as rival claims to *aretē*, "excellence," and *kleos*; "glory," and it intensifies with the passing of time and dialogue, particularly in Odysseus's long account of his travels and in the kind of identity he generates for himself in shaping that account.

Claims to *Aretē* and *Kleos*

As the hero who led the Achaeans to victory in Troy, Odysseus has a headstart in *kleos* over Alcinous, who lives in remote and unknown Scheria, and looks for an opportunity to assert it. Alcinous, for his part, tries to ensure that the *kleos* of the Phaeacians will ultimately reach beyond Scheria and pursues this goal with urgency and determination. Indeed, there is irony in Alcinous and Nausicaa's insistence that not many strangers come to their unknown and probably fictitious land. Odysseus must serve as messenger of their excellence, since he may well be the only available messenger. To complete the irony, Alcinous claims he knows that the Phaeacians will someday be cut off from the inhabited world, as if they were not already cut off, and wants word of their excellence as seafarers and athletes spread at this possibly unique moment while contact with the rest of the world is possible. Knowledge of those who are excellent seafarers—the Phoenicians, for example—usually spreads as a result of their own contacts with other peoples. But the Phaeacians have had little such contact. Therefore, since Alcinous wants to send Odysseus away quickly, he has not much more than one day to achieve his goal. Because he knows time is short, Alcinous avoids Odysseus's broad hints about his distinguished past until Odysseus has observed how brilliant his host's achievements are. There is, consequently, much sparring as each tries to impress the other and to show his superiority.

Odysseus's strategy for establishing himself as the lost hero of the Trojan War is gradual and circumspect. After supplicating Arete, yet failing to be taken under her maternal aegis as he expected, he is careful not to tell her his name, although asked to do so.[1] Alcinous, meanwhile, whose strength of mind is implicit in the popular etymology of his name, "Strength of Mind," is no less oblique in his dealings with Odysseus. If Frame is right (and if Homer had even the vaguest awareness of what was really right in Indo-European etymological theory!), the actual etymology of "Alcinoos" suggests the meaning "he who brings back by his might."[2] But given Frame's own contention of the relationship between *nous* and *nostos,* which we discussed in Chapter 1, the gulf between the Indo-European and the popular etymology may not be great.

Odysseus's mysterious appearance in the palace forewarns the king that this stranger is in some way special. Curious about his guest's guarded identity, Alcinous tries to play upon his vanity by suggesting that he may be a god. "Up until now the gods have appeared openly to us," he says in a speech to the Phaeacian counselors in Odysseus's presence; and he adds that the gods have usually been obviously recognizable (7.201–5). This statement should not surprise Odysseus or us (as outer audience), since it is suggested to Odysseus early in *Odyssey* 6 that he has achieved something few mortals have simply by arriving in Phaeacia. The Phaeacians, at least according to their claims, are used only to dealings among themselves or with gods. Nausicaa tells her maids within Odysseus's hearing that no mortal man has dealings, or mingles closely, *epimisgetai,* with the Phaeacians (6.204–5, 278–9). Yet the Muse soon undermines these claims by members of the royal family—notably, as we saw, their assertion that the gods move undisguised in their midst. The Muse also hints that we should note Alcinous's wiliness. He reads between the lines of what others are saying and is able to screen his own intentions from others.

Alcinous's oblique probing for Odysseus's identity does not escape Odysseus. Yet, though Odysseus poignantly asserts his mortality, he does not reveal his name. He dwells on his sufferings and tries to elicit pity: he is tired, hungry, and grief-laden, ready to die once he sees his native land again (7.208–25). The famous lines in which Odysseus expresses his hunger were for centuries taken to indicate unexpected "bad manners" on his part. But surely they are subtly calculated. He is unlikely really to be driven by ravenous hunger, since Nausicaa has fed him not long ago. On the other hand, he does have good reason for worrying that his hosts genuinely mistake him for a god. Twice since his arrival in Scheria the

Phaeacians have claimed not to have much experience with strangers other than divine visitors. Odysseus's remarks about food, then, are a calculatedly brusque affirmation of his mortality.[3] He is not a god. He needs real food. He needs help to get back to Ithaca. The Phaeacians seem to catch at least something of his point. They are not offended by any perceived rudeness. On the contrary, they praise his words (7.226–27).

Having established his human rather than divine status, Odysseus makes clear that he belongs to a high echelon of human society, one which is as routinely in contact with the divine as the Phaeacians claim to be. His pathetic self-portrayal to Arete as a woebegone survivor of divine captivity and as a target of divine wrath also tells his hosts that he is accustomed to the presence of gods. He has spent seven years living with one. Similarly, his mortality established, he ensures that he does not slip to the bottom of the scale in their estimation. He is a *free* human, not a slave, with his own possessions and slaves in his native land (7.211–25). While less than divine, he is not *simply* human.

From this point on his chief helper in building up the specific and heroic nature of his humanity is the bard Demodocus, who obliges, the following day, with a song about Odysseus's quarrel with Achilles. The setting seems perfect. Odysseus has been offered (however cagily) Nausicaa's hand, and a feast is held in his honor. He ought to be well on the way to gaining acceptance of his identity as a famous hero from the Trojan War. But Alcinous concedes ground reluctantly. Whereas Menelaus quickly discerns from Telemachus's tears that his young visitor in *Odyssey* 4 is Odysseus's son, Alcinous either genuinely fails to read the clues that Demodocus, sometimes with Odysseus's prompting, is feeding him or declines to satisfy Odysseus by acknowledging he has understood the clues, and tries, rather, to force Odysseus into overt self-declaration. Alcinous has his own agenda to establish, as Odysseus recognizes implicitly when he declares that Alcinous will attain *asbeston kleos,* "unquenchable fame," when he returns to his native land.[4]

The Muse adds a slightly sarcastic twist to the phrase *asbeston kleos* in this context, for the sake of the outer audience. She has already put these very words in Menelaus's mouth, when he tells Telemachus how, when stranded in Egypt, he heard of his brother's death. He raised a mound, he says, to his brother's memory, to give him *asbeston kleos,* "unquenchable fame." How much glory a burial mound would give Agamemnon in Egypt—much less in Greece—is unclear. And this dedicatory gesture is about the extent of Menelaus's aid to his brother's family on his return to Sparta. He is in the process, as he talks, of marrying his daughter to Neoptolemus, Achilles' son, not to Agamemnon's son, Orestes (her usual mythic groom).[5] Similarly, Odysseus does not expend much effort on Alcinous and the Phaeacians once he reaches his native land, perhaps because he is adopting the rhetoric of disguise as a beggar, perhaps because there is a certain fictional quality about the Phaeacians themselves. Although he briefly mentions the Phaeacians to Telemachus and Penelope, he does not mention Alcinous after landing in Ithaca.[6] He usually substitutes Phoenicians or Thesprotians for Phaeacians when talking about his travels. Alcinous is lucky that he has Homer's muse, not just Odysseus, to tell his tale.

Odysseus's allusion to the eternal glory, *kleos*, Alcinous will have when Odysseus returns to Ithaca is, however, immediately noted by Alcinous. From this point on the king dwells on the fame Phaeacia may attain by sending Odysseus back to Ithaca. True, it is not entirely clear whether Alcinous's hopes of being remembered in Greek lore are genuine rather than just a good rhetorical pretext for sending Odysseus away. But Alcinous is persistent on this topic: he seeks, at least three times, his guest's promise to spread the name of the Phaeacians in his native land. Similarly, Nausicaa's parting words to Odysseus are a plea not to be forgotten. The struggle for *kleos* is under way.

The Phaeacians and Troy

Alcinous's failure to deduce Odysseus's identity, despite the latter's prompting, leaves Odysseus curiously isolated among the Phaeacians.[7] Neither Nausicaa nor Arete (despite wedding plans) displays knowledge of or interest in the world Odysseus comes from. Odysseus has strayed out of myth into fiction, where a people no one has ever heard of give the impression that they do not know him. And, whether or not readers accept our hypothesis that the Phaeacians are the Muse's invention, no one is likely to suggest that they had a contingent of warriors at Troy. On the basis of what Alcinous says to Odysseus, we might easily conclude that they are, on the whole, ignorant not only of the Trojan War, but even of Troy's existence. If Euboea is, as Alcinous claims, the most distant of lands, then Troy is well beyond the limits of Phaeacian cartography.

There are, however, counterindications that force us to conclude either that Alcinous is not candid or that he is oddly ignorant of what is known to at least one resident of his court, the blind bard Demodocus. Demodocus's song about Odysseus's quarrel with Achilles betrays familiarity with the protagonists of the Trojan War. The bard's choice of topics almost suggests that he has figured out who the visitor is, even if, for obvious reasons, he does not observe Odysseus's tears. But the bard is alone in his awareness of Troy.

In separating the roles of raconteur and host in Phaeacia, as she does not in Sparta, the Muse creates a more complex scenario. If Alcinous, reading between the lines, does not recognize Odysseus earlier, Demodocus's song should serve as a prompt to him as well as to Odysseus. Demodocus, we infer from the pattern established in *Odyssey* 4, is making the stranger's identity as evident as possible to his king while letting Odysseus know he has figured out who he is. Demodocus tells Odysseus that he is already a subject of a song: "a mythical hero." Thus, paradoxically, while Odysseus labors to establish his mortality (to accompany his request for a speedy return to the world of mortals), Demodocus is planting him in the timeless world of mythic song. Demodocus's choice of topic, the quarrel between Achilles and Odysseus, is particularly appropriate, since it portends, either intentionally or with unconsciously deconstructionistic prophetic insight, the rivalry of the two great epic tales of the Trojan War. One recalls again the disconcerting greeting the Irish hero Bran receives on his return after years of voyaging. He discovers that he is no longer "real" but part of Irish traditional lore.

Trying to escape mythic discourse is harder than one may think, especially if one is a mythic character in a possibly fictional environment. Our point is not as facile as it may seem. To be mythic is to be part of a discourse familiar and traditional to one's own society. But it does imply a certain dislocation in time, a transcendancy of simple historicity. To be fictional is to be part of an invented world which can become mythic only if somehow integrated with the traditional stories of one's own society.

As Demodocus sings his song of quarrel, Odysseus draws his cloak over his head and hides his face:

> About these things the famous minstrel sang; but Odysseus, pulling his big purple cloak with his heavy hands, drew it over his head, and hid [*kalypse*] his handsome face: for he was ashamed of shedding tears in front of the Phaeacians. (8.83–86)

The Muse's claim that Odysseus acted as he did so the Phaeacians would not see his tears is probably partially true. It certainly spurred a theory postulated early in the scholarly tradition by Eustathius: namely, that it was not good manners for a guest to express sorrow at his host's banquet.[8] Whether it was better manners to express grief by sitting at a banquet with a cloak over one's head and groaning aloud, however, is a moot point. By explicitly noting Odysseus's purpose in covering his head, the Muse draws attention to the rules of etiquette and propriety and tells us Odysseus is trespassing their bounds.

Yet that Odysseus is weeping at all and that no one appears to notice his grief is most remarkable. Perhaps his are Proustian tears, as he goes back over time past and lost. But they are curiously restrained tears, and thus both like and unlike those Telemachus sheds at Menelaus's court. It is hard to avoid drawing a parallel between the two incidents, but when Homer's muse draws parallels or generates similes, her concern is usually to show how *different* the things compared really are. The detail of their similarity accentuates the chasm that yawns between them. Menelaus seems deliberately to have provoked Telemachus's tears by talking of Odysseus, to test his recognition of the young man. The tearful response and the attempt to hide it show Menelaus his hunch is right. Telemachus, by contrast, is not trying to get Menelaus to recognize him. The tears are a spontaneous reaction to the contrived narrative stimulus. Only when his first tears actually fall does he pull his cloak up to conceal them (4.113–16).

Odysseus, on the other hand, pulls up his cloak as he starts weeping, almost in anticipation (8.83–86). Perhaps the hope of recognition subtends Odysseus's response to Demodocus's story. But nothing of the sort happens. The Muse says none of the Phaeacians notice either Odysseus's emotional reaction or his attempts to conceal it. In short, the outcome of the situation is quite different from that of its apparent forerunner in *Odyssey* 4. The superficial similarities underscore the differences in the situations and warn us that poetry imitates life in its defiance of predictable symmetry.

Odysseus, unlike Telemachus, does not shroud tears in his cloak only once. Demodocus's song, which is represented as lasting longer than the Muse's synopsis, breaks off periodically. During these breaks Odysseus calms down. He resumes crying when Demodocus resumes the song.

> Yet, as often as the divine minstrel ceased his singing, Odysseus would wipe his tear and draw the cloak from his head, and taking the two-handled cup would pour libations to the gods. But as often as the minstrel began again, and the Phaeacian nobles encouraged him because they enjoyed his song, Odysseus would again cover [*kalypsamenos*] his head and groan. (8.87–92)

The motif of covering the head, with its echoes of the nymph Calypso, the "Concealer," in the participle *kalypsamenos*, "covering," as in the previous verb form *kalypse*, "he covered," remind us of Odysseus's paradoxical existence for much of the *Odyssey*. To emerge from the obscurity of concealment, he must conceal himself and his reactions. One must be veiled to be unveiled.

Although Alcinous eventually notes Odysseus's behavior, the other Phaeacians never observe the repeated connection between Demodocus's song and Odysseus's tearful response. On the contrary, they encourage the minstrel to continue singing, because they enjoy the song. And when the Muse finally comments on Alcinous's reaction she does not explain it:

> Alcinous alone marked him and grasped what was happening, for he was sitting next to him, and heard him sighing heavily. (8.94–95)

But Alcinous shows no overt reaction. As Arete did not react to Odysseus's supplication, so no one now asks Odysseus the reason for his tears and groans. He is not given the prompt he seeks before he identifies himself as the hero whose deeds are already canonized in the repertoire of bards.

Odysseus the Athlete

The closest Alcinous comes to responding to Odysseus's veiled tears is to change the nature of the court activities from poetry to athletics. The banqueters are to leave the palace and compete in games so Odysseus can tell his friends about Phaeacian preeminence in boxing, wrestling, jumping, and running. As yet Odysseus has been provided little basis for praising Phaeacian activity in any capacity other than the blind Demodocus's proficiency as a bard. Alcinous, therefore, wisely shifts the focus from passive listening to tales of glory about other people to activities which will highlight Phaeacian physical prowess:

> But let us go out and try all kind of sports, so this stranger may tell his dear ones, when he returns home, how far we excel other men in boxing, wrestling, jumping, and speed of foot. (8.100–103)

Alcinous's plan backfires. Once the first phase of the games ends, and before there is an opportunity for Odysseus to compliment the contenders on their performance, Laodamas, beloved son of Alcinous, praises the strong shape of Odysseus's body and invites him to join in the competition. His justification is both curious and significant:

> For there is no greater fame for a man so long as he lives than what he achieves by *his own* hands and feet, *his own*. (8.147–48; emphasis added)

In the Greek the expression we have rendered "his own" is repeated at the end of both of the lines. Laodamas's statement is, perhaps, a sarcastic comment on poets (such as Demodocus) or even visitors (such as Odysseus) who rely on words to represent prowess. Men must prove themselves. Reliance on reports is not sufficient.

Laodamas's remark challenges Odysseus to prove he deserves fame not only in the remote (and past) world of Greeks and Trojans, but in the present context of Phaeacia. The suggestion of games and the challenge issued to compete may indicate that the Phaeacians, despite their impassivity, detect that Odysseus is trying to establish, obliquely, a warrior identity for himself. His tears have not gone unnoticed or unrecognized: they are simply, and perhaps deliberately, not acknowledged.

Odysseus responds to the challenge as if insulted. He reminds his hosts of his sufferings and his longing to return home. Then Euryalus delivers a blow Odysseus cannot ignore. The stranger, Euryalus claims, does not look like an athlete, but like a shipowner whose business is in the profit of his cargo (8. 159–64). Heroic pretensions are crushed. Odysseus, angered, rebukes Euryalus for his unkind words and claims he is skilled in sports and that his unimpressive appearance results not only from sufferings at sea but also from sufferings in war. Although he does not specify which war, he refocuses attention on his own identity.

The challenges by Laodamas and Euryalus force Odysseus out of the role of a passive observer whose task will be to acknowledge or praise to the world Phaeacian *aretē* in sports. He must prove he is as good as, if not better than, the Phaeacians on their grounds and in their terms. Rather than enter the competition officially, Odysseus leaps up as he is, wearing his big cloak, seizes a discus and hurls it beyond the marks achieved by the Phaeacian discus throwers. Impressive as his feat is, however, the Muse ensures that we know it was not achieved without the help of Athena.

Encouraged by his success, Odysseus invites all Phaeacians, except Laodamas, to compete in boxing, wrestling, even running. His exclusion of Laodamas is both tactful and insulting. He does not wish to compete with Alcinous's son because Alcinous is his host, yet he makes no move to exclude Halius and Clytoneus, the king's other sons. Since Laodamas is Alcinous's favorite, and thus potentially his most powerful son, Odysseus's refusal to compete with him both demonstrates that he has no intention of rivaling his position in the state and implies that he would beat Laodamas if he tried to compete. Odysseus's position becomes a little more precarious. Indeed, he may even be wearing Laodamas's best clothes. There is now tension between Odysseus and Laodamas as well as between Odysseus and Arete, Nausicaa, and Alcinous. He is working against the wishes of each in one way or another as he tries to secure his safe return to Ithaca.[9] Odysseus proceeds, then, with allusions to his Greek identity. After summoning the Phaeacians to compete in sports with which they are familiar, he suggests he is good in archery too—though inferior to Philoctetes. He can also throw the spear farther than any other man can shoot an arrow. He is aware, he says, that he may be defeated in running by the Phaeacians, since he lacked nourishment on his ship. Yet as he catalogues his skills and deficiencies, he hints to the Phaeacians much more about himself than he has yet let them know. The allusion to Philoctetes suggests he fought at Troy and was second in proficiency with the bow to the man whose archery was crucial to the capture of the city.

His assertions are a mixture of boastfulness and caution: he will not compete with heroes of former days, such as Heracles or Eurytus, but in bragging that he can throw a spear farther than anyone else can shoot an arrow, he claims not only that he can do the impossible, as any archer will recognize, but that he is a better spearsman than Achilles or Hector, and a better overall warrior than Philoctetes, the best archer.

What are we to make of this speech? It is unlikely to be simply an outburst of anger, as George Dimock suggests.[10] By now Odysseus has proved his point: he is not merely a businessman. Euryalus was wrong. Thus there is no continuing reason for him to be angry. In fact, we should be cautious when Odysseus, master of covert innuendo, resorts to the explicit. He is, throughout the *Odyssey*, in complete control of his emotions in public situations. He rarely has (or talks of having) outbursts that betray his interests or plans unless, as in the case of the Polyphemus narrative in *Odyssey* 9, it suits his rhetorical purposes to do so. That he says Euryalus's words angered him does not mean he continues to be angry as he speaks (8.205). He may, of course, wish the Phaeacians to believe he is still angry; if they do, they may be less attentive to his rhetorical ploys.

Odysseus's words are, rather, carefully calculated. He focuses on the more aggressive sports Alcinous mentioned among those in which the Phaeacians are expert: boxing and wrestling. To these he adds archery and spear throwing, warlike sports, and thus less likely to be widely practiced among the allegedly "peace-loving" Phaeacians. If they accept his challenges here, they subvert their claims to be peace loving and, worse still, afford him an additional opportunity to prove his superiority. Odysseus completes his rhetorical triumph by not outrightly declining to engage even in lighter sports in which he has already seen the Phaeacians excel and in which he admits the possibility of defeat. He is prepared to be tested "even in the skill of feet" (8. 206), though acknowledging that "in skill of feet alone I fear someone among the Phaeacians may surpass me" (8.230–31). Odysseus's qualification of his excellence in running is particularly cunning. Those familiar with the *Iliad* will remember the funeral games in which Odysseus beat both Ajax and Antilochus in the footrace, although they were younger than he (*Iliad* 23.740–92). In some variants of the Odysseus myth, in fact, he won the hand of Penelope by outrunning the other suitors in a race arranged by Penelope's father, Icarius.[11] Odysseus thus has an excuse for not winning if he competes, and an opportunity to humiliate the Phaeacians if he wins.

Before anyone can accept Odysseus's challenge, Alcinous heads off potential disaster with a convoluted and double-edged apology:

> You have not spoken ungraciously among us, but you wish to display your excellence [*aretê*] which attends you, since you are upset that this

> man standing next to you at the games insulted you, in a way that no man, who knows how to speak right in his heart, should find fault with your excellence [*aretē*]. (8.236–40)

First, Alcinous prevents Odysseus from demonstrating his "excellence" by *not* taking up the general challenge. Second, he indicates that he recognizes Odysseus's attempt to capitalize on the opportunity afforded by the insult.

To mitigate Odysseus's anger he suggests a rather odd cure:

> But come now and listen to a word of mine, so that you may tell it to another hero when you are dining with your wife and children in your home, remembering our excellence: it is about the kind of accomplishment Zeus has continuously afforded us from the time of our ancestors. For we are not excellent boxers or wrestlers, but we run fast with our feet and are the best with ships, we always have a pleasant feast, a lyre, dances, a change of clothes, warm baths, and couches [*eunai*]. (8.241–49)

Alcinous is not really conceding any ground. He dismisses Laodamas's suggestion that heroic stature and fame come with prowess in the games, and thus negates any triumph Odysseus might feel as a result of his recent success. He withdraws the Phaeacian claim to excellence in more aggressive sports, boxing and wrestling, as if downgrading what Odysseus and the Phaeacians had seen shortly before, and avoids any reference to throwing the discus, in which Odysseus has proven himself, or to archery or spear throwing, in which Odysseus claims to excel. He seizes, instead, only on the untested areas in which Phaeacians might claim superiority over Odysseus by his own admission: running and sailing. Odysseus has admitted he can be beaten in running, and his shipwreck suggests his inferiority as a sailor.

Alcinous appends a few comments about Phaeacian prowess in living the "good life" to the full, along with a list of entertainments that do not offer any competition a man such as Odysseus might be interested in.[12] What is usually taken as Phaeacian proverbial luxury and "soft" existence is, in fact, a contrived statement by Alcinous to discourage Odysseus from staying among the Phaeacians. Odysseus never mentions any interest in dancing, feasting, and high living. Although he does allude to his hunger, he does not, even on his second day in Scheria, ask for a warm bath. Baths and changes of clothing are not among his priorities now or later when he returns to Ithaca. Alcinous either ignores or is oblivious to the meaning of the attire Odysseus was given by Nausicaa. In short, Odysseus's tears during the banquet may suggest to Alcinous that his guest does not care for the high living, banquets, music, and couches Phaeacians enjoyed.[13]

Given Odysseus's response to life with Calypso, Alcinous may, in fact, be correct.

The word *eunai*, which Alcinous uses of the couches on which the Phaeacians recline, carries sexual overtones throughout the Homeric poems. Odysseus's lack of interest in sexual relationships while in Phaeacia, despite overtures from Nausicaa, would not pass unnoticed. Most mythic heroes (including Odysseus in other traditions) rarely miss sexual opportunities. Hence Alcinous's comment that Odysseus will be returning home to his *wife and children* not only emphasizes, perhaps for Arete and Nausicaa, that his visitor is married but suggests that Odysseus lacks the hero's traditional zest for heroic recreation. He offers, then, a complicated, obscure, and slightly insulting panacea for a quite straightforward insult.[14] He neither gives significance to Odysseus's *aretē*, his excellence, nor accords him further opportunity to demonstrate it until he secures a promise that Phaeacian *aretē* will be a part of his homecoming tales despite the recent debacle.

Odysseus's oblique revelation that he fought at Troy is not, however, lost on Alcinous—though he minimizes the effect of this disclosure.[15] In his earlier plea to Odysseus to spread word of Phaeacian *aretē*, Alcinous referred to Odysseus's home audience simply as "close friends" (8.101). Now he redesignates them as "heroes" (8.242). Yet, while thus conceding that Odysseus moves in heroic company, he diffuses the effect by referring to the heroic company he will enjoy on his return *at home* (with his wife and children), not to the heroic company he enjoyed during the Trojan War.

As Alcinous orders the lyre to be brought again to Demodocus, he takes care that Odysseus does not choose the song again: it will be a tale of love and marital infidelity, not of war. He will experience what Alcinous claims the Phaeacians most enjoy: banqueting, lyre playing, dancing, and (a story about) sex. A change of clothes and warm bath will follow.

The Unfaithful Wife

Alcinous's orders are quickly fulfilled. Although Odysseus watches the quickly twinkling feet of the nine dancers and marvels at heart (8.265), he keeps his admiration to himself. After the dance, Demodocus obliges with a song about Ares and Aphrodite whose humorously irreverent nature raises interesting questions about the singer. Regardless of what Alcinous and other Phaeacians have or have not observed, Demodocus has shown, even in his first song, that he knows about Odysseus and the Trojan War. He is the only Phaeacian to mention Troy and Odysseus by name up to this point. Perhaps he, with a poet's skill, has divined Odysseus's identity.

The Muse says that Odysseus enjoys Demodocus's song as he listens (8.368), although its theme, given Demodocus's more than Iliadic knowledge of the Trojan War and its protagonists, might disturb him a little. The story of Ares' lovemaking with Aphrodite during her husband Hephaestus's absence might turn Odysseus's thoughts to the young Penelope he had left, some twenty years ago, to the vicissitudes of human nature and fate. He might well wonder about her faithfulness, since his own instructions to Penelope were not to wait beyond the sexual maturity of their son, which should have occurred not too long ago.

Striking parallels between Hephaestus and Odysseus emerge as the song proceeds, notably Demodocus's emphasis on Hephaestus's *dolos*, his cunning skill (8.276). No mythic hero is more famous for such skill than Odysseus. In fact, Odysseus will soon ask Demodocus to sing about Odysseus's *dolos* when he brought the wooden horse into Troy. If Odysseus takes offense at Demodocus's tale of Ares and Aphrodite, neither he nor the Muse gives any overt sign to that effect. Read allegorically, in fact, Demodocus's tale assures Odysseus that if Penelope has been unfaithful to him, he will be able to retrieve her by his tricky artifices and even increase his wealth through a penalty imposed on the adulterer. The problem is that Hephaestus's skill and cunning in punishing the adulterous couple leave the master of *dolos* looking foolish and unheroic. People may laugh at Odysseus, too, as Apollo laughs at Hephaestus. Even if Odysseus, like Hephaestus or Menelaus, who takes back his notoriously wayward Helen, is prepared to take Penelope back if she has been unfaithful, he can do so only, if like them, he is prepared to sacrifice his heroic stature for the benefits he stands to gain. Still, financial compensation is never lost on Odysseus, as Alcinous will soon learn to his people's cost.[16]

Whatever the resonances of Demodocus's story, Odysseus makes a point of construing it in his own favor and a show of enjoying it. At least the song reassures him that one man in the court probably knows who he is, even if that man is using his knowledge to mock him. Besides, given the amount of Hephaestean craftsmanship in evidence around Alcinous's court, Alcinous himself may be at least partially targeted by the bard.

Play It, Demodocus

After the song about Ares and Aphrodite, Odysseus is again offered an opportunity to recognize and acknowledge Phaeacian prominence in dancing. An elaborate dance is performed by Laodamas and Halius, two of Alcinous's sons. At this point Odysseus accords the Phaeacians the long-awaited recognition of their talents:

> Lord Alcinous, renowned above all men, you bragged that your dancers are the best, and indeed your words are made good. Wonder holds me when I look on them. (8.382–84)

Alcinous does not delay his expression of delight, though his response is addressed not to his guest, but to his fellow Phaeacians, as if to vindicate himself in their eyes:

> Hear me, leaders and counselors of the Phaeacians. This stranger really seems to me *pepnymenos*—a man of straightforward speech. (8.387–88)

Alcinous thinks he has finally achieved what he desired all along. The stranger has acknowledged Phaeacian *aretē* in dancing and will presumably spread word of it in his native land. But it is a small victory.

His words are selected with some care. *Pepnymenos* indicates mental vigor in speaking, not diplomacy or propriety. The Iliadic and Odyssean heroes referred to by this epithet, such as Antenor, Meriones, Antilochus, Polydamas, Telemachus, Peisistratus, and Laertes, do not hesitate to express views boldly and forthrightly, without prior calculation, and without concern for pleasing those to whom they speak.[17] It is hard to think of a situation, however, in which Odysseus could be considered a "straightforward" speaker. Not only in the Homeric poems, but throughout literature, his obliquity and deviousness are proverbial. He is the antithesis of the "straightforward" speaker, as Achilles implies in *Iliad* 9. 311–13, when he declares to Odysseus that he hates as he hates the gates of death a man who says one thing and means something else, as Odysseus usually does.[18]

It is, however, to Alcinous's advantage to take Odysseus's long-withheld compliment as sincere, following the shambles of his Phaeacian Games. He compensates the stranger's acknowledgment extravagantly. Each lord must bring a newly washed cloak (like those laundered by Nausicaa), a tunic, and one talent of gold. In addition, Alcinous provides the best chest he has, a golden cup, and (finally) a warm bath. Odysseus will now participate in most of the activities Phaeacians favor: the banquet, the lyre, the dance, the change of clothes, and a warm bath. Sex (*eunai*) is still omitted. Nausicaa waits as he emerges gleaming and freshly clad from the tub, but does not try to allure him, as at their first meeting, though the situation and narrative sequence suggest the opportunity. Rather, she bids him farewell. Of the possibilities implicit in the Greek *eunai*, only the literal (and unusual) meaning prevails. Not much later (in extent of time if not of narrative), Odysseus, still uninterested in the pleasures of the bed, is ready to stretch out on the deck of the ship which takes him home.

Since both Arete and Nausicaa now refer to his departure, Odysseus is left with only one dilemma: his unacknowledged identity. There is a danger the Phaeacians will never know who their guest was, though he, for his part, has conceded Phaeacian superiority in dancing and promised to worship Nausicaa as a goddess once he gets home. The imbalance between his and their recognition of *aretē* still needs adjustment. Only one person at court can prepare the way tactfully: Demodocus. So Odysseus asks him to sing about Odysseus's *dolos*, his most cunning scheme: the construction of the Trojan horse and how he brought it into Troy. Such a narrative would make him the architect par excellence of Troy's fall. Odysseus promises Demodocus worldwide fame if he will oblige:

> I will immediately tell all people that the god, of his own goodwill, bestowed on you the gift of divine song. (8.497–98)

Odysseus speaks in full confidence of prompt departure, and he shows how fully he understands the importance of fame, of *kleos*, for the Phaeacians, severed as they are from communication with other humans.

Demodocus does not fully comply with Odysseus's request. He omits Odysseus's *dolos*, his cunning plan for the horse, and begins when it is already in the Trojan agora. Then he focuses on Trojan discussion as to what to do with it. He sings of the various heroes who emerged and sacked the city, but mentions Odysseus only at the end, and then says nothing about the cunning resourcefulness on which the hero prides himself. Rather, coupling Odysseus with Menelaus, he tells how "Odysseus, like Ares, went with Menelaus to Deïphobus's house," where Odysseus "dared the most terrible fight and finally won with greathearted Athena's help" (8.517–20). Odysseus's role in the capture of Troy is not highlighted, as he had clearly hoped, but limited, as in no other version of the Trojan saga, to accompanying Menelaus as he retrieves Helen. Although the recovery of Helen is, of course, the object of the Trojan War, and although Demodocus is at least overtly showing Odysseus's role in the achievement of that object—he fights bravely in the battle to get the unfaithful Helen back—Odysseus is relegated to a supporting role in a narrative in which he had hoped to star. Demodocus further suggests that Odysseus's success owes much to the help of Athena—a statement which compliments the hero for receiving divine aid and, at the same time, minimizes the role of his intellect in carrying out the action.[19]

When Odysseus, master of tearful reaction, weeps, we need not assume he is fully satisfied with and moved by Demodocus's song. The Muse appends an ironic simile comparing him to a woman captured in war:

> But Odysseus was melting, a tear wetted his cheeks below his eyelids. And, as a woman cries while flinging herself upon her husband, struck down in front of his city and people while trying to ward off from his city and children the day of not pity; as she sees him dying and gasping

> for breath, she clings to him and shrieks aloud, while behind they are poking her with spears in her back and shoulders. They lead her away to captivity, to bear suffering and sorrow and her cheeks waste away with most pitiful grief; so Odysseus shed a pitiful tear from beneath his brows. From all the others he concealed the tears he shed; Alcinous alone noticed him and understood the situation, since he was sitting close and heard him groaning heavily. (8.521–34)

The simile, as usual, is wonderful not only in its power but in its paradoxical force: Odysseus, whose role as pitiless enslaver of the women of Troy is the subject of several ancient tragedies and numerous other poetic allusions, weeps as if he were the victim of the atrocities he himself perpetrated. Scholars have struggled to account for Odysseus's tears and the curious simile. It has been variously suggested that the tears are prompted by nostalgia, a contrast between his former achievements and his present ignoble state, sorrow for his lost comrades, simple grief, or grief that paves the way for him to cross from the world of fantasy to reality, even the simple memory of past toils.[20] Yet Odysseus is hardly a person to break down for any of these reasons. Emotional restraint is a major characteristic of his behavior which enables him to deploy his wiles and resourcefulness to maximum effect.[21] He does not weep for joy on seeing his son. He does not shed a tear while watching his wife cry over the memory of her absent husband (19.209–12). He endures the misery of his old and weak father, who mourns his lost son, and, instead of hugging him as he would like, addresses him with "insulting words," lying to him and calling him a slave (24.240–79). If he does not weep at the memory of lost times and lost loves, it is curious that he should weep at the memory of past *successes*. Unless there was something between Odysseus and Helen that is lost to tradition, the only element in Demodocus's song that could sadden Odysseus's heart is his own diminished role in the saga of the horse. In this sense the connection in the simile between the sacker of cities and his victim is particularly significant. Odysseus has become a casualty of the narrative he himself requested—a narrative that is itself, if fully set forth, a tale of shocking brutality as well as of skillful contrivance. And, from the Muse's point of view, there may be something else: *The Sack of Troy* is not her epic. As the simile implies, it is a tale already familiar to the audience.

Most likely Odysseus's crying is as carefully orchestrated as was his scheme of the wooden horse. It is his attempt to draw attention to himself and, by doing so, to precipitate his self-disclosure as the (albeit now reduced) hero of the song. If this is his aim, he meets with some success, since he eventually forces the reluctant Alcinous to stop Demodocus's song, which, though it brought pleasure to him and to the other banqueters, pained Odysseus. It is much better, he notes, when both hosts and guest make merry (8.542–43). Alcinous, however, does not say he has divined from his guest's reaction that he must be Odysseus. On the contrary, he declares that he still has no idea who his visitor is and that Odysseus must not evade with "crafty thoughts" (8.548) the questions he now proposes to ask.

The master of innuendo and oblique speech must be explicit. Alcinous asks his guest his real name—the name by which his parents and his people refer to him, "since no one is without a name: *anōnymos.*" To encourage a prompt, explicit response, he reassures Odysseus that he will be sent home despite all obstacles, because Phaeacians have magical ships which respond to the *thoughts,* rather than to the words, of those they convey. There is a covert threat here. Verbal dissimulation, useful in normal human company, will be no defense against Phaeacian mind-reading vessels.[22]

Yet even as he makes this statement, Alcinous adds a significant aside—a detail of Phaeacian lore. His father, Nausithous, he says, once foretold that the Phaeacians would be cut off by Poseidon from the inhabited world at some future point when returning home after transporting a stranger to his destination. The Phaeacians will, after Odysseus leaves, be unreachable by other outsiders. If we assume that Alcinous is telling the truth (insofar as anything said in the *Odyssey* is true), we may catch some sense of the urgency in his request that the fame of his people be narrated to the world at large, for this may be the last opportunity for the Phaeacians to make contact with that outside world. Odysseus is himself their safeguard against being *anōnymoi,* without name or identity. Thus there is, perhaps, a touch of poignancy as well as acidity in Alcinous's claim that no man is without name. Alcinous relies on Odysseus's sensitivity to innuendo to ensure the effect of his oblique insult. He does not elaborate his aside but presses Odysseus to tell about his adventures, the countries he wandered through, and why he wept as he listened to the fate of the Achaeans before Troy. Odysseus, of course, obliges with a lengthy narrative of his travels. But he never fully accedes to Alcinous's desire to spread the *kleos* of the Phaeacians.

Indeed, few features of the *Odyssey* have drawn more attention than Odysseus's substitution of Cretans, Phoenicians, and others for the Phaeacians when he tells, upon his return to Ithaca, the tale of the benefactors who brought him home. We owe our familiarity with the Phaeacians to Homer's muse. But it is surely worth reminding ourselves, before we discuss the tales Odysseus spins for the Phaeacians, that we also owe our familiarity with these to the Homeric muse rather than to "Odysseus" himself, for these are tales, overheard by the Muse, that Odysseus told in the no-longer accessible world of the very Phaeacians he declines to mention when he returns to Greece. They have not only all the marks of fantasy that characterize the Phaeacians themselves but the marks of a narrative motivated to at least some extent by the desire of the guest to exculpate himself from blame for the loss of his troops and to make at least gentle mockery of his hosts.

The reason for Odysseus's mockery is not simply wanton rudeness on his part. It is a defensive kind of counterattack to offset some innuendoes in Alcinous's remarks at the end of book 8. Just as we try to account for Odysseus's tears as he listens to Demodocus's song of the Trojan horse, so does Alcinous. Perhaps, he wonders aloud, Odysseus lost a relative in the fighting at Troy. We may, of course, simply attribute that suggestion to Alcinous's ignorance. But before we just sweep it aside, it is worth noting that the relatives he mentions in his speculations are not blood relatives, but relatives by marriage: Odysseus's daughter's husband, or his wife's father (8.582–83). He is downgrading Odysseus's grief: the loss of such in-laws would, arguably, cause *less* intense personal sorrow than the loss of one's own son or one's own father. Further, the suggestion that Odysseus had a daughter who was married at the time of the Trojan War implies that Odysseus is somewhere between ten and twenty years older than he actually is—quite possibly older than Alcinous himself, all of whose children are still unmarried, almost a decade after the war ended.

Alcinous's suggested in-laws killed in the fighting include father-in-law and son-in-law but not brother-in-law. Yet, as he proceeds with his list of those for whom Odysseus might be weeping, Alcinous notes that his guest may indeed be lamenting a comrade like a brother who was lost in the war, for, he declares, "not a bit worse than a brother is a comrade who speaks his mind [*pepnymena*]" (8.585–86). What makes this comment even more troubling is that Odysseus tells, in the narrative of his travels, of a comrade who is prepared to speak his mind and who also happens to be his brother-in-law: Eurylochus. Eurylochus, in fact, figures prominently in Odysseus's account of the events on Circe's island. Odysseus says he sent Penelope's brother to Circe's house on one of the most perilous expeditions and depicts him as a dissident voice among his crew, often openly critical of his leader's behavior.

Whether Odysseus assumes Alcinous's comments are based on ignorance of Troy and his travels or on concealed knowledge of the same, he has some reason to suspect that his host's intent is at least covertly malicious. Yet his strategy, in reply, is not to deny any shortcomings that Alcinous may have heard of, or that may have survived in other mythic traditions of his *nostos*, but to place them in a rather different causal nexus where they seem more laudable or at least more explicable. He does not deny, for example, a certain unjust harshness in his treatment of Eurylochus: but he assigns their conflict not to the period of the Trojan War, but to the voyage home. The tale Odysseus reveals in books 9–12 shows him as a person who consistently, out of curiosity, endangers his close comrades. Yet he obliquely but constantly hints that his valor and prudence far exceed Phaeacian valor and prudence. He modifies not only what happened in his past, *but what happened in the Phaeacian past.*

Although Odysseus controls his own narrative among the Phaeacians, his shaping of that narrative must take into account such features of the Odysseus tradition as he suspects are too widely known to be denied. His rhetorical dilemma is that Alcinous's dissimulation has left him unclear as to what the Phaeacians actually know about Odysseus's past activities. In the numerous traditions of Odysseus that emerge outside the *Odyssey* there is a great deal of unflattering detail which surfaces again and again, not only in the *Iliad* but also, more savagely still, in the texts of Greek and Roman tragedy. Even the Odyssean muse depicts her hero as a ruthless man whose son, wife, and father are instruments enabling him to reacquire position and possessions. The Odyssean Odysseus is sophisticated enough in the art of reinventing himself to grasp that it is better to recontextualize the negative tradition of his conduct than to confront it directly or deny it. Thus Odysseus suggests that whatever differences he may have had with his companions, including his brother-in-law, and whatever folly he may have been guilty of, occurred not at Troy, but in the shadowy world of his homeward voyage, to which only he, the narrator, really has access.

If Odysseus's tears at Demodocus's songs were, then, an expression of genuine grief over some loss at Troy rather than a studied rhetorical gesture, the cause of that grief is lost beyond recovery. We may postulate that Alcinous knows something no one knows nowadays: that there was some tradition that held Odysseus responsible for the loss of his men, including Eurylochus, at Troy and that Odysseus's narrative strategy is to transpose those catastrophes to the tale of his homeward journey. Perhaps that is why Odysseus begins the tale of his travels with his arrival among the Cicones. The Cicones are the only people Odysseus mentions in the course of his travels whose existence is supported by other narratives that are not arguably derived from the *Odyssey*. They are, in this sense, liminal: they stand on the border between tradition and invention, between myth and fiction, between epic "truth" and epic "lies."

Seaborne Destruction

The Cicones are known to us from the *Iliad* as allies of the Trojans (*Iliad* 2.846–47). That Odysseus falls among them can be seen either as an instance of bad luck—that he should be born by the winds to unequivocal enemies—or as an indication that he was not a skilled seaman. Later writers usually situate the Cicones in Thrace. If this is the case, Odysseus's further note that he could have sailed straight from their settlement of Ismarus to Ithaca, had it not been for the north wind, is preposterous. But, given Alcinous's apparently vague sense of geography and the king's own statement that Phaeacian ships need no pilots or steering oars, since they can read the minds of their travelers, it may also be an ironic jest. If Euboea is to Alcinous the most distant limit of the known world, Odysseus need not worry about being caught in "geographical incompetence." He may even be testing the Phaeacians for a reaction.

The Ciconian episode shares three main features with the majority of Odysseus's other narratives of his adventures. First, whatever he devises for his squadron is successful as long as his comrades follow his commands. Second, although he commands all the ships of the Cephallenian contingent, his orders are not always obeyed. Third, his comrades' failure to follow his advice causes them to suffer mishaps and casualties.

Odysseus is thus, in his own narrative, responsible mainly for successes, not for the disasters that strike his expedition—though he occasionally admits some responsibility, probably to give a sense of balance to his picture. *He* sacked the city of Ismarus, Troy's ally. *He* pursues Greek goals even on his homeward journey. In his narrative he astutely underscores his role by using the first-person pronoun, rarely used in Greek unless the speaker wants to focus particular attention upon himself in contrast to others: *I* destroyed the city and killed the men; *they*, the rest of the contingent, took the women and the treasures which they divided equally (9.40–42). *I* ordered my comrades to flee immediately; *my comrades* refused—with catastrophic results (9.43–44). The men drank much wine and feasted on the cattle, so the Cicones called on their neighbors for help. In the ensuing battle six comrades out of every ship were killed. But, of course, it was their fault, not his. In this respect Odysseus seems, at first, to be only slightly modifying the injunction to the Muse in the first ten lines of the *Odyssey*. But he is modifying them. At the outset he makes it plain that the major part of his squadron was lost well before he reached the land where Helios kept his cattle: all but one ship, in fact. His men are plundering and devouring cattle: but they are the cattle of the Cicones rather than the cattle of the Sun.

Although Odysseus is the only Greek commander who lost all his comrades, and not in Troy but on the homeward journey, he is not to be blamed (as he begins his story) for their misfortune. He moves toward this rhetorical goal of exculpating himself by way of a variety of tactics. In the case of the Cicones, he camouflages the magnitude of his losses by counting them on a per ship (and surely averaged) basis: six deaths per ship sounds better than seventy-two killed, since he has not yet told his audience that he had twelve ships. In fact, the size of his squadron is not mentioned until the third adventure, and then slyly, in sort of an accidental way not required by, and even cloaked by, the immediate context: his arrival on Goat Island (9.159). The chances that anyone among his listeners will remember the "six dead comrades per ship" during the high adventures on Goat Island are slim. And we still do not know how many men there were on each ship.

Odysseus's second ploy is to emphasize his deep distress for lost comrades (though the only comrades he names among his crew are Eurylochus, Elpenor, and Perimedes), and his narrative usually underscores his disagreements with them. He describes them as *deiloi hetairoi*, "wretched (although adventurous) comrades." The epithet *deilos*, routine in heroic descriptions, is used with *hetairos* only in association with the dead Patroclus in the *Iliad*, where it occurs repeatedly.[23] The Muse thus lets Odysseus invest, for the benefit of his inner audience, his description of his dead comrades with an echo of the Iliadic mourning of Achilles for Patroclus. It is a delicate touch, suggesting that grief for an impetuous friend's death outweighs any criticism of his recklessness.

Lotus Eaters

From this point, Odysseus's tales take his audiences into a never-never land marked off in his narrative by a nine-day drift which could have taken him almost anywhere in the Mediterranean—perhaps even outside it. It certainly removes him from definite geography. After the nine-day drift, he and his men reach, he claims, the land of the Lotus Eaters—a friendly folk who share their food with his crew. This second adventure has a different tone from the Cicones episode. There is nothing in it about his (or his comrades') heroism, for their hosts pose no threat of violence. The Lotus Eaters' friendliness, however, is as perilous to Odysseus's homecoming as is the Cicones' hostility. Eating the honey-sweet lotus fruit makes the men forgetful of their homes and homeward journey.

The story seems to have two functions in the architecture of Odysseus's narrative. First, it underscores his determination to get back home, even if that means he must bind his comrades and drag them to the ships against their will. Second, it introduces the theme of the fateful consumption of food, which becomes more prominent (and more destructive) as his narrative proceeds.

The Lotus-Eaters episode presents, again, a degrading picture of Odysseus's comrades as the echoes of Patroclean mourning subside. In this sense, Odysseus's narrative strategy of persuasion remains much the same as it was in his tale of the Cicones. He talks sometimes of himself, as if he were traveling alone, sometimes of himself and his men together, and sometimes of his men as a totally separate group. His arrival at the land of the Lotus Eaters is a case in point:

> From there for nine days *I* was carried by terrible winds over the sea teeming with fish; but on the tenth day *we* set foot on the land of the Lotus Eaters, who eat its flowers as their food. There *we* went ashore and drew water, and soon *my comrades* took their meal near the swift ships. (9.82–86; emphasis added)

The transition to third person plural in line 86 strikes scholars as brusque and puzzling. W. B. Stanford notes the problem but offers no solution: *helonto* (took) "is a curiously isolated 3rd person in this first person narrative"; P. Cauer takes the word as a relic of an original third-person version of the incident.[24] The most obvious explanation, surely, is rhetorical: Odysseus wants to separate himself from his crew in his narrative, just as he does in the tale of the Cicones. His crew are as much an obstacle to his (and their own) return home as are the peoples and creatures they meet along the way. And when he finally gets his crew within striking distance of Ithaca, their greed and folly, in opening Aeolus's bag of winds, robs both him and them of a successful return. Whatever his own shortcomings, the ultimate responsibility for the loss of his crew lies with his men, not with him. And it certainly does not diminish his heroism at Troy, since none of the losses occurred in the Iliadic context of the Trojan War.

Odysseus's retailoring of his past, as he describes himself sailing from myth into a more fictional environment, is but one goal of his narrative rhetoric in *Odyssey* 9–12. More remarkable is his success in reinventing the Phaeacians' past, a process which we must now examine.

[4]

Cyclopes Reinvented

Epic narrative is a complex rhetorical strategy and was recognized as such by rhetoricians in antiquity. It requires our careful attention to the identity of the inner narrator and to the circumstances under which he is speaking. As we have already seen in the case of Helen and Menelaus, we must consider both what we think the Homeric muse may wish to suggest to *us* and any other hypothetical external audiences and what the various inner narrators seek to suggest to their various "inner" audiences. These two sets of considerations are not, of course, entirely separate, since external audiences will necessarily perceive the work as a whole in terms of the various internal narratives. But it will help our enquiry to separate those internal narratives both to make our argument a little clearer and, especially, to keep in mind that any given character will not necessarily represent himself or herself in the same way to different people. Indeed, there is at least one further rhetorical complexity. In addition to trying to account for, say, the persona Odysseus presents to the Phaeacians, as opposed to that which he presents to Eumaeus or Telemachus, we must also take into account the different ways in which the Muse herself presents Odysseus to internal and external audiences. Finally, after noting such tensions as arise between the persona of Odysseus as presented by the narrator-poet and his muse to the external eye and the various personae he presents to his internal audiences, we must ask whether these internal and external personae coalesce at some point.

Truth and Lies

A narrative within an epic is not "simply" a vehicle for conveying information, least of all in the *Odyssey*. Odysseus, as narrative mythmaker, especially when in the company of the probably fictional Phaeacians, presents himself as he does because he is in an environment where "truth" cannot be factual discourse and factual discourse cannot be truth. Indeed truth, in our narrowly literal and unpoetic discourse, has little meaning in epic. The Homeric Odysseus's special claim to fame is his mastery of narrative, his ability to invent himself anew for each audience he confronts.[1] To call such fictions truth is to misuse the English word. To call them lies is to undermine the basis not only of Odyssean myth but of Christian parable. It is, therefore, wiser to avoid the incorrect distinction some scholars make between the "truth" Odysseus tells the Phaeacians and his later Cretan "lies." Odysseus's truth—which Homer vouches for in *Odyssey* 16.226—is, as Alcinous recognizes earlier (11.368–69), a *poetic* rather than a literal "truth": it is a narrative, a *mythos,* stated with understanding by a bard.[2]

The problem with Odysseus's narrative to Alcinous is that he is talking of people and events that are, even by Herodotean standards, improbable. And this is precisely what the possibly fictional Alcinous and the Muse are drawing our attention to. When Alcinous says that Odysseus is unlike other people who tell of people and places no one has ever seen, he leaves open at least two possible inferences from his words. The first, and that most often made by critics, such as Clay and Ford, is that Odysseus really was an eyewitness to the events he has described: that he is telling the literal truth. The difficulty is, of course, that what Odysseus claims to have witnessed is, by and large, incredible to any reasonable person, ancient or modern—unless one takes his truth to be a kind of allegorical, poetic truth (which would be unrecognizable as truth in any conventional sense). The second inference is that Odysseus is constructing a narrative which has a way of capturing the essence of things without being literally true at all: the poetic truth about life, human nature and so forth.

Alcinous's tone is hard to discern. But when he prefaces his remarks with the observation that no one would call Odysseus a liar, even though what he says resembles the kind of things liars (of which the world is full) say, the Phaeacian kings shows that he is not unskeptical; hence his assertion that Odysseus is not an inventer of fictions or lies but a rhapsode relaying songs. He is a Demodocus, but with a difference. Demodocus's traditional stories are about others, not about himself.[3] Odysseus, however, has inserted himself into the traditional narrative of epic encounters with the famous dead and monsters of the geographical unknown. Since Alcinous, who offers the comment, is himself, in all likelihood, a fiction of the Homeric muse, his observation is superbly ironic. He is as much an intruder into traditional epic as Odysseus is an intruder into the domain of Scylla and Charybdis, the Otherworld, and even the fictional Phaeacia.

We would do better to talk, in reference to the *Odyssey,* of "that which persuades" rather than of "that which is true." Though philosophers may quarrel with us here, we maintain that, in rhetorical, poetic terms, "truth" means little more than what a given person or group is prepared to believe or trust at a given time. The English language generally represents the world in more positive terms than does Greek. Where we talk of "safety," the ancient Greek talked of *asphaleia,* "that which does not trip one up." The Greek assumption is that a situation in which one is not tripped up is sufficiently anomalous that it needs to be described with caution. Similarly, the Greek notion of *alētheia,* which we generally translate as "truth," is also a negative rather than a positive concept: "that which is not forgotten, that which does not escape our notice."[4]

The most elaborate development of this notion of *alētheia* occurs at the end of Plato's *Republic,* in what is known as the Myth of Er, which Socrates prefaces with the comment that this is "no long tale of Alcinous." There Plato recounts Socrates' narrative of a narrative Socrates says derives from a man named Er—an almost certainly fictional creation of Plato or Socrates. At the very least, it is a narrative three removes distant from its reputed source. In it, Er is reported to have claimed that he returned from the dead, but that, unlike other souls returning from the underworld in their new bodies, he remembered what he had seen, before his return to life, of that world of pre- and post-corporeal existence. All the other souls drank from the river Lethe, "Oblivion," before reincarnation, but he was able to make the transition *without* drinking of Lethe. Thus his report is based on observations that are not overwhelmed (as almost everything is) by *lēthē.* It is *a-lētheia.*[5]

Our term "truth," by contrast, is a *positive* notion, deriving from the same root as "trust." It is a product of the English language, which was shaped in a world already Christian. Although scholars have tried to free "truth" from its links with belief rather than knowledge, the result has been, in practice, an uneasy equation of "truth" and "fact" which is more at home in the discourse we describe as history than in that which we describe as poetry.[6]

The Blameless Odysseus

Throughout the *Odyssey,* Odysseus appears reluctant to take a forthright, "truthful," approach in his exchanges with those around him. Whatever the goals of his self-presentation are, he usually alludes to most of them obliquely or leaves them for his listeners to infer, rather than stating them explicitly. Although he is quite explicit about his desire to return home, he is cautious about mentioning who he is or where his home is. His aim seems to be to provide clues for his interlocutors to piece together to infer his identity. He also realizes that his situation demands a certain amount of obliqueness in the interests of his own personal safety (of not tripping up) and of diplomacy and common courtesy.

When the Muse notes the actions and words of members of the Phaeacian royal family, she shows us that communication by innuendo is the norm in Phaeacia. Alcinous knows why Nausicaa wants to do the palace washing. No less important, the Phaeacians, even if they are meant to be Greeks, are at the very edge of the Greek world and live a life sufficiently different from that with which Odysseus seems familiar that he needs to define himself in Phaeacian rather than in traditionally Greek terms. This may be why, when he tells Alcinous's court about his adventures, he lays so much stress on his encounters with Cyclopes and Giants.

The Phaeacians, we will recall, offer gifts of guest-friendship, *xenia,* to Odysseus, even though there is, in their view, no hope for an exchange of hospitality. What they want in return is fame, *kleos,* in seafaring and athletics in the larger and more open world to which Odysseus will return. For his part, Odysseus is unwilling to promise to spread their *kleos* until they recognize his claim to fame too. After employing the various tactics we have already discussed, however, he is forced into explicit self-revelation. In a rare slip of tongue, although an oblique one, Alcinous indicates that Odysseus's deviousness is not lost on him: "Do not hide with crafty thoughts whatever I shall ask you," he tells Odysseus after the second instance of the hero's crying (8.548–49).

Obliged to abandon obliqueness, Odysseus proclaims:

> I am Odysseus, the son of Laertes, who is known to men for all kinds of wiles, and my fame [*kleos*] reaches the skies. (9.19–20)

This is not a humble assertion; in fact it carries a certain undertone of menace. Odysseus has already tried to draw attention to his wiles by prompting Demodocus to sing about his craftiness, his *dolos,* in bringing the wooden horse into Troy. Demodocus, as we have seen, does not do exactly as bidden and focuses rather on Odysseus's combat in the house of Deïphobus. Odysseus is thus presented as more threatening in fighting inside a house than in scheming to bring about the fall of the city as a whole. Demodocus's change of focus underscores the way in which Odysseus threatens the Phaeacians as well as the Trojans, and in which he will ultimately threaten (and destroy) those in his palace on Ithaca. Alcinous too seems to sense the danger of violence on Odysseus's part. He removes any remotely aggressive sport from the list of contests in which Odysseus might compete.

To ensure his prompt dispatch from Phaeacia, Odysseus needs to draw attention to a characteristic of his behavior which would not appeal to, and might even disquiet, the Phaeacians so that the wish to have him gone might outweigh any pressure (on the part of Arete or Nausicaa, for instance) to detain him. His *dolos,* whether in practice or in theory, might prove effective in prompting them to send him on his way. In a sense, of course, the essential "truth" about Odysseus is that he is the antithesis of truthfulness in its etymologizing Greek sense of "that which does not elude you." He is an elusive, tricky character.

To emphasize his concern for an assured departure, Odysseus, immediately after describing himself as a man of *dolos,* hastens to make explicit his yearning for home. Against the orderly sequence of what is to be his own narrative, he mentions the beautiful goddesses Calypso and Circe, who wanted him to stay with them and be their husband, and his refusal to succumb to their temptation. His intent may be to communicate, by innuendo, to Arete and Nausicaa that a man who can resist a goddess can resist a princess. From here he plunges straight into the most important subject for him at the moment: his "woeful homecoming" from Troy (9.37).

Odysseus's choice of narratives may seem surprising, considering that he has not yet completed his return journey and that his narrative must therefore also be incomplete. What he is doing, surely, is generating an epic story which his hosts will have the opportunity to bring to its fulfillment, thereby ensuring their importance as participants in his "epic" narrative. But his rhetorical difficulties are considerable, because Alcinous has not, so far, overtly revealed any awareness that his visitor comes from Troy. Odysseus's assumption that the Phaeacians know about Troy (based on what he gathers from Demodocus's song) is, perhaps, also his way of suggesting that Alcinous and others are concealing their knowledge of him and of Troy for reasons unknown. At least for his narrative purposes, his Trojan past and the Trojan War in general are of no particular use because they are of little interest to his immediate audience. That is probably why he takes pains early in the narrative of his travels to describe an encounter with the Cyclopes, whose mythic existence is well documented outside the Odyssean tradition and whose "reality" is accepted by the Phaeacians, who have claimed, in his hearing, to be related to the Cyclopes. The way Odysseus narrates his encounter with the Cyclopes serves not only to engage the attention of the Phaeacians, but to warn them of how they themselves may figure in a later narrative if they do not act as responsible hosts.

As Odysseus plunges deeper into a narrative that has all the marks of fiction dressed as folktale, he cunningly constructs it not only in such a way as to exonerate himself from responsibility for the deaths of most of his men, but as to make it acceptable—if not always entirely credible and satisfactory to the audience he is addressing. The sketchy information about the Phaeacians that Odysseus has derived from Nausicaa, from the girl (Athena) who led him to Alcinous's palace, from Alcinous in his addresses to the Phaeacians, and from his own observations gives him some sense of his hosts and what they believe about themselves and the world. They see themselves as close to the gods, as possessing magic ships, as on a par with the Cyclopes and the Giants. In sum, they see (or at least portray) themselves as a quasi-mythical people who still enjoy discourse and a close relationship with gods. They therefore cannot react with skepticism to Odysseus's narrative of Cyclopes and gods, since these beings are part of their own claimed "reality."

Scheria, as we have seen, is characterized by a strangely double nature, symbolized by the half-wild and half-cultivated olive bush under which Odysseus hides. Is this a culture emerging from savagery to civilization or a culture turning from civilization to savagery? In general, Greek writers tend to assume cultural entropy; but we should at least examine the possibility that the Homeric muse of the *Odyssey* does not share the Hesiodic and Nestorian view that the world is in decline. Although the Phaeacians trace their origins to the wild Giants and claim to be related to the Cyclopes, they present to Odysseus the facade of a tranquil and technologically advanced people, timid enough to have fled their original land in the previous generation to escape their menacing relatives. In short, they, like Odysseus, have been (and are still in the process of) reinventing themselves. Yet, while the Phaeacians claim to be removed both physically and spiritually from the ways and norms of their ancestors and relatives, there is much that suggests their Cyclopean origins.

We glimpse here one of the many paradoxes that confront us with this curious people. The Phaeacians seem ineffably remote, living in a small, closed community which, though they claim it has been visited by strangers before, is sufficiently out of touch with the rest of the world that an outsider is instantly detectable. Although Scheria, as the Muse always calls Phaecia, is a lively harbor city where the coming and going of strangers should be routine, both Athena and Nausicaa are sure Odysseus will stand out among the city people and therefore need protection. Strangers, even the king's guests, run the danger not only of being harassed by the local population if they come unaccompanied into the city, but also, as Arete warns, of being robbed by her own sailors while they sleep on a palace-sponsored homeward voyage. Odysseus should see to it that his treasure chest is sealed with a special knot, she advises. Similarly, although Alcinous declares that the Phaeacian habit of conveying strangers to their homes will eventually bring them punishment from Poseidon, the only guest Alcinous mentions that they conveyed anywhere is the Cretan Rhadamanthus, who belongs, at the very latest, to the mythic generation of Alcinous's father, Nausithous: to a time before the Phaeacians arrived in Phaeacia.

While the king represents the Phaeacians as remarkable seafarers, we—and presumably Odysseus, who has sailed much of the Mediterranean and even built his own ship on Calypso's island—quickly grasp that the strength of Phaeacian seamanship lies in their vessels rather than in themselves. Alcinous claims they need neither pilots nor steering oars, since *the ships* understand the thoughts and minds of their travelers. They know the cities the travelers want to go to, and they reach their destinations covered in mist, with never a fear of harm or ruin for their passengers (8.557–63). It is probably just as well that they do, for Alcinous's boast about Phaeacian excellence in seafaring has already been undermined by his description of Euboea as the most distant of lands, which it cannot be in any Greek navigator's reckoning.[7] The integrity and the competence of Phaeacian sailors are also suspect. Alcinous's reassuring words hardly mesh comfortably with Arete's warning to Odysseus about the dangers of being robbed by the sailors. Even if we make light of her words on the grounds that they may be merely a rhetorical ploy to discourage Odysseus from leaving, the "oar-loving" Phaeacian sailors do little other than provide muscle to propel the ships: they are men in the service of machines which are themselves employed to aid other (mostly foreign) humans. Their fabulous, thought-reading ships read the minds of *travelers* not of the *sailors* who sail them. Curiously enough, however, when it is time to go, Odysseus has to tell the Phaeacians where he wants to travel—though perhaps to satisfy their curiosity rather than to serve any undetected needs of the mind-reading vessels.

The excellence of the Phaeacians, like that of their cousins, the Cyclopes, resides in their brawn if they are, as Alcinous says, "oar-lovers"—*philēretmoi.* They provide the power for ships that think for themselves and take their prompting from the travelers.[8] The Muse herself, with perhaps a touch of irony, reserves the epithet "oar-loving" for the counselors and leaders of the Phaeacians rather than for those among the people who provide the oar power (8.96, 386, 535). Alcinous is himself set apart from these counselors, as is evident in Odysseus's farewell address, where Odysseus directs his words specially to Alcinous, although addressing the "oar-loving" Phaeacians as a whole (13.36–37).

Alcinous's decision to send Odysseus home on one of his magic ships will prove as disastrous for further direct communication between Phaeacians and the rest of the world as the decision of his father, Nausithous, was in the preceding generation. Nausithous, whose name is identical with that of one of Odysseus's sons by Calypso in other traditions, not only transported his people away from their original land, close to the Cyclopes, but brought some unspecified ruin upon them (6.1–10; 7.60). This point is particularly interesting if we bear in mind that Nausithous's name, "Swift in Ships," indicates his naval power. The ship Alcinous sends to convey Odysseus home will be stopped in its course and rooted to the seabed on its return, never to be a swift ship again. Alcinous's own, more abstract name sets him apart from the twelve "oar-loving" lesser kings he rules and who take their orders from him, even though it is not his mind but his thinking ships that make decisions on the high seas. Among the important Phaeacians, only Alcinous, his wife Arete, and their "beloved" son Laodamas have names which are neither "shippy" nor indicative of some physical singularity. Perhaps, in Alcinous's case *nous*, "mind," is a substitute for *naus*, "ship," since the two words are so close in sound and frequently the subject of wordplay in Greek.

Whether the Phaeacians know any more about building ships than about sailing them the Muse does not say. It is not at all clear who builds the Phaeacian ships. One may argue that it must be the Phaeacians themselves who do so. Yet it is not impossible that their naval design is (or is believed to be) the work of the gods who, Alcinous claims, freely engage with the Phaeacians. Hephaestus, after all, fashioned the remarkable gold and silver dogs guarding Alcinous's palace (7.91–93). There is indeed something strikingly postmodern about the Phaeacians: they not only live in a world of technology they do not understand but have little control over the technology at their disposal. One of the oddest aspects of Demodocus's story of Ares and Aphrodite is that it so obviously mocks the hapless craftsmanship of the god who designed and built Phaeacia's most remarkable works of art. Hephaestus's fine mesh net merely serves to lock Ares and Aphrodite in what Apollo finds a quite enviable embrace.

There is, in fact, a bizarre relationship between the palace of Alcinous, his gardens, the dancing floors, the agora in Scheria, and the pictures on the shield of Achilles, another work of Hephaestus (*Iliad* 18.478–608).[9] On the shield Hephaestus depicted earth, sky, sea, sun, moon, and constellations (484–89) and two cities: a city at peace, with weddings and a lawsuit in progress, and a city at war, with a siege, some inhabitants marching out to ambush their enemy's herdsmen, and a general battle (490–540). There is a field being plowed, with a man offering the plowmen wine as they reach the end of the field (541–49), and a king's domain, where laborers harvest the crop while the king looks on in silent joy as a meal is prepared (550–60). There is a vineyard where young men and women gather grapes to the accompaniment of a young man's music (561–72). There is a herd of cattle, and two lions attack one of the bulls and are pursued by the herdsmen and their dogs (573–86). There is a sheep pasture (587–89), a dancing area filled with joyful dancers (590–606), and Ocean at the shield's rim (607–8).

The shield made for Achilles is a model of an idealized world, and it makes a sadly ironic and strangely ineffective gift for Achilles, who will never set foot in a city again. He will not live long enough to enter Troy when it is captured, much less return from war to enjoy the pleasures of city life in his homeland. The shield, then, represents a universe from which its bearer is perpetually excluded, not only because he is not himself a Hephaestean artifact, but because the warrior life he has chosen precludes his entry into that universe even if it should prove, by some artistic magic, accessible. The reminiscences of Achilles' shield in the *Odyssey*'s description of Phaeacia are not without irony either, for Odysseus was heir to the Hephaestean arms of Achilles, including, in most accounts, the shield. Those arms, along with all Odysseus's other prizes from the Trojan War are, of course, long lost by the time he arrives in Phaeacia—though Sophocles suggests in the *Ajax* that the actual shield of Achilles went to Neoptolemus. Instead of being the bearer of the Hephaestean shield of Achilles, Odysseus finds himself a figure in one of Hephaestus's larger-scale works. He is in danger of being ensnared, as was Ares in Demodocus's narrative, by its voluptuous, even enviable, delights. His task now is to escape the Hephaestean chains and find a way back to the traditional, mythic (but at least geographically real) world where he belongs.

Perhaps we are witnessing yet another respect in which the *Odyssey* consciously rivals and seeks to surpass the *Iliad*. Although the Phaeacians themselves deny they engage in war (as do the denizens of the city on the shield), their city is, like that on the shield, fortified as well as idyllic, and reference is made to people captured as prizes in warfare. Although Odysseus escapes the fictional, artificial world upon a ship guided by his own thoughts, it is only his contact with that world that gives it any reality. Like the shield of Achilles, Phaeacia is lost forever in the seas and mists of Odysseus's homeward voyage, its memory preserved only in a poet's words.

The Wild and the Cultivated

The Odyssean muse, then, takes what appears, in the *Iliad*, to be an idealized picture on an artifact and puts life in it, in the person of Odysseus, who makes his first appearance in the Hephaestean palace, appropriately enough, phoenixlike amid the ashes of the hearth. Upon reaching the palace of Alcinous, Odysseus enters the hall and, after supplicating Arete with no apparent results, places himself on the hearth, in the ashes by the fire (7.153–54). Odysseus is thus presented to the Phaeacians in a kind of liminal no-man's-land between civilization and savagery which recalls his first point of refuge in Phaeacia beneath a half-wild and half-domesticated olive bush. There, under the bush and the leaves, he was compared by the Muse to a firebrand that saves the seed of fire for a lonely distant dweller (5.488–500). Now, on the palace hearth, Odysseus likewise is the rather curious and fiery seed of civilization, which one would not expect to find missing in a culture related to that of the masters of fire, the Cyclopes, and so generously endowed by the fire god Hephaestus.

The Phaeacians in the palace seem utterly at a loss as to what to make of this curious apparition in their midst. As Odysseus shelters himself on the hearth among the ashes, the Phaeacians are hushed in silence until Echeneus, an elder, speaks up. The Muse tells us he not only is well skilled in speech but also "knows many things of old" (7.157). Echeneus finds it necessary to tell the king, Alcinous, what one might have thought self-evident: that it is improper to let a *xenos,* a guest, sit among the ashes. He instructs Alcinous to set the guest on a silver-studded chair and to pour a libation of wine to Zeus, who watches over the rights of strangers and guests. Echeneus, being a Phaeacian elder statesman, still recalls the proper etiquette of guest reception from the times when the Phaeacians lived closer to "men who live on bread."[10] He also knows that Zeus oversees the proper treatment of guests. His remarks, however, suggest some anxiety that his king neither knows how to receive a guest nor realizes that the god in charge of guests is Zeus.

The measure of Phaeacian civilization—whether they themselves are wild or cultivated—will be assessed and determined, ultimately, by their guest and his Muse. The fact that the Phaeacians seem to have had no contact with their Cyclopean ancestry within the present generation affords Odysseus an interesting opportunity to reinvent their past while reinventing his own, for when he claims to have visited the land of the Cyclopes he exercises a free hand in redefining Alcinous's Cyclopean relatives in a manner that does little credit to Phaeacian intelligence or behavior. His portrait of the Zeus-defying, guest-eating Cyclops Polyphemus owes something to his perception of Alcinous and how the Phaeacians treat him when he is their guest. Phaeacian behavior suggests a remarkable lack of clear etiquette in the reception of visitors. And Nausicaa forewarns Odysseus of possible problems he might have as a *xenos,* a foreign guest. She herself does not wish to come to the city accompanied by the stranger Odysseus, since, she says, there are "insolent [*hyperphialoi*] men among the people" (6.274) who might not like seeing her associate with a man from afar. Odysseus, curiously, uses the same adjective to describe the Cyclopes: "We came to the land of the insolent [*hyperphialōn*] lawless Cyclopes" (9.106). Similarly, the goddess Athena, in her concern for Odysseus's safety among the common folk of the Phaeacians, wraps Odysseus in a mantle of thick mist to veil him from the Phaeacians so none of them will mock him with harsh words or demand to know his identity.

A Cyclopean Paradise Lost

Odysseus begins his account of the Cyclopes with an overview which ought to remind the Phaeacians of themselves. The Cyclopes are, he says, *hyperphialoi* and *athemistoi,* "arrogant" and "lawless." Theirs is a curiously paradoxical world, for they live on wheat, barley, and vines yet do not need to plough and sow, because the gods (for whom at least one of their number expresses contempt) provide their fields with the necessary crops. This almost Elysian picture of their easy life surely recalls, for the Phaeacians, the elaborate agricultural images of their own fields, which do not need the toil of mortal agriculture either: it is the Hephaestean world of Achilles' shield—at least insofar as the relationship of land and inhabitants is concerned.

In other respects, however, the contrasts between the Cyclopes and the Phaeacians, as they emerge in Odysseus's account, are impressive. Unlike the Phaeacians, the Cyclopes do not have assembly places, *agorai,* where people take counsel, nor is there a governmental system with prerogatives for rulers.[11] They live on the peaks of lofty mountains in hollow caves. Each individual rules his own children and wives, without any concern for a community at large. In contrast, Alcinous's palace is so spectacular that Odysseus is amazed by it, and the Phaeacian agora, as Nausicaa describes it, is elaborately built (6.266–67). At the same time, Homeric contrasts are rarely absolute. The Phaeacian agora is near the temple of Poseidon, who is not only their divine ancestor, but also the divine ancestor of the Cyclopes. Indeed, according to Nausicaa's description, the temple's construction bears, as we will see, a curious resemblance to the structure of the Cyclopean cave. In a few lines, Odysseus manages both to describe the Cyclopes to his audience and subtly to introduce points of similarity and dissimilarity between these two related peoples.

Suddenly, retreating to a point before he encounters the folk he has just described, Odysseus goes on to depict an island, the significance of which is never explicitly stated, but which is not too difficult to deduce. The island

> spreads, away from the harbor, neither close in to the land of the Cyclopes nor far out from it; it is forested, and wild goats beyond number breed there, for there is no coming and going of humankind to disturb them, nor are they visited by hunters, who suffer hardships in the forest as they haunt the peaks of the mountains, neither again is it held by herded flocks, nor farmers, but all its days, never plowed up and never planted, it goes without people and supports the bleating wild goats. *For the Cyclopes have no ships with cheeks of vermilion, nor do they have builders of ships among them, who could have made them strong-benched vessels. Yet these, if made, could have run them sailing to all the various cities of men, in the way that people cross the sea by means of ships and visit each other, and they could have made this island a strong settlement for them.* For it is not a bad place at all. There are well-watered meadows by the shores of the sea, where one could have a good crop of vines. There is plowland of rich soil promis-

> ing good harvests in season. There is an easy harbor with no need for a hawser or anchor stones thrown ashore or mooring cables; one could just run ashore and wait for the time when the sailors' desire stirred them to go and the right winds were blowing. Also at the head of the harbor there runs bright water from a rock spring, and there are black poplars growing around it. (9.116–41)

Odysseus says he and his twelve ships came upon this miraculous place by accident. Some god, he notes, must have guided them there, since it was a pitch-black night and thick fog enveloped the vessels; the moon did not light up the scene because it was covered by cloud. No one—*ou tis*—spotted the island before they beached their ships on it (9.146). Nor did anyone note the current which could account for running the ships ashore.

If we look carefully at lines we have italicized in the passage, it is apparent that Odysseus is adding some barbs, at the expense of the Phaeacians, to his narrative. Even before he highlights the tale of an improbable Cyclops who is, nonetheless, part of Phaeacian national tradition, he obliquely but effectively ridicules the whole tradition of the Phaeacian migration to Scheria in their magical ships. The Phaeacians, the Muse reports at the beginning of *Odyssey* 6, had to leave their former abode in Hypereia, "Beyondland," because of the violent behavior of the more powerful Cyclopes. Yet there was, Odysseus says, a fabulously rich island right next to where the Cyclopes lived. Though inaccessible to the Cyclopes, who could not build ships, it was surely within the reach of the miraculous ships and seamanship of the Phaeacians. Phaeacian emigration to the far ends of the earth, away from other humans (6.8), when a safe and fertile land was available close at hand becomes, if not inexplicable, at least ridiculously unnecessary.

It may, of course, be argued that the myth-history of the Phaeacians of the previous generation, available to us as an external audience, is not explicitly said to be available to Odysseus himself. But Odysseus certainly knows from what Athena tells him at 7.56–66 that Alcinous's father was Nausithous, child of Poseidon and Periboea, and that Periboea was daughter of Eurymedon, who ruled so arrogantly among the Giants that he brought some unspecified destruction on his people. Odysseus also knows from what Alcinous tells him at 7.205–6 that the Phaeacians are near kin to the Cyclopes as well as to the Giants. And, according to the Muse and to Odysseus himself, Poseidon is the father of the Cyclops Polyphemus. He may also reasonably infer from his own experiences that the land of the Cyclopes is some distance from Phaeacia. Alcinous is, then, Polyphemus's nephew.

It is fairly clear that so-called Goat Island, the paradisiacal island near the land of the Cyclopes, is Odysseus's narrative fabrication. To begin with, there is a conflict in important details between what Odysseus says, at two different points, about the anchorage Goat Island affords his ships. The harbor was so tranquil that no large waves were noticeable as markers for the seashore, and the harborage so perfect that there was no need to tie the ships with stern cables. He simply beached his fleet on the island (9.136–48). Some forty lines later, however, as he departs for the land of the Cyclops, Odysseus commands his comrades to loosen the stern cables and set sail (9.178). Even if we assume that despite his assurance that such mooring was unnecessary, he had nonetheless used stern cables as an extra precaution, the fact that he had secured it *by the stern* poses a problem. It was, of course, usual practice to throw the anchor over the bow and secure the ship to the shore by the stern. In this position the bow faces the exit of the harbor, and the stern faces the shore. By tying the stern to the shore the ship is prevented from drifting around its anchor. But since Odysseus's ship was simply beached, and its bow was on the shore, securing the stern to the shore by cables makes no sense even as a measure of extra security.

This narrative slip might simply be shunted aside as a glitch resulting from "oral transmission" if it stood alone. But it is only the first phase of what appears to be a deliberate line of impromptu narrative fabrication. Other slips follow. Odysseus, we recall, claims that the Cyclopes enjoy wheat, barley, and vines without sowing and tilling their land, since they are ignorant of basic agriculture (9.108–11). Yet, when describing Goat Island only few lines later, Odysseus says that though it is fertile and would bear all things in season, it is unsown and untilled, since the Cyclopes do not have ships to get to it. If the Cyclopes do not know how to sow and till the earth, their ability to reach the island is inconsequential as far cultivating the soil there or anywhere else is concerned. Odysseus's point is, surely, that the Phaeacians, who could cross the sea, could also have easily avoided the Cyclopes by moving to a nearby island with rich and fertile soil instead of migrating to out-of-the-way Scheria.

Odysseus's ploys here are (or should be) transparent and easy to detect for the outer audience and perhaps for the Phaeacians also. Perhaps the Phaeacians are too enmeshed in their own narrative traditions of past unfortunate dealings with the Cyclopes to be alert to such subtle points, but one cannot be sure, since the Muse gives no indication of the reactions of Odysseus's listeners to this narrative. Then again, Alcinous and the Phaeacians generally show no active and particular response to other stories they hear, except when they express their approval of Demodocus's tale of Ares and Aphrodite and when Alcinous, much later, voices polite skepticism about Odysseus's narrative as whole. Odysseus's tacit juxtaposition here of the Phaeacians' failure to stand up to the Cyclopes and their (unnecessary) flight with his personal ability to outwit and defeat Polyphemus was, however, unlikely to elude a people whose tradition told them of their need, because of fear of their relatives the Cyclopes, to relocate in a new and distant land.

At the Island of the Cyclops

Odysseus says that on leaving Goat Island he gathered his company together, rowed across to the Cyclopes' land, and hauled his ship up on the shore (9.194). He not only fails to suggest that he received any divine guidance but gives the impression, as he narrates, that he lacked any precise plan or guidance after his departure from Goat Island. The journey seems random: and its chronological sequence difficult to track. The tale is marked not only by constant prolepsis—that is, by anticipation of later events in the narrative of their antecedents—but also by nebulous descriptions of key points. One can, of course, explain away such apparent contradictions as "inconsistencies," oral suturing, or poetic confusion of character, narrator, and time. But why rule out the idea that Odysseus has a purpose, a narrative strategy in generating such a complex overlay of perspectives?[12]

Polyphemus's cave will serve as an example of what we mean. Odysseus's company observed the cave, he says, when they arrived at "a place close to it" (9.181). The immediate impression is that they have disembarked and reached a place where the cave and its surroundings are clearly visible. We soon learn, however, that they saw the cave while still at sea. Odysseus represents the physical location of the cave as close to the water's edge and visible in its fine details from the waves. It appears to be at sea level (or perhaps lower), since, in spite of its prominence and height, Odysseus and his men notice the laurel trees covering its roof. Odysseus says he discerned from his ship not only the high court surrounding the cave but also how the court was built—with stones set deep in the earth—and even distinguishes between two kinds of tree that surrounded the courtyard—tall pines and high-crested oaks. He also observes that the flocks grazing in the area consist of both sheep and goats. The rest of the detailed description, given from the crew's view of the cave from the sea, even includes information about the sleeping habits of the flocks and of the Cyclops himself.

Odysseus's introduction of Polyphemus and his cave, in short, offers a kaleidoscope of different perspectives both chronologically and visually. As he approached from the sea Odysseus could not have known who he was about to meet on the island or in the cave, yet he tells the Phaeacians that a monstrous man (whom he has not yet seen) slept in the tall cave and that this monstrous man shepherded his flocks alone and over a great range, not mingling with others but living apart, his heart set on lawlessness. He even adds that this monster was not like a man who feeds on bread, but like a wooded peak of lofty mountains, standing out in solitary splendor, apart from the rest.[13]

We may infer, therefore, that the Cyclops's cave was close to the sea and not much elevated above sea level. Yet if Odysseus's ship was sufficiently close to the Cyclops's cave for Odysseus to observe details of its construction on arrival, and, later, as he departs, to overhear personal conversations, prayers, and soliloquies, why did Polyphemus not see the ship when Odysseus first arrived?[14] How did Odysseus get away with his lie that his ship was dashed to pieces on the rocks (9.283–84)? And, if the cave was at or near sea level, how did Polyphemus, when blinded, manage to break off a peak of a "high mountain" and hurl it into the sea (9.481–82)? Is it because Odysseus is seeking to establish from the outset that what and how one observes depends not only on one's perspectives but upon one's size? He and his ship are so tiny, from a Cyclopean perspective, and Polyphemus so huge, that his arrival could easily pass unobserved. The same, of course, would be true of the Phaeacians in Polyphemian eyes, if they are of Odysseus's human dimensions, as we are given every reason to suspect—in which case these oar-loving people had even less reason to flee to the ends of the world to escape the Cyclopes.

Maro's Wine

After choosing twelve of his most reliable comrades to accompany him inland, Odysseus sets off, taking with him a goatskin full of the exceptionally strong, dark, sweet wine which, he says, Maro, son of Euanthes, one of the Cicones, gave him in Ismarus. The number twelve is interesting here since it corresponds not only to the number of Odysseus's ships, but to the number of wine amphoras given him by Maro.

The allusion to Maro's wine may seem, at first blush, an irrelevant digression to a modern audience. Yet the inner connections were probably lost neither on the inner audience nor on the various external ancient audiences. Odysseus explains that Maro was Apollo's priest, who dwelt in a wooded grove in Ismarus, and that he spared him, along with his family, when he pillaged the city and land of the Cicones. In return, he says, Maro gave him splendid presents, including twelve amphoras (around five hundred liters) of red, honey-sweet wine—enough to anesthetize his entire crew several times over. What is odd, however, is that when Odysseus narrated his sack of Ismarus he made no mention of Maro or his wine. It does not help to argue that the poet would not wish to repeat himself.

Neither Odysseus nor the Homeric muse is averse to repetition in similar instances.

Wine, nonetheless, plays an important part in Odysseus's first account of Ismarus and the Cicones. Overindulgence in its abundance caused his men to become drunk, indiscriminate in their slaughter of sheep and cattle, and so lax in their vigilance that the surviving Cicones, the city's inhabitants, were able to return, with help from their neighbors, and wreak vast destruction on Odysseus's expedition. Yet Odysseus does not mention, in his account of the Cicones, Maro's gift of twelve amphoras of wine. And for good reason. Since Odysseus has twelve ships, Maro's gift would have meant one amphora per vessel of a brew which, Odysseus tells the Phaeacians, Maro used to mix in a ratio of one part wine to twenty of water when preparing it for consumption. Had Odysseus mentioned Maro's wine in his first account, the debacle at Ismarus might be construed rather differently.

Maro's generosity might, under such circumstances, seem less an act of unselfish gratitude and kindness for mercy shown than a calculated effort to destroy the very people who had plundered his city by getting them drunk— in much the same way as Odysseus is able to overcome Polyphemus by making him drunk with Maro's wine. Further, by mentioning his acceptance of the wine, Odysseus shifts at least some responsibility for the ultimate drunken debacle away from the crew to its commander. He should have known better. In short, the sparing of Maro and his family, if told in connection with the sack of Ismarus, would emerge as an act of folly comparable to the Trojans' clemency to Sinon, which permitted the wooden horse to enter the city. And, as Vergil's Aeneas suggests, Troy was "entombed in sleep and wine" after celebrating the false Greek departure, when the Greeks returned (*Aeneid* 2.265). Such a debacle would never do, rhetorically, especially since the encounter with the Cicones follows closely on the fall of Troy, accomplished thanks to Odysseus's stratagem of the wooden horse. It would show Odysseus being damaged by a similar stratagem shortly after his own most famous achievement in the war.

By omitting all mention of Maro's wine at 9.39ff., Odysseus is able to represent the sack of Ismarus and the butchering of its men as his personal achievement. The killing is his; the capture of the wives and the seizure and partition of the city's treasures he concedes he shared with the rest of his squadron (9.40–42). By reserving at least enough from one of Maro's twelve amphoras to fill a goatskin on a later occasion, Odysseus is able to concentrate the lethal effects of Maro's brew on someone other than himself and his crew. He not only robs the cunning Ismarian of his claim to fame and clears himself of an embarrassing error but expropriates Maro's cunning for himself and his own aggrandizement. By redeploying Maro's wine at the Cyclops's cave he limits his personal liability to six dead as the result of his curiosity, but many saved by the brew, as opposed to seventy-two casualties to be charged to his account if he introduces Maro's amphoras at Ismarus.

Odysseus redirects his listeners' attention from the narrative past to the narrative future. He alludes to his sense of foreboding when he takes the skinful of Maro's lethal brew "that soon enough a man would come to me clothed in gigantic strength, a savage man who does not know of ways of justice and paths of law" (9.214–15). Yet wine is an odd weapon to choose for battle with a giant. Under most circumstances in fairy tale or real life, a hero tends to arm himself, when anticipating combat with an exceptionally strong and hostile individual, with, say, a sizable club rather than a skinful of wine—unless he applies the wine to himself as a tranquilizer. His comment on the Cyclops's lawlessness is itself ironic, given his own crew's barbaric and unprovoked onslaught on the Cicones, which cost him six men per vessel (or per amphora). Maro's wine, then, is saved for the moment when Odysseus prepares his audience for the monstrous Polyphemus neither they nor he (in narrative terms) has actually encountered yet. Even before we (or even Odysseus and his inner audience) meet the Cyclops, Odysseus suggests that Polyphemus is a loner: lawless, unjust, and, apparently, more easily dealt with when rendered drunk (much as his own men were at Ismarus).

By inserting, in advance, information about the Cyclops's cave, the dweller, and his daily routine, Odysseus not only generates a sense of ominous anticipation on the listener's part but uses the unhappy (and possibly traditional) associations of Maro's wine to endow himself with a special quality of prescience. It is quite likely that the Homeric muse and Odysseus are here conspiring to filter out, or at least minimize, a tradition which underscores the drunken folly of the commander and the crew during their encounter with the Cicones. Instead, the audience is induced to fear for the group as it makes its way from the ship to the Cyclopean cave, but led to suspect that Odysseus will find the means of overcoming the peril. Odysseus employs what is still the classic strategy of a narrative of suspense and horror, as in Bram Stoker's *Dracula.* He makes his listeners become increasingly tense as they hear about the company remaining in the cave, kindling fire, offering sacrifice, and feasting on the cheeses they find there, knowing all along that a frightening creature will return at any moment. Odysseus is not just using the Cyclops narrative as a means of ironic comment on the Phaeacian past. He is also using it to mask the catastrophic dimensions of a previous incident in his own voyage home and perhaps to suggest something even more impressive about himself. When retelling the story of Ismarus and Maro's wine within the Polyphemus episode, he conveniently associates himself with Apollo, who, in many Greek traditions, killed either the Cyclopes themselves or else their sons to avenge the death of his son Aesclepius, killed by a thunderbolt fashioned for Zeus by the Cyclopes.[15]

Turning the Tables

Of all the audiences for Odysseus's narrative none could be more affected than the Phaeacians themselves, who are thereby introduced to one of the very Cyclopes from whom, according to their own tradition, their fathers had fled in terror. It is interesting, therefore, that Odysseus tells the Phaeacians that his comrades advised him to take the cheeses, the kids and the lambs, and head for the ship as swiftly as possible (as they should have done at Ismarus and as Alcinous's father had done a generation earlier), whereas he himself insisted on remaining in the cave out of curiosity.

The rhetorical ploy is magnificently effective for several reasons. First, it enables Odysseus to give narrative form and context to a creature of the Phaeacians' own folk-fears and imagination. Second, it enables him to represent his own courage and curiosity (and his own superiority to the Phaeacians of the previous generation) not so much in terms of obvious self-aggrandizement, but, ironically, in terms of ill-advised rashness and folly. Throughout the Polyphemus episode, Odysseus compensates for his barely covert mockery of the Phaeacians by tastefully (but not ruinously) undermining the validity of his own decisions and leadership. Instead of praising himself, he credits his comrades with unusually levelheaded recommendations. Third, his approach to the narrative enables him to account for some of the losses he endured on his voyage. After all, the most difficult dimension to justify in Odysseus's claims to heroic stature is his failure to bring even one other member of his crew as far as Phaeacia, much less home.

Taking his cue, perhaps, from the "significant" names of the Phaeacians, Odysseus calls the one Cyclops he actually identifies Polyphemus—"The One Who Speaks Much" or, perhaps, "The One Much Spoken Of." This curious name strongly contrasts with the kind of names Hesiod uses for his Cyclopes: Brontes, "The Thunderer"; Steropes, "The Lightning Maker"; and Arges, "The Shining One" (*Theogony* 140–41). All Hesiod's Cyclopic names are appropriate to the roles they fulfill in the *Theogony,* where they are the creatures who bestow on Zeus the thunder and the thunderbolt. In the *Odyssey,* however, the name Polyphemus underscores the Cyclops's relationship to Odysseus not his nature as Cyclops. "Polyphemus" makes no allusion to the Cyclops's profession as a shepherd, nor to his preference for human flesh, as we might expect by analogy with

Hesiod. Indeed there is a strong possibility that Polyphemus's name is Odysseus's invention rather than a traditional appellation.

If Polyphemus means "the one who speaks much," it contrasts starkly with Odysseus's own epithet, Poly*mētis*: "the one who is full of thinking" or "the one who is intensely no one." If, rather, Polyphemus means "the one much spoken of," as many contend, then Odysseus, by so naming him, vouches for the Cyclops's fame and so successfully immortalizes his misfortunes in front of the Phaeacians as to demonstrate to the fame-hungry Phaeacians that it is in *his* power to act as muse: to make men known or to obliterate them from memory. Polyphemus is "much spoken of" not because of his own achievements, but because of Odysseus, who not only defeats him but also sings a song of victory over him. In these opening episodes of his travels, Odysseus has said little that would indicate anything special about his identity or his name. It is only when he comes to his Polyphemus that he begins to play with his own name and its resonances. The name Odysseus gives to himself when asked his identity by Polyphemus is Outis, "No Man."

Curiously enough, Alcinous, when challenging Odysseus to reveal his identity before the hero begins his narrative, had observed: "No man is nameless" (*ou. . . tis.. . . anōnymos,* 8.552)—a statement that is an odd combination of common sense and idiocy if one explores its rhetorical possibilities as Odysseus proceeds to do in *Odyssey* 9. Indeed, he attributes his success in outwitting Polyphemus to his use of Outis, "No Man," as if it were his own proper name. By the end of his Cyclopean narrative, Odysseus has shown Alcinous how much one can achieve by making a name of one's anonymity.

What Odysseus does not say about the Cyclopes is almost as interesting as the negative comments he actually has to make about them. Odysseus represents them, we have seen, as destitute of constructive skills in building ships or homes and lacking any system of civil justice or simple camaraderie. But he makes no mention at all of what is their most obvious feature in most other traditions: their mastery of fire and their collective factory teamwork on Zeus's divine armaments. On the contrary, as Odysseus tells it, Polyphemus will lose the light of his eye to the primitive weapon Odysseus fashions in the Cyclops's own fire.

But inconsistencies slip out from time to time which suggest that Odysseus is aware of other traditions about the Cyclopes. Thus, although he contends at first that each Cyclops lives by himself, without caring for others apart from immediate family, he later subverts that claim. From Odysseus's own description it emerges that Polyphemus, whom the wily hero has described as a lonely cave-dweller, is actually living among other Cyclopes who are settled round about in caves "among the windy heights" (9.399–400). The area must be densely populated indeed, since Polyphemus's neighbors were able to hear his cries of pain emitted from within his cave. Further, in spite of Odysseus's claim of mutual Cyclopean negligence, he now says Polyphemus's neigbors responded immediately and massively to his cries.

Has Odysseus forgotten his previous claims, or is he charting a sophisticated course for mocking his hosts, the Phaeacians? What begins as a struggle between Odysseus and a single lonely monster ends up as his confrontation with a whole community of monsters whom he eludes not by force, of course, but by what he wishes to be known for: his ruses and resourcefulness.

Odysseus's Phaeacian audience must have expected to hear about a multitude of Cyclopes, not just one. Their fathers had to leave Hypereia because they were oppressed by a whole tribe of Cyclopes. Odysseus thus redirects his story, at least in part, to fulfill his audience's expectations. He also, of course, gains status for himself by successfully escaping not only the one monster he has blinded, but the many others who still have their sight.

"We, You Should Know, Are Achaeans . . . "

When Odysseus tells of his first meeting with Polyphemus, he sets himself in a rather curious light. He and his men, he says, were caught by the Cyclops in the latter's cave where they had been feeding on the cheeses stored there. Polyphemus, as Odysseus tells the story, is surprisingly polite, considering that he has come home to find uninvited "guests" hiding in his cave after consuming his food. Instead of simply killing them on the spot he asks them who they are and whether they have come on some constructive business or are pirates risking their lives to bring death and destruction on other peoples (9.252–55). The question is especially interesting in the light of the observation by Phaeacian Euryalus that Odysseus looked more like a tradesman than a warrior—a statement he appears to have intended as (and which Odysseus certainly construed as) an insult. In short, Odysseus permits Polyphemus to ask good questions which he would find difficult to answer directly without admitting that, on the basis of his own account, he is more of a pirate than a trader.

Odysseus's response to Polyphemus, as he reports it, is oblique but informative:

> We, you should know, are Achaeans from Troy, driven wandering by winds from all directions on the great gulf of the sea, seeking home, we have come by another way, by other paths. So Zeus wished to devise. We declare we are the men of Agamemnon, son of Atreus, whose fame is now the greatest thing under heaven. (9.259–64)

Odysseus comes close to identifying himself to Polyphemus in their very first exchange. His Phaeacian audience would surely note the contrast with the reticence he had shown in their presence and might well take offense, since there is already some cause for irritation in what Odysseus has said about the Cyclopes. Alcinous, eager to have Odysseus spread the fame of Phaeacian technical wizardry, would hardly appreciate Odysseus's reduction of Phaeacia's feared adversaries and relatives, the thunderbolt-making Cyclopes, to the status of single-eyed, troglodytic shepherds. And Odysseus has already diminished Phaeacian prestige by suggesting that their flight from Hypereia was an extreme action which any thinking people would have realized was unnecessary.

Our suspicions that Odysseus has an ulterior motive here should be aroused by the apparent directness of his answer. His answers to pointed questions elsewhere in the *Odyssey* are usually much more disguised than this. By mentioning his involvement in the annihilation of Troy he is, in effect, conceding that he has led a more than piratical existence, destroying other people's lives and property much as he is now, as an uninvited guest, devouring the Cyclops's cheeses. While the identification Odysseus offers is short on helpful specifics, it is still sufficiently bold to warrant a justifiably violent reaction from Polyphemus.[16]

The first clue as to the deviousness underlying the apparent directness is Odysseus's magnanimity toward Agamemnon, whom he now mentions for the first time in the presence of the Phaeacians. He accords Agamemnon the same fame he claimed for himself at the beginning of his narrative when he proclaimed he was Odysseus, son of Laertes, "whose fame reaches up to heaven" (9.19–20). As we see in 9.263–64, cited above, Odysseus sets Agamemnon on an even higher celestial pedestal in almost identical words. Such elevation of an epic companion or rival by Odysseus is unparalleled.

Polyphemus does not respond in anger. In fact, he hardly reacts at all. Troy and Agamemnon mean as little to him as they do to Alcinous, because neither takes Odysseus completely seriously. Odysseus's boastful, if edited, heroic credentials are greeted by Polyphemus with a deflating indifference that makes Odysseus seem to be a *miles gloriosus* rather than an epic hero. Polyphemus's lack of response is probably calculated to excite a laugh among the Phaeacian audience to compensate for the potential offensiveness of what Odysseus had said just moments earlier.

Odysseus could have handled the situation differently. He could have disclosed a detail which would make his boast seem not only bolder and rasher, but sufficiently ominous to suppress any laughter in his audience. He later has Polyphemus claim to have received a prophecy from Telemus, son of Eurymus, that he will be blinded by someone named Odysseus (9.509–12). The suppression of this information at this point in his narrative is, of course, justifiable on the grounds that Odysseus himself was not aware of the prophecy when he answered these first questions of Polyphemus. But we should offset that justification with a reminder that Odysseus has, from the outset of his narrative, routinely employed prolepsis, when it serves his rhetorical interests, offering, even showing himself as acting upon, information he could not possibly have known at a given moment. Advance reference to Telemus's prophecy would spoil his rhetorical strategy. It would make Polyphemus seem more tolerant than he already appears to be of this intrusion upon his dwelling. It would make him, rather than Odysseus, seem stupid, and more important, a little pathetic, because he did not make the connection between the prophecy and the stranger. Polyphemus's present indifference to Odysseus's boast is, as we learn later, a product of his disastrous assumption that such a lilliputian creature could be no threat to him or anyone else of importance. A "man of destiny," as suggested in Telemus's prophecy, has to be a larger, worthier opponent.

To mention the "man of destiny" prophecy now would be to ruin his jest. Odysseus reserves it for a moment when it will be not an ominous moment of irony for Polyphemus but a humorously deprecating comment uttered by Polyphemus about Odysseus's heroic stature. Odysseus keeps it, in short, for a situation in which it will complement the humorous reaction he seeks to provoke at his own expense in this opening verbal encounter with the Cyclops. By arranging his presentation thus, he also launches two effective barbs in the direction of the Phaeacians, who will be tempted to snigger at Polyphemus's double deflation of Odysseus's boast and stature. Alcinous too is worried about the arrival of a "man of destiny" who will, in effect, break off Phaeacian communication with the outside world and thus render the Phaeacians even blinder than Polyphemus. They will be both unseeing and unseen. But it has not yet occurred to Alcinous that Odysseus might be precisely the man who will bring this prophesied doom to accomplishment. Though the Odyssean muse will spread their fame to the world, Odysseus will entomb them forever on his departure. No Greek hero will ever again set foot in their fictional land until Alexandrian times. Even though Odysseus's last and most sardonic laugh is at their expense, the Phaeacians can at least take consolation in the fact that had it not been for him and his muse, they would probably never have existed at all.

From Trojan Horse to Cyclopean Ram

Odysseus's ironic self-deprecation in his Cyclopean narrative serves several rhetorical purposes, the most important of which is probably to convey to the Phaeacians the sense that he is not helpless even when in a situation much more obviously menacing than that of the Phaeacian palace. Polyphemus thinks him a much more insignificant person than even the most contemptuous of his Phaeacian critics. And Polyphemus pays dearly for underestimating him.

Odysseus, we must remember, cannot be sure Alcinous will really release him. Certain details in his narrative, then, may be inserted more to trouble Alcinous than to describe Polyphemus. In describing his behavior toward Polyphemus, for instance, Odysseus is careful to convey his capacity for dissimulation. He tells Alcinous he lied to Polyphemus about his ship, saying his vessel had been destroyed when it had not been harmed at all. What, then, are the Phaeacians to make of his claim to them that his ship has been destroyed and that he is the solitary survivor of his crew? It is possibly his intent to warn the Phaeacians, in case they think they have him at their mercy, that he is as capable of concealing a ship from them as from Polyphemus. After all, if they had failed to notice that the Cyclopes had no ships (and Cyclopean ships would have to be of such enormous size that they would be hard to miss), they might be sufficiently open to the suggestion that he possessed a ship which had eluded their detection. It is, of course, a bluff. But Odysseus determinedly conveys his unpredictability and his skill at improvising and shows that he plays a shrewd hand when he concentrates. By insinuating the idea that he is capable of pretending to have no ship when he actually has one he is attempting to transfer some of his own insecurity to his hosts.

The Cyclopean narrative seems calculated to show that, for all the Phaeacians' disinterest in Troy, Odysseus is a man in every way capable of devising the stratagem of the Trojan horse. But he demonstrates his point by showing that he is just as shrewd at breaking out of a place where he is imprisoned as he is at breaking into a city which is carefully defended. To parallel his traditional, but to the Phaeacians irrelevant, stratagem of the Trojan horse, he generates the "Cyclopean ram" underneath which he escapes from enforced confinement and inevitable death.

He introduces the stratagem as an apparently improvised afterthought. He was ready, he declares, to attack the Cyclops in his sleep, after Polyphemus feasted on two of his comrades, but—and this is something he rarely does—he notes that he changed his mind upon realizing that he and his comrades would be unable to move the boulder blocking the exit from the cave (9.299–305). Instead, he determined to blind the Cyclops physically as well as verbally, and he goes out of his way to represent his actions as meticulously planned but necessary savagery, carried out with fierce courage and resolve. The change of plans does not reflect, in his account, any failure of nerve: he first approached the sleeping monster; he groped with his hand at the giant's belly to find a suitable spot to strike with his sharp sword (9.300–302). But to deal with the problem of an adversary of such size he needs to come up with a larger, if cruder, weapon and a means of disabling rather than killing Polyphemus. He uses, in fact, the Cyclops's own weapon against him and then employs the very strength with which the Cyclops imprisons him as the means of escaping from the cave. As a final touch, it will be Polyphemus's flocks and, in his own case, Polyphemus's especially beloved ram, that will serve as their escape vehicles.

He seizes, therefore, upon a huge staff of green olive wood which the Cyclops has left to dry out next to the sheep pen to serve him as a club. What Polyphemus was preparing to use in his own defense becomes the instrument of attack upon him. Odysseus describes his preparation of the weapon: "Standing near it [*parastas*], I [*egōn*] cut from it as much as a fathom length and handed it to my comrades ordering them to taper it; and they made it smooth, and I (*egō*) standing by (*parastas*) sharpened it, and then I took it immediately and hardened it in the blazing fire" (9.325–28). Odysseus's own activity in the process is highlighted by the personal pronoun *egō*, rarely used unless for emphasis, and by what might appear to be a wholly redundant participle, *parastas* : he obviously could have not cut the tree trunk or sharpened it without standing next to it. Why does he make these points?

By restating and emphasizing his position he underscores the personal nature of his role in forging the weapon with which he will strike. Trapped in the cave of a Cyclops, he becomes a Cyclops himself. As the wood hardens in the fire inside the Cyclopean cave, it is Odysseus who plays the Hephaestean role of master craftsman. In Polyphemus's world of gigantic, if less than Hesiodic and rustic, Cyclopes, Odysseus describes himself as in control and able to devise weapons from unexpected sources and in unexpected ways. While others, on hearing of the large tree trunk, might have cherished more Archimedean thoughts as to how to use it—to pry away the boulder that blocks the door, for example, or even to do the job of a battering ram—Odysseus uses it to rob Polyphemus of his sight. Then he effects his escape by using not the military *krios* a soldier might employ against a city wall, but the ovine *krios* that is the pride of Polyphemus's flock. *Krios,* "ram," is both ram and battering ram (so Xenophon *Cyropaedia* [Education of Cyrus] 7.4.1).[17] The episode is a deliciously ironic reworking of Odysseus's famous siege skills for the benefit of an audience of allegedly nonmilitary people. This time Odysseus escapes from, rather than breaks into, a fortified place, and that place, among his rusticized Cyclopes, is a shepherd's cave rather than a city with gates.

Subdividing Cyclopean Tradition

In Hesiod and other writers, the Cyclopes are skillful artisans who live below the earth and who provide not only Zeus with the thunderbolt, but Pluto with his helmet and Poseidon with his trident. Indeed, it is thanks to their craftsmanship that the Olympians established their supremacy over the Titans.[18] Cyclopean craftmanship also benefits humans, as the massive fortifications that the Cyclopes are credited with constructing at the cities of Tiryns and Mycenae bear witness.[19]

The Cyclopes, in short, enjoy a much better reputation outside *Odyssey* 9 (and works which are clearly derived from or based on it). Homer's Odysseus represents them as savages without advanced skills in building and totally ignorant of agriculture, navigation, or any kind of social structure which would enable them to have a civilized life. They live in mythically primitive and pastoral surroundings, dependent on their father Poseidon for rain and crops (not usually his particular area of expertise) and having nothing to do with Zeus, whose special technological experts they are in most other traditions.

Yet even as Odysseus relegates the Cyclopes to the status of cavemen, he leaves, as do the walls of Mycenae, unmistakable traces of their almost certainly earlier and more remarkable Cyclopean origin. We will recall that before he lands in Cyclopean territory or sees a Cyclops, Odysseus, while still on his ship, comments on a curious feature of the Cyclops's cave—its courtyard. First, it is odd that uncivilized cavepeople would have courtyards. But what shepherd's cave has ever had a courtyard, much less "a tall courtyard constructed upon foundation stones set deep in earth" (9.185–86)? There are traces of the high-tech Cyclopes here.[20]

Why does Odysseus barbarize the Cyclopes yet leave traces of their traditional skills? If we bear in mind that the principal audience for which the description is intended is the Phaeacians, the glimmer of an answer emerges. Had the Phaeacians fled from a thunderbolt-manufacturing advanced society whose skills had brought down the Titans and Giants (the latter, of course, are Alcinous's grandparents), their flight would have been not only comprehensible but laudable. But, as we have already seen, Odysseus seems interested in suggesting instead that the Phaeacian migration was unnecessary, since the Cyclopes were extremely primitive in comparison with almost all other peoples mentioned in the *Odyssey*, especially the Phaeacians, who are represented as having the most advanced technology (outside of Olympus). In fact, if we can credit some of this manipulation to Homer's muse as well as to Odysseus, we might suggest that she has taken the more usual Hesiodic Cyclopes and subdivided their talents between Polyphemus and his fellows, on the one hand, and the Phaeacians, on the other.

Would the Phaeacians perhaps recognize a distorted reflection of themselves in the Cyclopes? Odysseus's description of Polyphemus's courtyard must certainly have seemed strangely familiar to them. Like Polyphemus's courtyard, the Phaeacian agora was "constructed upon foundation stones set deep in earth," if the detail proudly noted by Nausicaa in her description of the city to Odysseus in 6.267–68 is correct—and no one has suggested that it is not. This architecture, seemingly crude and suggestive of fortifications, does not appear to be quite right for the Phaeacians. The entranceway to their king's palace is not blocked by a "mountainous stone which twenty-two four-wheeled wagons could not move," such as Polyphemus used to stop up his cave, but has golden doors mounted on doorposts of silver and set in thresholds of bronze watched over by gold and silver statues of dogs, illuminated by torches in the hands of golden youths standing on well-built pedestals.

Yet the Stonehenge-style architecture of megaliths set in earth is peculiar to the Cyclopes and the Phaeacians in Homer. Is it, then, a more or less isolated architectural marker of their common inheritance—a symbol of previous achievement in the case of the Cyclopes and a reminder of an older ruggedness in that of the Phaeacians? The Cyclopes as Odysseus represents them are certainly not currently capable of the cooperation required for such building, let alone the workmanship involved. They live in caves not houses; they do not build ships or cross the sea. The overall impression is of simpleminded, cumbersome, and powerful giants. Polyphemus lifts peaks of mountains or two men at once, and his club is the size of a ship's mast. Yet he is as unable as Odysseus may have been at Ismarus to see through a foe's ploy of making him drunk, and neither he nor his fellow Cyclopes, as we will see, can keep pace with the deadly word-playing rhetoric of Odysseus.

Cyclopes Civilized and Uncivilized

The Hesiodic and Homeric muses present us with two distinct kinds of Cyclopes. Hesiod offers us sophisticated artisans, who furnish Zeus with thunder and the thunderbolt, creatures in whose works strength, might, and craft are imbedded (*Theogony* 146; cf. 139ff., 503ff.). They are born of earth and are immortal, godlike, "Polyphemian" in only one respect: that they have "just one eye only set in the midst of their heads."[21] The Homeric muse presents us with a very different picture: the rural, destructive monsters of Odysseus's narrative. Odysseus's Polyphemus has no technical capacity or skill at building ships or houses and is also unable even to till the earth. He is a cave-dweller living on the milk and meat that his sheep provide; he has no regard for Zeus but claims the sea god Poseidon as ancestor, ironically enough, since he is no seafarer. Yet he lives amid the remains of a more technically competent Cyclopean society, as suggested by the technology of his cave, much as the Mycenaeans did in the centuries following the collapse of their high civilization.

In this sense, Polyphemus is, in fact, suggestive of a third kind of Cyclops found in later Greek historians and poets of the classical period: the builders and artisans who constructed the walls of Mycenae, Tiryns, Nauplia, and other cities whose rulers imported them specifically for this task.[22] Nothing specific is said about their appearance, although their name implies identification with the mythical creatures who had a single round eye in their foreheads.[23]

Classical writers generally associate all varieties of Cyclopes with Sicily. Thucydides mentions them together with the Laestrygonians as the earliest inhabitants of the island (6.2). In Aeschylus's *Prometheus,* we find them as blacksmiths in Hephaestus's shop inside Mt. Aetna. Their connection with Hephaestus is common to most ancient accounts. There is, in fact, something Cyclopean about most early builders and workers in metal in Greek tradition, incorporating awe not only at the size of the structures which they erected, but at their mastery in smelting the metals which were so important in the progress of ancient society. The only clear-cut differences between Hephaestus and the Cyclopes, aside from their number of eyes, are in their social status. Hephaestus is the Olympian (if unattractive) boss; they are the divine, but low-level (and differently unattractive) workers.[24]

Gods or Men?

In the *Odyssey,* Odysseus, in collaboration with the Homeric muse, has taken the Hesiodic, mythic Cyclopes and created out of them two separate but opposingly similar Cyclopean cultures: that of Polyphemus and his circle and that of the Phaeacians, who have, in effect, migrated not only in space but in time. The split of the two aspects of the proto-Cyclopeans into the uncultured and monstrous and the cultured and beautiful is set in the generation before Alcinous. Inhabiting the ruins of the Cyclopean land are those who have regressed into savagery. Flourishing in an unreachable, ageographical mystery land are the beautiful and intelligent. These different Cyclopes are, in fact, the twofold aspect of what we would now call the Greek Bronze Age, as viewed from a later period in which people are conscious that their civilization has declined and that the ruins of their "Cyclopean" past are now merely the shelters for aggressive and simpleminded shepherds.

In *Odyssey* 9, Odysseus holds up a mirror to the lost world of the Phaeacians, showing the reality of what they, in a sense, have become. The "advanced" but in fact lost Phaeacians belong more to Calypso's world than to the world of Ithaca to which Odysseus returns. They will be blocked from further contact with the world of men (from which they are already remote) by the Gibraltar-like mountain into which Poseidon their ancestor will convert their ship. The transformation is reminiscent of Polyphemus's unsuccessful attempt to destroy Odysseus's ship by hurling a mountaintop upon it.

As Phaeacian building resembles that of the Cyclopes, so too does their agriculture. Before Odysseus enters Alcinous's palace, he notes the spectacular fruit garden next to the palace, full of tall, luxuriant pear trees, pomegranates, apples, figs, and olives. It is a kind of Garden of Eden. The fruit fails in neither winter nor summer but lasts throughout the year. All the trees are abundant in fruit (7.114–21). The vineyard is divided seasonally. In one part, men gather ripe grapes; in another, they tread them into wine. In still a third, as-yet unripe grapes shed their blossoms; in a fourth, they are turning purple (7.122–26). A herb garden with similar properties borders the vineyard. Although Odysseus sees men working in the vineyard, no labor is involved in making the fruit grow, only in the harvesting. There is no tilling of earth, no sowing or planting. The trees, vines, and herbs grow by themselves. Although the Phaeacians eat bread, the Muse does not mention any crops of wheat and barley in their fields or any preparation of the grain or baking. They live apart from "grain-eating men" (6.8), which is usually taken to mean "men that live by toil," and enjoy the gifts of the immortals. And, as the Muse sums up in 7.132, "such were the glorious gifts of the gods in the palace of Alcinous."

The difference between Phaeacian and Polyphemian agriculture lies in the greater abundance and variety of the Phaeacian crop, and in the use to which they put it, not in its spontaneous production. This difference proves catastrophic for Polyphemus. While the Phaeacians are practiced in viticulture and routinely drink wine, the story of Polyphemus's inebriation suggests that though he knows about grapes, wine is, if not unknown to him, at least missing from his usual diet. His usual drink appears to be "unmixed" sheep's milk, not unmixed wine. In fact, it is not at all clear whether he knows anything about wine making. Polyphemus is thus especially vulnerable to the potent brew supplied to him by Odysseus from Maro's stock, which is normally watered down in a ratio of one part wine to twenty of water.

If, as we have suggested, the *Odyssey* presents a division of the Hesiodic Cyclopes into two groups, the Polyphemian and savage and the Phaeacian and civilized (but effete), it may be worth examining the detail of Odysseus's size relative to both the Cyclopes and the Phaeacians. Many details of the Polyphemian narrative, including Odysseus's description of Polyphemus's disenchantment at being blinded by a man who is "puny," a nothing, a weakling, when Polyphemus had expected his conqueror to be strong and "tall and handsome" (9.513–15), show that the savage Cyclopes are much larger than their human visitors. We might, then, expect that the Phaeacians, whom the Muse describes as kinfolk of the Giants and the Cyclopes, would also be larger than Odysseus. But, in general, the description of Odysseus in Phaeacia suggests that his proportions are roughly similar to those of his hosts. If the Phaeacian girls were as big in proportion to Odysseus as was Polyphemus, or as Glumdalclitch was to Gulliver in Swift's *Gulliver's Travels,* they would hardly had fled in terror from Odysseus on the beach, unless they were reacting to his presence as a Victorian lady might to the appearance of a mouse. Nonetheless, there is some residual suggestion that Odysseus needs to be made not just generally "greater," *meizona,* as Athena makes him when he appears before Penelope after the slaughter of the suitors (23.157), but, more specifically, "longer," *makroteron,* and "thicker," *passona* (8.20), before he is presented at the Phaeacian assembly. Athena is clearly worried about how the Phaeacians will react to him. Earlier, in 7.16–17, she shrouded him in a thick mist "so that none of the greathearted Phaeacian should mock him, on meeting him, and ask him who he was." Why would they mock him? Perhaps it is enough to say that he cuts an incongruous figure as an unknown foreigner wearing a royal wedding robe. If there is something alien in his appearance that would provoke their derision, the Muse does not need to elaborate on it. Although relatives of the Cyclopes and Giants, the Phaeacians are not of such massive size if Odysseus can wear one of their princely robes without looking utterly preposterous.

Echoes in Phaeacia

If we follow the chronology provided by Odysseus, he comes to Phaeacia *after* his adventures with Polyphemus, even though we, as readers, encounter the Phaeacians before we encounter Polyphemus. If we continue as we have so far to allow for the possibility that Odysseus is adapting the tale of his adventures to his specific audience, the Phaeacians, we might notice that there are additional motifs in his Polyphemus narrative that seem to develop from observations he has made about the Phaeacians themselves. And not without reason. In Phaeacia, as among the savage Cyclopes, Odysseus is judged negatively (by Euryalus, for instance) on the basis of his unimpressive stature and appearance, in spite of Athena's efforts at a make-over.

Odysseus's employment of the motif of blindness is particularly noteworthy, since the Muse has pointed out that the Phaeacian bard, Demodocus, who sings, perhaps not entirely to Odysseus's satisfaction, tales of Troy in which Odysseus plays a rather minor part, is himself blind. Athena, disguised as a man and assuming the role of an umpire, is perhaps alluding to the bard's blindness during the games which follow Demodocus's narratives. She comments in reference to the remarkable discus throw which Odysseus has made (with her help): "Even a blind man, stranger, could distinguish this mark groping with his hands" (8.195–96). The feat is such that even someone who could not see it with his own eyes (and might therefore be skeptical about it) could detect its greatness by touching the spot where it struck the ground.[25] Since Demodocus is the only blind person mentioned as being present in Alcinous's court, it would be hard for him or others to fail to see in the hypothetical blind man to whom the goddess refers at least a hint of an allusion to the official recounter of heroic deeds at the court.

The discus episode, in fact, suggests an even more complex association with Odysseus's story about the blinding of Polyphemus. When his discus flies past the marks of all other contenders, Odysseus, ignorant of the divine help extended to him, challenges the young Phaeacians to surpass his throw. He excludes, we will recall, Alcinous's son Laodamas from his challenge. "Who would quarrel with one who is near and dear to him? That man is foolish and of no account [*outidanos*] who challenges the host who receives him in a foreign land" (8.209–11). The word *outidanos* occurs only three times in the *Odyssey*: here and twice in Odysseus's later narrative of Polyphemus. In both instances in the Polyphemus narrative Polyphemus himself uses the word. In the first instance he complains to his beloved ram of "No Man, *Outis*, who is of no account, *outidanos*" (9.460). In the second, he reminisces about Telemus's prophecy that predicted his blinding. Polyphemus complains that he has suffered his fate at the hands of a weakling "of no account, *outidanos*" (9.515).

We have already noted how Odysseus turns Alcinous's observation against him with the wordplay on *Outis*, "No Man." In this case the irony is even more savage: Odysseus never behaves as an *outidanos*, challenging a host. Yet, as the Phaeacians will soon learn, he has not only challenged but blinded one former, albeit unwilling, host. The tale Odysseus tells among the Phaeacians about the blinding of their not especially remote relative Polyphemus (whose name itself means "one who speaks much" or "one who is much spoken about") would certainly have an effect on Demodocus. As Demetrius points out in his treatise *On Style* (293), allusions to Polyphemus were dangerous in the court of Philip II of Macedon (who was blind in one eye). Demodocus, however, cannot retaliate.

The verbal correspondences between the judgments passed on Odysseus when he was among the Polyphemian Cyclopes and those that are (or that he assumes are) passed on him by the Phaeacians suggest either that Odysseus construes his past in terms of what he feels are his present circumstances or, if we are uneasy with such a rhetorically skilled, fictionalizing Odysseus, that his present circumstances lead him to highlight those incidents from his past that hold up before the Phaeacians a distorted reflection of themselves.

[5]

The Ironic Lord of Death

Odysseus's narrative of his voyage to the far western land where he encounters the ghosts of the famous dead solidly establishes his heroic credentials not only with readers of the epic but among his immediate listeners, the Phaeacians. In designing the scenario, the Homeric muse, through Odysseus's narrative, sets him not only on a par with but above many of his epic competitors, situating him, for the first time in the *Odyssey*, amid an audience of his heroic predecessors and rivals, who know him and acknowledge, by their presence, words, or actions, his equality or superiority to themselves. To treat the journey as primarily a quest for information about Odysseus's future would be to misrepresent its nature, since Odysseus tells us that Circe, from whose land and at whose prompting he sets forth to consult the dead, knows both the past and the future and thus, presumably, has access to any of the information he would acquire during such a visit (10.457–59, 487ff.). On the contrary, we, like the Phaeacians, might more reasonably ask why Circe bothers ordering Odysseus to go to the Otherworld to learn what she could have told him herself. There are, in fact, other and less explicit motives for sending him there (488–95).

Let us begin by reminding ourselves that Circe, who orders Odysseus to go, does so within the framework of Odysseus's own narrative. That is to say, her voice is a creation of his own. Odysseus's Circe tells Odysseus to consult the seer Teiresias, who will tell him, she says, "the way and the measures of your path, and of your return, how you may go over the teeming deep" (10.539–40). This Teiresias indeed does, also through the intermediacy of Odysseus's own voice. And we can glimpse the economical continuity that ensues from the common narrative genesis of both Circe and Teiresias. Circe does not tell Odysseus what he should ask the seer, and Teiresias simply assumes, without waiting to be asked, what Odysseus wishes to hear: "You seek after your honey-sweet return, glorious Odysseus" (11.100). Indeed, as Teiresias proceeds, he omits the main details of Odysseus's return which Odysseus supplies in Circe's voice *after* he and his men have returned from the Otherworld.

With the exception of a warning about Thrinacia, Teiresias focuses, rather, on Odysseus's actual arrival in Ithaca and, more significantly, on his subsequent second departure from home for other adventures which will culminate in a second homecoming and his death. Odysseus's death, of course, lies beyond the narrative scope of Homer's muse in the *Odyssey* but is, in traditions of Odysseus outside the *Odyssey*, closely intertwined with his association with Circe and their son Telegonus. All that is retained in the Odyssean version is the strong sense that Circe is connected with Odysseus's encounter with the dead and the knowledge of his own death. And instead of any mention that Circe bears him a son, we have Odysseus's mention of the warning given by Hermes that Circe may actually castrate him or render him impotent—a threat which Odysseus takes seriously enough that he makes her swear that she will do no such thing before he goes to bed with her (10.296–301, 337–47).[1] In fact, the voyage to the threshold of the Otherworld of the dead begins with a solitary and accidental death—the only *accidental* death in the entire epic—that of Elpenor.

The Hasty Elpenor

The whole of Odysseus's adventures from his first arrival in Aeaea to his second departure claims only Elpenor's life, despite the temporary porcine metamorphosis of some crew members in Circe's land, the perilous journey, and the encounters with ghosts. There are no other casualties. Odysseus and his followers come back to Circe and Aeaea unscathed.

Although Elpenor is marked by Odysseus as a man neither very courageous in battle nor of sound understanding (10.552–53), he enjoys a curious prominence in Odysseus's narrative of his adventures in Circe's land. On the morning after Odysseus is urged by his comrades to leave the island and head for home, Elpenor loses his life in a singularly unheroic manner. After a day of feasting on abundant meat and while "heavy with wine" (10.555), he seeks a cool place to spend the night and chooses the palace roof. While sleeping on the roof of a house is common enough even today during hot weather in Mediterranean lands, there is, perhaps, a touch of the droll in sleeping on a *palace* roof. Awakened in the early morning by the bustling of his friends, gathered by Odysseus for an immediate departure, he forgets he needs a ladder to reach the main hall, falls headlong from the roof, and dies instantly of a broken neck. As Dimock observes, "Next to Thersites, Elpenor is the most unheroic person in Homeric epic."[2] Death resulting from a broken neck, in fact, is often associated with hanging, which, in ancient Greek literature is usually a woman's way of committing suicide or suffering execution.

What is troubling about Odysseus's account is that the same kind of carelessness which leads to Elpenor's death characterizes much of Odysseus's own behavior during his departure from Circe's abode to travel to the land where he can consult the dead. The immediate cause of Elpenor's death, of course, is the amount of sweet wine he and his comrades consumed the previous day and early evening. But his very Bacchic immoderation surely owes something to the fact that he had no reason to suspect Odysseus was intending to leave so abruptly that morning after a year's soft living with Circe. Odysseus decided on departure during the night following his comrades' protests. He gave the crew no indication of his decision until the morning and offers no explanation for his hurry to set sail immediately for the Otherworld. Odysseus's haste seems, in fact, unnecessarily impetuous. His account leaves (probably intentionally) the impression that he has, once again, sacrificed his close comrades to his own curiosity. He leaves so quickly that not only is he, in part, responsible for Elpenor's death; he also fails even to notice that Elpenor has died, much less offer him proper burial or notice his absence during the subsequent voyage.[3]

The irony of Odysseus's narrative here rests on several aspects of the relationship he posits between his own actions and those of Elpenor. Both are setting out for the world of the dead, one deliberately (if impetuously), the other unwittingly and carelessly. But Elpenor, though left behind as Odysseus sails, arrives among the dead before his leader not as the result of heroic endeavor, but simply by dying ludicrously. Odysseus thus postulates a bizarre and wittily ironic parallel between the heroic and the banal, between the subtle intellect of a man famous for his wiles and the simple mind of a minor personage whose name, Elpenor, suggests the fragility of "mortal hopes" and aspirations.

Odysseus develops the comparison between himself and Elpenor with an intricate and suggestive vocabulary when he describes his encounter with his comrade's unhappy ghost. In reporting Elpenor's plea that Odysseus bury him, Odysseus has Elpenor refer to himself as *dystēnos* (11.76), and uses the same epithet of him in his reply to his dead friend. This use of *dystēnos* is unique in the *Odyssey*. Elsewhere the adjective is reserved exclusively for Odysseus either when he is making reference to himself (7.223, 248) or when others are referring to him as "wretched" in his presence and absence.[4]

Elpenor's request that he be buried on the shores of the grey sea and that his grave be marked by the oar with which he rowed is likewise oddly reminiscent of Odysseus's fate as he reports it predicted by Teiresias. Odysseus will himself never be separated from his oar once he has slain the suitors and set out on his wanderings again. Before journeying home a second time, he is destined, he has Teiresias claim, to carry it to a place so distant and among people so ignorant of the grey sea, ships, and oars that when he sets it up as a marker, a wayfarer will mistake it for a winnowing fan (11.75–78, 121–30).[5]

Odysseus thus subverts, by his references to Elpenor, the very heroic claims to fame and heroism he makes at the outset of a narrative in which he declares he has achieved something no other hero has ever accomplished before: a direct encounter with the dead and a safe and immediate return. No part of him will remain in Hades, as even part of Heracles does.

The Great Odysseus

Boastfulness in an orator is neither an endearing quality nor one that carries much conviction with an audience. That is why it is often useful to soften the effect of extravagant claims by the judicious use of self-deprecating humor. That same deployment of humor is useful when the speaker is criticizing or attacking his audience in some way. While his intent may be to establish his greatness and his audience's smallness, it is vital that he not utterly alienate his listeners with his comments. Odysseus's aim is to keep the Phaeacians at bay, not to enrage them to the point that they will attack him.

As, then, Odysseus aggrandizes his own persona vis-à-vis his Phaeacian audience, he subtly and humorously undercuts it here, as he does in the Polyphemus narrative, probably to temper what might otherwise seem offensively boastful. While telling the Phaeacians that he is important enough to be the subject of prophecies given to a Cyclops and to a goddess, that he is a man Hermes personally helps, and to whom the ghost of the famous Teiresias predicts events yet to occur, he makes himself, at same time, humorously small: a disappointment to Polyphemus, a runner-up to Elpenor in reaching the land of the dead. Other details of his narrative are of a similarly complex texture. Teiresias's prediction about Odysseus's wanderings among people who do not know of the sea echoes Phaeacian fears of future isolation from the sea and obliquely reminds them that their hope for *kleos*, for glory, based on nautical excellence and miraculous ships, will not impress such a remote inland people any more than will his own tale of voyages and less meticulous seamanship. In fact, given Poseidon's predictions for the Phaeacians, Alcinous's own descendants, cut off from the sea, may themselves be as unimpressed by nautical prowess as those who think an oar is a winnowing fan. Odysseus reminds all his audiences, both internal and external, that a narrative of exploits means little to an audience to whom the very basis of those exploits is unintelligible. Fame demands receptive hearers as well as skilled poets.

Because Odysseus's oar will be set among people who will think it an agricultural implement for the rather unadventuresome occupation of sifting harvested grain (and a people who also do not seem to eat meat), it may be an even less significant marker than Elpenor's oar. At least Elpenor's oar will be planted where someone knows what an oar is—among *un*exceptional people who know of the sea and who "eat meat."[6] Among such unexceptional people, Elpenor merits status not only because he belongs to the common folk—his death followed a feast on "abundant meat" (10.477)—but because he himself was almost turned into a pig or a boar and thus was designated for consumption himself. His misfortune as he reaches the world of the dead before Odysseus is heightened by the fact that he is condemned, because his corpse lies unburied, to wander aimlessly and homelessly for ten times as many years as Odysseus does on this return to Ithaca.

Anticleia

The extent to which Odysseus's self-subversion is part of his narrative intent rather than the Muse's mockery of his unintentional or unconscious "slips"—much less any occasional nodding of her own—is sometimes hard to tell. Readers determined to view the *Odyssey* as a work of almost accidental genius will certainly be predisposed to treat anything that is not explicit as fortuitous. But if we are prepared at least to allow for the possibility of some conscious artistry and design in the epic, some details Odysseus gives of his exchanges with the ghost of his mother, Anticleia, may help sharpen our sense of how far and how deep the intentionality of design could run.

Odysseus's account of his meeting with Anticleia's ghost is one of the most powerful, if oblique, arguments to convince the Phaeacians (and us) that he is telling the truth about his travels. Even a mildly superstitious person would balk at Odysseus's fabricating his mother's death. The introduction of Anticleia's ghost, then, is a moment of great rhetorical power, as well as of great pathos, in Odysseus's narrative. Yet even as he introduces her ghost into his tale and tells the Phaeacians of his sorrow at discovering that she is dead, he mentions *her* surprise at seeing *him* there: not because he is still alive, but because one needs a ship to cross the Ocean that separates the realms of the living from those of the dead

(11.159–60).[7] Although Anticleia mentions his ship as part of his return from Troy with his companions, the words Odysseus attributes to her suggest she thinks her son might lack either the expertise or a sufficiently durable ship for such a supremely heroic voyage:

> My child, how did you come under the murky darkness? For it is difficult for those who are living to see these realms, for in between lie great rivers and terrible streams, Oceanus first, which in no way can one cross on foot; one must have a well-built ship. (11.155–59)

Anticleia's remarks are fully consonant with Odysseus's frequent belittlement of his own navigational skills.

When Odysseus reports Anticleia's description of how Telemachus is faring in Ithaca, however, the effect is more puzzling. She assures Odysseus that no one has usurped the throne and that Telemachus has not only full use of his father's possessions, but a share in the palace banquets. He is, she says, the invited guest of many men (11.184–86). Since Anticleia envisages Telemachus as a young adult, her words refer to some period not long before Odysseus lands in Phaeacia and therefore not long before Odysseus actually returns to Ithaca. Her report, then, runs counter to what the Muse tells us in her narrative voice throughout the epic. Even before he sets out for Nestor's palace and Menelaus's Sparta, Telemachus's position is anything but secure. His attempts to appeal to the Cephallenian assembly reveal his isolation and contradict Anticleia's claims that he is "invited by many." Further, we are soon to learn that when Odysseus arrives in Ithaca, Telemachus, having narrowly eluded an ambush set for him on his return from the Peloponnese, has great difficulty participating in the palace banquets, which are run by the suitors. He appears to be lonely. Of all the comrades he has in his homeland, only Peiraeus, whose friendship he gained on his own and not as an inherited family connection from his father, remains on his side.[8] Telemachus, in fact, is left almost as much to his own resources as is his father.[9]

The "reality" of Telemachus's position is so different from what Odysseus has Anticleia suggest that one is tempted to argue either that there is an inconsistency at this point in the *Odyssey* (perhaps explicable by its patchwork, "oral" state or the Muse's nodding) or that Odysseus is simply fabricating these words (and perhaps the entire encounter with Anticleia). Both Odysseus and the Phaeacians are, in this matter, less informed than the external audience. He and they have no additional basis for determining what is or is not true about the domestic situation in Ithaca and would not necessarily see the contradictions evident to the external reader. Thus we cannot rule out the possibility that Odysseus is, in fact, inventing words to put in his mother's mouth to express his hope that all will be well on the home front, at least insofar as Telemachus is concerned.

At the same time, we cannot rule out the mythic "truth" of Odysseus's encounter with Anticleia. If we grant that Odysseus is reporting things heard rather than things he has invented, she may herself be softening the harshness of what was happening so as to minimize Odysseus's anxieties. She may even have died before the suitors moved into Odysseus's house and thus be unaware of later developments. Of the characters Odysseus meets among the dead, only Teiresias appears to have knowledge of events subsequent to his own demise.

Most scholars, however, agree that the words Odysseus attributes to Anticleia indicate that she knows about some of the problems in Odysseus's house, notably about the suitors courting Penelope. The scant basis of this consensus is 11.178–82, where Odysseus asks whether Penelope has stayed at home with her child or whether some leading Achaean has married her. Anticleia says Penelope remains faithful and has not remarried. These minimal interchanges are hardly impressive indications that she knows of a houseful of suitors consuming Odysseus's substance.

Odysseus himself, by contrast, *does* know about the suitors. Some fifty or so lines earlier he reported that Teiresias told him about them. If Odysseus gets back to Ithaca, the seer says, he will find proud men devouring his livelihood, wooing his wife, and offering gifts to entice her to marry them (11.115–17). Teiresias's remarks not only make the presence of the suitors clear but imply that Penelope will remain as Odysseus's wife at least until he gets back to Ithaca. The questions Odysseus asks Anticleia, then, are redundant—if Odysseus believes Teiresias, from whose observations he could readily deduce that Penelope is still waiting for him. Thus Anticleia's brief and more reassuring picture of the state of affairs at home seems most likely to be her attempt to offer a less disturbing vision of what awaits her son.

Nonetheless, the possibility that Odysseus is, for his own rhetorical purposes, fabricating the story about the Otherworld, putting into Teiresias's mouth things he already knows or surmises have happened looms large. After all, he knows, as he speaks to the Phaeacians, that he will have to come home, if he comes home at all, on someone else's ship, since he has lost his own. The words he attributes to Teiresias endow the ruin of his squadron with a certain religious respectability. Losing all one's comrades and all one's ships is less ignoble if such losses are *fated* to occur and thus are not entirely one's personal responsibility. Further, if Odysseus does not know what the situation is in Ithaca, it is arguably wisest to allow for all possibilities in his narrative—hence, perhaps, the rather different observations on Penelope's fidelity by Anticleia, Teiresias, and, later, Agamemnon's ghost.

Given the length of his absence and the terms of his agreement with Penelope before their departure, Odysseus has to admit that Penelope may have succumbed to the overtures of others. Hence the suitors could well emerge in his mind from a consideration of what might have happened just as easily as from knowledge of what has happened. His extreme caution in his dealings with Penelope on his return to Ithaca (matched by her extreme caution in dealing with him) suggests that even if Odysseus did encounter the ghosts of Teiresias and Anticleia, as he claims, he knows their words are sufficiently contradictory as to render the collective impression unreliable. Besides, he cannot be sure whether the Phaeacians themselves know something of the situation in Ithaca, despite the impression they convey of ignorance about the events and geography of the Greek world.

Odysseus is consistent in portraying himself as a proud and hopeful father of the only child he or the Muse mentions in the *Odyssey*: Telemachus. Yet unless Circe broke her promise not to unman him, the notion that Odysseus produced no offspring as the result of his encounters with her must have seemed strange to an ancient audience whether or not it was familiar with their child Telegonus. Sexual relations between humans and gods are otherwise invariably fruitful in Greek myth, resulting in a child or children of special magnitude, as Odysseus himself confirms later in book 11 in his tale of Tyro and Poseidon, which we will discuss in more detail below. Odysseus reports Poseidon's assurance to Tyro that, after their sole encounter, she will bear two children in the course of the year: "for the embraces of the immortals are not weak" (11.249–50).

Odysseus, of course, would rhetorically undermine the self-portrait he gives to the Phaeacians of a man who wants to return to his family if he admitted having fathered (and abandoned) other children during his travels. Postulating that Circe might have been, unknown to him, with child at the time of his departure, casts their sexual relationship in mortal rather than immortal terms. The extraordinary power of the *Odyssey* becomes even more evident if we envisage the Homeric muse as editing down the more fertile Odysseus of tradition than if we envisage the original Odysseus of tradition as being a uniquely infertile hero despite his prolonged encounters with goddesses. The most terrifyingly consistent feature of Odysseus in the *Odyssey* is his ability to bring death and destruction, not life and new hope, upon everything he is associated with.[10]

The Killer of Anticleia

Anticleia's misleading depiction of Telemachus as growing happily and peacefully to manhood underscores for the external audience, if not for the Phaeacians, the effects of Odysseus's absence on those in his family who got to know him and still miss him. Indeed, in the early and later books of the *Odyssey*, Telemachus has one curious advantage over others in his household: he does not remember his father in any way. He thus seems free of the sadness which pervades, for example, the life of Penelope. Anticleia's terse observation that Penelope is still Odysseus's wife does not begin to tell the tale of her suffering as we discover it in Ithaca. She is locked in a kind of suspended and unappealing existence. Her nights are woeful, and during the days she cries constantly. The common interpretation, reinforced by editorial assurances from the Muse, is that she longs for and misses her beloved husband. But there are also suggestions that she mourns the passage of her own life and that her grief is mixed with fear of leaving Odysseus's halls. She knows him well. The consequences of her infidelity, should he return, could be terrible.[11]

Odysseus's father, Laertes, the second family member Odysseus asks Anticleia about, "remains" in the fields. The same verb, in fact, is used to describe Penelope's presence in the halls and Laertes' in the fields: *meinei* and *mimnei*. Critics tend to glamorize their existence more than the Muse does. Anticleia does not say that Laertes *retires* to the fields (as a Victorian Englishman might retire to his garden), though modern scholars and readers usually take her words to mean precisely that. Rather, she implies that his existence, like Penelope's, is static and frozen. He is still where he was when Odysseus left, just as Penelope is where she was. Later on, Eumaeus tells Odysseus that Laertes lives in the fields and supervises the work there (16.135–45).

It is never made clear in the epic why Odysseus rules Ithaca while his father is still alive and active and why (or by what right) Odysseus makes his father leave for the fields and supervise the work there, with permission to come to the city when he wanted to. His domestic arrangements seem quite the opposite of those set up by the suitors who compete for Penelope's hand. Their fathers, not they themselves, rule the family estates. If Odysseus's treament of Laertes seems somewhat ungenerous before his return, what he does after his return seems even more heartless. When he needs his father's acknowledgment of his identity, he forces a recognition through contentious words (*kertomiois epeessi*). He upbraids the old man and causes him to cry for his son as if he were dead, and only when Laertes has broken down does he disclose who he is. He achieves this desired acknowledgment, in short, by verbal ruthlessness, as if this were the salient characteristic of the son that his father will remember. Odysseus is never said to resemble Laertes as Telemachus resembles Odysseus. Indeed there is a Cyclic epic tradition that Odysseus is the child of Sisyphus, who raped Anticleia before her marriage.[12]

Anticleia's suffering, however, has ended. She died, she says, because of

> yearning for you [*sos pothos*]; and your counsels [*sa mēdea*], brilliant Odysseus and your honey-sweet gentleness [*aganophrosynē*] robbed me of my soul. (11.202–3)

Her words express a strange oxymoron between the love they imply and their ultimate message, which is blunt and paradoxical. She tells her only son that he, in effect, caused her death. But the harshness of this statement is muted by the kind and flattering words in which she phrases it. By using the noun *pothos* and not *achos,* which Eumaeus, for example, uses later in his description of her death (15.358), she attributes the reason for her death to the length of Odysseus's absence and thus puts the blame on him.[13] The longing for a son can be easily construed as a reason for a parent's death. Sophocles' Oedipus, in fact, realizes that Polybus's longing for him may have caused the old man's death (*Oedipus Tyrannus* 969–70). The only other Homeric parallel for this use of *pothos /pothē* is in the famous words of Achilles as he mourns his friend Patroclus:

> But now you are lying here pierced, but my heart fasts from drink and food, although they are beside me, because of yearning for you [*sē pothē*]. (*Iliad* 19.319–21)

Odysseus, in having Anticleia thus echo Achilles' words, reverses the import of a famous Iliadic scene: it is not the living who long for the dead but the dead who long for the living. Odysseus will take this theme further in the context of Achilles' heroism a little later in his narrative when he describes Achilles' ghost as declaring that he would rather be a poor living man than king of the dead. Again the theme will be the sense of loss among the dead rather than among the living.

The inversion of ideas in Anticleia's statement, then, is underscored by her curious use of *sos pothos.* Her use of "your counsels," *sa mēdea,* poses some problems too.[14] Odysseus, of course, is the character who is known above all others for his "counsels."[15] Yet there is certainly nothing in the structure of this phrase that allows the usual translation of *sa mēdea* as "longing for your counsels," as if the idea of longing in *pothos* necessarily carries over into *mēdea.*[16] The expression, in fact, is curiously ambiguous, for if we read the words as written, it is Odysseus's counsel, his plans, not deprivation of such counsel that brought about his mother's death. This is not to suggest that he plotted her death, but rather that his pursuit of his plans cost her dearly.

Odysseus's schemes, plans, and counsels in the *Odyssey* are either designed to cause harm to others or to protect himself. In both Homeric epics, in fact, the term *mēdea* has rather menacing resonances, since *mēdea* are usually employed in the interests of their employer to achieve an end regardless of means.[17] The "counsels" Odysseus is best known for and most prides himself on are those which lead to the capture of Troy by the stratagem of the wooden horse.

Our puzzlement should be further increased by the third cause Anticleia adduces for her death: Odysseus's "gentleness" (*aganophrosynē*). The only other occurrence of this word in Homer is in Helen's lament for the dead Hector, who, she says, would restrain his brothers, sisters, and their spouses from reproaching her in the halls of Priam "out of the gentleness of his soul," his *aganophrosynē* (*Iliad* 24.772). Hector, like Patroclus, is described by others as gentle and considerate of those around him. Nowhere, however, does Odysseus—or Achilles for that matter—claim to be gentle, nor does anyone else attribute gentleness of heart or soul to either of them.[18] What makes Odysseus weep tears of grief like those of a woman about to be marched off into captivity is the memory of when he marched women off into captivity, not sympathy for their plight.

The Muse, in fact, has rather curious ways of describing what might seem, at first glance, sympathetic reactions to others on his part. She compares, for instance, his reaction to the sight of his housemaids mating with the suitors to that of a bitch groaning at the sight of a stranger while protecting her young (*skylakes*) (20.14).[19] It is an odd simile in many ways, since Odysseus is, in effect, the stranger in this scene and since the bitch is, in Greek literature, no more famous for sexual fastidiousness than are Odysseus's housemaids. If we contend that the imagery suggests he feels some kind of parental sympathy for the girls, we should remember that, in the wake of his slaughter of the suitors, he orders all the maids to be put to the sword after they have cleaned up the carnage. And Telemachus goes him one better by having them hanged instead (22.437–73).

The imagery of bitch and whelps, besides, is rarely one which evokes any modern sentimentalism in Greek literature. Hesiod mentions the sound of whelps among those that the many heads of Typhoeus were able to emit, and describes them as "astonishing to hear" (*Theogony* 834). Similarly, Odysseus compares the voice of Scylla to that of a newborn *skylax* (whelp)—which is curious not only because her own name has canine resonances, but because of other traditions which suggest her recent metamorphosis from woman to doglike monster (12.86). Odysseus, in fact, thinks of puppies as creatures to be ruthlessly destroyed. He says the Cyclops grabbed two of his comrades and smashed them on the floor as if they were *skylakes*, puppies or whelps (9.289–90). Since Polyphemus devoured these men he killed like puppies, Odysseus may also be thinking of the Lydian practice of eating young whelps.[20]

One of the characteristics of Odysseus that allows him to survive his ordeals is, in fact, his ruthlessness. Athena calls him *schetlios*, which usually implies harshness and cruelty, when enumerating his various characteristics upon meeting him on the seashore in Ithaca (13.291–93). This epithet, more common in the *Odyssey* than in the *Iliad*, replaces the epithet *nēleēs*, "pitiless," which unequivocally indicates ruthless cruelty.[21] Among other characters with whom Odysseus shares the epithet *schetlios* are Polyphemus, who is said to have *nēleēs thymos* (pitiless spirit); Achilles, who is called both *schetlios* and *nēleēs* (*Iliad* 16.33, 204); and Penelope.

Gentleness is hardly a characteristic of Odysseus's family either. Indeed, of the few characterizing epithets and phrases shared by Odysseus and Penelope, *schetlios* and *tetlēoti thymōi* (of resolute spirit) are perhaps the most remarkable, as we see, for example, in 23.149–51. There the Ithacans, hearing music coming from their ruler's estate, believe it signals Penelope's wedding, not knowing that it camouflages the aftermath of the slaughter of the suitors by the *schetlios* master. They comment:

> Surely someone has wed the queen courted by many suitors. Cruel one! She did not have the heart to keep the great house of her wedded husband to the end, until he came back.[22]

Odysseus describes himself as *tetlēoti thymōi*, "of resolute spirit," during the escape from Polyphemus's cave in 9.435. The phrase indicates both callousness and stubborn persistence, which stand in direct antithesis to *aganophrosynē*. Anticleia and Eumaeus use it to describe Penelope's resoluteness in resisting the suitors' overtures (11.181, 16.37), and both Telemachus and Odysseus use it to indicate Penelope's harshness in refusing to acknowledge Odysseus's identity after his miraculous return (23.100, 168).

Neither Odysseus nor Telemachus show much overt gentleness even toward family members. While disguised as as beggar in Eumaeus's hut, Odysseus passively witnesses his son's return to Ithaca after avoiding the suitors' ambush. It is Eumaeus who greets the youth as if he were his son. We may, of course, account for Odysseus's emotionless behavior in the hut as tight-lipped caution. But Telemachus's behavior is more difficult to explain. When safe in the swineherd's hut, he asks Eumaeus to go to the city and notify Penelope about his return. Eumaeus gently hints that the same message should be given to Laertes, who had stopped eating and drinking and had remained seated, groaning and wailing while the flesh wasted from off his bones, ever since his grandson left (16.136–45). Telemachus does not permit Eumaeus to make the extra journey to the fields but instructs him to tell Penelope to send a handmaid with the news. Eumaeus himself must return to the hut as soon as possible. Telemachus's excuse is as follows:

> This is rather sad, but we shall let him be for all our sorrow, for if all things were somehow given to mortals according to their wishes, we should choose first my father's day of homecoming. (16.147–49)

Telemachus has no good reason for failing to go to Laertes himself, much less for denying Eumaeus this chance to alleviate Laertes' sorrow. He does not yet know that his father has returned and now needs the swineherd's help in planning an impending battle with the suitors. Eumaeus's prompt return to the hut will not speed Odysseus's return and is of no consequence at that moment.

What is even more striking is that the Muse does not suggest any unease in Telemachus's father, who witnesses the scene and whose own feelings for his father might be stirred, we would expect, if he is indeed a man of *aganophrosynē*, gentleness. Yet after his self-disclosure to his son, Odysseus instructs Telemachus to keep his return secret not only from Penelope, who might reveal the secret to the suitors and thus endanger him, but from both his old father and Eumaeus (16.302–3). Odysseus seems not to trust those who know him and feels safe only with his son who never got to know him.

The final verbal echo of the *Iliad* that emerges in Anticleia's words about her death occurs when she laments the loss of *meliēdea thymon* ("honey-sweet life," 11.203). The adjective *meliēdeēs* (honey-sweet), though not rare in the epics, usually appears in connection with food or drink, mostly wine.[23] But the phrase as we see it here is unusual in Homer. The closest parallel is the description of Diomedes' actions in *Iliad* 10.495, when he butchers the sleeping Rhesus, king of the Thracians, along with his troops. The next closest is the phrase *meliēdea thymon,* "honey-sweet life," describing Euphorbus's threat to kill Menelaus if the latter does not let go of Patroclus's corpse (*Iliad* 17.17). Anticleia's death, then, though she claims it results from longing, is expressed with words charged with undertones of violent killing in the *Iliad.*

The Call of Alcinous

After parting from his mother, Odysseus describes the various heroines he encountered. Tyro, daughter of Salmoneus and wife of Cretheus, is the first. Since both Salmoneus and Cretheus are sons of Aeolus, Tyro is both daughter-in-law and granddaughter of the god of the winds.[24] The choice of Tyro to head Odysseus's list may be something more than a simple reiteration of a traditional catalogue of heroines. Odysseus claims to have met her father-in-law and grandfather, Aeolus, whose name conjures for him memories both pleasant and bitter. The god entertained Odysseus and his company lavishly on his bronze-walled, floating island before sending them on their way with a bag in which all the winds, except the one which would blow them safely home, were safely contained. But when Odysseus's comrades break open the bag, thinking it contains treasure, and release the winds, Aeolus angrily and contemptuously refuses them hospitality a second time when the consequent storm blows them back to his island.

There are, then, two distinct aspects to Odysseus's encounters with Aeolus which underscore the sudden reversals which occur in dealings with the winds (or their god) and other human or divine circumstances. What is friendly one moment may become implacably hostile the next. This contrast emerges again when we compare Odysseus's picture of Aeolus's family and daily life in book 10 with what he implies in book 11. The scene in book 10 is one of great happiness. Aeolus lives with his faithful wife in a splendid palace. His six sons are married to his six daughters, and they all live with their dear father and mother, spending their days amid feasting and cheer (10.1–14). The scene, in fact, is reminiscent of the Phaeacian world in which Odysseus tells his tale. But, in book 11, Odysseus's account of Aeolus's daughter-in-law Tyro among the dead offers a stark contrast with the previous image of Aeolian domestic bliss. There, Tyro is said to have fallen in love with the river god Enipeus, her future husband's brother, and to have frequented his streams. Not only is her desperate passion not reciprocated by Enipeus, but her beloved helps Poseidon to impersonate him and rape her. He even arranges to conceal himself and watch the rape.[25]

Tyro's traditional misfortunes do not end with the deceitful rape which is the culmination of her tragic passion.[26] After giving birth to the twins Pelias and Neleus, whom Poseidon fathered, she marries, in some traditions, her uncle Cretheus, who raised her. Tyro's father, Salmoneus, and her stepmother, Sidero, torment Tyro for her rape by Poseidon until Pelias finally kills Sidero.[27] Although Homer's Odysseus describes Salmoneus as "blameless"—in contrast, say, to Vergil, who condemns him to Tartarus—and does not allude to the hateful relationship between Tyro and her father, Salmoneus (which probably explains her need to be brought up by Cretheus), the implication was unlikely to be lost on an ancient audience familiar with multiple traditions.

If we try to accommodate these two pictures of Aeolus's household in Odysseus's narrative, we must either postulate that the misfortunes of Tyro belong to an earlier and less blissful period in Aeolian domestic life or that a lot has happened during the year or so since Odysseus left Aeolus's island. Tyro was able to produce not only the twins Pelias and Neleus by Poseidon, but also Aeson, Pheres, and Amythaon by Cretheus, Aeolus's son. The latter scenario is highly improbable for a number of reasons (unless we postulate that mythic voyages allow one to move about in the geography of time-space, as they do in Irish epic or in Vergil's *Aeneid*). Tyro's sons are of great mythological importance. Neleus is the father of Odysseus's friend Nestor, and Aeson's son, Jason, sets out to search for the

Golden Fleece on the *Argo* in a mythic voyage which rivals Odysseus's tale of his own return from Troy. That Jason's ancestry should be traceable to a god who lived on a floating, walled island is itself a beautiful touch. Even more beautiful, however, is the subtle and oblique way in which Odysseus, by his allusion to Tyro's fate, invites comparison between his own voyage and that of Jason. Since he encounters, particularly in books 10 and 12, many perils either identical to or similar to those encountered by Jason in the Argonautic tradition, he invites his audience to make a comparison between himself and his nautical predecessor. And by the time he has finished his catalogue of women, he has encountered ghosts associated with most major epic traditions from the Battle of the Gods and Giants to the adventures of Theseus and the *Thebaid*.

The contrasting pictures of Aeolus's family match the contrasting images of Aeolus as the gentle host and the contemptuous dismisser of his erstwhile guest. Odysseus knew all along that the picture of bliss presented to him on the floating island kept at least something hidden, much as the overt display of concord and happiness in the court at Phaeacia masks internal tensions. This darker side of Aeolus's family should give the Phaeacians, no less than ourselves, an indication of the extent to which the narrator controls the way we perceive the subjects of his narrative. An idealized domestic scene can be turned, in a matter of seconds, into a tale of corruption and humiliation. And the catalogue of heroines becomes a pointed reminder to Odysseus's audiences, both internal and external, of the depths to which sexual intrigues can bring people. After that catalogue, Odysseus intrudes upon his own narrative and insists he needs sleep. Night has already fallen.

[6]

Alcinous Strikes Back

The most immediate effect of Odysseus's narrative on Arete is that she wants him even more as her son-in-law. By shrewdly suggesting that he be given more gifts, she seeks, as we have seen, to delay his departure and even to minimize the chances he will actually go. Alcinous, however, seems all the more determined to get rid of him. With the help of the wise Echeneus, he insists that Odysseus must be sent home. When Odysseus slyly suggests that he is willing to stay up to a year if it means that he can amass more treasure, Alcinous cannot restrain himself and makes his famous comment that "in no way do we think of you as a dissembler and a thief, such as the black earth breeds scattered far and wide" (11.363–65). The king misses neither Odysseus's immediate scheme of gaining more gifts nor the fact that Odysseus is telling him a mixture of fairy tale and reality tailored to his immediate needs. He gently compares Odysseus to a skilled minstrel but goes on to dismiss his claimed need for sleep and declares he would be happy to stay till dawn. If the piper must be paid, then the piper must play. And this time Alcinous attempts to call the tune. He bids Odysseus tell no more about the sufferings he underwent and "all the Achaeans" did but asks:

> Tell me this and recount exactly, whether you saw any of your godlike comrades, who went to Troy under your leadership and there met their fate. (11.370–72)

Alcinous is finally requesting a narrative which has some bearing on his guest's claim to have participated in the Trojan War. He is not interested in a Hesiodic catalogue of famous heroines. Nor is he interested in the general fighting between Greeks and Trojans. In fact, when he says Odysseus has already told them about his sufferings and those of "all the Argives," he is not accurately summarizing what has passed, since Odysseus has made precious few observations about the Trojan War. Alcinous wants to be introduced to some of the ghosts of Odysseus's own contingent who actually died in combat at Troy. This is a request which Odysseus cannot fulfill, as the external audience will appreciate and as Alcinous himself may either know or have deduced. Odysseus left Troy with the same number of ships he had when he arrived—twelve in all.[1] And if we cast about in the *Iliad* looking for members of Odysseus's squadron who died at Troy, we come up empty-handed. Odysseus, however much he persists in evading the issue, is forced to continue a narrative from which the disaster of his nautical leadership—the loss of all of his ships and comrades—cannot be omitted:

Although Alcinous is very specific in his request that Odysseus tell not about other heroes at Troy, but about his own "comrades," scholars commonly assume that Odysseus's ensuing description of his encounter with the ghosts of the great Greek warriors fulfills the king's demands. These were the people "who had been his comrades in war; and so the scene is set for the account of Odysseus's meeting with Agamemnon, Achilles, and Ajax," observes A. Heubeck.[2] But this is not the case. The phrase *hama hepesthai* with a dative implies in both epics following a leader, joining someone who is a commander or following him as an escort.[3] It is commonly used in the *Iliad* to indicate troops following a leader to the Trojan War. Odysseus's answer, then, evades rather than fulfills Alcinous's request, as did his responses to Arete's questions in *Odyssey* 7.237–39.

The Comrades: Agamemnon

Odysseus's first step is to rephrase Alcinous's demand. He announces that he is going to tell about the woes of his comrades "who died afterwards, who escaped from the fearful battle-cry of the Trojans, but died on their return through the will of an evil woman" (11.382–84). He proposes to develop a heroic pose despite the total loss of his retinue. But as he proceeds he does not follow even this modified outline. The only major personage who perished in the course of his *nostos* and because of the wicked determination of a woman is Agamemnon, killed because of the scheming of his wife, Clytemnestra.[4] Achilles and Ajax died at Troy one in combat, the other of self-inflicted wounds. And, of course, not one of the three could remotely be described as part of Odysseus's squadron.

Odysseus starts the tale of his meeting with Agamemnon's ghost with a carefully thought-out comment to the effect that people do not think he looks the part of the great hero. Ever since Euryalus mentioned that Odysseus's appearance does not mesh with his notion of a noble man (in spite of the outer audience's knowledge that Athena did her best in this regard), Odysseus seems defensive about his personal appearance.[5] When Arete tries to compliment his stature and comeliness in her address to the king during her efforts to keep Odysseus in Scheria (11.336–37), Alcinous hints, as we have seen, that he inclines to Euryalus's assessment of his guest's looks. Odysseus mocks such doubts, based on physical appearance and on the kind of figure he cuts, by having Polyphemus express disappointment at being blinded by such a paltry man. But he still faces the problem that he does not match up to the image Alcinous has of what a real hero should have achieved.

Odysseus, we see from the first moments of his encounter with Polyphemus, assumes that Agamemnon will be the most instantly recognizable Greek name of the Trojan War era to those he encounters, and speaks of him in honorific superlatives which he usually reserves for descriptions of himself. To establish his own identity more securely among the Phaeacians, then, he emphasizes that Agamemnon's ghost recognized him the moment he saw him among the dead (11.390). Yet Odysseus introduces Agamemnon not with pomp and glory, but in an atmosphere of lamentation and grief. The ghost of the lord of men is weeping pitifully and reaching arms without strength toward Odysseus. Not even in his most desperate moments does Odysseus himself appear so utterly abject.

What follows, however, is a subnarrative, attributed to Agamemnon himself, of a series of catastrophes in comparison with which the various misfortunes that led to the death of Odysseus's followers seem less discordant with heroic grandeur. Most of Odysseus's crew died either at the hands of virtually invincible semidivine monsters or by the implacable forces of heaven and the elements, even though their demise was often hastened by their own (or Odysseus's) folly. Even Elpenor's life was claimed by an accident, however unheroic. But Agamemnon was murdered, during a feast, through the trickery and plotting of his unfaithful wife, who aided and abetted the hand of her lover. Thus his wife and her lover triumphed, and he and his mistress perished.

Odysseus heightens the rhetorical effect by asking which of a series of heroic catastrophes overwhelmed Agamemnon. Was it a storm sent by Poseidon, enemy troops ambushing him in the middle of a cattle raid, or death during the siege of a city (11.397–403)? In short, he plays Alcinous to Odysseus's Agamemnon. In reply, Agamemnon describes the humiliating circumstances in great detail. He was butchered like an ox at the manger, and all his comrades were slain during the feast, like "white-tusked swine, which are slaughtered in the house of a rich man of great might at a marriage feast, or a joint banquet, or a rich drinking bout" (11.412–15). Odysseus has Agamemnon allocate a full three lines to the slaughter of the comrades, but does not accord them the determined heroic resistance they displayed in the event according to Proteus's story in *Odyssey* 4. We will, of course, remember that there Menelaus is reporting Proteus's words, and that he has good reason to represent his brother's death in high heroic style, if only to account for his own failure to render help to his brother's family–a topic about which he seems acutely sensitive. So when Proteus, according to Menelaus, declares that none of Agamemnon's followers survived the feast, nor did any of Aegisthus's (4.536–37), we should be at least a little skeptical about the veracity of his account.

Odysseus too has his own agenda: to point out that unheroic death was not reserved for his squadron alone in the aftermath of the Trojan War. And he uses Agamemnon's ghost to make the point quite explicitly: "You [Odysseus] have been present at the slaying of many men, killed either in single combat or in the press of the battle, but at heart you would have felt the greatest pity had you seen that sight: how about the mixing bowl and the laden tables we lay in the hall, and the floor all swam with blood" (11.416–20). The larger irony, of course, is that Odysseus will himself cause precisely such a slaughter when he returns to Ithaca, and feels no pity at all.

A safe *nostos* guarantees neither survival nor a heroic death. Agamemnon's successful return with his troops leads only to his murder and their wholesale massacre. Odysseus, though he has lost his troops, is at least still alive. And the potential exists for him to be the agent of massacre in his own halls, not its victim. The ghostly Agamemnon's voice drives home the point, assuring Odysseus that Penelope will never plot anything similar against him. She not only is sensible but shares with Odysseus the knowledge of "counsels" (*mēdea,* 11.445). As Odysseus reports the matter, Agamemnon is almost envious of the homecoming he foresees for Odysseus, which he senses will be the opposite of his own (11.444, 450–53). The main lesson that Odysseus should learn, according to Agamemnon—and thus, of course, according to Odysseus—is never to trust anyone. Agamemnon validates that characteristic of Odysseus highlighted throughout his narrative, that he never trusts even his closest comrades with anything—even with knowledge that could have saved their lives (the contents of the bag of winds, the advice about Scylla and Charybdis, Teiresias's warning about Thrinacia). He is a loner who trusts only himself.

Most curiously, Odysseus says Agamemnon warned him not to moor his ship openly on the shore of Ithaca, advice which, since it implies he will return in a vessel of his own, appears to contradict Teiresias's prediction that he will not arrive in Ithaca on board his own ship. Again, Odysseus shows his masterfully devious subtlety. With a nice touch of realism,

Agamemnon is not made privy to Teiresias's prediction. At the same time, Agamemnon's narrative serves as oblique advice to the Phaeacians about how to get Odysseus safely home: by bringing the ship to shore secretly.

Agamemnon's ghost, then, is deployed to great effect. Not only does he serve to put Odysseus's own current situation into a heroic perspective; he also, with his own voice, elevates Odysseus above himself. Odysseus is not satisfied in pressing his advantage over Agamemnon through the latter's assurance of his own safe homecoming and the prudence of his wife. Agamemnon's allusion to the pitiful death of Cassandra, daughter of Priam, at his side, is a reminder that there is a certain hypocrisy in his complaints about female infidelity and treachery. Odysseus, by contrast, will not be bringing any foreign courtesans home with him and has pointedly distanced himself even from what could be a union by consent with Nausicaa. Further, he, unlike the "king of kings," will, as he has already implied through other speakers, find his son in the ranks of men and be welcomed by him—hence, perhaps, his resolute silence on the matter of any rival sons he may have had by Circe and Calypso. There will be no Telegonus ready to kill him on the shore of Ithaca.

Odysseus's power of invention and judicious editing should not escape us here. He has Agamemnon tell him what he wants the Phaeacians to hear. His technique here is similar to the method he uses in his "retelling" of what his comrades said about him while he was asleep on their way from Aeolus's floating island: "How beloved and honored this man is by all men, to whose city and land he comes!" (10.38–9). Since he was asleep he cannot know what they said, but he does not lose the opportunity to suggest that their envy was provoked by the positive impression he made on the dignitaries visited and their consequent generosity.

Odysseus's presentation of Agamemnon, then, can indeed be read as fictionalized. Agamemnon, after all, reached his home very shortly after the end of the Trojan War, and Homer's muse establishes from the epic's opening lines that the story not only of Agamemnon's death but of Orestes' vengeance was in circulation before Odysseus left Calypso's island.[6] Although Odysseus denies any knowledge of Orestes' fate (11. 463–64) and makes a point of his ignorance of Agamemnon's own demise, he has clearly picked up something of the various *nostoi* of the Trojan heroes. Odysseus is very cagey in reporting his responses to Agamemnon's ghost. As Dawe notes, he "appears to ignore everything except the question whether Orestes is alive or not."[7]

Odysseus tells the Phaeacians that Aeolus questioned him "about each thing, about Troy, and the ships of the Argives, and the return of the Achaeans [*noston Achaiōn*]." "And," he says," I told him all the tale in due order" (10.15–16). Since Agamemnon was, in most traditions, one of the first to return home, it is unlikely that Odysseus really does not know about the attendant circumstances. He conceals the full story he told Aeolus from the Phaeacians.[8]

The story of Agamemnon's murder, brought to mind as the *Odyssey* opens, must have been a standard component of the bardic repertoire, like the stories of Tyro, Oedipus, Alcmena, and others. Once again, Odysseus tailors the song to his personal, rhetorical needs. By the end of his encounter with Agamemnon, Odysseus cuts a much more heroic figure than his famous commander in chief: he is more fortunate than the great lord who returned home quickly with his troops and with no trouble from the vicious Poseidon (11.399–400, 406–7). Alcinous's cutting remarks about Odysseus's loss of comrades and unprepossessing appearance are thus counterpoised. And he has not even finished his work yet.

The Dead and the Living

From Agamemnon Odysseus moves on to the hero par excellence of the *Iliad*: Achilles. He not only ignores, once again, Alcinous's request to hear about the comrades who followed him personally to Troy and died there, but breaks his own promise to tell of the woes the heroes suffered *after* they had escaped the dread battle-cry of the Trojans. Achilles clearly died before the war ended. Why then does Odysseus introduce him?

We will remember that, on his second day in Scheria, Odysseus learned from Demodocus's song that he himself had become a mythic character and the subject of song. But he presumably also gathered that the Phaeacians might have a different perspective on what were the most memorable incidents of the Trojan War. Rather than viewing it through the prism of the ingenious stratagem of the wooden horse, as Odysseus would prefer, or through the quarrel between Agamemnon and Achilles, as it is set in the *Iliad*, the Phaeacians and their bard want to see it through the *neikos* (quarrel) between Odysseus and Achilles (8.75).[9] The first words Odysseus assigns to Achilles indicate the latter's great respect for him by noting not only his patronymic, Laertiades, but his descent from Zeus. Although 11.473 is a formula found elsewhere in the *Odyssey*, it assumes a specially live pertinence in this context, uttered as it is by the ghost of a man who, in most traditions, would have rivaled Zeus himself if his mother, the goddess Thetis, had had sexual relations with the lord of Olympus. That Achilles is now among the dead owes much to the fact that he himself is *not* of Zeus's blood, as Odysseus is. In case the Phaeacians miss the point, Odysseus addresses Achilles, in reply, as "son of Peleus" (11.478).

The allusion to Odysseus's craftiness in Achilles' formulaic line also assumes a live force in this context, since the characteristic of Odysseus that Achilles immediately focuses on is his capacity not just for plotting but for *ruthless* plotting. It is interesting that Odysseus represents himself as being called by such a harsh epithet as *schetlie,* "ruthless," since, as we have already noted, this is an epithet Odysseus shares not only with Polyphemus and Penelope, but with Achilles himself, who is called both *schetlios* and *nēleēs,* "pitiless" (*Iliad* 16.33, 204). In the mouth of someone who did not pride himself on his own ruthlessness, *schetlios* might be an insult. On Achilles' lips it is a compliment. We see from the outset, then, that if there is to be a quarrel between the two heroes after this introduction, it will be a battle of compliments. Achilles' admiring reaffirmation of Odysseus's deviousness combined with a touch of his own ruthlessness undermines the Iliadic tradition of Achilles' dislike for Odysseus.

Achilles' reply also instantly establishes the point around which the entire interchange will pivot: that the dead are without sensation and, in effect, of no account. Why would any living person willingly venture among them? Odysseus appears, at first, to ignore this undertone in his reply and, in effect, to contradict it. He came to seek Teiresias to find out how to get home, to Ithaca. Like Achilles, he has not returned home. What is implicit, but unsaid, of course, is that Odysseus's absence is temporary. Achilles will never get back to his native Phthia.

Odysseus loses nothing in these circumstances by praising Achilles as the warrior supreme. He contrasts his own ill luck which dogs his attempts to return to Ithaca with Achilles' good fortune:

> But, no man was ever before nor will be in the future more blessed than you, Achilles. Since in the past, when you were alive we, the Argives, honored you equally to the gods, and now that you are here you rule mightily among the dead. Therefore, do not grieve for your death, Achilles. (11.482–86)

Several points seem odd in this address. No one has said or implied that Achilles rules among the dead. In fact, there is nothing majestic at all about him. He is depicted as unhappy and rather isolated, accompanied only by Patroclus and Ajax—hardly an image of a mighty ruler. Second, Odysseus's assertion that Achilles grieves for his own death shows that he has not missed the undertone of self-pity in Achilles' words. This observation undermines the congratulatory tone of the hollow compliment preceding it. Achilles' soul is lamenting, *olophyromenē,* Odysseus says, as he later claims Heracles' soul is lamenting (11.616).[10] Now the participle need not imply the notion of grief over one's own death. Nowhere else in the Homeric epics does *olophyromenē* or a related form refer to the speaker's own death, only to someone else's.[11] Indeed, the audience will remember from the *Iliad* that Achilles is ever grieving and mourning after the death of Patroclus. Nothing can assuage his grief and console him.

Nonetheless, Odysseus is quite correct. In Achilles' case, death is a cause for grief, since he traded off the possibility of an undistinguished but long life in favor of a brief but heroic existence. In his response to Odysseus, he makes it quite clear that this is a choice he would not make now if he had the decision over again. Odysseus claims that the ghost of Achilles, the great Achaean hero, declared he would rather be a hired hand of a poor but living man than king of the dead (which, of course, he is not anyway). Achilles' achievement in becoming the greatest hero of the Achaeans is thus reduced to pathetic disillusionment. In spite of his greatness, Odysseus tells us, *Achilles is dead*, whereas he, Odysseus, although not so great an Iliadic hero as Achilles, although not yet home, and although without his troops, not only remains alive but subsequently declines Calypso's offer to make him immortal, as he has already told the Phaeacians. While Achilles, once dead, regrets his choice, Odysseus, though he has seen death face-to-face and has seen Achilles' reaction to death, nonetheless insists on maintaining his mortality.

Yet Odysseus goes still one step further in his triumph over Achilles and in advancing the claims of his Odyssean heroism over that of the Iliadic Achilles. He says he was able to console Achilles at least a little by telling him of the achievements of Neoptolemus when the ghost asked him how things were going with his son and his father, old Peleus, who are in the world of the living and thus unreachable by Achilles. We should add, of course, that young Neoptolemus's excellence is expressed in terms of his achievements in warfare dominated by Odysseus's presence. Neoptolemus was third in oratory after Odysseus and Nestor (11.512) and the most eager of the Greeks within the wooden horse (the opening of whose exits was, of course, controlled by our narrator [11.523–32]). Odysseus glosses over what would, no doubt, have been a troubling piece of information for Achilles: that he himself, and not Neoptolemus, had won the right to wear Achilles' armor. His failure to mention this issue is more than just a matter of tact. It would remind the Phaeacians that his legacy as Achilles' successor was, by this point, lying somewhere at the bottom of the Aegean, unless, of course, he subsequently turned over the armor to Neoptolemus of his own free will, as he does in some later traditions.[12] But most versions, notably that of Sophocles' *Philoctetes*, suggest that there was some unresolved tension between Neoptolemus and Odysseus on the matter of Achilles' arms.

In short, Odysseus depicts himself providing for Achilles the sort of information Teiresias provides for him, but in a narrative that shows his own superior position to Neoptolemus. In this matter the Muse lends something of a hand herself, for we will recall that, in *Odyssey* 4, the Muse not only fails to allow the son of Achilles to meet the son of Odysseus but says nothing at all about Neoptolemus other than to note that Hermione is being sent off to be his bride. Odysseus and his muse do to Achilles and Neoptolemus in the *Odyssey* what Lucian does, centuries later, to Odysseus in his *True Story*. They make rivals, real or potential, their footnotes. Lucian tells how the ghost of Odysseus came up to him with a letter addressed to Calypso in which he expresses his regrets now for having turned down her offer of immortality and promises to slip away to see her if the opportunity ever arises (*True Story* 2.29, 35–36). By the end of his account of the Otherworld, Odysseus has even suggested that he is, at the moment of narration, outdoing Heracles, the all-powerful son of Zeus whose descent into Hades to capture Cerberus was the mightiest of his famous labors (11.623–26). Heracles, though translated to Olympus, is still, in some partial sense dead. His ghost, like those of Theseus and Pirithous, will not see the sun again. And he too laments his death to Odysseus, as Achilles had done (11.616).

Ajax

If Odysseus's rhetorical vault over his Iliadic rival is a tour de force, his encounter with the ghost of Ajax is hardly less impressive. In the first place, Ajax and Achilles are very much alike: straightforward (in comparison to Odysseus) military men. Ajax understands Achilles and knows how to approach him. In the *Iliad*, Achilles changes his decision to abandon the host and return to Phthia only after Ajax's short, but poignant address. That Ajax shares Achilles' dislike of Odysseus, though feeling it more intensely, is clear from the *Iliad*. When the embassy sent to Achilles arrives, Ajax looks to Phoenix to open business, although, according to the instructions given by Nestor, Odysseus was supposed to lead off. It has been suggested that Ajax makes a stupid mistake (scholars seem to regard him as thickheaded), or that Homer "even intends an ironic hint that Odysseus will overreach himself and his contribution will not be a success."[13] But surely the point is, rather, that the initial selection of Odysseus was made by Nestor, Odysseus's friend, and overlooks the simple rhetorical principle that the speaker must have credibility with the person to be persuaded. As the episode unravels, Ajax emerges as anything but a thickheaded or stupid man. We see, rather, that he dislikes Odysseus and senses that Achilles does too. He substitutes Phoenix for Odysseus to prevent the embassy's failure.

Odysseus, in *Odyssey* 11, anchors the hostility between Ajax and Odysseus to the competition for Achilles' arms—which turned out in Odysseus's favor and led, Odysseus notes obliquely, to Ajax's death. In short, the matter of Achilles' arms, scrupulously omitted in the discussion of Neoptolemus, is raised now, but in an unusual way. In the first place, Odysseus puts no words at all in Ajax's mouth. Odysseus does the speaking himself, in an attempt at what he claims is reconciliation. He represents himself as showering his old rival with compliments as "the best in comeliness and form of all the Danaans after the peerless son of Peleus" (11.469–70, 549–51). He regrets that he won the contest (though he never says he did not deserve to win) and contends that the whole situation was devised by the gods in their desire to weaken the Greek cause. The only response he shows Ajax giving is resistance to his attempts to bring about a post mortem peace and his retreat into the darkness, in implacable anger. Then, tantalizingly, Odysseus hints that Ajax might have come around to discussing the matter, but he, Odysseus, was not interested in him anymore:

> Then he would nevertheless have spoken to me despite his wrath, or I to him, but the heart in my breast yearned to see the spirits of those others that are dead. (11.565–67)

Odysseus has more important figures to visit, more pressing business to attend to. He has made his gesture of magnanimity. And it is enough. By offering reconciliation and having it rebuffed, he triumphs yet again over Ajax.

The Otherworld and the Aftermath

When Odysseus draws back from his contacts with the realm of Hades and Persephone, he is still with his faithful comrades, he tells his audience. By now it should be clear to the Phaeacian listeners that he lost his comrades on the way back from Troy, since he has introduced none of their ghosts and said nothing about their deaths on the battlefield. He knows he still owes Alcinous an explanation of how the rest of his crew died, and it is must seem possible to him that Alcinous will not give him an escort to Ithaca without being told how he managed to achieve what no other Greek hero who fought in Troy did—the loss of all his troops. Having sailed into Phaeacian myth, thus establishing his credentials in terms of what he thinks is acceptable to his "inner" audience, he proceeds farther into the realms of the fantastic. But he remains on guard. Alcinous has already hinted, obliquely and politely, that he is a liar and dissembler. What Odysseus does is to use this assumption that he is a liar and dissembler to show that he is a potential menace and threat to the king.

The Second Departure from Circe's Island

A less notable selection of mythic (and overtly Argonautic) variants seems to be present in the depictions of dangers Odysseus has to undergo after leaving Circe's land of Aeaea. Circe, in fact, pointedly refers to the voyage of the *Argo* at 12.70–72. Some of the hazards in Odysseus's adventures seem to reflect in some way those he managed to avoid when he first came to Circe under the aegis of Hermes' advice. As Circe's songs lure Odysseus's unsuspecting companions into her house and animal metamorphosis in 10.222–31, so, Circe warns Odysseus in 12.39–54, sailors who are unwittingly beguiled by the Sirens' song become heaps of dry bones surrounding the Sirens' meadow. The persuasive, seductive magic of song can be lethal. And, curiously enough, the Sirens' song as Odysseus reports it is the song of Troy—the lure, if you will, of the musical reenactment of his own past, his own self, his own reflection, his own narcissism (12.184–91).

Similarly, as Circe overpowers her victims with drugged wine which turns them into animals that can be consumed, Scylla and Charybdis are physical, geographical equivalents to Circe in their potential to devour or swallow humans. No wonder, then, that Odysseus hopes to defeat Charybdis with sword in hand as he defeated Circe, for although Scylla is in one sense a rocky reef and Charybdis a whirlpool, both are described by Circe as menacing female personages with some animal and human features. If Odysseus is composing here against the background of traditions which emerge not in Homer but in later writers, the audience may have been aware that Scylla is the by-product of Circe's witchery. Ovid, for example, tells of a once-beautiful Scylla turned into a monster by Circe out of her jealousy for Glaucus's love. Thus Scylla's destruction of some of Odysseus's comrades who have been spared by Circe becomes, in a way, an act of retaliation for her own deformation by Circe.[14]

It is, in a sense, the song (or the sound) rather than the singer which beguiles, as Odysseus tells the story. It makes no difference whether the singer is beautiful (as Circe) or of uncertain appearance (as the Sirens) or so monstrous that not even a god would be interested in her (as Scylla).[15] The song that lures may be the saga of one's own existence (as in the case of the Sirens) or the pathetic yelping of puppies (as with Scylla). Not only is Odysseus, in the Homeric manner, careful never to suggest that he felt any sexual attraction for Circe (or Calypso, for that matter). He also leaves out any hint that Circe felt any strong, emotional attachment for him. Though their relationship is sexual, it is quite unlike the tale of passion in the Argonautic tradition between Jason and the enchantress Medea, Circe's niece. Odysseus, unlike Jason, leaves his passionless enchantress in her own world, which she manifests no desire to leave and from which he shows no inclination to take her.

From the moment he meets Circe, Odysseus seems to suggest that he has lost any freedom to decide where he sails next. He represents himself as trapped in a kind of mythic subnarrative which she controls. Circe's directives and predictions are clear and detailed. First he must go to the Sirens who cast a spell with their voice and song on sailors and lure them to death. Then he must row past the Sirens, after sealing his comrades' ears with wax so they will not hear their voice. The only option Circe leaves him is whether he himself will listen to their song. If he does so wish, he must have his own freedom of movement restricted. He must submit to being bound hand and foot to the mast. Although, he says, Circe tells him he can choose his route to Thrinacia—either via the Clashing Rocks or between Scylla and Charybdis—she does not explain how to bypass the Clashing Rocks and focuses only on the alternative route between Scylla and Charybdis, thus leaving him really no prudent course but to accept the alternative route.[16]

Circe's instructions, in fact, are so detailed that they render much of what Teiresias says redundant. The major additions Teiresias makes above and beyond what Circe says are that Odysseus will return on another's ship to a difficult situation at home and that he must resume his travels shortly after his return. Perhaps Odysseus feels that Teiresias's authority will be enough to persuade Alcinous to guarantee his conveyance. In other matters, however, Circe, like Teiresias, insists that the conduct of Odysseus and his crew on the island of Thrinacia is crucial to the success of his homeward voyage. But her information is fuller and more precise. She gives Odysseus the exact number of Helios's flocks, their size, and the number—even the names—of their shepherds. Like Teiresias, she warns Odysseus to control himself and his men and not to touch Helios's cattle. If they harm his herds, disaster will fall upon the ship and his comrades. And even if Odysseus himself escapes the general ruin, his return will be late, and he will lose all his comrades.

Presenting himself as a genuine and caring leader, Odysseus tells his comrades, once they sail for the second and final time from the shores of Aeaea, that it would not be right if only one or two people knew about Circe's revelations. He is going, he says, to tell them her predictions "in order that knowing them we may either die or, shunning death and fate, escape" (12.156–57). Yet, not only he does *not* tell his comrades all she said, and chooses, as he admits later, to suppress that additional information, but he reshapes and misrepresents those portions he actually communicates. Thus, although he repeats Circe's warning not to come close to the Sirens, he claims that Circe *ordered* him alone to listen to their song (12.160). Yet, not more than a hundred lines earlier he told the Phaeacians (and us) that Circe left it to him to decide whether to listen to them or not (12.49). More perplexing still, Odysseus does not mention anything to his crew about Scylla, Charybdis, or Thrinacia.

It makes little sense to excuse these omissions on the grounds that Odysseus lacks the necessary time to elaborate them because of his ship's prompt arrival at the island of the Sirens, speedily wafted by favoring winds. If Odysseus were interested in giving his crew the full information, he could have told them about Circe's predictions before they set sail. In fact, he later admits, he did not tell his crew about the dangers of Scylla and Charybdis so as not to discourage them from rowing forward (12.223–25). Yet to gain that forward progress without discussing the nature of the perils as forecast by Circe is, in effect, to lure his men on to their doom. His periodic revelations and periodic silence when dealing with his crew not only show a captain's traditional reluctance to trust his comrades with warnings about all the dangers of their mission but mirror his equally edited presentations to Alcinous and the Phaeacians. Again, Odysseus seems to be reminding Alcinous that he is capable of manipulating and hurting his loyal crew, and thus, by inference, a wary host. He is also making it plain to any, such as Arete, who worry that a Phaeacian crew might harm him on his way home, that he, on the whole, is more dangerous to a crew than a crew is likely to be to him.

Thrinacia

After losing six comrades to Scylla, as predicted by Circe, Odysseus and his crew approach the island of Thrinacia. The tale of Thrinacia continues the narrative distortion found in Odysseus's accounts of all his adventures in the aftermath of the Otherworld. Although he told the Phaeacians of the warnings given by Teiresias and Circe about harming the cattle of Helios on Thrinacia (11.110–11, 12.136–37), he maintains now that both the seer and the goddess told him to shun the island of Helios altogether (12.268–69). They said nothing of the kind. An attentive Phaeacian might have noticed that both Teiresias and Circe cannot envision Odysseus's return without a halt on Thrinacia.[17]

It has been claimed that "Odysseus has extracted from Circe's warning words which she did not in fact use: *nēson aleuasthai.* His idea is to escape temptation by avoiding the island altogether."[18] The suggestion that Odysseus now or at any moment in his narrative wants to escape temptation should be suspect. It wins more scholarly acceptance than it should probably because it attributes to Odysseus the noble intent of saving his comrades at all costs, an intent he has hardly exhibited anywhere else. The general tone of his tale suggests, rather, the opposite. He seems often to use his comrades as a means of providing him with experiences they are themselves denied. They must convey him past the Sirens and their alluring song with ears blocked while he keeps his own ears open. Had his men unstopped their ears, as well they might if curiosity prompted, both they and he would have been lost.

Having passed the island of the Sirens without being able to land, having lost six comrades in the terrifying encounter with Scylla, having been exposed to, but without loss, the suctioning vortex of Charybdis, any exhausted sailor would wish to land and rest. Odysseus's demand that they not land on Thrinacia predictably meets with objections from his crew, especially since Eurylochus is still alive and on board. Eurylochus usually spots Odysseus's intent to endanger his comrades or treat them unfairly. Although Odysseus now warns his men about Thrinacia, he does so only in a general comment to the effect that Circe told him "a most terrible evil is on the island" (12.275). He says nothing at all about the cattle of Helios but surely could not have been so naive as to expect his crew not to notice the herds, since he himself heard their bellowing and bleating while still on his ship at sea (12.263–66). Yet he says nothing about any prohibition against killing a cow or a sheep until after Eurylochus's tirade against him. Although, after the tirade, he mentions that eating the cattle is dangerous and repeats the warning on their second day on the island, he never mentions precisely *why* it is so dangerous for them to do so, even though there is no reason to withhold such information now. On the contrary, Teiresias's and Circe's warning that if they do slaughter Helios's cattle, they will never return home safely might be a deterrent for the crew. His men, after all, seem to miss home more than he does. They remind him during their stay at Aeaea that they, unlike he, have not forgotten their native land (10.472–74). Dawe argues that "the whole point of the story is that Odysseus will remain guiltless."[19] We suggest that, in the course of his self-exculpation, elements show through which cast doubt on his pose of guiltlessness.

In spite of Odysseus's claim that they should shun the island altogether, and in spite of warnings that his comrades must not touch the cattle, he allows them to stay a whole month on the island—until they have eaten all the provisions Circe gave him. At this point they have to look for food on the island. His claim to the oar-loving Phaeacians (who would know the fickleness of winds) is that the South and East winds blew unceasingly, thus preventing them from leaving. By this time, Helios's cattle become an irresistible temptation, as we learn form Eurylochus's comment in 12.348–51, where he avows that he would rather be struck down by Helios in his ship for devouring the god's cattle than perish of hunger. All excuses aside, however, Odysseus walks away from his comrades to another part of the island at the critical hour when he knows they are desperately looking for food, under the pretext that he wants to pray to the gods to show him a way out of the situation. This, Dawe rightly observes, is "the weakest part of the story."[20] Under the pretext of piety, Odysseus seeks to absolve himself of responsiblity for his comrades' act. Let us grant that he needed to leave his men and go some distance away to pray to the gods. Yet the nap he takes after he has prayed (and which he says the gods sent upon him) is of considerable duration. It lasts long enough not only for Eurylochus to make a subversive speech to the crew which convinces them to kill the cattle but long enough to allow for the killing, flaying, roasting, and consuming of the herd (12.340–70).

Odysseus, by controlling the flow of information as he does, makes it almost inevitable that his men will eat the cattle of the Sun. In fact, we cannot rule out the possibility that he has used his foreknowledge of their catastrophe, based on the prophecies of Circe and Teiresias, to maneuver them into bringing that very catastrophe to pass.

Odysseus's expedition is so diminished in numbers and effectiveness by this point that, from his own perspective, it might now be safer not to bring anyone back than to bring back a tiny fraction of the whole contingent. His aide, Eurylochus, is never intimidated by him and has been free in his criticism of Odysseus's leadership. No less significant, Eurylochus is both a relative of Penelope and, potentially, a rival narrator, who could immensely complicate Odysseus's return to claim his estates and position in Ithaca. By leaving the narrative of his travels and the loss of his comrades open to such a construction, Odysseus shows Alcinous and his Phaeacian audience not only how skillfully he can manipulate his companions to their demise, but also how skillfully he can describe the process: allowing the naive to be taken in by its apparently disingenuous nature and the more alert and suspicious to see what a formidable manipulator of words he is, capable of destroying anyone with whom he comes in contact. He thereby plays on Alcinous's fears and suspicions that the man in front of him is as dangerous to his house and daughter as he is to everyone else he has ever met.

Whichever reading of Odysseus any given Phaeacian makes, he or she, if we allow for Arete's and Nausicaa's reactions to these later phases of his narrative, will emerge with the impression that he is a man who regards his personal survival as of the utmost importance and ensures it with a mixture of bravado and calculating ruthlessness, a man who will experience and achieve whatever he can experience or achieve regardless of the cost to others. Even a listener who might dismiss him as a dangerously irresponsible leader might discern within his narrative the menace of a man who can get rid of companions who might attest to his irresponsibility. He is, in fact, the Greek hero par excellence: his greatness is such that you would prefer the honor of his tomb to his living presence.

[7]

Recognizing Discrete Identities

Recognition is a complex process involving several phases of reaction, and as commentators from antiquity on have pointed out, the *Odyssey* involves a constant process of recognition.[1] For this reason it is perhaps better to divide that process of recognition into at least two separate elements. We will use the terms "recognize" and "recognition" to indicate only that a given person has grasped, or strongly suspects, that he or she knows the identity of a newcomer. The overt statement of that recognition we will call "acknowledgment." On this matter it is possible to be a little more precise in English than in Greek (ancient or modern), since *anagnōrisis* encompasses both notions. Aristotle defines *anagnōrisis* in terms resembling "recognition" but uses it only in reference to those moments when the recognition is made public.

A character in an epic or tragedy may recognize another character and yet not wish to have his recognition acknowledged either by himself or by the recognized character. Or vice versa. There are of course recognition episodes which do not involve identity but bring about a further realization or understanding of events. To facilitate our discussion we can divide recognitions into two main groups: inductive recognitions and deductive recognitions. An inductive recognition is one in which someone realizes, on the basis of appearances, who an unknown person must be. Helen, for example, recognizes Telemachus inductively in *Odyssey* 4. In a deductive recognition, someone assembles and analyzes the facts available and, at the moment of recognition, decides what they mean. Menelaus's recognition of Telemachus in *Odyssey* 4 is such a recognition. Deductive recognition involves reasoning and is less simply intuitive than inductive recognition. But, we will recall, Menelaus, who identifies Telemachus deductively, declares that he has also recognized Telemachus on the basis of his resemblance to Odysseus (i.e., inductively), and, more important, the Muse tells us he was debating with himself whether or not to communicate that recognition at the very moment Helen arrived, looked at Telemachus, and declared that he must be Odysseus's son.

Since it has more episodes of recognition than any other work of Greek or Latin poetry, the *Odyssey* offers numerous instances of deductive recognitions, inductive recognitions, and a mixture of the two. One of the first recognition episodes in the epic, is, in fact, a mixture of the two types. Athena visits Telemachus when his life is in disarray, appearing to him disguised as Mentes, a family *xenos,* (guest and friend). After raising the issue of Odysseus's return, Athena says: "And you must be the son of Odysseus" (1.207). Although she, as a god, knows who Telemachus is, she justifies her recognition in mortal terms on the physical similarity of Telemachus to his father—that is to say, inductively.

Athena's task is not to figure out who Telemachus is but to convince him that she has some personal basis of knowledge for making that recognition and that he really is Odysseus's son. She must get *him* to recognize who he is. Since he would not recall his father, his only basis for accepting that he is Odysseus's son is what people have told him. Athena therefore tells Telemachus that he resembles Odysseus in the beauty of his head and eyes. And, to show she knows what she is talking about, she mentions her frequent encounters with Odysseus at Troy. Telemachus, however, resists her efforts at persuasion:

> So, stranger, I will tell you everything frankly. My mother says I am his child, but I do not know; for no one ever really knows his father himself. (1.214–16)

Athena's attempts to persuade Telemachus of his identity meet with only limited success. She knows he will not be a dependable guardian of his father's interests until he accepts more certainly that Odysseus really is his father—hence her logic in prompting him to assert himself in the household and to journey to Pylos and Sparta as much in search of his own identity as Odysseus's son as for news of Odysseus. Telemachus cannot possibly recognize inductively that Odysseus is his father. But he may be able to deduce from the inductive and deductive recognition of others that he is Odysseus's son.

Athena's visit readies Telemachus for the deductive process. Although she is disguised as Mentes and goes unrecognized during their discussion, Telemachus deduces, on her departure, that she is a god, though he does not know which god. He is thus left to resolve a paradox of some complexity: a visitor who is not who he claims to be is attempting to convince him that he himself is who he suspects he may not be. The process of recognition is not going to be straightforward; and it involves complex interweavings of what we (and he) take to be truth and lies.

Homer's muse not only challenges the characters with problems of deductive and inductive recognition; she challenges the audience from the outset by setting up patterns of action and behavior for us to observe. When Zeus, in *Odyssey* 1, discusses mortals' tendency to blame the gods rather than themselves for their troubles, he adduces the case of Aegisthus, who ignored the warnings of the gods and killed Agamemnon. And throughout the *Odyssey*, Agamemnon's return, his wife's infidelity, his murder by Aegisthus, and Orestes' vengeance remain menacing examples of what might befall a returning hero and his family. It lurks in the consciousness not only of Odysseus, Telemachus, and Penelope, but also of the reader, who, the Muse assumes, is familiar with Agamemnon's return. The threat that this pattern will subsume the lives of Odysseus and his family is exacerbated by the knowledge that he is returning alone to a household occupied not by a single lover but by over a hundred suitors (and their relatives) who have an obvious interest in preventing the reestablishment of the previous regime.

From the outset, then, this pattern guides us to interpret Odysseus's *nostos* in the light of Agamemnon's. We come to expect the evolving plots to shape themselves in terms of the example because the epic's characters do so and adjust their actions and attitudes accordingly. Telemachus does not trust Penelope. Neither does Odysseus, because of the precedent of Clytemnestra. And Telemachus's awareness of Orestes' example makes him potentially threatening to Penelope. Their collective and individual recognition of the similarity between their situation and that of the house of Agamemnon threatens to reproduce the events of Mycenae in Ithaca if the participants do not grasp how they, individually, differ from those in the Mycenaean archetype. That is why Telemachus's visit to Sparta is important. It provides another pattern of what can happen to the returning hero.

There are many other instances of patterning in the *Odyssey* which affect our perceptions of what is happening and modify our understanding of what recognition means in the Homeric environment. Uvo Hölscher, for instance, observes that a stranger in the *Odyssey* often finds persons he meets spontaneously speaking to him about precisely those matters that touch or concern him most.[2] His observation seems to be so generally correct as to constitute a predictable pattern within the narrative. But what makes the pattern of spontaneous coincidence of interests between narrator and listener more remarkable than, say, the iterated archetypal *nostos* pattern discussed above is that it runs counter to normal human experience. We don't usually find strangers talking about specific events that have shaped our individual lives when they don't know who we are.

That a phenomenon which we would regard as a rare coincidence or accident should be a predictable pattern of interchanges in the *Odyssey* makes for something of a critical dilemma. Yet there is little doubt that Hölscher is right in his observation.

In Alcinous's banquet hall, Demodocus begins to sing, in the presence of the as yet unidentified Odysseus, of the quarrel between Odysseus and Achilles. True, he is invited to sing by Alcinous. But the choice of subject is his own, prompted, the Muse tells us, by herself (8.73). Much the same is true of Odysseus's first encounter with Eumaeus. He has barely arrived in Eumaeus's hut when the swineherd begins to lament his lost master (14.40–41). Similarly, Eurycleia, when called upon to wash the apparently unknown beggar's feet, bewails Odysseus's fate (19. 369), and Penelope regrets her lost beauty and describes her long fidelity to her apparently unrecognized husband as he sits before her (19.124–28).

Such behavior ought to imply that there is a glimmer of recognition, however half-conscious, on the part of the speaker, of the apparently unknown stranger's identity. But most critics (Hölscher, for example) make no allowance for the possibility that Eumaeus, Eurycleia, or Penelope (much less Demodocus) recognize, or half-recognize, their disguised visitor as Odysseus, let alone the possibility that Odysseus is himself attempting to encourage at least partial recognition of his identity. This recurrent pattern of reminiscences of Odysseus in his disguised presence tends to be dismissed as mere chance.

Aristotle sensibly objected to plots which rely on chance. And, in an epic which shows such carefully integrated interaction between human and divine, so should we. If we detect, as Hölscher does, a repeated schematic pattern, it seems unlikely that such a pattern is the product of chance alone and thus purposeless. While patterned structures do not necessarily presuppose a particular purpose or design, they should not be ignored by the critic any more than the traces of what might have been a wall should be ignored by the archaeologist.

Critics of the *Odyssey* often deny that Eumaeus and Penelope can recognize Odysseus, even though the narrative builds toward such a recognition. Yet if Odysseus is to gain the support or at least the neutrality of his wife, son, and swineherd, he must be recognized by them (or they have no reason to gamble their lives on association with him). Dawe, in commenting on 19.479, where Athena diverts Penelope's attention and prevents her from being forced to recognize Odysseus, argues that "the poet has painted himself into a corner, and this is his abjectly incapable way of trying to extricate himself."[3] He is right: the logic of the scene leads one to expect such an acknowledgment. But must we assume authorial incompetence? Fenik, by contrast, argues that Penelope does not recognize Odysseus, "because the thematic logic of the situation *requires* that Penelope not guess the truth. A fundamental aspect of this and all the related scenes is that one not recognize that which is before him, that he grieve for that which is lost while it is already found."[4]

When Penelope bewails her lost beauty before the disguised Odysseus, we are reminded that time has not stood still for either husband or wife. Her young husband and her own youth are lost. When Penelope sets up, and Odysseus accepts, an open contest for her hand on the basis of ability to use Odysseus's bow she is stating that whoever wins her must be a match for the Odysseus that was. And Odysseus, by agreeing to her terms, accepts that he must prove he still *is* the Odysseus that was. So aware is he, in fact, of how things change, that one of his first concerns when he enters the contest is to check the bow to make sure that bugs have not eaten into it and weakened its structure.

Characters in the *Odyssey* know that there is much more to recognizing someone than applying a name to face. Odysseus is no more the same person he was twenty years ago than any of us are. He left as a youth with a squadron of ships and men. He returns not merely *as* a disguised, friendless, and aging beggar: he *is,* in reality, more or less what his disguise suggests. True, Odysseus is not a beggar in the classic mold. He has a treasure chest on the beach. But he can't buy back house and family or pay off the suitors. To regain his position he must show he is equal to the tasks that would face Odysseus if Odysseus were to return under the prevailing circumstances: that the Odysseus that *is* more than equals the Odysseus that *was.* If he proves no more than an over-the-hill fighter trying to make a comeback, those who back him will be ruined.

It makes sense for all parties concerned to be cautious and to test each other. Awareness of Agamemnon's doom will have alerted Odysseus to the dangers of an overt homecoming, even if one has an army in support. For their part, Eumaeus and Penelope may be in trouble if they acknowledge that the stranger at their gates is at least in name Odysseus. They would be reaffirming their status as *his* social inferiors at the perilous moment when he is, in fact, *their* social inferior—a beggar in his own house and on his own estate. There is no guarantee that he will be able to reestablish himself. On the face of it, it seems more likely that he will bring himself to ruin and will ruin anyone who allies himself or herself with him.

Thus each outright acknowledgment of Odysseus by his household occurs when a person has more to gain than to lose by offering it or risks being harmed by Odysseus if acknowledgment is withheld. In short, there is some reason to believe Eumaeus and Penelope recognize the beggar as Odysseus before they acknowledge the beggar as Odysseus. The difficulty is that scholars incline to assume that recognition and acknowledgment occur simultaneously: if not, then recognition has not occurred. The fallacy should be evident from our daily experience. Most of us, at times, recognize people on the street but pretend not to see them. We avert our eyes or hurry to get out of their way. It is not always in our perceived interests to acknowledge that we have recognized them. It would also be naive to suppose that our failure to acknowledge the persons we avoid goes unnoticed by them. The averted eyes, the crossing of the road, are, in fact, signs of recognition, not signs of nonrecognition.

Odysseus, then, is both recognizable and unrecognizable because he both is and is not "Odysseus." When he approaches Eumaeus's hut, the dogs sense only the presence of a stranger and would tear him to pieces if Eumaeus did not intervene. The dogs would all have been born long after Odysseus left and have shared the usual canine indifference to human laws of prior ownership. Only the aging Argus, sole surviving hound from the old days, will recognize Odysseus. Argus, who guards Odysseus's property until his master crosses its boundaries to resume possession, is the first nonimmortal to recognize him. And the dog promptly dies.

There is strong irony here embedded in paradox. But it is not a *straightforward* irony, as Fenik suggests. "Irony demands," he says, "that the audience know something the fictional characters do not; we can see, but they are blind."[5] But literature also knows an inversion of dramatic irony which arises when characters know or see something never made explicit to the audience.[6] Eumaeus and Penelope may well see in their beggarly visitor signs that he is what has become of the man they knew two decades earlier. Indeed, in their exchanges with Odysseus, we find much to suggest their half-conscious recognition of him. Yet if we call their recognition half-conscious, we underestimate the complexity of their observations and interactions and of the nature of identity itself. As in Aeschylus's *Persians*, where Xerxes will not really become the Great King again until he is symbolically reclad as monarch and the disasters of Salamis and Plataea are put behind him, so, in the *Odyssey*, Odysseus does not become Penelope's husband again until he has demonstrated that he is as powerful and cunning as he used to be and has vanquished the suitors.

The Cretan Odysseus: Phase I

In *Odyssey* 13, Odysseus is deposited, asleep, in Ithaca by the Phaeacians. The scene marks the transition between his long sojourn in a fantastical environment of gods and dubiously real people and geography and his reestablishment in what should be the familiar geography of his native land. But Odysseus, on awakening, has no idea where he is. Fortunately, Athena, disguised as a young shepherd, is on the beach to explain where he is. Her presence is not as unthreatening as that of Nausicaa in Phaeacia. True, Odysseus is now well clothed and has much treasure. Still, a solitary man with a treasure chest on an unknown shore has reason to be afraid.

Athena is banteringly ironic as she explains to Odysseus where he is. She treats him as if he has never heard of Ithaca rather than as if he does not know this is Ithaca: "Surely it is not nameless. Many do know it fairly well, both those who live toward the dawn and the sun, and those who are behind, toward the murky darkness" (13.239–41). Her reference to Ithaca as not "nameless" (*nōnymos*) —an epithet rare in epic— has intriguing resonances. It echoes Alcinous's comment, made while he is prompting Odysseus's self-identification and his travel: no man is "nameless" (*anōnymos*, 8.550–52).[7]

The echo invites comparison between the response Odysseus gives Alcinous and the one he gives Athena. It prepares us for a narrative in which Odysseus will establish an identity through tales of adventure. But this narrative, like Plato's Myth of Er, will not be a long tale told to Alcinous, but a much briefer narrative, a prelude not only to several further small narratives, but to a scenario in which the hero's narratives are subsumed into a larger, overarching account, given by the Muse, of his interactions with his household and with the community in Ithaca.

Homer's muse, of course, faces something of a problem. While Odysseus generates an identity of sorts in his narrative to the Phaeacians—an audience as otherworldly and elusive as the narrative he addresses to them—such an approach will not work for an audience in Ithaca who inhabit a "real" place in a world of relatively clear geography. It belongs, if not to history, at least to the context of myth-history. Thus fiction cannot be passed off as the reality "the poet tells (or invents)." Removed from the context of fiction, a fictional statement becomes false. Homer's muse adapts to this new environment by describing what Odysseus tells the young shepherd as *lies.*[8] At the same time, the shepherd who tells Odysseus "the truth" (that he is in Ithaca) is neither male nor human, but female and divine. Thus Athena's fictional persona, speaking the truth, confronts a "real" Odysseus who, the Muse assures us, is telling lies.

In his "lies," Odysseus tells the shepherd first that he has as much treasure overseas in Crete as he has in Ithaca; then that he is exiled because he killed Orsilochus, Idomeneus's son and the fastest runner in Crete, who tried to take away his share of Trojan plunder.[9]

> I heard of Ithaca even in broad Crete far over the sea; now I myself have arrived with these possessions after leaving even more to my children when I fled, since I killed the dear son of Idomeneus, Orsilochus, swift of foot, who in broad Crete surpassed in swiftness of foot all men who eat bread, since he intended to rob me of all this booty from Troy, for the sake of which I suffered many toils in my heart, having experi-

> enced the wars of men and the grievous waves. You see, I would not oblige his father by becoming his squire in the land of the Trojans, but commanded comrades of my own. (13.256–66)

He lay in wait, he says, for the young man and killed him at night as he returned from the fields, then escaped to a ship of the Phoenicians, who, in exchange for some booty, agreed to carry him and his treasure to Pylos. A strong wind thrust them ashore at Ithaca. They landed on the beach, where he fell asleep. While he was asleep, the Phoenicians took his goods out of the ship, set them by him, and returned to Sidon.

We fall into a rhetorical trap if we accept the Muse's assurance that this story is a lie.[10] Although it contradicts the narrative of Odysseus's return, loaded with treasure, from the magical land of Phaeacia, if one simply substitutes (historical) Phoenicians for (fictional) Phaeacians, the substance of how Odysseus arrived is unchanged from what we have just been told in *Odyssey* 12. Then the only improbable element in Odysseus's story (as he obliquely admits) is that the Phoenicians did not rob him when he fell asleep on the shore (13.271–86). Phoenicians are not noted in the *Odyssey* for scrupulous dealing, even by Odysseus in his other Cretan tales.

The "truth" (if that is what it is) is even more incredible than the lie. Those elements in Odysseus's story that are lies represent adjustments in his explanation of what has actually happened that will bring his account closer to probability. He turns Phaeacians into Phoenicians and has them transport him, for an ample payment, to a mistaken destination rather than free of charge to the exact place he wishes to reach. Odysseus grasps that truth is not a simple matter of fact and nonfact. Unless truth is noticeable, noticed, and believed, it is, in a practical sense, irrelevant. Sometimes, therefore, truth must be so tailored as to coincide with the listener's ability to believe that it will strike the more scient reader and the omniscient Athena as a lie.[11] But such a lie is only a refraction of the "truth."

Several other rhetorical tactics are detectable in Odysseus's tale. Having heard the young shepherd mentioning Troy as one of the most remote geographical points the name of Ithaca has reached (13.248–49), Odysseus hastens to put himself in the context of the heroes who fought at Troy: the context of Odysseus. Nor does he disguise what one would have thought he would most want to disguise—that he has treasure with him. The picture he presents is not remote from the truth, for if the other warriors have returned to their homes years ago, as we are several times assured in the *Odyssey*, the only person he can possibly be is Odysseus.

But there is more. Odysseus establishes his identity within the stories of war and adventure known to the "shepherd." He also seeks to impress upon the youngster that he is a wealthy, well-connected man with children in Crete: a warning that there are people who will avenge him if harm befalls him. Odysseus portrays himself as a dangerous man who has ambushed and killed someone who tried to rob him (as the shepherd might be tempted to do), a man who was the fastest runner of all. The detail is well calculated. Odysseus recalls how fleetness of foot is cherished among the young (8.120–23), and how his appearance does not strike youngsters as athletic (8.159–64). To offset any advantage the shepherd might imagine he holds, Odysseus points out that such superiority did not help a previous robber, who, he implies, was faster than the shepherd appears to be.

Odysseus's response is a mixture of disguise and disclosure. If word of his arrival should spread, the rumor will be that a wealthy, well-established warrior from Crete, a veteran of Troy, has arrived. No one should hope to steal his treasures and get away without being punished. Of course, anyone interested in news of Odysseus would want to seek him out.

Critical to the strategy of Homer's muse is that she not only calls Odysseus's narrative to the disguised Athena a lie, but has Athena, when she reveals her identity, also insist it is a lie—even though she, in Alcinous's manner, does so while praising his skill as a liar. Muse and goddess combine to do to us what Odysseus has done to the putative shepherd. They induce us to accept, by reminders of help rendered in Phaeacia (13.302, 322, 341–43), the improbable stories of Odysseus's adventures as if they were true: that he was indeed among the Phaeacians (whoever they may have been), that he triumphed over monsters of more than Herodotean implausibility.

With the exception of the mythical Phaeacians, virtually no one, not even Herodotus, believed in the existence of one-eyed monsters. The Phaeacians accepted that Cyclopes existed because they were part of their national mythology: they were their pretext for coming to the ageographical Scheria. Lucian, as if predicting later generations' gullibility, warns us in *True History* 1.3 that "the guide and instructor in this sort of imposture is Homer's Odysseus, who tells Alcinous and his court about winds in bags, one-eyed-men, cannibals, and savages, creatures with lots of heads, and the drug-induced metamorphosis of his companions. This the stuff—and there's lots more of it,—is what he used to befuddle the ignorant Phaeacians." Herewith the fundamental irony of the *Odyssey*. Everyone knows there were Phoenicians; when he speaks about them, and other plausible beings and events, however, Odysseus tells "lies," but when he tells of implausible beings and improbable places, he speaks "the truth."

Alcinous is less credulous than we tend to be. He understands, as does Lucian (though he is more polite), that Odysseus's narrative is fictional. Odysseus, says Alcinous, is skilled at the "shaping of words" (*morphē epeōn*), the ability to fashion a convincing tale (11.367). That shaping makes lies fiction (and thus noble rather than ignoble): hence Alcinous's reference to Odysseus's *phrenes esthlai,* his noble intent (11.367). Greek *alētheia,* we recall, is not so much our "truth" as the notion that something "does not elude." Hence the eternal problem of the narrator, whose words, if they are to have effect, not only must show that things have not eluded him but narrate them in such a way that they do not elude his audience. In such a scenario, our notion of truth is simply irrelevant.

What we see in Odysseus's encounter with the disguised Athena is characteristic of his self-narration when he returns to Ithaca. He routinely replaces the Phaeacians and other mythic peoples he has encountered with Phoenicians and Egyptians, with peoples within the range of experience and credibility not only of a shepherd (13. 256–86), but of a swineherd (14.199–359), of suitors (17.415–44), and of his wife (19.165–203). He shapes his narrative differently on each occasion to suit each particular "audience" and situation. To all except the suitors he represents himself as a Cretan (a native of a land proverbial for its liars in later Greek tradition), elevating his social status in each successive narrative, and always associating himself with the Cretan king Idomeneus. The link with Idomeneus is noteworthy. Nestor tells Telemachus that Idomeneus lost not a single man from his forces on the way home (*Odyssey* 3.191–92). If Nestor is right, there could hardly be a greater contrast between Idomeneus and Odysseus, who lost all of his men. Yet, as we shall see, Odysseus depicts his relationship with Idomeneus differently in each of his "Cretan" narratives.

The Cretan Odysseus: Phase II

Odysseus also presents himself to Eumaeus as a Cretan and the illegitimate son of a wealthy man and a concubine:

> I declare that my family line is from broad Crete; I am the son of a wealthy man; and many other sons were born and bred in his halls, legitimate sons by his wife; however, the mother that bore me was a concubine, but Castor, son of Hylax, who I declare was my father, honored me as equal to his legitimate sons. Then he was honored as a god among the Cretans in the land because of his possessions, his wealth, and his glorious sons. But the apportioners of death came and carried him away to the house of Hades; and his proud sons divided his estate among themselves. To me they gave a small portion, and allotted a dwelling. (14.199–210)

Thanks to personal valor, he improved his fortunes by marrying a wealthy woman. He was never a family man, however, and did not enjoy the mundane life of a farmer but preferred to wage war far from home and, before embarking for Troy, led his troops nine times in ship-borne attacks against foreign peoples. He amassed thereby a great fortune and became so respected among the Cretans that they asked him to join their king Idomeneus at the head of their contingent to Troy:

> They urged me and glorious Idomeneus to lead the ships to Troy; and there was no contrivance available to refuse, for the voice of the people was adamant. (14.235–39)

He thus advances from the role of Idomeneus's rival to that of Idomeneus's equal in military stature and prestige and removes any suggestion of evildoing on his own part. He is not the murderer of a king's son and the ambusher of a robber. There is no sense here that Odysseus feels threatened by, and therefore needs to threaten, the person he is now addressing. What is puzzling, however, is his assertion that there was "no contrivance [*mēchos*] to refuse, for the voice of the people was adamant" (14.238–39). In view of what he says about his zeal for fighting overseas and his lack of interest in staying at home farming, the idea that he wanted to avoid service at Troy makes no sense.

The remark may, rather, allude to Odysseus's famous contrivance, not mentioned in the *Iliad* or *Odyssey*, of feigning madness and tilling his fields obsessively to avoid joining the Trojan expedition. Only when the infant Telemachus was placed in the path of his plow, the tradition runs, did Odysseus cease plowing and accompany the recruiters. The word *mēchos*, which he uses to describe his unspecified scheming here, though rare in the epic, is etymologically connected with and evocative of *mēchanē*, "contrivance" or "plotting," the defining element in one of Odysseus's most common epithets: *polymēchanos*, "man of many devices."[12]

If, as we shall see, there are other elements in Odysseus's early communications with Eumaeus that suggest he is trying to prompt the latter to recognize him without actually revealing too much too directly, then the purpose of this contradictory comment may be precisely to trigger Eumaeus's recollections of the "plowing trick" from earlier days and thus nudge him toward grasping his identity.

Yet there is a warning, or perhaps a word of encouragement, for Eumaeus here—since the swineherd has prospered during Odysseus's absence. Teiresias, we recall, has predicted that Odysseus will not stay long in Ithaca after his return there—and Odysseus seems prepared to set forth again shortly after he has slaughtered the suitors. So when he alludes here to his dislike of farming and his haste to leave home again after returning from Troy, he is pointing out that he is not a man of the land (as Eumaeus is) and will not stay around after he has reclaimed his home and estates. Eumaeus will be on his own again.

Odysseus's allusion to the month at home before he resumed his travels is important for another reason too. It reconciles his Idomenean identity with the tradition that the Cretan expedition returned from Troy intact. His men, all of whom are lost, were, he says, eventually killed in Egypt. In fact, he saved his own life only by begging the Egyptian king for mercy and gaining his protection (14.235–84). He spent seven years in Egypt reamassing great treasures (14.285–86). But in the seventh year, he sailed with a Phoenician to Phoenicia where he spent a year before being sent on a ship bound for Libya. The same Phoenician gave "lying counsels so that I should convey cargo with him, but in truth that when there he would sell me and get a vast price" (14.295–96). The ship, however, was destroyed en route, and Odysseus eventually arrived among the Thesprotians (14.315), a people who live not far from Ithaca. There King Pheidon, whose name means "sparing," looked after him as his own and gave him clothing—a mantle and a tunic—and sent him home. It was there in Thesprotia (in Epirus), he says, that he heard that Odysseus (whom he had met earlier at the wall of Troy) was on his way home with enough loot for ten generations. But the Thesprotian sailors who conveyed him planned, as the Phoenician did earlier, to enslave him. He escaped them by swimming and hiding.

In contrast to what he told the disguised Athena, Odysseus here represents the sailors who transported him as untrustworthy and dishonest. He also abandons his pose as killer of Idomeneus's son, Orchilochus. Why these changes? To suggest they are the random inconsistencies of an inventive liar is to accord both Odysseus and his muse little credit and to dismiss the conflicting statements without examining their possible intentionality. Odysseus is a schemer. We must see what indications of schematic purpose subtend these adjustments.

Aristotle argued that what is persuasive, *to pithanon,* is what is persuasive, *pithanon,* to a particular person (*tini*). So let us consider what the Muse's external audience might think it knows about Odysseus's return from other versions of the myth.[13] Odysseus's allusion to his return from Thesprotia in Epirus might trigger reminiscences of other accounts of the hero's homecoming, such as those found in Sophocles' lost *Euryalus* and his fragmentary *Niptra* and *Odysseus Acanthoplex.* The English-speaking reader will find them most conveniently summarized in D. Sutton's *Lost Sophocles.* In this tradition, Odysseus arrives in Ithaca from Thesprotia in Epirus rather than from Phaeacia. While in Epirus he seduced Euippe (or Callidice), the daughter of his host, Tyrimmas, and had a child, Euryalus, by her. Euippe eventually sent her son in search of his father, but the boy, unfortunately, arrived when Odysseus was away, and Penelope, unhappy at his presence, tricked Odysseus into killing him on his return on the grounds that Euryalus was plotting against him. Further, while Odysseus was returning from Thesprotia, another illegitimate son, Telegonus, came in search of him and inadvertently killed him.[14]

By setting the tradition of Odysseus's return from Thesprotia in the context of Odysseus's "lies," his Cretan fictions, the Muse acknowledges its existence in a backhanded kind of way and, simultaneously, shunts it aside.

While the Muse is persuading the external audience to dismiss the Thesprotian tradition as fiction—with resounding and general success—she has Odysseus further undermine its credibility by integrating it into the fictional Cretan persona he adopts in Ithaca. At the same time, if the Phaeacians are the Muse's fictions, there is a countervailing rhetorical dilemma to be faced in presenting internal, Ithacan audiences with an identity based on residence among a people no one (other than the external audience) has previously heard of. With the most astonishing rhetorical dexterity, then, Muse and hero convince us that the Phaeacians are real and that Odysseus's residence among the Thesprotians and Cretans is a lie. The Homeric text convinces both the internal and the external audiences of opposing notions at the same time.

Nor is this the limit of the Muse's achievement. Each of Odysseus's Cretan tales and the situations in which the addresses are made take into account not only the Ithacan—that is, the mythically traditional—environment of the later books, but the particular response to be elicited from the specific individual to whom the tale is addressed. As noted, Odysseus feels threatened by, and therefore obliged to generate a menacing persona in his conversation with, the disguised Athena. He has only just awoken, he is alone, he does not recognize his interlocutor, and he does not know where he is. When he is with Eumaeus, however, he is fully alert, though still alone. He does recognize his interlocutor and knows exactly where he is. Even more to the point, there is nothing in any way threatening about Eumaeus's demeanor. On the contrary, the swineherd has just saved him from being mauled, possibly even killed, by a pack of dogs.

Odysseus's narrative, therefore, needs not offer counterthreats, since there are no threats to answer. And, since he has already learned of the special affection of Eumaeus for Telemachus, it would do much more damage than good to describe himself as the killer of a king's son (even if he had actually killed a king's son). To mention to Eumaeus the murder of Orsilochus would be, to say the least, rhetorically ill-advised.

The different representation of the sailors raises a more complex problem. Why should it make any difference to Odysseus's rhetorical effect on Eumaeus whether the sailors are trustworthy (as he indicates to the disguised Athena) or untrustworthy (as he indicates to Eumaeus)? Is there anything in Odysseus's knowledge of Eumaeus that might prompt him to make the seamen of his Cretan narrative unreliable rather than reliable? At first, the answer seems to be negative. But, there again, we do not, at this stage, have sufficient knowledge of Eumaeus's background to be sure. The light dawns only after we hear Eumaeus's account of his own life story, which we will explore in Chapter 9. Its "truth" or "falsehood" is, on the whole, irrelevant. In all likelihood it is a blend of fiction and fact (in whatever proportions you wish) which Odysseus has probably heard before he left for Troy. There is no reason to suppose that he was utterly unfamiliar with Eumaeus's life story, however fictionalized it was.

The idea that Odysseus tailors his Cretan narrative to each specific listener for a specific purpose should not strike the reader as in any way strange or anomalous, even though this particular rhetorical dimension of his presentation has drawn too little scholarly comment. It would be far more surprising if Odysseus were to maintain a consistent persona in his interactions with the shepherd, Eumaeus, and Penelope. His stories have a purpose beyond providing information or disinformation, as do those of Menelaus, who manages his tale of Odysseus in the Trojan horse to Helen's rhetorical disadvantage. Carl Trahmann showed in an important article over forty years ago that Odysseus's lies are purposeful and that they change according to the audience Odysseus is addressing. He saw Odysseus's familiarity with Eumaeus's past as a reason for his portrayal of the Phoenicians as scoundrels and argues, to our mind convincingly, that the *Odyssey* has a unity "far subtler than unity of plot construction."[15]

The setting of the third phase of Odysseus's Cretan identity—the version he narrates to Penelope—involves a more detailed examination of circumstances than we can offer at this point. We will therefore defer it until our discussion of Penelope. By way of preliminary comment, however, we might note that the so-called Cretan lies are a series of interconnected and powerful narrative devices of self-presentation, adjusted to suit the specific situation and the specific interlocutor. Through them Odysseus seeks not so much to seal off his identity from detection, but to provide a credible facade which he can make as opaque or transparent as he wants it to be. They well illustrate Demetrius's "formidable" style, where the listener is encouraged to search beneath what is said for that which lurks unsaid or half-said. Or to reecho Quintilian: the judge is always more persuaded by what he thinks he has discovered for himself despite our attempts to cover it up. The whole point of revelation is that what is to be revealed must first be concealed, to catch the audience's attention.

Odysseus's Cretan tales, then, are no more or less lies or truth than his tales to the Phaeacians. His goal is not to adhere to any particular series of facts, but to convince his listeners of his reliability, resolve, and truthfulness. To be considered truthful, paradoxically, one must sometimes tell lies—when one suspects that presenting the raw truth (whatever that is) will bring doubts rather than conviction to the listener who is to be persuaded. It is, as Alcinous grasps, the *intent* of the narrator not the *factuality* of his narration that determines its truthfulness. What Odysseus's "real" adventures were and where he "really" spent the ten years after the Trojan War are not only unknowable but irrelevant. One of the reasons, we suspect, that Odysseus generally takes so long to identify himself in almost any situation is that he knows how complex the process of recognition is and how dangerous it is to be known by others before both you and they have had a chance to assess one another.

In Ithaca, Odysseus needs Eumaeus and Penelope more than they need him. Eumaeus certainly seems to dine well and to stay warm. Penelope has the option of marrying someone else, someone young and powerful. Only Telemachus stands to lose personally if Odysseus does not return. So it is no surprise that he is the first person to whom Odysseus fully discloses his identity, even though the skeptical Telemachus has no possible basis for recognizing Odysseus.

[8]

First Encounters with Eumaeus

No formal recognition and acknowledgment between Odysseus and Eumaeus occurs until *Odyssey* 21, even though the two men have been in close contact and companionship from their meeting seven books earlier. The formal acknowledgment of Odysseus by Penelope is similarly slow. She first comments on Odysseus's presence in 17. 511 but does not acknowledge him as her husband until book 23, after all the suitors have been killed. In each case, the groundwork is meticulously prepared. As we will see, understanding of each other by the parties concerned grows steadily throughout their interchanges. Curiously enough, the speed with which acknowledgment occurs in the *Odyssey* tends to be in inverse proportion to the amount of prior association. With Telemachus, who has no real basis for recognizing Odysseus, the process is almost perfunctory in its swiftness. Such is also the case with the cowherd Philoetius. The only exception to this generalization is Eurycleia, who recognizes Odysseus by his hunting scar and provokes from him an almost murderous reaction.

The contrast between Odysseus's caution in his treatment of Eumaeus and the speed with which he accepts Philoetius is especially remarkable, since both are herdsmen with strong ties to the family estate. Odysseus formally discloses his identity to Eumaeus just before the contest of the bow. And he does so in Philoetius's presence, even though Philoetius has made his first appearance in the epic as recently as 20.185. The major difference in status between the two herdsmen is that Philoetius is, it would appear, a free man, who feels it within his discretion to leave Ithaca and take service elsewhere (20.222–25), whereas Eumaeus is Laertes' slave. If Philoetius allies himself with Odysseus, then, it is a matter of his free choice. For Eumaeus, it is a matter of more complex obligation. Philoetius differs from Eumaeus not only in status but in general demeanor. His most notable characteristic is his immediate outspokenness and candor. Arriving fresh on the scene, he instantly and vocally sympathizes with the plight of the disguised Odysseus, who, he declares, shows signs of nobility through his rags and stirs memories of his benefactor Odysseus. He inveighs against the malice of the gods in general and of Zeus in particular and forthrightly expresses his resentment of the parasitic suitors and the way Telemachus is treated. The only thing that has made him remain in Ithaca instead of seeking service elsewhere is the hope that Odysseus will return. When the disguised Odysseus promises that Philoetius will have the chance to see the suitors dead, the latter exclaims:

> Stranger, if only the son of Cronos would fulfill this word of yours. Then you would know the quality of my strength, and my hands would follow suit. (20.236–37)

Philoetius's unqualified enthusiasm immediately wins Odysseus's confidence. The cowherd, who is rather younger than Odysseus, has in no sense been financially impoverished by the prevailing situation in Ithaca. He has nothing apparently to gain, and a great deal to lose, by expressing overt disapproval of the suitors. His actions are guided by principle rather than self-interest, and Odysseus takes Philoetius totally on trust—something he does with no one else in the *Odyssey.* Why does he not do the same with Eumaeus, whose loyalty is never overtly questioned?

The Canny Eumaeus

Odysseus's closest encounter with death on his return to Ithaca occurs when he is approaching Eumaeus's hut and is attacked by the swineherd's dogs. It is Eumaeus's intervention that saves him from, at the very least, a savage mauling. We might expect, following this incident, that Eumaeus will quickly earn the confidence of the cautious hero. Indeed, the Muse, by means of various devices, including verbal echoes, prepares us for an instant resumption of old ties between the two men even before Eumaeus comes to the rescue. When Eumaeus's dogs are about to attack, for instance, the Muse says: "But Odysseus in his shrewdness [*kerdosynē*] sat down" (14.30–31).

The use of *kerdosynē* not only reminds us of Odysseus's resourcefulness, ingenuity, and shrewdness but hints at the motif of recognition. Its only other occurrence in Homer is in Helen's tale about her recognition of Odysseus when he entered Troy disguised as a beggar. Helen claims she alone recognized and questioned him, but that, in his *shrewdness,* he sought to avoid her (4.251). The noun *kerdosynē,* then, occurs in association with the penetrability of Odysseus's disguise. Moreover, words derived from the base *kerd-* occur in every scene in which Odysseus is recognized through his disguise. Alcinous tells him not to hide his identity with *noēmasi kerdaleoisin,* "crafty thoughts," and proceeds to inquire (and obtain an answer) as to who he really is (8.548–49). When Odysseus tries to hide his identity from the disguised Athena, the Muse remarks on his employment of *polykerdea,* "much cunning" (13.255). Similarly, when Eurycleia tells Penelope she recognized Odysseus in the bath, she adds: "In his great shrewdness [*polykerdeiēsi*] he would not permit me to speak" (23.77). Finally, when Odysseus reveals himself to Penelope, she accuses him of *kaka kerdea,* "wicked cunning" (23.217). Words from the base *kerd-* are important to our understanding of the process of recognition, as we shall see shortly. But they are not the only verbal clues prompting us to expect quick recognition between master and swineherd.[1]

Eumaeus's first address to Odysseus is introduced by the words "and he addressed his lord [*anakta*]" (14.36). The listener hesitates for an instant as to whether these words are merely the Muse's editorial comment or whether they suggest that Eumaeus addresses Odysseus as his master.[2] After all, the listener learns from Athena that the disguise she provides for the hero will fool Penelope, Telemachus, and the suitors—though it is not perfectly successful in this regard. But nothing is said of its potential effect on Eumaeus, even though the goddess mentions him right after her prediction (13.402–5).[3] Eumaeus is no less *kerdaleos* than his master, no less ready to play the cautious, waiting game.

There are glimmerings in Eumaeus's own response to the stranger which suggest he sees resemblance between the stranger he rescues and his long-lost master. His opening words offer a rather startling "double take." "Old man," he says, "the dogs almost tore you apart and you'd have caused [*katecheuas*] me to get a bad name. And indeed the gods have given me other troubles and reasons to groan; for I, tearful and groaning [*acheuon*], await my godlike master" (14.37–40). Eumaeus's reaction is not just to the folly of his aged visitor, but to the damage his own reputation would suffer if someone were mauled on his premises. Yet he almost instantly changes course and comments on the godlike master whose absence grieves him. The shift in attitude is captured by the verbal similarity between *katecheuas* ("you poured <censure> down on me," 14.38) and *acheuon* ("groaning," 14.40).

It is noteworthy that Eumaeus relates, in the second sentence after he has set his eyes on the stranger, the misfortunes of Odysseus's household, without being asked or in any way encouraged to do so:

> . . . while I rear fat swine for other men to eat, while he is wandering searching for food round the land and city of some men of foreign speech, if indeed he still lives and sees the light of the sun. (14.41–44)

The only parallel in the *Odyssey* for a host's disclosure of the misfortunes or blessings of his house before asking the stranger to identify himself occurs when Telemachus apologizes to the disguised Athena for the suitors' conduct, which necessitates his seating her apart from them (1.132–34, 158–68).[4] We could, of course, be witnessing a phenomenon noted by students of modern Greek society: the greater willingness to entrust a secret to a casual passerby than to a relative or neighbor (who may, of course, use it against one).[5] It is perfectly sensible behavior, especially in a small community. But to be so open on one's very first encounter is more peculiar.

Eumaeus, his response more friendly and discursive than in his first comments, adds that his godlike master is probably wandering the earth hungry, then invites his wanderer-visitor into his hut for food, wine, and an opportunity to tell his story. Odysseus's thanks take the form of a benediction: "Stranger, may Zeus and the rest of the gods reward you with what you want most" (14.53–54) It will not be long before he finds out what Eumaeus wants most, for, as Odysseus enters the swineherd's hut, Eumaeus makes a lengthy speech, the content of which we will now examine.

Eumaeus follows Odysseus in using the appellation *xeine,* "stranger, guest, host," to redefine their relationship. He addresses the supposed beggar, whom he had, at first, simply called "old man," with qualified deference and respect:

> Stranger, it is not right for me, even if someone more lowly than you would have come, to slander a stranger. All strangers and beggars are from Zeus, and a gift though small is dear from us, for that is the way for those of us who are servants, ever filled with fear when ruled by masters who are young [*neoi*]. (14.56–61)

"Wretched as you are," Eumaeus is saying, "I'd look after you even if you were worse." But the next statement sets an immediate limit on what he is prepared to do. His proclaimed adherence to Zeus's laws might not be total. The adjective *neoi,* which Eumaeus uses to describe his masters, means "new"—primarily in the sense of "young." If we take it, as Stanford does, both as a general allusion to the proverbial harshness of young masters and as a specific allusion to Telemachus's harshness, we will find no shortage of indications later in the epic to justify such a view of Odysseus's son. There is no punishment that the women slaves think Telemachus incapable of contriving (18.338–42), and events prove their suspicions are well founded. Telemachus does not like to see the maids consorting with the suitors. Yet, since the suitors themselves are both new and, on the whole, youthful, we should not exclude them from Eumaeus's picture either, for he is, however reluctantly, collaborating with their occupation of Odysseus's house.

In these remarks of Eumaeus, Odysseus would find no expression of resolve like that later expressed by Philoetius. Eumaeus wants it to be known that he is both cautious and fearful, as if to say to his visitor: "I am only a slave. I am afraid of my new masters. I cannot be held wholly to account." He would have needed to rehearse such an explanation in the event that Odysseus returned. His use of it now, combined with the other indications he gives that he is constantly adjusting his approach to the stranger, suggest he has at least an inkling that the person he saved from the dogs might be Odysseus.

Eumaeus underscores, at first, not the extent of his collaboration with the suitors, but how he lives as best he can in accordance with the hospitable traditions of Odysseus's household, of which we see much in the *Odyssey* (14.388–89, 402–6). Similarly, Penelope and Telemachus not only tacitly allow the disguised Odysseus into their home but also provide him with the necessities of life (16.44–45; cf. 1.119–20). Eumaeus, however, makes it clear that Odysseus's household is his household too by using the first person plural of the possessive, "our" (14.59). And he clearly expects an even more personal interest in it in the future, as he enumerates the rewards he expects from Odysseus upon his return:

> For indeed the gods have stayed the return of the man who would have loved me now with all his heart, and would have given me possessions, such things as a kind master usually gives: a house, piece of land, and a wife courted by many. He who toils much, god makes his labor prosper, as this labor of mine to which I pay attention prospers. Therefore my master would have rewarded me richly, if he had grown old here at home. (14.61–67)

The rewards described here are precisely the rewards Odysseus promises Eumaeus and Philoetius later at his formal self-revelation in 21.214–16. Like the greeting that preceded it, this codicil makes most sense if we assume Eumaeus has guessed he is addressing, if not Odysseus himself, at least an emissary from Odysseus. His wish list looks like a statement of his terms for risking the wrath of the "young masters."

Eumaeus's skill in covert allusion is less surprising when we note that he detects, or thinks he detects, in Odysseus's words, much the same sort of oblique request. Odysseus's mention of the cloak he was supposedly given during his travels prompts the offer of a cloak from Eumaeus, even though Odysseus has made no direct request to that effect. As in modern diplomacy, where governments negotiate terms with each other before according official recognition, so too do Odysseus and Eumaeus. Both parties must feel satisfied with the terms. But negotations would never have opened had the parties not, in normal, nondiplomatic parlance, really recognized each other beforehand.

Along with his wish list, Eumaeus accounts for his stewardship during Odysseus's absence. The Muse has already said he has built a big outer court for himself and his swine with huge stones and a coping of thorn on top of it. From the outside he has secured the court by poles. Inside the court he has built twelve sties for the swine. And he did all this "without the knowledge of his mistress and the old man Laertes" (14.9). He has also bought a personal slave without the knowledge of Penelope or Laertes (14.449–51). While no Trimalchio, he has not ignored his own interests while serving his master's (and those of the suitors, who have been well supplied with pork). One might even argue that he has taken advantage of his master's absence and the consequent lack of supervision. Eumaeus is resourceful, he is *kerdaleos,* as he himself attests: a man who knows how to use opportunities when they arise.[6]

Words derived from the base *kerd-* are employed by the Odyssean muse in a calculated and sparing manner and applied exclusively to Odysseus's family, household, and sponsoring deity when there is some reason for distrust or suspicion. Although most often used of Odysseus, they are also used of Athena and Penelope. Odysseus obviously does not completely trust Athena, who vouched for Eumaeus's good disposition toward him (13.405). He feels he must handle her with care. Similarly, he guards his secrets from Penelope, though Agamemnon's ghost, Anticleia, and Athena all assure him of Penelope's fidelity (11.181–82, 444–46; 13.336–37, 378–81). Among Odysseus's dependents, only Philoetius and Telemachus earn his complete and unconditional trust. Remarkably, no *kerd*-based words are used of Philoetius; and Telemachus is upbraided by Penelope for *not* wielding *kerdea,* although as a child he used to demonstrate resourcefulness (18.215–16).[7]

Odysseus's reluctance to trust people is usually explained as a generic result of his suspicious nature.[8] In fact, he is most distrustful of those he knows resemble him in their capacity to turn a situation to advantage. By the same token, people like himself, if they intend to survive—and surviving in Odysseus's company is itself a heroic accomplishment—must approach him with caution. Eumaeus and Penelope are resourceful. They understand that if he returns in his classic disguise as a beggar (penetrated, so she claims, at an earlier stage, by Helen) he has an advantage over them. While he may not be able to kill all the suitors, he has the ability to dispose of those members of his household he thinks have betrayed him. To protect themselves, they resort to the only disguise they have available: disguise of their recognition of him. Such disguise enables them to do two things. First, they are able to maintain a technically superior position to Odysseus, since he is, by all appearances, a beggar, and they have a fixed status in the social structure of the island. Second, they can use the pose of nonrecognition as a means of demonstrating their loyalty to a master who is "still missing and probably dead."

Competing with the master of *kerdea* is an immense strain. Penelope needs Athena's help to avoid being compelled to acknowledge Odysseus too early. Eumaeus manages better than Penelope because he has more to gain than she does by Odysseus's return. From the first encounter between master and swineherd, the Muse demonstrates why Odysseus is apprehensive and cautious in his dealings with his slave, but leaves us to determine the reasons for the slave's caution in dealing with his master. Odysseus has known Eumaeus for many years and is, in effect, his older brother (*ētheion*), or very close friend, since Eumaeus was raised in the family along with Odysseus's younger sister, Ctimene. Eumaeus can help or to harm Odysseus more than most others precisely because of their closeness. Thus Eumaeus's comment about his fear of new masters in the household reminds Odysseus not only of the difficulties the household is experiencing, but of the damage Eumaeus could cause if his courage failed. He could, under duress, inform the suitors of Odysseus's arrival, for instance, much as he has fed them over the years. Eumaeus's reminder is, in its own way, something of a threat.

Disguise and Appearance

The more Odysseus resembles the man he was when he left, the more likely Eumaeus is to give overt recognition. Grasping this, Athena changes Odysseus's appearance before he enters Eumaeus's courtyard:

> Athena touched him with her wand. She withered the fair skin on his limbs and destroyed the yellow hair on his head; all about him she put the skin of an ancient old man. She made dim and dark his eyes that were beautiful before. (13.429–33)

She also clothes him in a ragged cloak and tunic and a deerhide stripped of hair. He picks up a staff and a wallet full of holes slung by a twisted cord. In this attire and appearance, Odysseus is seen by Penelope, Eurycleia, and Philoetius. Remarkably, for all this secrecy and disguise, the Muse implies on several occasions that inductive recognition is possible. Time, after all, would itself produce some of the effects achieved by

Athena's wand. Yet Penelope, Eurycleia, and Philoetius are all immediately struck either by the beggar's similarity to Odysseus or by his princely demeanor. Penelope orders Eurycleia to wash her master's "contemporary" and notes in his presence: "Odysseus must by this time have the same hands and feet as he does" (19.358–59). Eurycleia observes as she is about to bathe the beggar: "Many exhausted strangers have come here, but I declare I have never seen one as like as you are to Odysseus in form, voice, and feet" (19.379–81). Even Philoetius, never particularly close to Odysseus before his departure, compares the beggar's form to that of a royal prince (20.194). Cold sweat covered him when he saw him, he says, since he was immediately reminded of his long-absent master (20.204). Odysseus's awareness that his disguise can be penetrated is, at least partially, the reason he presents himself to Penelope after sunset, when she and others would have a harder time making out his features with certainty (17.570, 582).

Similarly, Odysseus worries that Eumaeus may see through his rags and notice the physique of the man lurking behind them. His anxiety here is complex. Though still strong, his physical strength is not always evident to others even when neither he nor Athena is making an attempt to disguise it. When among the Phaeacians, Euryalus and other youths find him unimpressive. He does not strike them as an athlete until he demonstrates, by hurling the discus, that appearances deceive. And even as he disguises his identity before Eumaeus, he declares his prowess undiminished, even if his looks suggest it is: as a youth he married a wealthy wife despite the meager possessions his brother allowed him. He explains that the marriage came about

> because of my valor, since I was not a weakling, nor a coward in war; now indeed all of this is gone. I think, in fact, that you can still perceive the stubble [i.e., the relics] of my former strength. For misery came upon me in abundance. (14.212–15)

Odysseus is saying two opposing things at once: "I am not the man I used to be" and "Don't underrate me utterly." He will have to fight for his inheritance, as he and Eumaeus both know. He cannot, therefore, so present himself that the swineherd will dismiss him as the shadow of a great name and think him no match for the suitors. For his part, Eumaeus withholds acknowledgment until he ascertains whether what is left of Odysseus is up to the tasks awaiting him.

Unlike others who knew Odysseus prior to his departure, Eumaeus never comments on the beggar's resemblance to Odysseus, though he was closer to his master than the other slaves and thus more likely to notice such similarity. Eumaeus is more likely suppressing, either consciously or subconsciously, recognition of Odysseus than failing to recognize him.[9] We think the recognition is conscious. Cedric Whitman's statement that Odysseus starts his self-revelation with the lower ranks but not with Eumaeus is true only to the extent that master and swineherd treat each other with amicable caution.[10] Eumaeus, who spends three days with Odysseus in his hut, has ample opportunity to recognize him.[11]

In Eumaeus's Hut

Eumaeus proceeds, once he has taken the beggar under his wing, to behave and to speak with increasing deference and consideration. In giving Odysseus a detailed account of the suitors' exploitation of the household, he provides important information and uses the occasion to reiterate his deep affection for his master. Given his expressed fear of the young (new) masters, such an overt statement of his devotion could be troublesome. A vagabond might report such remarks to the suitors and jeopardize Eumaeus's standing. Eumaeus trusts that his visitor will not report what passes between them to hostile ears.

Odysseus himself, while in Eumaeus's hut, alternately, and sometimes simultaneously, hints at his identity and denies it, depending on the extent to which Eumaeus indicates that he has guessed or suspected his identity, as if testing the swineherd's reactions and measuring his responses. In response to Eumaeus's complaint that his master will never return, Odysseus answers on oath and insists, ironically, that deceitful tales are hateful to him (14.151–64). On the surface, he tells Eumaeus a deceitful tale—that Odysseus *will* return—implying that he has not yet come back. But his statement that Odysseus "is in the very process of returning" (14.152) is in the present tense, not the future.[12] Eumaeus wavers momentarily and suggests they leave the subject of his master and turn to other matters (14.168–70). Yet in the next verse he returns to that very subject, claiming that, along with Penelope, Laertes, and Telemachus, he wishes Odysseus would return. There is, then, tension between what Eumaeus says he is going to do and what he does. Eumaeus goes on to complete his account of the suitors' misconduct and informs his hearer of their scheme to kill Telemachus and bring an end to Odysseus's line (14.179–84). Such information might indeed be expected to produce some overt reaction if the beggar is indeed Odysseus. It gives Odysseus another chance to reveal himself and could well be, as are Menelaus's remarks about Odysseus to Telemachus in *Odyssey* 4, a prompt to such revelation.

The beggar's unemotional response to Eumaeus is simply that he has heard Odysseus is returning either "openly or in secret" (14.321–30). Though telling the swineherd not to worry, he is clearly unready to reveal himself openly. Henceforth Eumaeus's failure to acknowledge Odysseus may be as much a ploy to inspire his master's confidence in his ability to keep a secret as to protect himself and his welfare.[13] Inopportune acknowledgment can be fatal. Argus, who acknowledges his master in his canine way, dies before he can strip Odysseus of his disguise; Eurycleia, later, almost loses her life when she blurts out her recognition (19.479–81). Odysseus wants to have his cake and eat it too. If he does not wish to be recognized, he should insist on being bathed by a young handmaiden, not by his old nurse. Similarly, if he wants anonymity in Ithaca, he should seek shelter with someone who does not know him, not Eumaeus. Clearly, Odysseus wants recognition, but not acknowledgment.

When Eumaeus says he does not believe Odysseus will return so soon and abstains from further probing of the beggar's identity, he shows he has taken the hint. In fact, he pushes matters to the opposite extreme by telling of a bad experience he had with a lying Aetolian who claimed to have seen Odysseus in Idomeneus's house and had declared Odysseus would be back by harvesttime (14.361–89). The incident is probably Eumaeus's invention. No one else mentions a recent Aetolian visitor, and the tale does not correspond fully with Odysseus's (or the Muse's) tales of travel. However, it does intersect with Odysseus's *Cretan* adventures and places the alleged informant just down the coast from Odysseus's Thesprotian, Epirote king, Pheidon. Eumaeus does not call Odysseus a liar, but he calls someone who told a similar story a liar.

There lurks within the text of Eumaeus's yarn about the Aetolian an implicit question concerning the major differences between what the Aetolian says and what the beggar says. The Odysseus Eumaeus mentions is repairing his ships and has his godlike companions with him. Eumaeus is either challenging the contention that Odysseus will return alone, implicit in the beggar's Cretan narrative, or suggesting that if the beggar is right, what can be done on his return will be severely limited.

How we construe Eumaeus's purpose in this fabrication depends on what we think he has deduced. If Eumaeus does not recognize his visitor, then he is dismissing, with oblique slyness, what Odysseus has told him. If Eumaeus has recognized him but has felt rebuffed in his efforts to prompt his visitor to self-disclosure, he is saying that he knows Odysseus is lying and challenges him to explain how he differs from the Aetolian.

The Language of Manipulation

The manipulative power of language is, virtually, the central theme of the *Odyssey*. Language charms, as the Homeric muse shows by her persistent use of words with the base *thelg-*, "beguile," which are deployed almost exclusively in connection with Odysseus, the master of verbal craft, and in a variety of contexts.[14] Calypso tries to beguile him with words (1.56–57), Circe is unable to beguile him with herbs as she beguiles others (10.212–13, 290–91, 317–18), the Sirens try to beguile him with their voice and song (12.39–40, 43–44), Telemachus claims his father is but a *daimon* (a divine spirit) who tries to beguile him (16.194–95), Odysseus promises Telemachus that Athena and Zeus will beguile the suitors' minds in battle (16.297–98), Eumaeus tells Penelope the stranger has beguiled his heart with his stories (17.513–14, 520–21), and Odysseus rejoices that Penelope has beguiled the souls of the suitors by setting up the bow contest and requesting gifts (18.281–82).

The base *thelg-* suggests the utter emotive helplessness of the person beguiled and his consequent inability to exercise rational judgment. Like Hermes' beguiling wand, such beguilement can make one sleep or wake up. Resistance to its power is beyond human will.[15] Whoever listens to the Sirens, even Odysseus himself, gives up all plans and stays to listen forever unless physically restrained from doing so. Telemachus, who is not so restrained, cannot fight his inner wish to believe his father has returned, although there is no logical or critical proof that the stranger is, in fact, his father.[16] The secret of beguilement is in the content and arrangement of words—their rhetorical force. Its persuasive force lies in the listener's obsession with (or desire to believe) what is said.

Like the English "beguile," *thelg-* is suggestive of lies, deceit, or the insinuation of ideas that are not in the best interests of those on whom the beguilement is exercised. Subtending most uses is the sense of seduction and flattery. The beguiler uses the desires or vanity of the victim against him, as the Sirens beguile Odysseus's ears by telling him stories about the Trojan War. Even a master of rhetoric such as Cicero fears the attack of the beguiling flatterer. Flattery is a kind of aggression; he who succumbs to it looks stupid in the eyes of others:

> There is no one who does not see *open* adulation, except for the man who is entirely out of touch with reality. So one must take very studious care that this shrewd and hidden flatterer does not snake his way into us.[17] (*On Friendship* 99)

We, as listeners and readers of the *Odyssey*, should exercise critical caution before believing all that is said by its beguiling muse and beguiling hero. Eumaeus knows the dangers and tells the beggar: "Do not try to please me or beguile me with lying words" (14.387). What part of Odysseus's tale he is referring to is not clear, since a puritanical judgment would describe almost everything Odysseus says to his listeners as beguiling lies.

Hog Wild

Despite yielding to Odysseus's wish for anonymity, Eumaeus becomes increasingly explicit in oblique expressions of his awareness of the stranger's importance. When Odysseus first arrives, Eumaeus offers him a meal of suckling pig and apologizes for giving him only the "food of slaves," explaining that the suitors eat the fatted hogs (14.81–82). The usual explanation for this improbable meal is to see it as a moment of irony or pathos: the contrast between Odysseus's present lowly position and the lavish banquet a returning hero might expect. But surely a dinner of suckling pig would have been beyond the wildest expectations of most slaves. Presumably a swineherd can get away with slaughtering a newborn piglet, whose existence would not necessarily be inventoried (14.73–84; cf. 14.13–22). Eumaeus is offering, it would apppear, the best dinner he can give.

Yet, following their initial interchanges and Odysseus's narrative, Eumaeus becomes more ambitious in his cuisine. For the second meal he orders his fellow slaves to slaughter the best fat hog for the stranger (14.414–17)—a meal befitting the returning master of the house, and reminiscent of the killing of the fatted calf in the Christian parable of the prodigal son. Similarly, the chine of a white-tusked boar is served to Odysseus in Phaeacia after he mentions he fought at Troy and just before he formally reveals his identity to Alcinous (8.474–76)

White-tusked boars were served only on festive occasions (11.412–15) and, in Ithaca, only to the suitors. Even when Telemachus and Odysseus openly acknowledge each other, they dine only on a year-old boar (16.454). A white-tusked boar would appear in any inventory—and we have already been told that the number of boars was far smaller than the number of female swine because of the suitors' greed (14.16–19). The slaughter of a white-tusked boar would hardly escape an overseer responsible for supplying the suitors' meals, so a slave-swineherd (who, by his own claim, is afraid of the suitors) would be ill advised to slaughter one in honor of a lowly guest unless he had reason to suspect his guest was not as lowly as he appeared. Eumaeus gives Odysseus the best animal he has in the pens and the finest cut of the roast—the long chine. The Muse says this sign of respect "exalted the heart of his master" (14.438).

Odysseus, who notes Eumaeus's stewardship of his part of the estate, never suggests that consumption of the master's swine by slaves and beggars is even less appropriate than their coerced surrender to the suitors. A butler who drinks the best wine in the cellar usually risks his position unless his master is a Trimalchio.[18] To comment negatively on Eumaeus's actions, however, would hardly be in Odysseus's interests, not least because such comment would show he had missed the significance of the swineherd's gesture. Rather than saying Eumaeus is going too far, he marks the swineherd's covert recognition of his status by contending that the good portion he has been offered exceeds what his low status merits:

> Eumeaus, may you be as dear to father Zeus as you are showing me honor now in spite of my condition. (14.440–41)

By offering the disguised beggar the master's portion of the master's finest beast Eumaeus is, as Odysseus realizes, virtually acknowledging his master's presence. And the fact that this feast is served by Eumaeus's secretly acquired personal slave, Mesaulius, adds a bourgeois, Petronian touch to this anomalous banquet in a swineherd's hut.

How can we feel sure there is mutual comprehension in this covert dialogue of signs? In Phaeacia, we recall, Odysseus's attempts to get Alcinous to recognize him by the ploy of weeping and hiding his head in his cloak met with no immediate success because Alcinous had his own reasons for declining to perceive who Odysseus was. Odysseus, however, has no cloak when he arrives home. In fact, Eumaeus tells him Penelope would almost certainly receive him warmly, as she has always received others who claim to have news about Odysseus, if only "someone would give him a cloak and some <decent> clothing" (14.122–32). Odysseus's lack of a cloak, then, has been noticed by Eumaeus and will prevent him from gaining access to the royal presence. But who is the "someone" who will provide the cloak that he needs? The most obvious potential donor is Eumaeus himself, though he does not now volunteer such a costly item.

It is Odysseus who brings up the matter of a cloak when the subject arises a second time. The butler, Mesaulius, has just cleared the table. The swineherd and his guest have had their fill of wine and boar. Then Odysseus tells a story designed to test his companion:

> Odysseus spoke among them, making trial of the swineherd, to see whether he would take off his cloak and give it to him, or tell one of his comrades to do it, since he cared for him so greatly. (14.459–61)

Odysseus does not request a cloak directly, even though the Muse has, rather unusually, explained exactly what his purposes are: to test Eumaeus and obtain a cloak. That is why this passage is of such importance. Established here is something we note again and again in the *Odyssey*: that a narrative of things past is itself only a cloak for bringing up a specific present need or intent. Odysseus wants to determine not only how far Eumaeus will inconvenience himself, but how capable he is of "reading between the lines" of a narrative to decode the request.[19]

Like the emperor Domitian, Odysseus rarely proclaims one thing without leading the listener to anticipate the opposite.[20] "I wish I were," he says, "as strong now as I was when I was young and we were setting up an ambush beneath the walls of Troy" (14.468–69). He, "Odysseus," and Menelaus were, he declares, carrying out their task on a cold, stormy, and snowy night—and he had set out without a cloak. During the third shift, he confessed to "Odysseus," who was near him, that he would probably freeze to death. Odysseus responded by sending a messenger, under the pretext of needing reinforcements, to Agamemnon. The messenger flung aside his cloak as he left, providing the narrator with cover for the night.

Some of Odyseus's rhetorical touches are worth underscoring. Odysseus is, as he speaks, preparing to ambush the suitors in Ithaca just as he and his companions were planning an ambush in his apocryphal Trojan tale. Second, the Odysseus of his narrative devises a means of getting a cloak without exposing the speaker's incompetence to any of his companions or making anyone else cold. The messenger will shed his cloak, and his companion will be protected both from the elements and from losing face. The dilemma is resolved without anyone, friend or foe, being aware that a dilemma existed, apart from "Odysseus" and the narrator.

Odysseus casts Eumaeus not merely in the role of the Odysseus of his story, but of someone even shrewder. The Odysseus of his story has to be told directly that the narrator is freezing before he springs into oblique and covert action. Eumaeus, on the other hand, is asked to decode the need as well as to remedy it. The approach is wonderfully flattering to Eumaeus, who is being asked to outdo his master. What will he do? Strip off his own cloak or make the butler give up his? Eumaeus begins his answer by stating that Odysseus has not in any way stepped out of bounds or discredited himself by his tale— even though the tale is testimony to the narrator's incompetence if taken at face value. And, he adds, this tale will not remain "unprofitable" (*nēkerdes*, once again the base *kerd-*):

> Old man, the story you told is blameless, nor have you uttered an unmannerly or unprofitable word. (14.508–9)

But then Eumaeus spells out *publicly* that he has discerned the covert request for a cloak (which "Odysseus" in the story does not do), and he refers to his guest as a suppliant (thereby putting himself even more ostentatiously than before in the position of the magnanimous host):[21]

> Therefore you will lack neither clothing nor anything else that a sore tired suppliant should receive—for now. But in the morning you will swing around yourself your rags. For there are not many cloaks here or changes of tunics to put on, but there is one for each man. But when

the dear son of Odysseus comes, he himself will give you a cloak to clothe you and will send you wherever your heart and spirit call you. (14.512–17)

By uttering these words Eumaeus, we suspect, fails Odysseus's test. He does not handle the request with sufficient discretion. He cannot be fully trusted, despite the banquet of white-tusked boar. The swineherd is saying that sponsorship beyond the temporary refurbishing of the stranger's wardrobe depends not on himself but on Telemachus. Since Eumaeus has already communicated to Odysseus something of Telemachus's plight, he does not need to reemphasize the conditional nature of his statement. Long-term help from Eumaeus is predicated on Telemachus's return. In the morning Odysseus must resume his rags.

This said, he makes Odysseus a comfortable bed of animal skins by the fireside (where the returning hero will sleep in the company of Eumaeus's attendants). He even throws over his visitor an extra, thick cloak which he kept as a change of clothing for particularly cold nights. Apparently, all previous claims about people owning only one cloak aside, Eumaeus has a spare, for he himself steps outside to spend the night in a hollow with his prized white-tusked boars, protected against predators, whether animal or human, by a sword and spear, and against the elements by *another* thick cloak. Is he standing guard primarily over Odysseus, his own companions, and his butler (who are toasting about the fire) or over the white-tusked boars? Or, given that he has divined at least something of his guest's importance, is it, perhaps, good for his image or simply safer to be outside? The Muse offers us no clear answer.

Although Odysseus feels confident enough to go to sleep, he does not feel fully confident of Eumaeus's support. This becomes clear in the swineherd's hut the following evening, when Odysseus searches again for a firmer commitment. But before turning to the second phase of their encounter, we must follow the narrative turn of the epic and pick up the fortunes of Telemachus.

[9]

Turning Points and Returns

The Muse begins *Odyssey* 15 in Sparta, reminding us of the narrative inversion in the epic. The first four books keep us waiting for Odysseus's *nostos* while Telemachus sets out in quest of news about his father. Now, in book 15, while Odysseus awaits Telemachus's return, the Muse takes us back to the day preceding Telemachus's departure from Sparta. Before arriving in Ithaca, Telemachus must negotiate (improbably) in a chariot the corkscrew mountain roads across the Taygetus Mountains to Pylos, set sail, and evade the ambush which the suitors have set for him en route. His departure from Sparta looks both backwards and forwards in the *Odyssey*. It is the critical link uniting various strands of the epic.

Athena prompts Telemachus's return by reminding him that his house and interests are unprotected in his absence. She also plays on doubts he has expressed about Penelope: Get back in time to find your mother still at home. Make sure she's not smuggled any family possessions out. Women do that sort of thing when they marry. She'll have no thought for her former husband and son.[1] That Athena should motivate Telemachus with fears about his mother rather than with the news that his father is (about to arrive) home shows the extent to which the goddess communicates with humans by shaping her arguments in the form of what their own thoughts and fears would take as well as by assuming human appearance. She is both a deity separate from the persons whom she helps and the prefiguration of their inner thoughts. Her approach is rhetorically sound, no matter how unfair it is to Penelope. Fear of the situation at home looms larger under such circumstances than hope that a father, gone for twenty years, is actually back at last. Oddly enough, it is Helen, not Athena, who prophesies Odysseus's return—a prophecy she says is inspired in her by the gods.

Helen, we recall, came off worse in the rhetorical exchanges with Menelaus in *Odyssey* 4. In book 15, the situation is reversed. When an eagle swoops down and carries off a large, white, tame goose from the courtyard, Menelaus is at a loss to interpret the omen. Peisistratus, Nestor's son, assumes the omen must apply either to himself and Telemachus or to Menelaus. Helen, however, claims divine inspiration for her suggestion: it refers to none of those present, but to Odysseus:

> Listen to me, and I shall prophesy, as immortals cast it into my heart, and as I think it will be fulfilled. As this eagle came from the mountain, where both his birthplace and his offspring are, and snatched up a goose that was bred in the house, so will Odysseus return home after suffering many toils and many wanderings, and he will take vengeance; or maybe even now he is at home, and he sows seeds of evil for all the suitors. (15.172–78)

In her explanation, the eagle symbolizes the returning Odysseus. The identity of the goose is less obvious. If it symbolizes the suitors, as is the case in the dream about Odysseus's return which Penelope narrates in book 19, its singularity is peculiar. If it symbolizes Penelope, it makes rather more, if disturbing, sense. Penelope's own name recalls the avian *pēnelops*: a wild duck or wild goose.[2] Given the tales of Helen's own birth as the result of Zeus's assault, in avian disguise, upon her mother Leda (see especially Euripides *Helen* 17–21, where Zeus approached Leda as an eagle pursuing a swan), the possibility that Helen reads (but does not communicate) the identification of the goose with Penelope is brought more securely within the horizon. Telemachus accepts Helen's words with alacrity and promises that if she is right, he will regard her as a god.

While the suitors' ambush of Telemachus is brushed aside with a wave of the divine hand, the reaffirmation of anxieties about Penelope's role (and fate) in Odysseus's homecoming adds new tension to the narrative. The parallel between Telemachus and the matricide Orestes was established at the beginning of the epic. And Telemachus is to be accompanied on his return journey by the "godlike" Theoclymenus, who makes no secret of the fact that he is on the run and hotly pursued in the Peloponnese because he has killed one of his own relatives.

Telemachus disembarks before reaching the port of Ithaca itself (15.492–557). The vessel sails on without him and puts in at Ithaca at 16.321–34. The treasures given to Telemachus by Menelaus are stored at Clytius's house, and a herald is sent to Penelope to inform her that her son is safely returned and will be staying with the swineherd Eumaeus.

City Lights

With Telemachus on his way, the Muse returns us to the swineherd's hut in Ithaca, where we find Odysseus, on his second day home, still probing the boundaries of Eumaeus's willingness to cooperate:

> Odysseus spoke among them, making trial of the swineherd, to see whether he would show him kind affection and invite him to stay on his farm, or would urge him to go to the city. (15.304–6)

Odysseus's goal now, the Muse explains, is to assess what progress has been made: whether the swineherd will come to show him some affection (*phileoi*) —something the latter had declined to do in their first meeting: "I shall not show you affection" (*oude philēsō,* 14.388).[3] So he outlines his plans: to go to the city in the morning and beg, then to see Penelope and to offer the suitors his services in tending the fire and pouring wine. If Odysseus recalls Eumaeus's comment that he cannot present himself at the palace without a cloak, he is implicitly asking for extended use of Eumaeus's cloak. At their first meeting, Eumaeus had told him that the following day he would have to resume his rags and give back the cloak.

Yet what Odysseus actually asks of Eumaeus is not clothing but good advice and a reliable guide—*hēgemōn esthlos* (15.309–10). He thus opens up an opportunity for Eumaeus to offer his services (16.272). It is an opportunity Eumaeus declines just as he declines to give him a cloak to go in. He does not agree to take Odysseus into town until ordered to do so by Telemachus. And even then he adds that had the decision been his, he would have left his guest at the hut to look after things there (17.185–96). Given the swineherd's reluctance to associate himself with his guest in public, Odysseus is wise to avoid making any further remark and wise not to reveal any information that might lead to a formal recognition by Eumaeus. Eumaeus already has enough information to identify his visitor, should he so desire. As it is, the swineherd shies from acknowledgment, while at the same time treating his guest in the most lavish manner possible. Eumaeus is, after all, caught between a rock and a hard place. To admit to himself, much less to anyone else, that his guest actually is Odysseus (especially before Telemachus has returned and has had a chance to meet and accept or reject the stranger) would be contrary to his interests on almost all counts.

Thus Odysseus maintains a necessary balance of uncertainties, keeping Eumaeus poised between recognition and denial, by continuing his alternately teasing self-revelation and explicit denial. Unable to proceed to the city at this juncture, Odysseus begins to press Eumaeus into something of a corner. He asks, apparently innocently, whether Odysseus's parents are still alive—a kind of lawyer's question to which he already knows, or has claimed that he knows, the answer (15.346–50). Eumaeus assures him, briefly, that Laertes is still alive and grieving for his son, but reserves the large part of his response for an encomium of the dead Anticleia, who was, he says, virtually a mother to him. From his account, in fact, one might conclude that Eumaeus was brought up, perhaps even born, to the household in Ithaca.

Now Odysseus springs something of a surprise. He enquires how Eumaeus came to be purchased, for a lot of money, as a slave—a detail of Eumaeus's background that did not appear in Eumaeus's account of himself. Odysseus refers to the buyer not as Laertes but as "this man" (*hode anēr,* 15.388)—an expression often used in Greek poetry by the speaker in reference to himself. It might well give Eumaeus pause that his guest knows he was purchased as a slave rather than born into slavery, and that the price of his purchase was high.

Eumaeus responds to Odysseus's ambiguous reference to his purchaser only after some 100 verses, at 15.483, where he finally states explicitly that Laertes bought him.[4] In between, he generates a royal pedigree for himself which helps explain his insistence on the close relationship he claims he enjoyed with Odysseus's family in Ithaca and the rather high style of life he lives (and enjoys) in his hut, with his feasts of boar, his two cloaks, the slaves he supervises, and his butler. And, granted that Eumaeus has some glimmering of who his guest is, why should he not be entitled to reinvent himself as his guest has been entitled to? His fictive autobiography is all part of establishing the new contract that must exist between former master and former slave.

Eumaeus's Autobiography

When Odysseus asks about Eumaeus's origins, he gives the swineherd a chance to invent himself anew by offering a whole series of scenarios to explain how he became a slave:

> Well now, you must have been very little, swineherd Eumaeus, when you wandered off from your native land and your parents. But come now, tell me this and declare it truly, was the wide-wayed city of men sacked, where your father and honored mother lived, or were you alone beside your sheep and cattle, when enemy men in their ships carried you away and sold you here to the house of this man, who paid a fair price for you? (15.381–88)

Odysseus's rhetorical assumption that Eumaeus was not born into slavery is flattering, suggesting that Eumaeus does not strike him as a man born to a servile lot. The present status of an individual, no matter how long it has prevailed, does not define him. He thereby allows Eumaeus either to invent himself as he sees fit or, if Odysseus already knows the story of Eumaeus's origins, to retell his tale.

Odysseus offers three possibilities for Eumaeus's enslavement: (1) he wandered away from his country and parents when he was a very small child; (2) his city was sacked; (3) he was kidnapped by pirates and shipped away while herding his flocks. Of the three possibilities the first—that he ran away from home as a child—is at once the oddest and the least dramatic. The second—the destruction of one's homeland—is a common mode of transition from freedom to slavery in both the Homeric poems and the real ancient world. The third—kidnapping—not unusual in antiquity, is the basic stuff of ancient novels and of Plautine comedy. Interestingly enough, the first possibility assigns ultimate responsibility for the misfortune to the baby Eumaeus, the second sets his enslavement in the realm of universal catastrophe for his people, and the third has him individually selected for slavery, tearing him from an otherwise normal, if merely pastoral, existence.

Eumaeus's story is a variant of the first and third possibilities: he was kidnapped when he wandered off from his parents' palace as a child. Yet he was no mere shepherd boy born to common folk; he was a prince. His father, King Ctesius, ruled a city on the (very idealized) island of Syria—abundant in flocks, wine, and wheat. There, people die only of old age, never of sickness or famine. The utopian setting for the tale of a king's son who becomes a slave has all the hallmarks of a fairy tale or fairy-tale-like wishful thinking. Granted that this need not be the first time Odysseus has heard the story, his purpose may be precisely to prompt its renarration, given his assumption that Eumaeus was not born a slave, and even to stir Eumaeus's recognition of himself by making that assumption.

Eumaeus continues: one of his parents' maids was a Phoenician slave woman, seduced while doing her washing on the seashore by a Phoenician sailor who arrived on the island. She negotiated with him and his crew, at the sailors' suggestion, to return with them to her home in Sidon. Although Eumaeus does not mention that they asked a particular price in return, she promised to bring as much treasure from the king's house as she could, including the young Eumaeus, who always followed her when she came outside, and would bring a good price in the slave market. Eumaeus then appends an elaborate account of how, a year later, a Phoenician seaman captured the parents' attention with negotiations over the price of an amber and gold necklace and tipped off the maid, who took Eumaeus by the hand, stuffed as much of the tableware as she could into the folds of her clothes, and headed for the ship. Although, Eumaeus assures Odysseus, the gods punished the maid with death at sea, he himself was borne off into slavery and sold to Laertes.

The improbabilities are numerous—though admittedly not so overwhelming as those in Odysseus's narrative to Alcinous, which critics often treat as truth. Why does it take the Phoenicians a full year to reload their ship? How did Eumaeus learn the antecedent causes of his parents' beguilement and his capture, given the prompt demise of his abductress and his own arrival in Ithaca within a matter of days? Although the story would probably carry little conviction with such a master of fiction as Odysseus, not only does Odysseus declare himself deeply moved in his spirit, his *thymos* (15.486), by this *mythos,* this tale, of what Eumaeus has suffered in his own *thymos,* but he also consoles him with the thought that for Eumaeus things turned out happily in that he became the slave of a nice man, whereas he himself is still condemned to wander.

Odysseus thus pointedly sums up the common nature of his own experiences and those of Eumaeus. The beggar and the swineherd (master and slave) share experiences of life and suffering, although, at least within his own rhetoric, his own sufferings are worse because they still continue. Indeed, this parallelism may well have been Odysseus's goal all along, for there is an odd coincidence of detail between Odysseus's self-narrative to Eumaeus and Eumaeus's self-narrative to Odysseus, which now admits of at least two possible explanations which go above and beyond mere coincidence. The first is that Eumaeus uses the occasion of Odysseus's narrative to remold his own past in a curiously parallel way. Because he has spent his whole adult life as a slave, of course, he cannot rival Odysseus's adult exploits. The second is that if we grant Odysseus had heard Eumaeus's tale before, his own earlier Cretan narrative of a treacherous Phoenician who entertained him for a year, like Eumaeus's Phoenicians who dallied in Syria for a year, then attempted to rob him, abduct him, and sell him into slavery, may have been deliberately fashioned to stir Eumaeus's sympathy, if not to win his recognition.

If the second explanation is preferable, the Homeric muse has managed a marvelous rhetorical feat. Not until Eumaeus tells his story does the audience grasp why Odysseus has modified the nautical details of his narrative and introduced the villainous Phoenician. The Phoenician is jettisoned (along with Crete) when Odysseus renarrates himself, in Eumaeus's presence, to the suitors in 17.415–44. Neither Crete nor treacherous Phoenicians are helpful to his purposes at that point.

Since, however, there is no reason to suppose Eumaeus tells his tale now exactly as he would have done twenty years earlier, there may be a little of both explanations at work in the dynamic of the text. If Odysseus's narrative is shaped by a memory of what Eumaeus has said about himself in the past, Eumaeus's present narrative is no less likely to be adapted to the occasion and the present audience than is Odysseus's. Eumaeus has already stated to the disguised Odysseus what his expectations are for himself and his own future in the event that his master returns. He wants a house, a bit of land, and a wife sufficiently attractive to be sought by many other men—in short, freedom and a decent (if not princely) standard of living (14.61–67). Odysseus, at that early stage of their reacquaintance, made no response and no promises. Yet beneath the surface of the interchanged and delicately fabricated résumés, a certain amount of hard, if covert, negotiation is taking place. Much has to be settled before either is prepared to trust the other far enough to move to overt acknowledgment.

From Odysseus's point of view, any attempt to force Eumaeus into open acknowledgment would be counterproductive. Eumaeus enjoys the role of patron rather than of client and openly displays his generosity before his fellow slaves and his butler. Fortunately for Odysseus the impasse with Eumaeus is bypassed because of the opportune return of Telemachus. And Eumaeus loses forever his chance to be *the* major partner in Odysseus's reestablishment.

[10]

Telemachus

Telemachus has sailed home to Ithaca with his curious, soothsaying companion named, appropriately, Theoclymenus, "the one who hears god." Unable to offer him hospitality in his own house because it is unsafe, Telemachus first tries to sends him to Eurymachus, whom he considers the leading contender for his mother's hand, then lodges him, when Theoclymenus protests, at the house of his personal friend Peiraeus, who voyaged with him to Pylos. Telemachus himself heads for Eumaeus's hut where he is a familiar and frequent visitor, it seems, because the dogs do not attack him as they attacked Odysseus.

Appropriately enough, it is Odysseus who comments on the canine reaction to the newcomer: "[He] must be a companion or someone they know, since they're not barking. They're fawning on him" (16.8–10). Our sense of the close relationship between Telemachus and Eumaeus is increased by the simile the Muse employs to describe how the swineherd greets his visitor: "as a father affectionately welcomes the son he loves who has come back in the tenth year from a distant land, an only son who has no siblings and for whom he suffered much sorrow" (16.17–19). The simile is magnificently ironic. Just inside the door sits (impassively) Telemachus's *real* father who has not seen his son or his own father for twenty years. Although Odysseus will soon be reintroduced to his son, Odysseus's father, Laertes, is not given an opportunity to see his son until some time after the latter's return. And even then Laertes is greeted by a lie and forced into tears before there is an embrace and acknowledgment.

In spite of Eumaeus's emotional welcome, his opening words to Telemachus undermine rather than reaffirm some of the sense of closeness between the two:

> You came, Telemachus, sweet light. And I insisted I'd never see you again, after you went in your ship to Pylos. But now come, please come in, dear child, so I can enjoy looking at you now you're here inside my house and returned from abroad. For you don't visit the farm or the herdsmen at all often. You stay in town, for it pleases your heart to look at the destructive throng of the suitors. (16.23–29)

Rhetoric is more likely to beguile humans than to beguile dogs. If Telemachus does not visit often, as Eumaeus claims, then the dogs are unlikely to react to him in such a passive and friendly way. The commentator Eustathius noted centuries ago (on 16.26) that the dogs' reaction proves Telemachus *was* a frequent visitor and adds that the suitors also thought he was. When he left Ithaca they assumed he had gone to visit Eumaeus. What Eumaeus says about Telemachus's rare visits is unlikely, then, to be strictly true. We may argue that Eumaeus, like the parent to whom he is compared, is never satisfied with the frequency of visits from his grown-up son. But, if so, we must also note the parental "bite" in the next statement: that he does not come often because he prefers the company of the destructive suitors. The warm greeting, in short, is qualified by a rebuke.

Telemachus does not defend himself on this matter any more than he defends himself against Theoclymenus's protest about being lodged with Eurymachus. Thus no further light is shed on his ambiguous relationship with the suitors. Of course, the fulsome elements of welcome outweigh the censure, and Telemachus has more pressing concerns than such innuendoes as his swineherd may interject. But Eumaeus's words reach not only Telemachus's ears but those of Odysseus, who must hear them just as surely as he heard the footsteps and the fawning dogs. Indeed, Eumaeus's words may have been directed as much to the listener within as to the youth in the doorway: it is not only Eumaeus who was involved with the suitors' feasts in the palace. While Eumaeus partially, fearfully, and reluctantly provisioned them, Telemachus *enjoyed* attending them. The son is no less guilty of fraternizing with the foe than is the swineherd.

Telemachus's response to Eumaeus's show of modified rapture is, in fact, perfunctory. He has come to the hut primarily for information about his mother, the suitors, and the palace. He quickly learns that the situation is, essentially, unchanged. Penelope still waits, faithful and weeping. At this point, Eumaeus takes Telemachus's spear, and the son crosses the threshold into the house. There his waiting father rises and offers him his place, which Telemachus courteously declines. He, unlike Eumaeus, addresses the stranger immediately as a guest, not as an old man.

Odysseus's reaction to this first impression of his son is impassive. He does not utter a word. The absence of conversation is notable, considering the dangers Telemachus faced and the possibility that he might be bringing news of Odysseus which, one would imagine, could be of interest to Eumaeus. Silence grips the hut while Eumaeus prepares a place for Telemachus to sit and brings in the leftovers from the previous day's meal: no freshly killed white-tusked boar for the returned and much imperiled son.

Telemachus finally breaks the silence with an enquiry addressed not to the stranger but to Eumaeus. Again, Telemachus refers to the newcomer by his status as a guest rather than by his age. With a weak jest, he suggests that the man must have been brought to Ithaca by sailors, since he could not have walked there. Perhaps Telemachus's first enquiry, like his initial silence, is prompted by the possibility that there is some connection between the stranger and his homicidal friend, Theoclymenus.

Eumaeus's reply, which he claims to be truthful, takes Odysseus's Cretan story and strips it of all its glitter and its importance. His visitor is a Cretan (but not a kingly man, the equal of Idomeneus); he has traveled through (but not sacked) many cities; he has arrived on a ship from Thesprotia (but not loaded with treasure); and he has run away from that ship. There is no mention that he claims to bring news of Odysseus's return—a subject surely of interest to Telemachus, who has just returned from an expedition whose purpose was to discover precisely such information. "He came to my farm; I now put him in your hands. Do with him as you please. He claims he's your suppliant" (16.66–67).

It is too harsh to say the truth takes a beating from Eumaeus. Yet certainly Odysseus has not declared himself anyone's suppliant (although Eumaeus has described him to his fellow herdsmen as a suppliant). And he could hardly miss the way Eumaeus's synopsis has reduced him to something like a runaway slave who jumped ship in Ithaca. But Odysseus remains silent. The reader or listener familiar with other tales of Odysseus's return and encountering the *Odyssey* for the first time might draw an apprehensive breath. In the tense situation on Ithaca father and son might inadvertently harm each other, as they do in the tales of Euryalus and Telegonus. And Eumaeus has not particularly helped the situation by downgrading Odysseus's status.

Telemachus is deeply troubled by what Eumaeus says. He has just been handed a second dependent that he cannot welcome into his home. He argues, interestingly enough, that he is still a youth lacking the power to defend himself against a grown man. But who does he think he will have to defend himself against? Since he offers the stranger a cloak, tunic, sandals, and a sword, possibly the weapon he himself is carrying, it is logical to assume that he believes the stranger to be something other than a beggar and certainly someone who poses no threat to him.

At this point Odysseus breaks out of his resolute silence into this conversation which affects his existence as both "beggar" and Odysseus. Telemachus and Eumaeus have conversed as if they were the only people in the room, as if he were an embarrassing object to be disposed of. The epithet *polytlas* (much enduring) used of him here never has more absolute justification (16.90). If it is a conventional "formula," that formula springs to resonant life in this line. Odysseus has just set eyes, after twenty years, on his only son, yet remained silent. He has seen his slave, who has declined to venture beyond the most covert acknowledgment of his presence, reacting to his son as a surrogate father yet attaching dubious qualifications to his effusive welcome. He has heard Eumaeus strip the royal clothing from his Cretan story to leave him as a beggar. Most disturbing of all, he has heard his son's fear about going into his own home—a fear which may deny him access to the palace as it denied Theoclymenus (16.85–89). If Telemachus cannot be moved on this last issue, Odysseus will be unable to confront the suitors and reestablish himself. His return will have been in vain.

Odysseus can take no more. His anger explodes into words charged with emotion in an outburst of hitherto unparalleled ferocity. He obviously does not come forth and declare himself Odysseus. Such precipitous action would be ruinous under the circumstances. His companions would not be ready to join him at this stage even if both were sure he was the returned master. He cannot upbraid them in such a way as to alienate them, but he must try somehow to shame them:

> Friend, surely it is right for me to answer; indeed my dear heart was torn to pieces listening to what you have said about the outrages the suitors were devising in your halls against your will in spite of the man you are. Tell me if you are willingly abused like this. Do the people throughout the land hate you, following the voice of a god? Or do you have reason to blame your brothers, in whose fighting abilities one trusts even when great conflict arises. If only I, with my courage, were as young as you are, either the son of blameless Odysseus, or Odysseus himself—should he come home from his wandering, for hope still remains. Any man could cut the head off my neck right away if I did not become the death of all of them, when I came into the halls of Odysseus, son of Laertes. And if they should overwhelm me by their numbers because I was alone, I would prefer to be slain and die in my own halls than to watch these shameful actions all the time: strangers rudely treated, men assaulting female slaves shamefully in the beautiful palace, and wine drawn and wasted, men eating up my bread in a thoughtless manner, without limit, with no end to their behavior. (16.91–111)

Even in his anger, Odysseus selects his words carefully. He addresses Telemachus as *phile*, "dear one," "friend." In fact, the normal sense of *philos* in Homer is "near and dear." He then claims he has the right to respond and adds that he is heartbroken by what he has heard. He explains his heartbreak, however, in terms of the suitors' behavior rather than as disappointment with his son and swineherd, although it rapidly becomes clear that his real purpose is to take Telemachus, in particular, to task. The issue is whether Telemachus endures the suitors' oppression willingly (16.95). Odysseus gradually narrows the focus: is Telemachus's problem with the community, his immediate family, or himself?

The catalogue of atrocities attributed to the suitors is judiciously fashioned from comments he has heard and from what he probably suspects are those aspects of the suitors' depredations most disturbing to his young son. His allusion to their consumption of *sitos,* his grain, his bread, neatly avoids reference to the swine they have consumed (and thus avoids directly insulting Eumaeus). His allusion to maids being dragged off into concubinage with the suitors seems based entirely on his own assumptions. No one else has mentioned the subject. Odysseus perhaps suspects that this is a sensitive issue to the youthful Telemachus, for unless one had a formidable wife, as Laertes did, the master of the house might feel as free as Menelaus did to console himself with one of the servants. Certainly Telemachus's later, brutal treatment of the maids who slept with the suitors shows he was more enraged by their behavior than by that of the male slaves, who, like Eumaeus, also provided the ingredients for an entertaining evening. Besides, Odysseus's own experience of dragging women off into concubinage (alluded to in the famous simile in *Odyssey* 8) probably gave him opportunity to notice the reactions of such males in the household as were still alive. Until Telemachus sees the situation in the palace as a matter of honor rather than of personal survival, however, there is no hope.

Telemachus responds to the less important of Odysseus's questions in order. No, the people don't hate me. I don't have any brothers. The problem is the suitors and, to some extent, Penelope's indecision. But he offers no response to the substantial but less explicit charge that his own irresolution is to blame. Instead he redirects the discussion and asks Eumaeus to bring news to Penelope of his safe return. Such action is superfluous. Telemachus's ship is already on its way to the port of Ithaca, and a herald will be dispatched (in accordance with Telemachus's own instructions) to bring Penelope precisely the same news. There is no reason for anyone else to go—unless Telemachus fears his crew will betray him, or unless he wants Eumaeus out of the way for a while. Telemachus may have guessed that this visitor has news about his father or even is his father, for reasons we will explore shortly.

Eumaeus agrees to go but wonders if he should not also visit Laertes who has been worried about Telemachus in the midst of his anxiety about Odysseus. The old man has stopped eating and drinking and has not been seen publicly since Telemachus's departure for Pylos (16.137–45). With a curiously enigmatic remark, Telemachus denies Eumaeus permission to visit to Laertes: "It would be better for us to choose the day of my father's return" (16.149). At first we might conclude that Telemachus does not want Laertes to learn of his own safe return. But it is quickly evident that Telemachus is not referring to himself, since he asks Eumaeus to instruct Penelope to send an unnamed handmaiden, possibly Eurycleia, on that errand instead. What is gained by such indirection? Is Telemachus afraid of stirring Laertes' hopes? Is he giving his grandfather a chance to spend a little time with the woman he would have slept with, but dared not, while Anticleia was still alive? This seems unlikely. The more likely reason for this oblique transmission of the news is that it filters out any other information Eumaeus might have to impart—in particular, the presence of the mysterious stranger now in Eumaeus's hut.

The chief results of this duplicate embassy to Penelope are that the troublesome matter of what to do with the guest, which had occupied much of their discussion, is dropped, and that Eumaeus arrives at the palace at the same time as the herald from the ship, bearing the same news. The difference is that Eumaeus knows about the stranger in his hut. Perhaps Telemachus assumes that Eumaeus will tell Penelope about him anyway. But there is a third and very important consequence of the double embassy: Eumaeus is removed from his hut. And while he is away, Odysseus reveals his identity to Telemachus and, with a little help from Athena, is able to get Telemachus to acknowledge that he is, in fact, his long-lost father.

Acknowledging a Youthful Father

Telemachus has had some time to evaluate the truculent stranger who challenges his courage and resolve. He has even, perhaps deliberately, contrived a situation where he can be alone with that stranger by sending Eumaeus off on an unnecessary errand. As Eumaeus departs, Odysseus steps outside the hut and encounters Athena, whose presence is noticeable only to himself and the dogs (who react in fear). The goddess, disguised (appropriately enough) as a woman skilled in handicrafts, tells him the time has come for self-disclosure to Telemachus and, with a touch of her wand, enlarges him, converts him into a much more youthful person, and dresses him more elegantly. Athena, who does not always read situations correctly, may have done precisely the wrong thing if, as we have suggested, Telemachus suspects that the beggar in Eumaeus's hut could be his father, for Telemachus, rather than being encouraged to accept this transformed vision as Odysseus, is terrified at the stranger's changed appearance as he reenters the hut. He assumes his visitor must be a god and offers him gifts and sacrifices. "Spare us!" he cries.

Telemachus is not at all ready to believe the stranger when he denies he is a god, declares he is Telemachus's father, and embraces him. Nor is his reaction surprising. If he had suspected, on the basis of what Helen and Theoclymenus had said, that his father might be home, the beggar's transformation might lead him to suspect he was confronting some divine mirage, a false Odysseus designed to deceive him. Telemachus's reluctance to accept the stranger as his father does not indicate that the possibility that this man is Odysseus had not suggested itself to him. Athena's miraculous remake of Odysseus, however, lessens rather than increases the possibility that the stranger is his father. If the stranger had earlier seemed too worn down and out of luck to be a father capable of reestablishing himself, he is now too young, too transformed, to be plausible as Telemachus's father or even as a human. Telemachus's earlier comment that "it would be better for us to choose the day of my father's return" (16.149) may suggest that he had grasped the possibility that Eumaeus's visitor was Odysseus.

Telemachus's hesitation does not last long. Once Odysseus assures him the gods can adjust human appearances as well as their own and convert them into youths or beggars at will, Telemachus breaks down and accepts him. No tokens of identity are provided, and there is nothing personal and secret the two men can share, since Telemachus was a baby when his father left. Perhaps Odysseus's transformation now resolves doubts Telemachus may have had about his father's ability to cope physically with the trials ahead, if not necessarily to win them.

Telemachus is confronted with a paradoxical inversion of his skeptical comment in *Odyssey* 1: not only does a man take his children on trust; a son takes his father on trust. The man must obviously have divine support to undergo such remarkable metamorphosis. He returns in disguise as a beggar according to the same formula Helen described to Telemachus in *Odyssey* 4. And now that Odysseus has been rejuvenated he is, in effect, Telemachus's mirror image. It was established early in the epic that Telemachus strongly resembles his father. Thus there is an element of self-recognition in Telemachus's response too.

As both men break down in their mutual acknowledgment and acceptance, the Muse intrudes a ghoulish reminder of what this acknowledgment means. She compares them to ospreys or vultures lamenting over their ravaged nests (16.216–17). The grief birds of prey feel over their lost young, the sorrow of ospreys who feed on others' young, and of vultures who feed on the dead, is disturbingly paradoxical in a context where father and son have just been reunited. It looks forward, relentlessly, to the havoc they will wreak among the intruders in their own nest, leaving the youth of the Ionian islands as carrion and their parents lamenting over their own plundered nests. Indeed, the conversation quickly moves from recognition to revenge. At 16.235–39 Odysseus asks: "Come, then, tell me the number of suitors, and tell me about them, so I can know how many there are, and which men are of them; and then, when I have pondered it in my faultless mind, I can decide whether we two alone will be able to face them without any help, or whether we must go looking for others." Eumaeus does not figure in his calculations at all.

Return of the Sty Lord

By the time Eumaeus arrives back at the pig farm after his visit to the palace, the entire dynamic of the situation has changed in both locations. The suitors are again plotting to kill the returned Telemachus, and Eumaeus, not Odysseus, is about to be the excluded third person in the trio within the hut. All kinds of curious details are adduced by the Muse to make it clear that the swineherd is now the outsider.

First, a meal (of yearling boar) is already in progress. Something is being celebrated, but not on such a lavish scale as the feast Eumaeus prepared for Odysseus on his arrival. The menu is bourgeois rather than imperial. Second, Odysseus is now redisguised as an old beggar. This last precaution is Athena's idea, devised through fear that Eumaeus will not keep his mouth shut and will tell Penelope. The goddess, like both Odysseus and Telemachus, is aware that Eumaeus has difficulty keeping secrets. Telemachus, in fact, opens up the conversation not by asking how Penelope received the news of his return, but whether the suitors who set the ambush are back or still en route. His thoughts are now on the proposed slaughter of his mother's wooers rather than on his mother or the material damage done by those paying her court.

Eumaeus answers gruffly that this topic was not on his mind or (implicitly) part of his mission. He seems irked that he was forestalled in the delivery of his good news by the messenger sent from the ship, but he adds that he did observe a ship putting in, full of armed men, which he assumed must be the suitors. Eumaeus's words are testimony to his powers of observation on the matter of his essentially futile mission and on the details of the ship which has just put in: had I grasped that you wanted information about the suitors, he implies, I would have obtained it for you. As it was, I did my job and hurried back.

Whether Eumaeus also observes that Telemachus greets the news of the suitors' return with a smile rather than with a shudder the Muse does not tell us. All she adds is that Telemachus avoided the swineherd's eye as he smiled, and that they all began to feast on the roast pork. But from this moment onward the changed relationship between the beggar and Telemachus could hardly pass unnoticed by one, such as Eumaeus, who had seen them together before. Now it is Eumaeus's turn to read between the lines of what Telemachus says. And this is precisely what he does.

At 16.85–89 Telemachus had ordered Eumaeus not to allow the beggar to beg at his palace. Telemachus modifies his instructions at 17.6–15 at least to the extent that he instructs Eumaeus to take him to the city and let him beg there. At the same time, he declares he is no longer responsible for the beggar and delivers his instructions to Eumaeus as if they mean that he is expelling Odysseus from the swineherd's hut. Nor does he give him the cloak, much less the promised sandals and sword. Telemachus officially renounces further obligation to the beggar.

Telemachus's instructions to take the beggar into town to ply his trade are not tantamount to ordering him to take him to his own palace in town. As the abusive goatherd Melantheus, who encounters Eumaeus and the disguised Odysseus on their way into Ithaca, observes: there are feasts in other houses besides that of Odysseus (20.182). There are other places to beg. Eumaeus, however, leads Odysseus straight to the palace, not just to the city (17.260–71). He would hardly have done so if he felt Telemachus would disapprove. In fact, as he says to Odysseus at 17.188–89, he must carry out his master's orders through reverence and fear of him. He does not want to earn Telemachus's censure, because the censure of one's lord makes life hard for slaves. Yet all Telemachus's overt verbal signals have suggested that he would not approve of such action. Eumaeus is therefore discerning the intent beneath the instructions and obeying that.

When Odysseus and Eumaeus enter the palace in 17.336–44, Telemachus summons the swineherd, takes a basket containing a whole loaf of bread and as much meat as his hands can hold, and tells him to deliver these to Odysseus. He also authorizes Odysseus to beg among the suitors. Eumaeus has not mistaken Telemachus's intent. He has deduced it accurately. Perhaps he has also deduced that he now has two masters, for as Eumaeus and Odysseus set out for town, Eumaeus addresses Odysseus as *xeinos*,"guest" (17.185), even though Telemachus's words severed any obligations of *xenia* that might be incumbent upon him. "I would rather have kept you on the farm," Eumaeus says (17.186–87)—though this is the opposite of what he had told Telemachus earlier. Eumaeus even insists that they make a prompt start because the day is passing and the beggar will find it colder at night. Indeed Odysseus will, for he now has neither the cloak Eumaeus lent him nor the cloak promised, but not given, by Telemachus.

Odysseus asks Eumaeus to guide him and to provide him a *rhopalon* to help him along the way. The term *rhopalon* is ambiguous, meaning either a staff to support one's steps or a club, such as that of Heracles. What Eumaeus gives him is described by the Muse as a *skeptron*, which is less overtly a weapon, but apparently stout enough to satisfy Odysseus (17.195–99). Along the way, Eumaeus contrives to act as a good scout, providing Odysseus with information about the situation in Ithaca. Thus when they meet Melantheus the goatherd, Eumaeus makes sure his companion knows that this herdsman, in contrast to himself, has deliberately destroyed Odysseus's herds (17.246).[1] And when Melantheus abuses and kicks Odysseus, Eumaeus challenges the assailant verbally, praying that Odysseus will return and punish him.

Once they arrive at the palace, Eumaeus gives Odysseus the option either of entering while he remains outside or of waiting outside while he enters first. In either case, he is inviting Odysseus to enter but is still trying to maintain some distance between himself and his "guest." Odysseus goes along with the latter suggestion, although Eumaeus implies that it will be the more dangerous. A hungry belly drives one to extremities, he declares. A curious remark. Having consumed, as Eumaeus well knows, the best part of a suckling pig, two white-tusked boars, and a yearling hog over the last two days, Odysseus is far from the brink of starvation. Yet this moment of ironic humor is immediately and brilliantly followed by one of the great moments of pathos in the *Odyssey*: Odysseus's encounter with his hunting dog Argus, who is old enough to remember his master.

Argus

The Muse tells us that Odysseus bred Argus but had no joy in him since he left for Troy. In the past, Argus accompanied young men on hunting expeditions, but now he lies old, full of vermin, and neglected, on a heap of mule and cattle dung in front of the palace. Argus struggles to show his joy at recognizing Odysseus but lacks the strength to approach his master. He thus becomes the first being, other than a god, to acknowledge Odysseus's identity unprompted. Sadly, but fortunately, for Odysseus, Argus dies immediately after drooping his ears in submission and wagging his tail for joy. The now cloakless Odysseus turns his head aside from the sight and wipes away a tear, which he easily hides from Eumaeus (17.304–5). This is an extraordinary response from a hero so capable of disguising his reactions in situations which surely stir his emotions. There are no tears when he sees Telemachus or Penelope after twenty years.

Although Odysseus disguises his tears from Eumaeus, he draws the swineherd's attention to Argus, observing that it is surprising to see this animal lying in the dung. The dog has a fine form, he says, but declares he is unsure whether he has speed of foot or whether he is a table dog for show (17.306–10). Odysseus is rather sly in his expression of uncertainty, for *Argos* means "swift," a name appropriate for a hunting dog not a lapdog. While Odysseus alludes to the old dog's speed, he avoids using the epithet *argos,* which is also the dog's name, since it might suggest he knows the dog's identity. When Eumaeus affirms that no creature could escape this dog in the thick of the wood because of his keen scent, he answers Odysseus's enquiry without falling back on the epithet for canine swiftness which would also supply the dog's name. He is as oblique as is Odysseus. In the recognition of the dog, then, lies the recognition of Odyseus too.

Since there is no suggestion that Argus has been *placed* on a dung heap, we must ask why he has stationed himself there. The critic in a hurry might respond: "Just to keep warm." But then we must ask why there is a pile of dung in front of the palace entrance. Slaves may need manure for the fields, but this is an odd place for a compost heap and a strange place for a dog to station himself, as Odysseus himself observes (17.306). Odysseus's comment to Eumaeus about Argus's place and condition and Eumaeus's reply give us a sense of Odysseus's first impression of his old home and its condition. To both of them, Argus symbolizes the situation as it affects them. Eumaeus suggests that since Argus's master has perished, the women give the dog no care: "Slaves, when their masters lose their power, no longer desire to do honest service; for Zeus, whose voice is borne afar, takes away half of the worth from a man, when the day of slavery seizes him" (17.320–23). A slave's human dignity is so diminished by his status as someone else's property that total loyalty can hardly be expected once fear of the master is removed. Eumaeus chooses his moment for this understandably bitter remark well. No one has given *him* freedom yet.

From Odysseus's point of view, Argus has a different symbolism. The dog, neglected by the whole household, including Penelope and Telemachus, is its only totally devoted guardian. The hero has been ejected and, in an almost legal sense alienated, from his own property. By allowing suitors to be present, Penelope has, in effect, placed the property on the market. The ancient Argus, then, is a kind of substitute for the absent hero, watching over the entrance to Odysseus's palace during his master's absence, like the Argive watchman in Aeschylus's *Agamemnon*—who compares himself to a dog. In fact, as the dog-head coins of the city of Argos show, there was a strong association in Greek minds between Argos and dogs (or persons who performed watchdog functions, such as the thousand-eyed monster Argus that Hermes killed).

The oddly situated compost heap may perhaps be where it is because of the dog's presence. A detail from the *Ancient Laws and Institutes of Ireland,* cited by Alfred W. De Quoy, provides a clue. If a dog is present on land long enough to relieve himself, he establishes a territorial claim for his master—a claim which demands legal recompense. Cow dung is used in an attempt to separate, ritually, dog and master from their claim to the property.[2] Thus one may envisage a scenario in which Argus is defying ritual attempts to alienate him—and through him, his absent master—from the estate in Ithaca. Argus dies as Odysseus crosses back into his territory to reclaim it. The watchdog is replaced by his master. His role in the epic and, in a larger sense, heroic Greek society is over, and he dies. It is noteworthy in this connection that in Irish epic tradition the relationship between hero and hound amounts to interchangeability. CuChulainn is obliged to take the place of the smith Culainn's dog, which he has killed—hence his name, "the dog of Culainn." Thus an attack on someone's dog can be tantamount to an attack on the hero himself, and a rejection of the hound to the rejection of the hero.[3] Perhaps there are residual traces of such a tradition in the *Odyssey*.

There is certainly a sense in which Argus is a curiously inverted image of Odysseus, a symbol of Odysseus's youthful past as a hunter, when he too ventured out in the company of swift hounds. And it is in terms of a wound from that hunting past that Odysseus will be recognized by Eurycleia (19.361–502). The presence of hunting dogs seems to confer princely stature in Ithacan society. At the beginning of the epic, when Telemachus needs to make an impressive appearance at the assembly and dazzle the Ithacans with his rank and princely status, he carries a spear of bronze and brings with him two swift dogs (2.11). Similarly, after his return from Sparta and Pylos, he sets out for the assembly carrying a spear of bronze and accompanied by "two swift hounds" (17.62, 20.145). The formula is identical. Perhaps the dogs are as essential a symbol of his standing as is the spear, if only to help him make a *bella figura* as a prince.

Is there also in the Argus episode (and generally in *Odyssey* 14–24, books replete with canine imagery) a relic of some older order of heroic narrative which focused on such hunting heroes? Homeric heroes have passed, on the whole, beyond the huntsman stage, even though the Greek word for "hunter," *kynēgetēs*, makes it clear that the hunter is unimaginable without his hounds. In Homer, "dog" is as often as not simply a term of abuse, as it is when appplied to Helen in the *Iliad* or when applied by Melantheus to Eumaeus in 17.248. Similarly, the wretched Dolon, in *Iliad* 10, for example, wears a dogskin cap. Greek myth outside the *Iliad* and *Odyssey*, however, is full of hunter-heroes. In one of the several major treatises on hunting (with dogs) which have survived from Greco-Roman antiquity, the pseudo-Xenophontine *On Hunting*, lists among the important students of Chiron the centaur, the patron of hunting, Achilles, Odysseus, Amphiaraus, Theseus, and Aeneas (1.1–5). Of these, however, only one, Odysseus, is shown, in Greco-Roman heroic epic, as having a special dog or dogs.[4]

The Homeric muse does not usually represent humans as affectionate toward any particular animal, though they sometimes wear animal hides as symbols of triumph or as a device to characterize their behavior.[5] The role of dogs in the society of hunter-heroes does not loom large in Homer as it does in the prose epics of medieval Ireland, where many important heroes are accompanied by remarkable hounds and bear doggy names: Cu-Chulainn, for instance. In fact, the Irish term for the most princely of dogs is Ar Cu, "Slaughter Hound," an animal whose ownership was restricted by law to the most important noblemen and who, in the heroic tradition, is usually represented as having brilliant and unreal coloring, like Bran's dog, which has blue feet, green paws, and a crimson tail.[6] In the medieval Irish version of the *Odyssey*, probably the oldest "translation" of Homer into any language other than Latin—its only rival is the Icelandic version—it is Argus's recognition of Uilix (Odysseus) which clinches Penelope's acknowledgment of her husband. To an Irish medieval reader, in fact, the notion of a prince's dog lying on a heap of mule and cow dung is unacceptable; so the translator changes the mise-en-scène and has Argus (endowed with white sides, a crimson back, a black belly, and a green tail) maintained in fine condition by a magical broth. Indeed, the odd resemblance of the Irish Ar Cu to the Greek Argus is worth noting. In the *Odyssey*, however, it is only the hero who can be miraculously restored to youth and vigor, not his dog.

Pressing One's Suit

Following Odysseus's suggestion, the swineherd precedes Odysseus into the palace, is spotted by Telemachus, and is summoned to his table with a nod rather than with words (17.328–30). The suitors pay little attention to Odysseus's arrival and when he begins to beg, they are sympathetic and generous until the goatherd Melantheus says he has seen this stranger before and that Eumaeus brought him. It is Odysseus's association with Eumaeus, established by his rival herdsman, that provokes the suitors' wrath. But the anger finds its expression not through Eurymachus, Melantheus's (and, curiously, Telemachus's) favorite, but through Antinous.

However popular Eumaeus may be with Telemachus, his name is despised among the suitors. The venomous verbal assault Antinous makes should convince Odysseus, if the encounter with Melantheus has not already done so, that Eumaeus is not on good terms with the suitors. Antinous's abuse, of course, is shot through with irony. He complains that there are too many beggars in the hall consuming Odysseus's food, and that Eumaeus is making matters worse.

Eumaeus, though a slave, answers boldly. He accuses Antinous of speaking unseemly words and points out that no one invites any outsider to his house unless that person can contribute to the well-being or pleasure of the household. This remark is both ominous and stinging. It is ominous in that Odysseus has come to reclaim the household for himself and to restore its well-being (from his point of view). The sting is that the suitors are uninvited outsiders par excellence who have absolutely nothing to offer the household. Eumaeus adds that no one invites a beggar to be a burden on himself and finally that Antinous, among the suitors, is particularly rough on Odysseus's slaves and especially to himself, though his hostility is a matter of indifference, as long as Penelope and Telemachus approve his presence.

Telemachus immediately silences Eumaeus, on the pretext that Antinous can do a lot of damage when provoked. But he may also be concerned about what is implicit in Eumaeus's statement: Eumaeus has invited this particular beggar into the palace, without Telemachus's explicit instructions. Antinous is right on that score. It would not be hard for Melantheus to convince the suitors that Eumaeus did, in fact, invite the beggar, should they wish to pursue the matter. The logical conclusion to be drawn, then, from the ominous undertones in Eumaeus's remarks is that the beggar is really not a beggar at all, as Telemachus knows perfectly well. More to the point, Eumaeus is himself conscious of the significance of these undertones. He has observed the change in Telemachus's attitude to the stranger. His impromptu and confident reply to Antinous reveals the extent to which he has lost the fear of the suitors he had expressed earlier.

During these exchanges, Odysseus, at Athena's prompting, makes his round and promptly becomes a victim of Antinous's anger at Telemachus and Eumaeus. Antinous throws a stool at him. The other suitors do not imitate his boorishness but give the beggar gifts and fill his wallet with bread and pieces of meat. Odysseus is about to return to his place on the threshold when he suddenly stops next to Antinous, praises his looks, and declares that he himself was once a rich man with a house and slaves, and in the habit of giving gifts to strangers. Zeus made him join pirates who went to Egypt, where he lost all his fellow buccaneers. Although in outline his narrative corresponds to the tale told in Eumaeus's hut, there are important changes. He does not say where he is from, does not mention Crete or the Trojan War, says nothing about treasure, and substitutes the more distant Cyprus, which had no connection with the Trojan War, for neighboring Thesprotia as the last place he visited before his arrival in Ithaca. He removes, in fact, all details which might bring Odysseus to mind. For the first time, he claims to have been a pirate (17.425), but not a pirate king or pirate leader, simply an individual member of a crew now lost.

Eumaeus could hardly fail to note that his guest's current version of his life story is sufficiently different from the version he had heard in his hut that, probably, neither is really true. Now, if Odysseus is as cunning as is generally assumed, he knows that although Eumaeus could contradict here, the swineherd will do nothing of the sort. Eumaeus can hardly call him a liar in front of the suitors, since he has strongly supported the beggar's presence and since Telemachus has publicly offered gestures and words to the same effect. Eumaeus's quarrel with Antinous is a public avowal of hostility to the suitors. He has taken his stand alongside Penelope and Telemachus, and he must stick with it whether he has grasped that the beggar is Odysseus or just been shocked to discover that the beggar is a liar. At all events, Eumaeus is at least neutralized.

Odysseus's narrative is not designed to please his listeners. There is nothing for the suitors to wonder at or to admire—just something to provoke minor anxiety about his piratical past and to cause distaste and contempt such as might justify the low opinion expressed of him by Melantheus and Antinous. Why would Odysseus want to antagonize the suitors? Perhaps because all except Antinous treat him with consideration. However much they have transgressed the laws of hospitality, their generosity to him now makes it more difficult to justify slaughtering them as they dine. They must be induced to turn against him in his disguised persona. He needs an immediate pretext for his planned butchery. As Aeschylus's Clytemnestra bullies Agamemnon into walking on beautiful tapestries and thereby symbolically reenacting his past hybris, his despoliation of beauty, so Odysseus lures the suitors into mistreating him.

What ensues is a crescendo of provocation on his part and of contemptuous response on theirs. Antinous underscores Odysseus's (self-admitted) worthlessness and the false nature of his fellow suitors' generosity: they are giving away what belongs to another man. Odysseus retorts that Antinous's brains do not match his beauty and that he has denied even a grain of salt, to a suppliant. Again Antinous hurls a stool at Odysseus. Odysseus, though seething, limits himself to a general response to all the suitors, yet his identity is barely concealed within his imperious words. A man fighting for his possessions does not feel pain. If there are avenging gods who interest themselves in beggars, may they bring death to Antinous (17.475–76). This curse seems disproportionate to the insult offered. Now it is Antinous's opportunity to show restraint: "Sit still or else young men will drag you away." He has, no doubt, read his audience's lack of support for his behavior, a disapproval that finds an unnamed voice among the suitors which attributes great seriousness to Odysseus's curse:

> Antinous, it was not good that you struck the wretched wanderer.
> Doomed man, what if he is some god coming from heaven? Indeed,

> gods resembling strangers from afar come in all forms, visit cities, watching over the violence and righteousness of men. (17.483–87)

Such boldness and such a manner of speech as the beggar has shown might indicate that their visitor is really a god in disguise.

Antinous is not appeased. When Telemachus remains silent, our attention is directed to a new voice expressing disapproval of Antinous's behavior and reechoing Odysseus's prayer for death upon the arrogant suitors—Penelope's. Though she is not in the hall, she is informed of what is happening. And she goes beyond the beggar as she even specifies which god should kill Antinous: Apollo, famous for his expertise with the bow (17.494).

[11]

Penelope's Intervention

Penelope's curse on Antinous comes as a surprise (17.494). She is usually more ambivalent and indecisive: constantly grieving for her lost husband, but still flirting with or tantalizing the suitors. Though her concern with the treatment of the beggar has led her to denounce at least one of them, she has not fully accepted the necessity to reject all the suitors outright. It is not clear what Penelope wants, to express the dilemma in Marylin Katz's terms.[1] Penelope's first action in the epic is an unsuccessful attempt to silence the bard Phemius when he sings of the heroes returning from Troy. Does she intervene because she is sad that Odysseus's story is not among them, or to prevent further narration of such voyages of return because they will include Odysseus's?

Generally, Penelope's chief concern is to maintain the status quo, even after her curse on Antinous. Her reluctance in selecting a husband from among her suitors is matched by her reluctance to acknowledge Odysseus. Her role is that of the waiting wife, suspended in time for the twenty years Odysseus has been away. Since her indecision controls many other people, however, she controls time rather than being controlled by time, and she defines the situation in which she exists rather than being defined by it. She is thus a figure of compelling mythic dimensions, for to be mythic is, to a large extent, to escape the limitations of time and space.

As we have observed already, Penelope resembles one of the Moirai, or Fates, in that she can weave the destinies of men as she weaves the shroud for Laertes. Indeed, she can, in a way, transcend the Moirai because she can unravel her own work as they cannot. During her three years of weaving and unraveling the shroud, the main threat she faces, aside from the discovery of her scheme, is from Laertes. If he dies inopportunely, she will be not only discovered but disgraced.

In the later books of the *Odyssey*, Penelope delays the resolution of the dilemma which she symbolizes and for which she is at least partially responsible much as Odysseus often delays, however unconsciously, his own return. Her skill with the loom, *histos,* enables her to generate as well as to survive the constant pressure of the suitors' courtship, much as the mast, *histos,* of Odysseus's ship enables him to sail at will, and, when the rest of his vessel perishes, serves as a life preserver in a storm. Penelope's presence in the palace has been, Telemachus realizes, as much the reason for its occupation by the suitors as is Odysseus's absence. The *Odyssey*, in fact, is as much Penelope's epic as it is Odysseus's, for she, flirtatious and faithful, decisive in her indecision, freezes time while her husband wanders between time and timelessness.

Penelope is the center of attention, the focus of ambition in Ithaca. That is her claim to mythic fame—and to that fame the absence of Odysseus is as crucial as is the presence of the suitors. If she marries Antinous or Eurymachus, she returns to the world of time. The mythic aspects of her role are over, as they are the moment she accepts Odysseus back as her husband. It is not the date of Odysseus's return that restores Penelope to sequential time but the moment she acknowledges his return.[2]

When Odysseus enters the hall and sits among the suitors, he leaves his world and enters hers. It will be easier for him to kill the suitors and execute much of his household than to win Penelope back. When he becomes her husband again, he does so in her time and, to some degree, on her terms. But a beginning is made with her prayer that Apollo may kill Antinous. It is uttered in the presence of Eurynome and her maids and is her most overt position statement up to this point. Her curse, made in the presence of the female slaves, some of whom are sleeping with the suitors, reminds us that there are two parallel and threatening worlds within the household: that of the men in the hall, where Odysseus and the suitors sit, and that of the women behind the scenes. Odysseus's return must be secured (and can be as easily jeopardized) by the women as by the men. The Muse conveys this notion by transferring our attention from the hall to the kitchen, from Odysseus to Penelope. This parallelism is reinforced in the next book when we see that the disloyal goatherd Melantheus has a female counterpart with a virtually identical name—Melantho.

The sudden shift from the male world of the hall to the female world "behind the scenes" is intensified by Penelope's overt expression of anger toward and hatred of Antinous, which follows so closely on Odysseus's curse that, for a moment, one may even have the illusion that Penelope must have been a witness to everything that happened in the hall. She prays for Antinous's death just after Antinous hurls a second stool at Odysseus. Her curse virtually coincides with Odysseus's, which is uttered after the same incident.[3] Readers may wish to take 17.492–93 merely as indicating that Penelope has heard Odysseus being hit (*tou . . . blēmenou*); but she utters her imprecation upon Antinous in the second person singular, as if she were in the hall, addressing him in person, not simply reacting to a sound she has heard or to a report delivered by someone else:

> If only Apollo the Archer would strike you in this way. (17.494)

Since Penelope is, at the time, with her maids and her confidante, Eurynome, one of them might have told her about it. It cannot have been Eurynome, since Penelope tells her about the incident. More likely, Penelope has seen it happen, because she describes precisely the place where the blow struck the beggar (17.501–4), soon after the incident occurs, and in exactly the same language as the Muse uses to report it in 17.462–63.

Odysseus's curse, rather than Antinous's hurling of the stool, makes the incident notable. That an apparently lowborn beggar should invoke the Erinyes, the avenging Furies, upon an aristocrat who has thrown a stool at him is remarkable. The Erinyes are not usually summoned to avenge minor hooliganism. Besides, upper-class arrogance is capable of much worse treatment of the "lower orders" and of avenging any, even purely verbal, affronts, as Telemachus pointed out earlier in a word of caution to Eumaeus. It is equally surprising that the assembled suitors should unanimously sympathize with the beggar rather than with Antinous and take the curse seriously. In most Greek communities, the only persons entitled to pronounce such a curse were the *basileus*, the "king," and, under certain circumstances, his wife, and priests—members of the local citizen aristocracy. A curse cannot be made by an outsider.[4]

After Odysseus has pronounced his curse on Antinous, the suitors (including Antinous himself) are cowed. The anonymous suitor who acts as their spokesman fears that it may indicate that a god is in their midst, even though no "king" or "priest" is present. A private citizen or foreigner would never dare such a curse, though disguised gods would. The suitor does not allow for the possibility that the beggar is, rather, the *basileus* returning in disguise: that the beggar who curses Antinous is Odysseus.

Eurynome, however, Penelope's attendant, who wants the suitors gone, prays for the fulfillment of "our" prayers that they will all be destroyed before sunrise. The intensity of her reaction to the news of the curse imparts a strong sense that she too suspects she is hearing the prelude to the immediate divine destruction of all the suitors—which will occur only if gods intervene or if Odysseus reappears. But Eurynome and other maids endure much more abuse from the suitors than the hurling of stools, and Eurynome does not formulate her wish as a curse. She re-echoes (and rather expands the scope of) Penelope's prayer which is formulated in the manner of a curse, as is within her rights as wife of the *basileus.* Yet, though Penelope advances beyond Odysseus's curse by specifying which god (Apollo) should destroy Antinous, with which weapon (his bow), her plea is less sweeping than Eurynome's apparent reaffirmation of it. Although Penelope agrees that all the suitors are enemies, she limits her curse to Antinous, whose likeness to a *melaina kēr,* "a dark demon of destruction," particularly merits her wrath. Her cautious wording shows she is not ready to go as far (or as quickly) as Eurynome. The maid wants to assimilate all the suitors to Antinous's insolence and to condemn them. Penelope wants to keep him separate from the rest. Given the disapproval the other suitors express about Antinous's behavior, Penelope's reaction seems the more just.

Yet the beggar's curse and Eurynome's response have stirred something else in Penelope: the possibility that matters may come to a head very quickly—perhaps before dawn. Indeed, the beggar's regal boldness in cursing Antinous suggests that his presence is divinely ominous. Penelope decides she must meet him to discover whether he knows about, or has even seen, Odysseus, since "he resembles someone who has wandered far" (*polyplanktōi gar eoike,* 17.508–11). Again Penelope speaks as if she has seen the beggar rather than just heard about him. She echoes a word Odysseus uses to the suitors in 17.425, claiming Zeus sent him with "far wandering pirates" to Egypt. The epithet "far wandering," *polyplanktos,* comes similarly to Philoetius's mind when he sees Odysseus and notes that gods bring misery to "men who wander far" (20.195).

The Muse now reminds us that Penelope and her maids are not present when Odysseus dines with the suitors, Telemachus, and Eumaeus. Yet, curiously, she says Penelope calls *Eumaeus* to bring the beggar to her (17.507–11). She might be dispatching a maid to fetch the swineherd from his seat close to Telemachus, where he was when he last had our attention. More likely, Eumaeus is already within earshot, for the Muse simply says Penelope called Eumaeus to her, something she could have done if the women's quarters, as in an Ottoman *sarai,* enabled the women to observe and communicate without being seen. A little later (17.541–42) Penelope hears Telemachus sneeze (and knows that it is he who is sneezing), and Odysseus instructs her to stay in the halls (*megaron*) till sunset, as if implying that her chambers were, in effect, an extension of the main hall where the suitors are dining (17.569–70).[5]

Penelope's instructions to Eumaeus are quite explicit:

> Go, godlike Eumaeus. Go up to the stranger and bring him over here, so that I can greet him and also ask if by any chance he has either heard of Odysseus of the steadfast heart, or has seen him with his own eyes. For he seems like a man who wandered far. (17.508–11)

Instead of simply complying with her request, Eumaeus seizes the opportunity to brief Penelope about the beggar:

> If only the Achaeans would keep silence, my queen! Indeed he told such stories that would beguile your heart. For I had him for three nights, and detained him for three days in my hut; for he came to me first when he fled by stealth from a ship. But he did not bring his tale of sufferings to an end. As when a man looks at a minstrel who has learned the songs of longing from the gods, sings them for mortals, and they yearn insatiably to listen to him, whenever he sings, so did he beguile me as he sat in my halls. . . . He says that he is an ancestral *xenos* [guest and friend] of Odysseus, that he dwells in Crete, where the race of Minos lives. From there he came here on this journey, suffering many woes, driven about from place to place; he insists he has heard of Odysseus, that he's near at hand, in the rich land of the Thesprotians, that he is alive and is bringing many treasures home. (17.512–16; 522–27)

Why does Eumaeus offer this briefing? Penelope has simply said: "Tell him to come here, this man who seems like someone who has wandered much." Perhaps he wants to give her a chance to reconsider her order, in the light of his perceptions, before he carries it out. He emphasizes the stranger's beguiling prowess as a storyteller; he offers a more favorable synopsis of the stranger's background than he gave Telemachus; he still modifies what Odysseus has told him; he accepts that the stranger may be a Cretan who enjoyed guest-friendship with Odysseus (and is therefore of some social standing); he is prepared (for the first time) to think Odysseus may still be alive and returning with treasure; he totally dismisses the autobiography given by Odysseus to the suitors and reported to Penelope.

Precisely what Eumaeus means when he wishes the Achaeans would shut up because the stranger is a good narrator eludes us, since there is nothing to suggest that the suitors are not, at this moment, quiet. The Muse usually mentions expressly when they are kicking up a ruckus (e.g., 1.365–71; 18.399–400). Besides, of the 133 uses of *Achaioi* in the *Odyssey*, only 19 refer to the suitors.[6] *Achaioi* most commonly (62 instances) denotes Greek heroes who fought at Troy. Further, the rather unheroic self-portrait Odysseus has given the suitors says nothing of Troy and marvelous experiences. Perhaps Eumaeus's point is this: "If only people would shut up for a moment on the topic of the Trojan War, they'd find something worth listening to here." A tale to rival the *Iliad*, in fact.

Eumaeus's synopsis of the stranger's life does not represent the outer limits of what he has heard about the stranger. Characters in the *Odyssey*, as in real life, rarely reveal everything they know. Even if the swineherd knows the beggar is Odysseus, his task is to assess and either kindle or mute Penelope's interest in meeting him. Eumaeus knows, and has told

Odysseus, that Penelope is receptive to strangers who claim to have news about Odysseus. This one has a good claim to her attention not only because he was a guest-friend of Odysseus, but because he is also a beguiling poet: good entertainment, if nothing else. Within this praise there lurks, of course, a veiled warning: Penelope must be on guard against a master of language who may beguile her with words.

Eumaeus's picture of the beggar contrasts with what Penelope has heard (or observed) about the man who has just cursed Antinous. If she has also heard (of) the autobiographical details the beggar has given publicly, she has no reason to suppose he has any social status, that he knows anything about Odysseus, much less that he is her husband's *xenos* [guest and friend], bearing news that Odysseus is coming home with a treasure chest. The beggar is not what he seems, but someone more important. Eumaeus claims special privilege for his account, since it is based on observation over three days and nights when he detained the stranger in his hut.

If there is force or truth in Eumaeus's claim to have detained Odysseus on the farm, we get a different sense of the swineherd's strategy. He willingly provides Odysseus with a (spare) cloak while he is in the hut, but will not lend it to him when he goes into the town. He even tells him he cannot enter the palace without a cloak (a claim which proves untrue). In short, Eumaeus's hospitality, like most acts of hospitality in the *Odyssey*, is a means of controlling the guest's movements. Why is Eumaeus cautious in his recommendation of Odysseus to Penelope? Perhaps because, as he suggested when he mentioned to Odysseus the visit of a honey-tongued Aetolian, he knows Penelope is susceptible to rogues with silvery tongues. Perhaps Eumaeus has sensed that his visitor brings trouble and may even be Odysseus.

Penelope, now described by the Muse as *periphrōn*, "able to think her way around" a situation, amply justifies that epithet in her reply. She reiterates her order to Eumaeus without the slightest overt hint that he has said anything of interest. If everything following her first command in 17.508 until she utters he second command in 17.529 were missing from our manuscripts, no one would suspect a lacuna. She restates her command with the verb she used when issuing the order: *ercheo*, "Go!" She wants to meet the beggar: "Bring him," not "Tell me about him."

Penelope registers what Eumaeus says despite her show of ignoring it. As she restates her order she attributes the havoc in her household to the absence of a man such as Odysseus used to be. Odysseus, she obliquely assures him, would be most welcome:

> Go call him over here, so he can tell it to me to my face. As for these men let them entertain themselves, either as they sit in the doorway, or

> here in the house, for their hearts are merry. For their possessions lie untouched in their homes: their bread and sweet wine, these their servants eat, but they frequent our house every day. They sacrifice cattle and sheep and fat goats, they feast and drink the flaming wine, recklessly; and they waste everything. For there is no man around like Odysseus used to be, to keep ruin from the house. But if Odysseus were to come and return to his native land, he, along with his son, would take vengeance on these men immediately. (17.529–40)

Penelope's allusions to the suitors' consumption of the estate's cattle, sheep, and goats are, partially, a jibe at Eumaeus's expense, though she, like Odysseus, makes no specific reference to the inroads the suitors have made into the pig population—pork is the only meat the suitors are described as eating.

Eumaeus still does not move. When Telemachus sneezes, which Penelope takes as a good omen, she orders him yet a third time to go on his errand. This time she promises to reward the beggar with a cloak and a tunic if she reckons he has told her the truth. Now, finally, Eumaeus complies. Yet when he reports what she has said to Odysseus, he does so in a way calculated to stir his guest's anger. He says that "the mother of Telemachus" (*mētēr Tēlemachoio,* 17.554), wishes to question him about her husband. If she finds that she is being told the truth, she will give him a cloak and tunic ("which you need most of all"), but for food he will have to go and beg throughout the land. The inference to be drawn is that Penelope will not feed as well as clothe him. But the addition about food is his own, so phrased as to seem part of what Penelope said. It is sophisticated lying.

Why is Eumaeus so discouraging to Odysseus? Perhaps to prepare his guest for rejection by Penelope, perhaps to shed favorable light on his own generosity, perhaps to encourage Odysseus to leave. As in a Western, the returning lawman is not always welcome because his chance of success against the villains appears so slim that his presence promises more havoc than order—and greater suffering for the townspeople.[7] But perhaps the real reason is to preserve his own importance as power broker by withholding just enough information or so modifiying it as to create some tension between Odysseus and Penelope.

When Eumaeus calls Penelope the mother of Telemachus, for instance, he identifies her in terms of her son not her husband. The characterization seems to rule out the possibility that Odysseus is still alive. We have only to contrast Odysseus's persistent address of Penelope when he meets her as "honored wife of Laertes' son Odysseus" (19.165, 262, 336, 583) to see how important this matter is to Odysseus. To compound the slight, Eumaeus comments that Odysseus needs a cloak most of all. Certainly Odysseus needs the cooperation of Penelope, now distanced as "the mother of Telemachus," more than he needs a cloak. What adds to the sting is that the remark is made by a swineherd who owns a spare cloak which he had lent his guest once but which he has not let him borrow again.

Odysseus also appears to ignore what Eumaeus says. He does not show overtly that he finds what Eurmaeus has said offensive, but he indicates in the details of his response that the undertones have not passed unnoticed. He refers to Penelope by her frequent epithet "she who can think her way around situations" (*periphrōn*). She is no fool. He also describes her as daughter of Icarius—not as "the wife of Odysseus," as he addresses her when they are face-to-face, nor as "mother of Telemachus," as Eumaeus has described her.

The form of address on each of these occasions is significant. When Odysseus calls Penelope "daughter of Icarius," he is defining her in terms of her ties outside the palace, outside Odysseus's family. He is distancing himself from her, as is appropriate, given his cautious handling of Eumaeus. Such a distanced address goes well with the fears he expresses that he is not safe from the suitors: he has been attacked in the hall, and no one, Telemachus or anyone else, has attempted to protect him. If Penelope's son will not protect him, Icarius's daughter will not protect him either. The "anyone else," of course, also includes Eumaeus.

But there is more to the phrase "daughter of Icarius" than we have yet mentioned. This is the formula the suitors use when they talk to Penelope, though for different, but no less valid, rhetorical reasons (16.435; 18.245; 285; 21.321). They want to bring her within range of their courtship. To call her "the wife of Odysseus" would be to admit their dubious position as suitors of another man's wife. Similarly, had Odysseus referred to Penelope as "the wife of Odysseus," he would risk breaking his cover in front of Eumaeus.

If Eumaeus has recognized, or suspects, who the beggar is, Odysseus's opening words tell the swineherd that he is avoiding even a covert claim that Penelope is his wife. Further, if Eumaeus repeats this formula when reporting back to Penelope, Odysseus's use of the suitors' formula will provide *her* with a pretext for maintaining *her distance* from him and, beyond that, for treating him on a par with the suitors rather than as her husband. This point is worth noting, because Penelope ultimately creates a situation where Odysseus must become her suitor once again in order to reclaim her hand.

Aware, no doubt, that Eumaeus will have noted the conflict between his life story as presented in the hall and his life story as presented in the swineherd's hut, Odysseus promises he will soon tell the queen the truth about Odysseus and pointedly reminds Eumaeus that he and Odysseus bore their afflictions together. "Order Penelope," he says, "to stay in the halls, eager though she is, until sunset. Then she can ask me about her husband's day of return" (17.569–71). Eumaeus is relegated to the role of palace messenger by both Penelope and Odysseus. It is one thing for the queen to send her loyal swineherd on errands; for a beggar to do so is rather more presumptuous, especially when the message he must bring is itself somewhat presumptuous: "Tell the queen to wait. And tell her to ask about her husband's return (not simply about news pertaining to him)."

In telling the queen she must wait, Odysseus compels her to meet him on his terms and at a time (and place) of his choice. He, not she, will be in control. Thus begins a battle of wills between husband and wife—a battle which Penelope will, ultimately, if temporarily, win. But now Odysseus conveys the impression that he is in charge. He is ordering her to do what he says, using the imperative "command" (*anōchthi*). In both the *Iliad* and the *Odyssey*, *anōchthi* designates a command from a person in charge to his subjects or characters of a lower status.[8]

The beggar behaves as master of the house. He gives directions as to where and how he should be seated during his sunset interview with the queen: nearer the fire, since his clothing is so threadbare, "as you yourself know since you were the first I begged help from." Odysseus reminds Eumaeus that he must insist on a position by the hearth because the swineherd has not permitted him continued use of his spare cloak. There is a rebuke here and, perhaps, a hint of menace. Although the business of the cloak is significant to the two men in different ways, it serves, at the same time, as a symbol of their relationship consequent upon Odysseus's disguise: that of host and suppliant respectively rather than of slave and master. By concluding his remarks to Eumaeus with a reminder of his suppliant status and of Eumaeus's reluctance to part with his spare cloak, Odysseus reaffirms his determination to maintain his disguise just as surely as Eumaeus maintains his resolve not to acknowledge who he is. Eumaeus has not yet received a promise of freedom, a homestead, and a much-courted wife. Each has reasons for behaving with calculated obtuseness.

The hearth, of course, is the proper place for a suppliant, as in Scheria. But in Ithaca the palace fireplace is actually the central place in Odysseus's own home. It will be ablaze, not just full of ashes like Alcinous's, because the weather is cool, as we are frequently reminded by all the allusions to the cloak. There may be more to Odysseus's strategy here than just keeping warm. He is taking up the place at the hearth which is his; he is standing where he is entitled to stand. His choice of sunset as a meeting time diminishes the possibility that he will be recognized. Similarly, his choice of the hearth as the backdrop to his conversation with Penelope will, if he positions himself with care, allow him a good view of his wife but make it more difficult for her to see him clearly.

Eumaeus, for once, does not question the instructions given him. He takes the message to Penelope immediately. Her suggestion about distracting the suitors with a party can be ignored, since the beggar is not going to meet her now. Perhaps Eumaeus realizes, as readers will, that the swineherd is no longer in control of the beggar's destiny.

The Contest Begins

Penelope is shocked that Eumaeus reappears alone: is it the beggar's fear or shame? she wonders aloud to Eumaeus. Eumaeus's response is cunning. He concedes that there is fear. As for shame, well, the proposed delay safeguards Penelope's reputation not just the beggar's. Eumaeus thus calms any feathers ruffled by the beggar's order (*anōgen,* 17.582) that the queen wait for him by pointing out that the revised arrangement is to her advantage. Penelope, able, of course, to "think her way around situations," *periphrōn,* acknowledges that the beggar is obviously not *aphrōn,* "feckless," himself. At first we assume she is referring to the forethought about her own reputation. But the following lines make it clear that she is noting the beggar's wisdom in not irritating the suitors, not accepting the swineherd's advice about her reputation. Which consideration weighed more heavily with her we have no means of knowing. Suffice it to say that she complies with the beggar's request and does not send Eumaeus back to confirm her rendezvous.

Eumaeus, nudged by all concerned from center stage, returns to the hall and announces to Telemachus his intent to go back to the farm and look after the pigs. Making the rhetorical best of the situation, he says to the young prince: "You take charge now." Telemachus suggests, however, that the swineherd dine with them before he leaves (as if everyone has not already gorged himself sufficiently by this point). Eumaeus complies. In fact, he does not leave until evening is falling, the suitors' party is in full swing, and the time for the rendezvous is approaching. Obviously it will not be as quiet in the palace as the disguised Odysseus had suggested it would be. But, there again, the sunset meeting, as we have suggested, was more of a power play by Odysseus than a genuinely practical arrangement. Penelope has waited twenty years. She can wait a little longer. And while she waits, the Muse begins a new book and introduces a new character: another beggar.

[12]

Comely Thighs and Broad Shoulders

Arnaeus, a well-known beggar-about-town with an insatiable appetite for food and wine, is consequently large and lacking in strength. The suitors call him "a male Iris," the Muse explains, because he runs errands for them; and it is by this name that he is identified throughout book 18. The detail is intriguing on two counts: first, we have just observed Eumaeus's conversion into an errand boy by Penelope and Odysseus; second, there is no suggestion, as yet, that the suitors have agreed upon a nickname for Odysseus, who has not given them a name for himself and whose presence has been remarkable, if of short duration.

Beggars and dogs, like returning princes, have a sense of what their territory is. It is not that Irus is pretending to a role he cannot fulfill, as some have suggested.[1] He is exactly what he seems to be: a beggar whose plumpness attests his professional success. The palace has been part of his beggarly domain for some time. If beggars come from Zeus, Irus has some right to protection and to the generosity of men. Not surprisingly, Irus is upset to discover another beggar in the great hall and orders him out before they come to blows. Odysseus points out that there is quite enough food for both of them (who share the same lot in life) and warns him not to provoke a fight, for if he does, Irus will not "return for a second time into the great hall of Odysseus, son of Laertes" (18.24).

The warning is ironic, ominous, and challenging. It is ironic in that Odysseus's claim that there is enough food for two beggars is more than amply justified. There is enough food for over a hundred suitors and household help in addition to Penelope and Telemachus. Although Eumaeus consumes the odd hog before it gets to table, there are still, Odysseus later claims, pigs running around outside the door. But Odysseus is no more prepared to share his territory with the suitors than Irus is to share with another beggar, though both have access to more than they need.

What is ominous and challenging is Odysseus's choice of words when he says Irus will not enter the hall *deuteron,* "a second time." Although Irus has often visited the hall before, this is his first visit since Odysseus's return to what Odysseus now pointedly identifies as Odysseus's palace. His reference to the lord of the manor is not just for Irus's benefit. It is Odysseus's first mention, in the palace, of his real name, a reminder to the suitors that the great hall is no more their territory than it is Irus's.

Antinous, still smarting from the curse Odysseus has placed upon him, proposes a fight. The winner will get a paunch of his choice filled with fat and blood, will always feast with the suitors, and will be the only beggar allowed to join their company and beg from them. It is a nice way of getting rid of Eumaeus's friend, since the odds obviously seem to favor the younger, if plump, Irus over the older and more ragged interloper. Exclusive rights to the palace are also Odysseus's goal. In setting terms for the fight among beggars, Antinous sets terms for the much bloodier struggle that will leave every suitor dead.

The remaining suitors concur with Antinous's proposal. When the cautious Odysseus remarks that the suitors might intervene on his opponent's side, they promise not to interfere and Telemachus offers his personal guarantee, as Odysseus's host, that there will be no foul play. Again, irony surfaces. It will not be much of a fair fight when Odysseus and his companions shoot the unarmed suitors down in the hall. Odysseus girds up his rags for combat:

> But Odysseus girded himself with the rags around his loins, and then he showed his comely and great thighs, and he showed his broad shoulders and his chest and heavy arms. Athena came near and made the limbs of the shepherd of the people greater. And all the suitors were astonished. (18.66–71)

The outcome of the fight is now predictable and becomes the topic of a grim jest among the suitors: Irus will soon be Ex-Irused. Unfortunately for him, Antinous's ego is at issue here. The suitor offers his quivering champion an incentive to fight hard: failure will result in deportation to Echetus, "Crippler of All Men," who will cut off his nose, then disembowel him. Irus is paralyzed with terror. The contrast between Antinous and Odysseus is striking. Antinous, though full of insolent words, likes to get others to do his dirty work. He suggested ambushing Telemachus (rather than killing the youth on the spot) but does not join the ambuscade. Now he does not simply kill Odysseus when the latter curses him, but uses a fat beggar as his substitute. If the beggar fails, he will have someone else mutilate the wretch. Antinous lacks Odysseus's cold ruthlessness.

Irus's fate is a matter of utter indifference to Odysseus. He decides not to kill him with a single blow for fear of arousing suspicions, and so he crushes the bones in his head and drags his bloodied body through the hall and out through the gates. Then he sets him against the wall and warns:

> Now sit there in your wretchedness, scaring away pigs[2] and dogs, and don't you be king of strangers and beggars in case you run into some greater evil. (18.105–8)

Antinous presents the rewards, without protest, giving Odysseus the promised paunch of fat and blood. Amphinomus, by contrast, not only sets two loaves of bread before Odysseus but drinks to his health and future good fortune from a cup of gold. He is impressed by the stranger's performance, and Odysseus by Amphinomus's gesture. But the considerate suitor does not heed the long and detailed warning Odysseus quietly gives him to leave the palace (18.125–50). Instead he returns to his place—destined, the Muse notes, for death at the hands of Telemachus. This most considerate suitor is, curiously, the first one marked for death at the hands of a specific member of Odysseus's group. It is a chilling moment in the narrative. From now on, such glimpses of the future massacre occur with increasing frequency. The suitors' doom is as inexorable as Odysseus himself.

Beauty Sleep

The Muse's anticipation of the massacre radically changes the atmosphere of the epic and thus sets Penelope's next appearance in a different light. Penelope puts on a "show of beauty" to counterbalance Odysseus's "show of muscle." Athena prompts her to make an appearance among the suitors "to set their hearts beating fast and win greater honor from her husband and her son" (18.160–62). Penelope, however, assures Eurynome that her sole purpose in entering the hall is to advise Telemachus. There is a sharp contrast, then, between what Penelope says is her motivation and what the Muse says it is. If Athena is a divine symbol of what is going on in Penelope's mind, the queen is coming out at least partly to flirt, as in her first entrance into the epic. Although she may have seen (and probably heard) the beggar's fight with Irus, she does not grasp, as Amphinomus does, how radically the situation has changed, even if (despite the Muse's assurances to the contrary) she suspects that the beggar is her long-lost husband.

To glimpse the tensions at work here, let us consider the Muse's comment that Penelope "laughs a meaningless laugh" (18.163), just before she addresses Eurynome. Scholars here seek meaning in what the Muse describes as meaningless. Theories abound. D. B. Levine claims the laugh expresses the queen's confidence in and appreciation of her own trickery regarding the suitors.[3] If he is right, then the laugh is most meaningful, and the Muse has lied to us. But it is surely strange that Penelope is laughing at all, as Clay notes, albeit obliquely, by suggesting that *achreion*, which we have translated as "meaningless," ought to be rendered by "uncharacteristic."[4] Penelope more often weeps (or claims to weep). Why does she laugh so meaninglessly or uncharacteristically at this moment? There has already been some ungentle laughter in book 18: the derisive laughter of the suitors at Irus's expense. Is Penelope also mocking someone in her laughter: the suitors, for instance, as Levine suggests? Or is hers a "dry," humorless, laugh—perhaps even an embarrassed laugh? She *is* coming down to flirt with the suitors whom she claims she wants out of her home.

Her behavior may seem somehow inappropriate. After all, the suitors are not alone. Telemachus is present. So is the disguised Odysseus. And the Muse has told us that her performance is designed to enhance her standing in their eyes too. But how? Such an appearance defies the instructions relayed to her from Odysseus, who did not want to meet her at this point. Her uncharacteristic, dry, humorless, and embarrassed laugh may well owe its origin to her entrance into the hall before sunset, before the suitors are gone. If Odysseus plans to have his first meeting with his wife, after so many years, in the dimly lit, private, and disguised intimacy of the blazing hearth, his expectation is shattered. There is a kind of poetic justice in this, since Penelope had offered the beggar a personal and private interview on her terms, which he refused. Now he will see her first from the sidelines as she makes a grand entry before 108 eager young suitors. We are witnessing a continuing struggle for control of the initiative between the beggar and Penelope. By this move Penelope regains the upper hand.

Penelope tells Eurynome that her heart longs as it has never longed before to show herself to the suitors. Yet she wants to advise her son against further conviviality with the suitors. Although there is a fundamental contradiction in these two purposes, Eurynome finds none. Perhaps the answer lies in her comment that Telemachus has reached puberty. This is the time when, according to Odysseus's instruction, Penelope should remarry if he had not returned. The reader has not yet been informed of this crucial detail, which Eurynome, presumably, knows. Thus the idea of warning Telemachus to get out of the suitors' company is to ensure he is not in the way while she is in the process of selecting a new husband. Penelope's appearance at this moment must seem to Eurynome an announcement that she is ready to remarry—hence the attendant's advice to wash her body and touch up her face, since her cheeks are marred by tears. (One would not want the men to lose interest).

The Muse obscures the situation by her maddening deployment of the split between what Penelope says she will and will not do, and what Athena does anyway. Penelope refuses to beautify herself, but Athena puts her to sleep and beautifies her much as she beautified Odysseus before his one punch fight with Irus. The goddess applies oil of ambrosia, such as Aphrodite uses, enhances Penelope's stature, and makes her skin like new ivory. The idea, surely, is to augment her attraction to men. Yet Penelope, on waking, prays that Artemis will kill her so she will no longer have to weep in yearning for the remarkable husband she lost at Troy. When she appears holding a shiny veil before her face, however, the suitors are overwhelmed by her erotic beauty.[5] Their limbs are loosened as limbs are traditionally loosened by Aphrodite:

> And the knees of the suitors were loosened and their hearts beguiled with desire, and each one desired to lie in bed by her side. (18.212–13)

There is a nicely ominous overtone amid the eroticism here: the suitors' *knees* are loosened—the joints loosened in Homeric death. This overtone is itself enhanced by recollection of the similarly surprised (though not erotic) response of the suitors to Odysseus's enhanced appearance when he tucks up his rags to fight Irus. This time Odysseus is part of the crowd. He sees his wife meticulously groomed with Autinoe and Hippodameia at her side and lacks our privileged knowledge that her ravishing appearance results not from conscious preparation on her part, but from the cosmetic skills of Athena, practiced while she slept.

Just as the Muse makes no explicit comment on Penelope's reaction to the powerful limbs beneath the beggar's rags, so she passes over Odysseus's reaction to the sight of his wife.[6] Her silence on both scores keeps us from grasping the full subtext of what is happening. Obviously Odysseus must notice the suitors' amorous reaction to his wife. But he has no means of knowing whether her present appearance is routine, undertaken of her own volition, or an occurrence which is, as Penelope assures Eurynome, rare in the sense that she has not often so actively *desired* to appear before them (18.164–65).

Odysseus does know that Penelope has acted against the spirit of his instructions if not against the precise details. She could, after all, claim that she would meet him privately and later, as he had asked. Yet she first presents herself before his eyes not as the grieving wife but as the dazzling beauty all men want to marry— and who may now be ready to choose. Penelope (and Athena) has devised a rather dangerous gamble. Odysseus is not noted for mercy toward those who oppose him.

My Son Is Fully Grown

Penelope's first action on entering is to chastise her son for his treatment of the beggar, for being less mature than he should be now that he has reached manhood:

> Telemachus, your mind and your thought are not steadfast anymore. You used to revolve more resourceful thoughts when you were still a child. But now, when you are grown up and you've reached the age of manhood, and someone from afar would say that you are the offspring of a rich man, just by looking at your stature and beauty, your mind and thought are no longer proper. What an event has occurred in the hall: you allowed a stranger to be so disgracefully treated. Now if a stranger, sitting in our house, endures being dragged around and ill treated, it is on you that shame and guilt will fall in men's eyes. (18.215–25)

Telemachus politely, but firmly, justifies his inactivity as best he can, but insists he is now a man. He thus corroborates in self-defense Penelope's claim that he is of age. She is thus technically free to remarry. And Telemachus has conceded that she is. Telemachus fails to grasp that he has fallen into a rhetorical trap, since he is more concerned with excusing his failure to intervene in the fight between Irus and the beggar. Irus, he notes, is lolling about loose-limbed and unable to move, and he wishes the suitors were themselves loose-limbed because they are hanging about in various places in the palace.

There is unconscious humor in Telemachus's words, since the suitors are at present loose-limbed under the spell of Penelope's beauty. His reply needs no response from Penelope, because Telemachus has simply missed the point of her maneuver. Instead, Eurymachus moves into the conversation, ignoring Telemachus's bloodthirsty comments and perhaps catching the hint that Penelope is ready to choose. To get into a quarrel with Telemachus (who favors his suit anyway) would be counterproductive. Instead, he flatters Penelope's beauty and her qualities of mind as well. Her appearance dispels all the anxiety stirred by Odysseus's trouncing of Irus. Ironically, then, Penelope's entrance makes the suitors' destruction more, rather than less, inevitable.

Penelope, like Eurymachus, ignores Telemachus, but she takes meticulous care to respond to Eurymachus's compliment:

> All excellence of mine, both of beauty and of form, the immortals destroyed when the Argives embarked for Troy, and among them my own husband, Odysseus. If he were to come and take charge of this life of mine, this way my fame would be greater and fairer. (18.251–55)

There is coquettishness in her reply: if you think I'm lovely now, you should have seen me twenty years ago! Yet this reference to times past quickly becomes a justification for what she represents as a word-for-word quotation of Odysseus's parting instructions: to remarry when their son reached maturity. Announcing that the time has come, she complains that the suitors have consumed her goods rather than brought gifts of their own, as one does when courting the daughter of a rich man.

The Muse does not give her own reaction, but Odysseus's. He has discerned, apparently correctly, that Penelope is soliciting gifts from them. And he approves:

> So she spoke, and the much-enduring, divine Odysseus was glad, because she drew gifts from them, and beguiled their heart with gentle words, but her mind was set on other things. (18.281–83)

But what are these other things he perceives to be on her mind? Antinous, aware of Penelope's deviousness, thinks he has the answer: she is trying to get them to leave the palace on the pretext of having them search out appropriate gifts. "We can send heralds for that purpose," he interjects. "But we're not leaving until you choose a husband."

Although heralds are promptly dispatched and Penelope's maids soon bear the fruits of her rhetoric away for storage, we have no assurance that Antinous has frustrated Penelope's real intentions, what it was Odysseus thought she had on her mind. It would not be difficult for them to go home and return with gifts just as quickly as their heralds do. As we will see shortly, they leave for the night anyway. Penelope's purpose might well be the opposite of what Antinous thinks: to ensure not only that the suitors bring gifts, but that they remain, rather than leave. Antinous has failed, so far, to outthink Eumaeus, Telemachus, and Odysseus. There is no reason to suppose that he can so quickly outthink Penelope.

In requesting gifts, Penelope has announced that she will marry soon. But why now? Since Odysseus approves whatever he discerns her strategy to be, he is unlikely to be hoping that she will marry someone else. Perhaps he thinks she has concluded that Odysseus will be back at any moment or is actually back now because she is forcing matters toward a resolution. She possibly figures that the returning Odysseus, contrary to what Eumaeus has said, may have no money, and thus she wishes to contribute new funds to the coffers to be on a par with him.

The Suitors Retire

As Penelope intrudes on the world of men, so Odysseus establishes his authority over the women as evening approaches. He orders them away to look after Penelope; he will see that the hall is lit with torches. He is taking charge in his palace, and he wants Penelope to know this and to remind her of their rendezvous. But as he takes over, he discovers the situation is more complicated than he had realized. Melantho, who, the Muse tells us, is in love with (and a lover of) Eurymachus, resents this exercise of authority by a beggar made overconfident, she assumes, by his thrashing of Irus. Odysseus frightens her and the other maids by threatening to report her to Telemachus, who will cut her to pieces. Odysseus has detected something in Telemachus's attitude toward the maids that makes his name feared among them.

Eurymachus takes up where his mistress Melantho has left off, taunting Odysseus for his unwillingness to work. Odysseus replies that he would happily compete with him in any kind of manual work, even a soldier's work with the spear. This last remark is tantamount to a challenge to fight and is ignored by Eurymachus, either because it is beneath his dignity to fight with a beggar or because he is afraid. Odysseus concludes with a biting taunt of his own: if Odysseus comes back, the hall's wide doors will be too narrow for Eurymachus to escape through. Eurymachus, when provoked, no more resorts to deadly violence than did Antinous. Both are better with words than deeds and fear physical confrontation with the beggar. Eurymachus is forced back onto the same rationalization used by his mistress Melantho: that the beggar is emboldened by his success over Irus. For physical action, he copies Antinous's feeble lead and hurls a stool at Odysseus, lacking originality in his offensive behavior and aim. He misses his mark, since Odysseus crouches down. But this time the suitors react with hostility toward the beggar not his assailant. Still, the menace disappears quickly when Telemachus suggests they go home for the night. And they do so. There is great irresolution among the suitors about how to handle this cheeky intruder.

The possibility that the suitors will ultimately resort to violence is not lost on Odysseus, who instructs Telemachus to store all weapons away. Telemachus tells Eurycleia to lock up not only the weapons but the maids. Odysseus is saved from countermanding Telemachus's order when Eurycleia notes that they will need people to light their way in the dark. Although Telemachus declares that his beggar-guest will do the job, he does not follow up his order that the maids be confined to quarters. His instruction is simply ignored. Odysseus wants to test the maids as he has tested the suitors, in a trial where the accused do not realize they are being tried. But Telemachus's suggestion again shows that the maids have reason to fear him.

Odysseus, now carrying a torch, is curiously concealed by the very light he carries. There is not a flutter of recognition from Eurycleia, who later that evening recognizes him. The Muse insists that we notice the matter of illumination. She tells us Athena became a torchbearer for father and son, shedding about the palace a light whose rays suggest to Telemachus the presence of a god. It is a beautiful narrative touch, for when Odysseus first disclosed his identity to Telemachus, his son suspected he was a god, not his father. Some such suspicion may linger in his mind despite his acknowledgment of the beggar as his father. As recognition does not necessarily imply acknowledgment, acknowledgment does not necessarily imply recognition. Odysseus, who probably discerns more good than harm in such confusion comments: "Control the thought: that's the way the gods operate. Now go to sleep. . . . I must provoke the maids and your mother a little more. She, in her grief, will ask me about each thing separately" (19.42–46). Here is his formula for the interview with Penelope—still his most immediate concern. It is not his intention to answer questions but to provoke them (19.45).[7]

My Beauty and Form

The party is over. The house is now in the hands of the women and, less obviously, at first, of Odysseus, the sole remaining guest still at large. For an instant we have an image of tranquil, upper-class, wifely domesticity. Yet, even as Penelope takes her seat in her fireside chair, inlaid with ivory and silver, she is reintroduced in the same paradoxical manner we noted in book 18: the Muse compares her to "Artemis or Aphrodite"—conflicting, juxtaposed images, disturbing in their mutual exclusivity. Artemis is as totally virginal as Aphrodite is promiscuous. A loyal wife is neither.

The continued presence of Odysseus among the women is a jarring anomaly. Understandably, Melantho is irritated at his insolence. She, unlike the suitors, has every right to be present and to fulfill her normal duties, such as lighting the hall. She therefore berates Odysseus, tells him to leave, and threatens to hit him with a torch if he does not. Odysseus's angry response that he is a beggar who begs out of necessity is not adequate justification for remaining after the guests have left, especially when he has been amply fed. His argument that he once owned slaves and had his own palace does not justify his taking up residence in someone else's palace.

Odysseus's most telling contentions are the following. First, Melantho should not irritate her mistress and lose her standing among the maids: Penelope is not objecting to his presence. Second, even if Odysseus never returns, she will have Telemachus to deal with.[8] Reckless maids do not escape him, "since he is no longer a child" (19.88). If Odysseus has deduced that Melantho is Eurymachus's lover, his words imply that her unseemly behavior is not limited to insulting beggars. Melantho is silenced. Her relationship to Penelope is already tenuous: Penelope is angry at Melantho's transferal of loyalty to the suitors, since she had looked after the maid when she was a child (18.322–23).[9] And if Eurymachus is Penelope's favorite suitor, as both Telemachus and Athena presume, things will be worse. (The Muse herself thinks Amphinomus is the leading contender!)

Penelope joins the conversation and affirms Odysseus's condemnation of Melantho. She calls the maid a bitch and announces that her "great achievement" is not unknown to her and that she will pay for it with her life. The usual explanation that Penelope is angry at Melantho for berating the beggar surely makes no sense. But such a minimal tongue-lashing hardly merits the death sentence. Only if Penelope has recognized Odysseus or is angry (or jealous) about Melantho's relationship with Eurymachus would such an extreme reaction make sense. Penelope may have 107 other suitors, but it is not nice to know that a leading (and possibly favorite) contender has slept with your (younger) maid. Penelope's explosion of wrath is an interesting reminder of what she has observed without comment or overt reaction. Penelope can hardly begin executing her maids when no one even goes along with Telemachus's efforts to have them locked in their rooms at night—surely his effort to keep them out of the suitors' beds. But if Penelope suspects that the beggar is Odysseus, she is surely agreeing to the placement of Melantho's name on the list of those to be eliminated, along with Antinous.

Odysseus's chastisement of Melantho is as much for Penelope's ears as for the naughty maid. There is an ironic latent symmetry to this scene. A maid is chastised for bedding down with a suitor by a beggar about to have a tête-à-tête with the queen while everyone else is in bed. Bewilderment, as much as fear, silences Melantho for good as Penelope tells Eurynome to pull up a chair for Odysseus and begins to question him.

Her interview starts formally:

> Stranger, this question I shall ask you myself: Who are you from among men? Where is your city, and where are your parents? (19.104–5)

Odysseus, instead of answering directly, says flatteringly:

> My dear woman, no one of mortals upon the boundless earth would find fault with you; for your fame reaches the broad heaven. (19.107–8)

Odysseus is usually more careful to employ more courteous terms when addressing a woman whose status is above that which he is assuming at the time. He calls Arete, for example, either by her name or by the title *basileia,* "queen" (7.146, 241), as Eumaeus addresses Penelope (17.513). The vocative *gynai,* when not used of wives, is reserved for conversation with women who are younger or of lower social status. Hence our translation, "my dear woman." Odysseus calls Nausicaa *gynai* in 6.168 and Melantho *gynai* in 19.81.[10] Although *gynē,* the generic term for an adult woman, is ambiguous, it never fails to suggest "wife" when used by a husband to his wife.[11] When Penelope cites, for the suitors' benefit, Odysseus's parting instructions about when she should remarry, she represents him as calling her *gynai* (18.259).

Odysseus's first words, then, acknowledge his relationship to Penelope and thus answer all her questions at once, if she chooses to accept them as an answer. And he persists in this vein: *gynai* is the only vocative form of address he uses when speaking to her either before his formal self-disclosure in *Odyssey* 23 or after it.[12] His next words tell her that no one could take exception to her conduct. He has nothing to fault. And when he adds that her fame reaches the heavens, he reiterates the grand formula he used when identifying himself to Alcinous in 9.19–20: "I am Odysseus, son of Laertes . . . and my fame reaches heaven." He thereby accords Penelope a heroic stature equal to his own or that of a "blameless king" (19.109), one who fears gods. Her achievements as a woman and a wife match those of the greatest male symbols of virtuous conduct.

Penelope must either conclude that her visitor is claiming to be her husband or that he is more arrogant than his detractors have suggested. Odysseus surely shapes his words toward that end—hence the compliments, whose very fulsomeness establish that he is not being rude. He is not forcing her to acknowledge him. But he is indicating that if she does, she will be regaining a husband who holds her in the highest regard. Odysseus's oblique self-revelation gives Penelope the latitude to respond as she sees fit, but conceals what he is saying from the maids, of whose presence both are aware. That is why the previous conversation between Odysseus and Melantho is important. Melantho "reads" the stranger as a presumptuous imposter. Someone so insolent to the leading princes of the area would be capable of calling the queen "woman." With the audience of maids in mind, Odysseus goes on to insist that Penelope not ask him about his family or native land, because he is a man of many sorrows and because it is unfitting that he should cry in another's house. Such behavior would lead one of Penelope's handmaidens to get angry and say that he swims in tears because he is drunk.

Penelope does not take offense but reacts modestly to Odysseus's praises, declaring that the gods destroyed her beauty when Odysseus left.

She acknowledges the paean to her excellence, her *aretē,* but then redefines *aretē* in more conventionally feminine terms which Odysseus has pointedly avoided: while others laud her beauty, he has made no allusion to her beauty at all. She reacts to what he leaves out as well as to what he says. Odysseus could hardly miss her point, since her reply is, apart from the opening vocative, exactly what she replied to Eurymachus's flattering compliment about her beauty in Odysseus's presence:

> Stranger, all excellence of mine, both of beauty and of form, the immortals destroyed when the Argives embarked for Troy, and among them my own husband, Odysseus, if he were to come and take charge of my life, greater would be my fame and fairer this way. (19.124–28)

She reminds her visitor that though her beauty is diminished, others have praised it. She is courted, she adds, by many princes from Dulichium, Same, Zacynthus, and Ithaca—against her will, of course.[13] Her fame is not just that of being a faithful, waiting wife, as Odysseus has implied.

Penelope now responds to excuse what she clearly suspects is an undertone of reproof in Odysseus's words: his maltreatment in her house. She excuses herself on the grounds of the same ever-present suitors whose attention to her beauty has just served her well rhetorically. Next, Penelope sets out in detail her wifely strategy of the loom, the symbol of her "fame which reaches heaven." She announced, she says, that she believed Odysseus was dead but kept her ardent young men at bay for three years by unraveling at night what she had woven by day until her maids betrayed her scheme. She calls her action, rightly and cunningly, *doloi,* "treacherous deceit," something for which Odysseus is famed and which he admires in others. The strategy of the loom is a strategy of delay. Perhaps she also hopes that her listener's admiration for her skillful handling of the situation will mask the fact that the strategy of the loom began and ended before Telemachus came of age, for the suitors have been in the house for years, but the announcement of Telemachus's coming of age has only just been made that very evening! The tale of the loom is a preamble to something more troubling.

Her apologia made, Penelope returns to her original question:

> Yet even so tell me of your lineage, where are you from? For you are not born from some mythical oak or from a rock. (19.162–63)

There is a strange infusion of irony and sarcasm in her repeated question. She has recast it now with a phrase suggesting that he cannot really be born of rock or from a tree. We might be tempted to pass it over without comment if the same phrase did not also occur in *Iliad* 22.126.

There Hector debates with himself about the need to engage in what he suspects will be fatal combat with Achilles (22.129–30). Part of him would prefer to avoid fighting. "I cannot," he explains to himself, "engage with him as if I were born from an oak tree or from a rock." Such, at least in gist, is what the phrase means in Greek, though commentators from Eustathius onward have had little success in making precise sense of it.[14] He can no longer flirt with doom, with Achilles, as a youth flirts with a woman. Most critics take the phrase to be a proverb, alluding to the folkloric origins of humans from trees or stone, as in the myth of human regeneration from stones in the story of Deucalion and Pyrrha.[15] If so, it is an assertion that he is a person of flesh and blood, not a creature of myth or the less sensate nonanimal or inorganic world, who is not governed by the laws of human life and death.

Penelope's use of the same phrase Hector uses may be her call to the disguised Odysseus to abandon the illusions of myth for reality. It is hardly less dramatic or less appropriate to the immediate situation than Hector's use of the same image, since Odysseus has been wandering for years in a much more mythic world than that of Hector's Troy, inhabited by fantastical subhuman and superhuman creatures. Odysseus's interview with Penelope sets the stage for the massacre of his enemies in the hall at the same point in the *Odyssey* as Hector's death occurs in the *Iliad,* book 22. If the *Odyssey*'s muse was aware of the *Iliad*'s muse, or vice versa, the rich resonance enhances both epics. If the *Iliad* is here refracting the *Odyssey* —for the phrase makes sense in and of itself in the Odyssean context— Hector's allusion to the flirtatious dalliance of man and woman would recall the cautious interchanges between Odysseus and Penelope in *Odyssey* 19 which serve as a prelude to their acceptance of each other. If we pursue the more traditional assumption that the *Odyssey* is aware of the *Iliad,* Penelope's imagery summons the disguised Odysseus to depart, like Hector, from the world of fantasy and face the harsh contest which he must undertake if he is to reaccommodate himself to the real world. The verbal recollection of Hector (rather than of Achilles) may be significant. It implies that Penelope sees her visitor as a person who, despite his disguise, is heroic, but who will, in all likelihood, lose the contest he must face, as Hector lost to Achilles.

Odysseus's response to her restated question is a modification of his first reaction. Previously he had begun: "My dear woman"(*O gynai,* 19.107). Now he begins more specifically and with less familiarity: "My dear chaste woman, married to Odysseus, son of Laertes" (*O gynai aioidoiē Laertiadeo Odysēos,* 19.165). The vocative running all the way to the caesura reaches directly from himself as speaker to her as listener—until modified by the distancing reference first to the patronymic Laertiades, then to Odysseus, both in the genitive case. If you won't accept me addressing you as wife, then let me address you, nonetheless, as wife of Odysseus.

His reaction suggests irritation: "Will you never leave off cross-questioning me about my lineage?" Her sarcasm and her strategy of delay have not passed unnoticed. But he has detected, or suspects he has detected, another undercurrent in her words, as we shall see shortly. With a show of resignation, he appears to accede to her request: "Well, I'll tell you everything. But you'll be presenting me with more pains than those that grip me now" (19.165–66). An audience on first hearing these words might well assume, as Penelope probably does, that they are a preamble to self-disclosure. Instead Odysseus puts on his most defensive mask—that of the Cretan.

[13]

Courting One's Own Wife

> There is a land called Crete, in the midst of the wine-dark sea, beautiful and rich, surrounded by water. There are many men there, past counting, and ninety cities. Their language is not the same but mixed. There are Achaeans, there are greathearted true Cretans, Cydonians, Dorians of the three tribes, and godlike Pelasgians. Among their towns is Cnossus, a big city. There Minos reigned for nine years, he who conversed with great Zeus, the father of my father, Deucalion, the son of greathearted Deucalion. Deucalion fathered me and the prince Idomeneus; but Idomeneus went to Troy in his beaked ships with the sons of Atreus, and my famous name is Aethon. I was the younger by birth, while he was the older and better man. (19.172–84)

Odysseus's miniature lecture on Crete's history and inhabitants suggests that Penelope has no idea where it is or what it is like. When he talks to the youthful, false shepherd and to Eumaeus, by contrast, he assumes his listener knows where Crete is and who lives there. He addresses Penelope as if she were the naive young woman he left twenty years ago, rather than the Penelope of the present day, matured in sorrow, for she is now assuming the former role: the bride-to-be who must be courted all over again. Odysseus returns sarcasm for sarcasm, disguise for disguise. Odysseus knows Penelope is not ignorant of Greek geography. Her son has just returned from Sparta, her husband has traveled to Troy, and she has interviewed visitors from all over the Greek world.

Odysseus takes his audience and Penelope back to a time before the Greek expedition arrived in Asia Minor, that is, shortly after Odysseus left Penelope. Not only does he claim he enjoyed prestige as Idomeneus's brother (his rank upgraded from that described to Eumaeus), but he gives his Cretan persona a name, identifies his father as Deucalion, and says he met Odysseus in Crete. Given Penelope's suggestion that he is not born of oak or stone, the name Deucalion neatly echoes the mythic Deucalion who regenerated the human race from stones.

The Cretan Odysseus: Phase III

Odysseus does not elaborate his identity and role as the Cretan Aethon. In contrast to the pseudoautobiographies he gives the disguised shepherd and Eumaeus, he here focuses on Odysseus. Since Idomeneus had already left for Troy some ten or eleven days earlier, it falls to Aethon's lot to entertain the visiting Odysseus, as he does most generously. Although Odysseus has resorted again to his Cretan persona, he does so in order to give Penelope a glimpse of Odysseus two decades ago.

The Muse now breaks in upon his narrative (which she describes as false explanations so like the truth) to show its effect on Penelope, whose stern and frozen face thaws into tears for her husband. Whatever her reaction might be to the middle-aged man before her (who looks so like Odysseus), he has evoked in her memories of Odysseus in his youth, when she last saw him. Though he pities her, his gaze remains fixed and hard, eyes like horn or steel between their lids (in contrast to the ivory to which Penelope is compared).

"What was he like then?" Penelope asks once her tears have subsided. "What was he wearing? Who was with him?"[1]

In reply, Odysseus describes Odysseus's garments in detail. What is surprising is how unsuitable they are for war. The slinky tunic and the fleecy, purple cloak seem more appropriate to a social evening with the ladies in Sidon—and lots of women gazed at him in admiration (19.235). Penelope in those days had a husband to inspire envy and jealousy. If she has her suitors and opportunities now, he was not without his chances either. Odysseus's brooch is given particular attention. He describes it in more intricate detail than would be credible to even the most observant and attentive host. Significantly, the brooch is dominated by a hunting motif: a hound (could it be Argus?) pouncing on a fawn—the right motif for a famous hunter who is first acknowledged on his return by his hunting dog and first overtly identified by a hunting wound.

Penelope weeps and acknowledges the accuracy of his observations but persists in maintaining that Odysseus will never return and in addressing her interlocutor as "stranger"—though she says she will move from pitying him to honoring him (19.253–54). Her response again evokes from Odysseus the formula "my dear chaste woman, married to Odysseus, son of Laertes" (19.262), defining her as the wife, rather than the widow, of

Odysseus. Coming close to the brink of self-disclosure, Odysseus picks up the threads of his Cretan narrative to Eumaeus: he has heard from Pheidon, king of the Thesprotians, that Odysseus's ship, loaded with treasure (which he himself has seen and is enough to last into the tenth generation), is awaiting his return from Dodona, where he is consulting Zeus as to whether he should return openly or in secret. Odysseus is coming home, begging his way around.[2]

Odysseus's narrative here is a mixture of elements drawn from arguably real experiences, his Cretan alter ego, and select details from his travels in books 6–12. Odysseus has been in Phaeacia—something he mentions to no one in books 13–24 but those to whom his identity is fully disclosed (Telemachus, for example, in 16.227). And Odysseus will be returning alone, for he alludes to Thrinacia and the death of Odysseus's troops in retribution for their eating of the cattle of the Sun. Although Odysseus tries to break down Penelope's resistance by pulling aside his Cretan mask in this way, the antiphony of "Stranger" and "My dear chaste woman" continues. Penelope gives ground without giving in.

Her first step is to get the beggar cleaned up so she can get a better idea of what he looks like. Then he is to be given bright coverlets, tunics, and cloaks. She suggests that her maids perform the honors. Given Melantho's attitude toward Odysseus, and Penelope's generally negative feelings toward her maids, such a proposal is unsettling. The example of Agamemnon, always in Odysseus's mind, as in the Muse's, gives cause for anxiety. Agamemnon's ghost told Odysseus he had been killed by Aegisthus after being lured into his house for a feast (11.410–11)—a gesture of apparent friendliness and hospitality. But Agamemnon's greatest rage was directed against his wife, Clytemnestra, who watched him die and did not offer the most basic rites to his corpse (11.424–30).

Penelope has manipulated the situation well. At first she was in some danger from the returning Odysseus. Now he is, at least potentially, in some danger from her. His reply is prudent and well calculated:

> My dear chaste woman, married to Odysseus, son of Laertes, indeed cloaks and shiny coverlets are hateful to me since I first left the snowy mountains of Crete sailing in a long-oared ship. I would rather lie down as I used to sleep in the past through sleepless nights; for I slept many nights in a foul bed and waited for the beautifully throned, godlike Dawn. (19.336–42)

Again he reminds Penelope she is Odysseus's wife, even as he dismisses fancy clothes and coverlets. He is not yet ready to shed his disguise. Penelope's strategy is clear: if she gives the stranger items from Odysseus's wardrobe to wear, she will be better able to assess his resemblance to her husband. And the fit will indicate how much he has changed.

Such transformation could be fatal to Odysseus now, however. He accepts only the bath, and that reluctantly, since it will diminish his disguise as the filthy beggar. He also insists that he not be bathed by one of the serving girls. They will not be permitted to touch his *pous,* his foot or leg (the word designates both):

> Nor do foot baths give pleasure to my heart: nor should any woman from those who are serving women in your house touch my foot. (19.343–45)

Most obviously this leaves Penelope as his potential bather. And if she is as shrewd as Helen, why does she not volunteer to wash his feet herself? Helen claims to have recognized Odysseus when she bathed him, despite his disguise as a beggar. Helen, of course, wanted to know who her visitor was and recognized him once the clothes and dirt were stripped away. Penelope's enquiries about her visitor show she is curious too. She is either more fastidious than Helen or not as inquisitive. Or perhaps she does not want to be forced to acknowledge him now.

Odysseus does not himself suggest that the queen bathe him but quickly modifies his prohibition against maidservants:

> Unless there is some grey old woman, who knows discretion, who has suffered in her heart as much as I have. I would not begrudge letting her touch my feet. (19.346–48)

Odysseus is, oddly enough, asking for someone who might identify him, as one of the younger girls could not—hence the significance that this request follows immediately after his mention of the word *pous.* It is by a scar on his leg that he will be recognized. Even before Eurycleia washes Odysseus's feet she observes:

> I declare I have never yet seen anyone that so resembled Odysseus as you resemble him in form, voice, and feet. (19.379–81)

Odysseus responds that this is "what all men who have actually seen both of us with their eyes have observed" (19.383–85). He is certainly not trying to discourage recognition.

Penelope, who knows her way around things, compliments the stranger on his shrewd behavior and prudent words. So she offers the services of Eurycleia who nursed Odysseus from childhood, and to whom, curiously, Penelope applies the same epithet, *periphrōn,* that the Muse uses of her. She addresses Eurycleia as follows:

> Wash him who is of the same age as your master; and Odysseus is somewhere looking exactly like this man in his feet, and exactly like this man in his arms. For humans age quickly in misfortune. (19.358–60)

Penelope acknowledges a modified, inductive recognition: the physical resemblance between the stranger and Odysseus. The nature of her resistance to that recognition finds partial expression in 360: "Humans grow old quickly in misfortune." The man before her is far different from the glorious youth of twenty years ago. Penelope must now choose between the youthful but feckless suitors and the wizened but intelligent older man. Her tears for the Odysseus who was young and handsome as well as intelligent are in vain. He will never return.

As Odysseus prepares to be bathed, he again arranges the lighting carefully. He sits facing away from the hearth for fear not that Eurycleia will recognize him by an old hunting scar but that she will make her recognition public (19.391). Her words and her demeanor show she is loyal. But it has been established that the maids are on the suitors' side and that Penelope has mixed feelings. When the battle comes, Eurycleia plays an active part, but Penelope has to be kept out of the way.

The mention of the scar prompts a lengthy digression by the Muse as to how Odysseus acquired it: when he, as an infant, was set upon his grandfather Autolycus's knees by Eurycleia, who declared that Autolycus should name him. It is odd that the important ritual of naming the child is decided not by father and mother, but by grandfather and nurse, especially since, we are told, the child was much prayed for.[3] The choice of Autolycus, famous for thievery (*kleptosynē*) and breaking oaths, as the child's namer, shows the family tradition Odysseus was expected to maintain. Thus Eurycleia's double role in the naming of the infant Odysseus and the identification of the returning adult Odysseus is remarkable.

For all Odysseus's management of the lighting, it is Eurycleia's sense of touch that proves critical in this situation. She finds the scar almost instantly, not only because she knew it was there, but because she already suspected the beggar's identity. Her reaction is immediate. She lets his foot slip from her hands into the bronze bowl with a clang, weeps, and declares her recognition to Odysseus:

> Indeed you are Odysseus, dear child. But I did not really know who you were before, before I [*egō ge*] had touched my lord all over. (19.474–75)

Her suspicions turn into knowledge because she knew what she was looking for to confirm them—hence her opening words, "Indeed you are Odysseus," and the modifying enclitic *ge* following *egō* in her second sentence. Eurycleia has time to go through all these reactions and speak these two lines before Odysseus reacts. Only when she looks toward and tries to signal Penelope does he grab her by the throat. He does not threaten to kill her on the spot, but only to include her in the general slaughter of the other maids after he has retaken his palace, if she communicates what she knows. Odysseus confirms the correctness of Eurycleia's deduction. Her declaration of that recognition is the problem.

Penelope, the Muse says, is prevented by Athena from noticing Eurycleia's significant glance. What is to be communicated by a silent glance, unless tacit confirmation of what both women have already observed, in each other's presence: the resemblance between the stranger and Odysseus as he would now look (19.358–360, 379–81). Is Penelope (or the other maids still present) also prevented from hearing Eurycleia's acknowledgment or Odysseus's vow to kill her and the other maids? Even if the old nurse voiced her discovery in a subdued whisper, the sound of Odysseus's foot falling, making the water spill and forcing Eurycleia to refill the basin, could hardly have passed unnoticed. Athena's intervention confirms that Penelope does not wish to acknowledge him now. The clanging basin tells her all she wants to know.

Penelope as Procne

Once Odysseus is washed and reclad in his rags, Penelope proposes to question him further. She finds her joy in sleepless mourning, she says, like Procne, the songstress nightingale, daughter of Pandareus, who laments the death of her son Itylus (19.518–23). Few myths outdo the tale of Procne and her sister Philomela in multiplicity of family brutality and horror. Penelope, however, bypasses the stages of that myth in which women are victims and moves to where vengeful women become perpetrators of horror upon innocent victims. Procne kills her son by Zethus, Itylus, *di' aphradias,* often rendered "unwillingly," "unwittingly," or by other expressions suggesting Itylus was killed by accident (19.522–23). The word *aphradia* means something closer to "thoughtlessness," "failure to think," or "madness," as Lattimore suggests. Yet it remains an understatement: Procne is usually described as killing Itylus and serving him as food to her husband.

Penelope postulates a disturbing similarity between herself and Procne which has a special force because Procne learns her husband's crime from her tongueless sister by means of a woven tapestry. Penelope too is famous as a weaver, as is at least one of the goddesses with whom Odysseus has dallied along the way—Circe. And Penelope, like Procne and Circe, has avian connections in many traditions. Her penchant for avian imagery should not surprise us, since her name, as already noted, is suggestive of the bird *pēnelops*, a goose or wild duck. The scholiast on Aristophanes *Birds* 292 notes that *pēnelopes* once saved Penelope from drowning.

If Odysseus knows anything about myths alluded to rather than fully developed in the *Odyssey*, as he does in the case of Ino (see Chapter 2, pp. 45–46), he may deduce that Penelope's mention of Procne and Itylus hints that Penelope poses a potential threat to their son, Telemachus. In fact, the first person Penelope mentions after alluding to Procne and Itylus is Telemachus. It may not be just absence of hunger but caution that makes Odysseus decline a meal she offers him (20.136–37). Indeed, other traditions ascribe to Penelope precisely such potential destructiveness. Sophocles' lost tragedy *Euryalus* seems to have described Penelope tricking Odysseus into killing his son Euryalus by Euippe, the daughter of Tyrimmas, the Epirote (Thesprotian) king.[4]

The Geese and the Eagle

Penelope tells Odysseus she is torn between two choices: either staying faithful to her husband's bed and popular sentiment or obeying her son's urging that she marry one of the suitors to end the devastation of the household. Missing in her statement is what she herself would prefer. The people stand on one side, her son on the other. Which should she obey? Before he can answer, she says she has had a dream which she would like her visitor to interpret:

> I have twenty geese in the house away from the water eating wheat; my heart warms as I watch them. But a great eagle came from the mountain with a crooked beak and broke the necks of all of them and killed them; and they lie in the house in a heap, and he was carried off to the bright sky. (19.536–40)

The symbolism is obvious: the twenty geese (domestic birds with greedy appetites) are the suitors and the eagle who attacks them and then flies up into the air is Odysseus. That Penelope not only likes watching the geese but weeps aloud because the eagle has killed *her* geese (19.543) is both understandable and worrisome. Indeed, her dream creates a dilemma as to her own fate in the aftermath of the eagle's attack. How pleasing Odysseus would find her "dream" is not clear. Perhaps that is why Penelope assures him that it was a dream. Given the association of her name with the wild duck or goose (*pēnelops*), her sympathy with fellow waterfowl and her unhappiness with the eagle are to be expected. Besides, her realm is domestic: her realm is the palace, her home.

Penelope does not leave interpreation of the dream to her visitor, as we might expect. On the contrary, she says that the plundering eagle assumed a human voice and explained it all as follows:

> Take courage, daughter of far-famed Icarius, this is not a dream, but a true vision of good, which shall be fulfilled. The geese are the suitors, and I, who was an eagle before, have returned once more as your husband—I who shall unleash a terrible doom upon the suitors. (19.546–50)

The dream eagle, claiming to be Odysseus, addresses Penelope not as her listening visitor does, but as her suitors do: "Daughter of Icarius" (19.546). He is not claiming her as his wife but classifying her as a woman under her father's authority. Given her affection for her (fellow) geese, what awaits her at Odysseus's hands? This is the only remaining question to be answered, since the dream is now not only self-explanatory but self-explained. Even if this narrative represents a genuine dream rather than Penelope's rhetorical fiction, the only conclusion left either to the listening Odysseus or to us is that Penelope is asking her visitor to confirm or deny whether the returning Odysseus will kill the suitors and to clarify what awaits her. She has framed her narrative as a dream because it lets her distance herself from the emotional response she attributes to herself: that the prospect of the wholesale slaughter of the geese—that is, the suitors—distresses her greatly.

We have already seen that Penelope, even when awake, is not ready to accept that all the suitors must die (as Eurynome is). Thus, even if Penelope is reporting a genuine dream, her reaction is not at odds with her waking response to the possibility of a massacre. If the dream's meaning is obvious to the talking dream eagle and to the listening Odysseus, it is also obvious to Penelope. What she is really asking is "Is this what Odysseus plans to do, and what does he plan to do with me?" Only Odysseus can answer with absolute authority. Here is his reply:

> My dear woman, it is impossible to turn this dream aside and give it another interpretation, since Odysseus himself told you how he will accomplish it. The destruction of the suitors seems sure. Not one of them will escape death and the fates. (19.555–58)

Again he addresses Penelope with the vocative *gynai* —"My dear woman." But now it lacks the fuller formula "married to Odysseus, son of Laertes." How reassuring this change of address is we (and presumably Penelope) find unclear. It gives no hint of what he will do with her. As to the more explicit issue, there is no other resolution. Each and every suitor is doomed.

Now that her visitor has confirmed at least one of her carefully phrased suspicions, Penelope draws a famous distinction between dreams which can be accomplished and those which cannot:

> There are double gates of dreams that do not stay: the first are built of horn, the second of ivory. Those dreams that come through those of sawn ivory [*ELEPHAntos*] deceive [*ELEPHAirontai*], for they bring words that cannot be made real [*aKRAanta*]. But those that come out through the gates of polished horn [*KeRAon*] bring real things [*etyma*] to reality [*KRAinousi*], whenever some mortal sees them. (19.562–67)

We have used capitals here to illustrate the play between the Greek word for "ivory" (*elephas*) and the verb "deceive" (*elephairontai*), and the similar play between the word for "horn" (*keras*) and words indicating accomplishment. Dreams from the ivory gate are unfulfillable, deceptive, the *etymo*logizing tells us. Dreams from the horn gate are real and fulfillable. And my dreams, she adds, did not come from the gates of horn. So regardless of what the dream means, it is simply fantasy.

With finesse Penelope covers her emotional tracks and establishes a link between horn and reality which she will soon develop further. Having thus demolished her own "dream" and her visitor's affirmation of its meaning, she announces that the next morning she will marry the winner of an archery contest in which a bow, *biós* (21.75), will determine the winner and render her previous way of life, *biotoio,* a dream. She thus continues her wordplay with a pun later immortalized by Heraclitus, who likened life, *bíos,* to a bow, *biós,* because of the pun on the bow's "name which is life but whose work is death" (frag. 48.1).

After years of waiting, her haste now is puzzling. She is, in effect, forcing Odysseus's hand. If the suitors are to be killed, they must be killed within twenty-four hours, because when the contest begins she is declaring herself officially free to marry—regardless of whether anyone wins it. As she outlines the competition, it becomes clear that nobody but Odysseus can win it. The suitors will all eliminate themselves from contention as suitors and can be sent home. Killing them will thus be unnecessary. The geese can fly back to their ponds.

The proposed contest, like those to which most mythic suitors are subjected, is technically impossible for anyone to win:

> For now I shall appoint for a contest those axes which he used to set up in line in his halls like props for a hull under construction, twelve all together, and he would stand far off and shoot an arrow through them. (19.572–75)

As any archer knows, even to hit a single bull's eye requires calculation of the arrow's trajectory with precision. To pass an arrow through a dozen small openings set in series one would have to place the axes so as to allow for the parabola an arrow makes over even a short distance. One needs not only skill, an accurate bow, and a true arrow but familiarity with the particular weapon to be used. Even if we assume Penelope is correct in saying Odysseus used to perform precisely such a feat, we must remember that he has not handled the bow for twenty years.

Odysseus's skill in handling a bow of horn, then, will determine whether Penelope's dream of the eagle's vengeance was an elephantine fantasy or a horned reality. He has to prove himself the equal of the Odysseus of twenty years ago or he has no more chance of winning than the suitors have. Odysseus has changed. So has the weapon. That is why, later, Odysseus inspects his bow to make sure no bugs have eaten through the horn (*KERA*) from which it is made (21.393–95). Curiously, when the bow is strung, its string sings not like a Procne, a nightingale, but like her sister Philomela, the unmusical swallow.

Odysseus approves Penelope's suggestion. He reverts from the simple vocative *gynai* to the fuller formula, taking note of her chastity and her status as wife of Odysseus, son of Laertes. Whether she is prepared to acknowledge him or not, he knows he alone can string and shoot the bow. And his renewed use of the fuller formula declares his confidence.

But Penelope is not left without further resources. She does not have to marry a beggar, even one who wins the competition for her hand.

It is time for bed she says. Yet again, she offers him accommodation in the palace, on the floor of the hall, even on a bedstead which the maids can set up. Odysseus does not reply but, as we see at the beginning of the next book, decides to sleep outside the great hall in the entranceway, where Eurynome covers him with a cloak. Penelope returns with her maids to her chamber and to the role we are familiar with from the first book of the epic: crying for her own husband Odysseus. Once she has fallen asleep, however, the maids troop out past the angry and wakeful Odysseus to sleep with the suitors in a final night of wantonness.

[14]

Prelude to the Massacre

Odysseus is angry, restless, and struggling with himself and his doubts as he lies sleepless in the entranceway of his house. He is aware, as he comments to Athena, who comes to cheer him up, that he is essentially alone in his enterprise and that even if he succeeds in killing the suitors with divine help, the repercussions will be disastrous. This preface to the denouement of the *Odyssey*, outlining Odysseus's psychological state at the last moment at which he can change his mind, is vitally necessary.

In rejecting the idea of killing the maids on the spot, Odysseus reflects on the forbearance he had to show in handling his dilemma in the Cyclops's cave, which, for some strange reason, he considers a tighter corner than the one he is in now. There are, of course, parallels between the two situations. But these parallels, on the whole, suggest that his present situation is worse rather than better. He escapes the Cyclops, after all, by blinding his opponent rather than killing him and by sailing away in the nick of time. Had he killed Polyphemus, he would have been trapped in the cave. Now he is set on killing his opponents and staying at least a while.

As Odysseus reveals more of his state of mind to the sympathetic but resolute goddess Athena, it becomes clear that he has thought ahead to the dilemma which actually confronts him after the massacre of the suitors. He has perhaps foreseen that the relatives of the slain youths will converge on his palace and threaten a complete and bloody vengeance, as he inflicted on the Cyclops. No less likely, he has realized, after his conversation with Penelope, is the possibility that she will not acknowledge him anyway. If she does not, he cannot resume his position as master of the house regardless of how many suitors he kills.

The analogy with the dilemma in the Cyclops's cave, if anything, makes more sense if we see Odysseus, in this instance, as Polyphemus. After all, the suitors are the numerous daytime intruders in his house, consuming his substance, and he is the one who, the next day, will bar the doors to prevent their escape. And Odysseus himself will emerge as bloody and subhuman in appearance as Polyphemus was after one of his grotesque meals. Little wonder that he is reluctant to sleep, bearing in mind that once he loses consciousness he is as vulnerable to others as the Cyclops was to him. It is only when Athena takes him to task for his unwillingness to trust her and urges him to succumb to sleep that he eventually complies. Even the ultimately distrustful skeptic must take some things on faith.

When he falls asleep, however, Penelope wakes up and prays to Artemis, either to shoot her with an arrow in her breast and kill her or to carry her away with a storm wind to where Ocean empties its waters, just as storm winds carried off Pandareus's daughters. The first image, that of the arrow, is marvelously appropriate, given her decision to have her future marriage decided by the flight of an arrow. The second similarly recalls her conversation with Odysseus, when the tale of Pandareus's daughters, Procne and Philomela, was on her mind.

Given their beauty, both daughters of Pandareus were destined by Aphrodite for wonderful marriages. But the intervention of the rapacious storm winds forestalled these plans and whirled them off to become the Erinyes' agents of vengeance. If the reference here is to Procne and Philomela, as we suspect, rather than to additional unnamed daughters, as Eustathius suggests, they go to far-off Thrace, land of storms, where they become both the instigation to and the means of punishment for the crimes of Zethus. And they continue to ride the storm winds after their avian metamorphosis. Procne, as Penelope noted, becomes a nightingale, a melancholy bird of the night, often heard but hardly ever seen. It is with Procne, rather than Philomela, that Penelope identifies in *Odyssey* 19. Philomela, as we learn in other sources, is metamorphosed into a swallow. Both, however, become migratory birds who ride the winds at the beginning of the stormy season to destinations far from their homes and their family crimes.

Here, then, are Penelope's two wishes, as the Muse sums up. That she may die by an arrow shot from Artemis's bow with the image of the Odysseus of twenty years ago (see 20.88–90) before her eyes, rather than be won by an arrow shot by a baser man in the contest which she herself has proposed. And that she could vanish from sight into the nightingale's nocturnal darkness, however ominous and guilt-ridden that darkness may be. She cannot maintain her fantasy of the lost Odysseus once she remarries, whether the winner is one of the suitors or her older, returning husband. She cannot reject the real, as opposed to the fantasy, Odysseus if he returns (whether he proves to be the beggar who so closely resembles

Odysseus or the man whose impending return the beggar forecasts) without alienating her son, who may become a threat to her existence much as Orestes was to Clytemnestra in that parallel of which we have all been aware since the opening of the epic. What Penelope does not take into account, of course, is a solution which almost presents itself the following day: Telemachus, who reminds Helen so much of the youthful Odysseus, enters the competition and almost succeeds in stringing the bow himself.

She cannot sleep peacefully, Penelope adds, in explanation of her prayer to Artemis, because she has had evil dreams:

> For this night one like him was lying next to me again, such as he was when he went with the expedition; but my heart was glad, for I told myself it is not a dream, but a true vision at last. (20.88–90)

In what sense are these dreams evil? Perhaps because they are the ultimate illusion, demanding either the reversal of time for their fulfillment or that they be fulfilled by marriage with Odysseus's son—Telegonus, his child by Circe, as in versions of the myth which are never explicit in the *Odyssey*. How we read the possibilities depends on our willingness to accept that the Odyssean muse was drawing from a pool of tradition larger than that explicitly stated in the epic.

The last words Penelope utters about the potential for truth in her dream coincide with the advent of dawn and with Odysseus's partial awakening from sleep. The Muse says he "concluded [*syntheto*] that it was the voice of the weeping Penelope" (20.92).[1] Odysseus, half-asleep, hears a woman crying, assumes—but is not necessarily sure—that it is his wife, then imagines she is next to him. But at what point has he taken note of her weeping? The Muse says Penelope stopped weeping *before* she began to pray (20.59). Either she has started weeping again or Odysseus has heard, drowsily, her weeping and her prayer.

The conclusion Odysseus draws from what he hears or half-hears is itself partly a dream fantasy:

> He began to ponder anxiously, and she seemed to his heart to be recognizing him and to have taken a position by his head. (20.93–94)

The hypnopompic imagery brought on by the sleep Athena induces comes upon him before he is fully awake and before he has risen from his resting place. In it, Odysseus believes that Penelope is beginning to grasp who he is. While this is probably true, she certainly is not yet ready to take her stand by his head in what would be, in effect, acknowledgment. Thus the image is both real and illusory at the same time. The present participle *gignōskousa,* "recognizing," makes it clear that such acknowledgment is, to his mind, in process rather than complete. It is, we think, significant that in his vision Penelope has come to him rather than he to her. His conversation with her the previous night shows that he wants her to accept him on his own terms rather than to be forced to go to her himself on her terms. It is worth comparing the effect imagined in his dreaming state with the actual awakening of the dreaming Penelope by Eurycleia in 23.1–9. There Eurycleia stands by sleeping Penelope's head to coax her awake and tell her that her dream has been fulfilled: Odysseus is home.

It is, in fact, a beautiful moment of pathos. Had Odysseus been fully conscious of what his wife was saying in her prayer to Artemis, he would have realized that, whether or not she was moving toward acknowledgment, she is unready as yet to stand close to him as he sleeps because she is unready to accept the unreality of her own fantasy of the youthful Odysseus. Though two ivoried dreams are shattered with the dawn, at least one will be fulfilled by the following evening.

Odysseus asks for a sign that all will be well and is promptly obliged by Zeus, who sends a thunderbolt from a clear sky. The omen prompts an exclamation from, of all people, a pathetically weak woman working in the estate's flour mills, who has had to stay up all night grinding her quota of grain. We are given a sudden, almost Apuleian glimpse of the oppressive effects of the continued presence of the suitors upon ordinary people. While Eumaeus has been able to keep the pigs breeding fast enough to accommodate their appetites, maintaining the supply of bread has been more difficult. Suddenly Penelope's dream of the suitors as her pet geese consuming grain becomes a little less harmless. Some will welcome the eagle for very personal and practical reasons.

This omen explained, negative impressions of Penelope begin to mount again. Telemachus, armed with sword and spear and accompanied by his two swift dogs, emerges and asks Eurycleia whether the beggar has been properly cared for. Penelope looks after the worse among men, he comments acidly, while sending the better, dishonored, away (20.132–33). So much for Penelope's anxiety about having to marry someone worse than Odysseus. Her son does not think much of her judgment. Eurycleia defends her mistress (and herself) by a skillful reshaping of what happened the previous night. The cloak that "we" threw over Odysseus was, in fact, thrown over him by Eurynome. Yet in one respect Eurycleia holds firm. Nothing in her response suggests for a moment that she has recognized Odysseus. But, as she and Telemachus go their different ways, she cannot resist noting, when ordering the available maids to spruce up the palace for the day's revelry, that this will be a "festival day for everyone" (20.156).

With consummate skill, the Muse assembles the cast, familiar and unfamilar, for that festival day: men haul in logs; Eumaeus brings in no fewer than three large hogs; Melantheus brings in the best she-goats, and Philoetius brings in a heifer and fat, imported she-goats. Pleasantries, insults, and encouraging words are exchanged. The suitors, meanwhile, still trying to dream up ways of killing Telemachus, are interrupted by the arrival of an eagle clutching a dove—an omen Amphinomus interprets, strangely enough, as unfavorable to their cause. There is no compelling reason for him to assume that the youthful Telemachus is not himself the dove in the omen. In this instance, the way in which the omen is interpreted tells us more than does the omen itself. Amphinomus has lost confidence in the situation and worries that the roles of predator and victim are about to be reversed. His conclusion is that they had better forget about plotting against Telemachus and concentrate on feasting.

How much Amphinomus, Telemachus, and the others know about the special day ahead is not clear, for Penelope, though she has promised to decide on a new husband, has told only the beggar about the proposed contest of the bow. Telemachus certainly knows nothing about it at this stage, and if the suitors have had advance warning, via the maids, the Muse gives no indication to that effect. The only indications that anything has changed since the previous day are the mixed signals Telemachus gives by seating the beggar at a special table on a humble stool which he places among the suitors. It is an act of provocation which makes the beggar virtually the equal of the noblemen and well above Melantheus and Eumaeus, who act as waiters. Telemachus advances that provocation by serving the beggar from a golden cup, vowing to defend him against ill-treatment, and eventually serving him a portion of meat equal in size to what he gives the suitors. This time it is the previously unnamed suitor Ctesippus who reacts. But in between the first provocation and the reaction a textual problem arises which we must briefly take into account before proceeding.

The Muse, in a bizarre and seemingly illogical transition, takes us out of the palace which everyone has just entered (20.276–78). We are told that a hecatomb in honor of Apollo, the god of archery, is being driven through the town to the god's shaded grove and that the Achaeans are gathered together outside. Unless we assume that the Achaeans alluded to are Ithacans other than the suitors now gathered in the hall, we have here one of the few passages in the *Odyssey* which defies integration into the sequence of a carefully composed literary narrative. The meat from the hecatomb will be brought into the hall in addition to the ample supply of goats, hogs, and other cattle brought just moments before by the herdsmen. It would be quite remarkable for such a sacrifice to be made without the presence of Telemachus and the high-ranking nobles. And when the suitor Ctesippus hurls an ox hoof at Odysseus (20.299–303), Telemachus, in his reply, would surely have been warranted in commenting on the inappropriateness of hurling chunks of a sacrificial ox at one of his guests.

But he does nothing of the kind. Rather he comments on how inappropriate his behavior is on an occasion when sheep are being slaughtered and wine drunk.

The symbolic rationale for the hecatomb to the archer-god Apollo just before the contest of the bow and the slaughter of the 108 suitors is self-evident. The problem is that the decision to hold the contest of the bow does not seem to have occurred until after sundown the previous day and was communicated only to Odysseus. The idea of offering a hecatomb was raised earlier by Telemachus, who ordered Penelope to vow hecatombs in the hope that Zeus would some day avenge the suitors' arrogance (in occupying the palace and in plotting to kill him). She vowed that she would (17.50–60). But the Muse makes no mention of her issuing instructions for such a large, ritual offering, which would require advance preparation and advance notice. There is no reason, apart from the three lines, to assume she issued such instructions.

True, Antinous later notes that the day of the bow contest coincides with the feast of Apollo the Archer celebrated throughout the land (21.258). We might even contend that Eurycleia has this festival in mind when she orders the maids to sweep the halls and throw purple coverlets on the chairs, observing that "this is a feast for all men" (20.149–56). Yet there is no indication that the suitors are celebrating the holiday with a hecatomb, or outside the palace. After both Leiodes and Eurymachus fail to string the bow, in fact, Antinous orders Melantheus to bring she-goats in the morning so the suitors can sacrifice thigh pieces on the altar of Apollo, and then try the bow again (21.265–68).

We may argue that Penelope and Telemachus must have made the arrangements alluded to and that it was with this festival of Apollo the Archer (and her proposed hecatomb) in mind that Penelope had publicly announced her willingness to marry soon and privately proposed the contest of the bow to Odysseus. Yet the difficulty remains that the hecatomb at the shrine of Apollo interrupts an otherwise logical development of the scene. The protagonists are already inside the palace, and there is not the slightest suggestion that they go out to the grove of Apollo to take part in the ceremonies. Eustathius noticed the problem and explained the passage as follows in his comment on 20.277:

> The Achaeans now in Ithaca: there will be no need for Odysseus to fear, while they are at the sacrifice, that the suitors might derive any help from that source in the fighting.

Eustathius's interpretation would be plausible if the Muse made even the slightest narrative connection between the Ithacans participating in the public hecatomb and the events in Odysseus's palace. But she does not. And there remains the problem of explaining why neither Telemachus nor Penelope supervises the hecatomb—a strangely negligent attitude on their part, since they were its initiators. Compare Eurycleia's comment about the hecatombs offered to Zeus by Odysseus, possibly on the occasion of Telemachus's birth, accompanied by the prayer that he would live to an old age and have a chance to raise his son (19.366).

Either the Muse is patching together pieces from two traditions, one of which involves a hecatomb and one which does not, or the three lines are an interpolation made by a later reader who noticed that events are proceeding without the hecatomb which Telemachus made Penelope vow. The notion of an interpolation is attractive simply because the presence of the three lines reduces the narrative sequence to nonsense. Telemachus has already served up the innards of the animals brought in by the herdsmen as a kind of hors d'oeuvre. Thus, when the meat itself is served in 20.279–80, it would, once the hecatomb reference is removed, be logical to assume that it is the meat of Philoetius's, Melantheus's, and Eumaeus's animals. Perhaps some scribe or scholar has spoiled the narrative by splicing in the apparently missing hecatomb.

Telemachus, after rebuking Ctesippus and the suitors in general, resorts to a little exaggeration. He accuses the men of dragging the maids around the house in a shameless way. Yet again we see his curious obsession with the maids' behavior and a totally false suggestion that the women are unwilling partners in all this. His words silence the suitors until yet another new voice, that of Agelaus, "Leader of People," urges the same old message upon Telemachus: that he should get his mother to marry. Telemachus, in reply, not only claims that he likes the idea of his mother remarrying but offers gifts of his own for the occasion. Yet he adds that it is not proper for him to force her to leave against her will. The suitors, prompted by Athena, burst into unquenchable laughter in this humorous as well as ominous moment in the text. Telemachus's witty anagram on the name of the suitor—*Agelae* (vocative) and *algea* (sufferings)—produces a reaction which itself affirms his wordplay: *gelōs* (laughter). Athena, with help from the Muse, adds divine zest to the jest, leaving the suitors hysterical with mirth. But another, unstated, wordplay lurks: *a-geloion*, "unfunny," for the situation is no laughing matter. Theoclymenus, whom we had almost forgotten, hastens to point out that the suitors are all doomed to die in a hideous slaughter that will blot out the sun. Yet the laughter continues, directed now at Theoclymenus, who walks out to the safety of Peiraeus's house before Eurymachus can fulfill a threat to have him removed. Telemachus, curiously, makes no effort to intervene, even though he is Theoclymenus's host. Encouraged, it appears, by Telemachus's failure to respond, the suitors now redirect their laughter toward him and toward his other guest, the disguised Odysseus. If they can rid themselves of Theoclymenus, they may also be able to rid themselves of the far more obnoxious beggar. While Telemachus remains silent, watching his father for an appropriate cue, Penelope, who knows her way around situations, so positions her chair in her room that she can listen to the words of each man in the hall.[2] Her attention has been drawn, as has everyone else's, to an immediately threatening crisis spelled out by the seer Theoclymenus, whose words would carry more force for Penelope than for the suitors. She had spoken with him just after Telemachus's return from the Peloponnese, and this is what he had said:

> Chaste woman, married to Odysseus, son of Laertes, he [Telemachus] truly does not understand clearly. Listen to my words, I will prophesy to you truly, and will not hide anything. Let Zeus be witness above all gods, and the hospitable table and hearth of blameless Odysseus, to which I have come, that Odysseus is indeed already in his native land, whether sitting still or moving around, learning about these evil things. He is here, and he is devising evil for all the suitors. Such was the bird sign I interpreted when I was sitting on the benched ship, and I told it to Telemachus. (17.152–61)

Theoclymenus, like the disguised Odysseus, addressed the queen as Odysseus's wife at that time and warned her that Odysseus was already in his homeland, preparing evil for the suitors. Now, in book 20, he is announcing that Odysseus's vengeance is imminent. If Theoclymenus is correct, Odysseus cannot be anyone other than the beggar on whom all eyes in the hall are now focused. As the book ends we naturally assume that he will now make the decision to act. But, as book 21 begins, we realize that, all appearances to the contrary, the initiative is not his but Penelope's.

[15]

Penelope and the Bow

At the prompting of Athena, the queen takes decisive action. The contest of the bow cannot wait another hour. She mounts the stairs to the armory, opens the doors, appropriately enough, with an ivory-handled bronze key, manipulating the sliding bolt with all the skill of an archer (21.42–50). The horn-bow locked away there is a relic of Odysseus's early manhood, when he was about Telemachus's age, even, perhaps, from the days before his marriage. It was a gift from Iphitus, son of Eurytus, who was killed by Heracles in Heracles' own house, where he was a guest. Because Odysseus cherished the bow as a token of his friendship with Iphitus, he did not take it to Troy.

The details are important here. The mention of Heracles invites a comparison between Odysseus's bow and Heracles's famous bow, which, in some versions of the fall of Troy, was as much the key to the city's capture as Athena's and Odysseus's stratagem of the wooden horse is in the *Odyssey*. The best-known version is in Sophocles' *Philoctetes*, where Odysseus plays a considerable role in bringing the Heraclean bow and its new owner into the war. Indeed, the comparison of these bows also invites a comparison between Odysseus and Heracles such as Odysseus himself had implicitly made in *Odyssey* 11. By noting that Odysseus did not take his bow to Troy, the Muse obviates any contrasts, unfavorable to Odysseus, between the relative merits of the two bows of the two heroes (and, no doubt, expects her audience to remember that the most famous exploits of Heracles' bow were achieved after his death, by Philoctetes).

Heracles, of course, is like most heroes, an ambiguous figure whose power brings almost equal measures of salvation and destruction. He kills guests in his house—among them the previous owner of Odysseus's bow. More ominously, Heracles's bow-wielding hands are, in some myths, turned in his madness against his own family. Odysseus's bow is not used against his family, but deployed against uninvited and unwanted guests .

Whether Penelope is aware of the bow's history is not clear. But she certainly knows that Odysseus has not handled it for twenty years. When she enters the storage room she takes the bow in its case from the peg, sits down, sets the case on her knees, and cries aloud (21.56). We might expect the Muse to interpose here and tell us what the bow symbolizes for Penelope. Was it memories of Odysseus before he set out for Troy? Such an expectation might be logical, since we learn that he used to walk about his land with it. But nothing of the sort occurs. Rather, the Muse alludes to Odysseus in his very early manhood, probably before Penelope knew him at all. Her tears, then, may be prompted by the recollection that her own taking up of the bow signifies the end of her role as the waiting wife and courted widow. When she removes it from its case and brings it to the suitors in the great hall she is putting her life (*bíos*) in the hands of others and of the bow (*biós*). And the shooting of the arrow (*diOIsteusei*) finds a syllabic echo in the word she uses to describe her thought (*OIomai*).

As she displays the bow she declares a contest for her hand:

> Whoever will string the bow [*biós*] most easily in his hands and shoot [*diOIsteusei*] an arrow through all twelve axes, him shall I follow, leaving this house of my marriage, a most beautiful house, full of life [*biotoio*], which I think [*OIomai*] I shall remember even in my dreams. (21.75–79)

Penelope's sound play on "bow" and "life" and on "shoot" and "thought" is as characteristic of her way of speech as such sound plays are of Odysseus's. And they are charged with irony, for the bow (like Apollo the Archer) is more usually (and in this case definitely) a bringer of death.

Penelope's preamble lays emphasis on the stringing of the bow rather than on using it to shoot an arrow through the twelve axes. In short, she underscores the only really possible part of the competition. It is a shrewd, rhetorical ploy, minimizing the apparent difficulties of the feat: several men, she implies, should be able to string it. Yet even on this matter she allows herself a fail-safe by adding that the winner must be able to manage the weapon effortlessly. There is always the danger that competitors, failing to complete the whole task, will insist on giving the prize to the one who accomplishes the first step.

The appearance of the bow has brought tears to Penelope's eyes. It now brings tears to Philoetius's eyes and to Eumaeus's eyes, as he is asked to set the bow for the suitors. Their reaction enrages Antinous, who admits nonetheless that stringing the bow will not be easy, since none of the assembled company is the equal of Odysseus as he was in bygone years.

Antinous, the Muse notes, will be the first to fall to Odysseus's bow, even though he is not the first to try. There will be more tears, and for different reasons, from the suitors.

Stringing the Bow

It is unclear what, if anything, Telemachus knows in advance about the contest of the bow. If he knows nothing, it is quite remarkable that he is, within moments, able to set up the axes in such a way that Odysseus (or anyone else) could shoot through the holes in twelve of them. Yet to discuss this matter at any length is pointless, given what seems to be the technical impossibility of the task. Heroes so routinely defy the common laws of nature and probability in fulfilling their labors in the Homeric poems, as in mythic tales worldwide, that foreknowledge on Telemachus's part hardly matters. Since Telemachus has suspected his mother all along of unseemly conduct and intentions, he is probably not entirely surprised by her new scheme even if he has not been notified of it beforehand. His reaction is sarcastic, if not crude:

> Alas! Indeed Zeus, the son of Cronos, made me witless! My dear mother, although she is wise, declares that she will follow another man, leaving this house. But I am laughing and I enjoy it in my witless heart. Come suitors, since this seems to be your prize, a woman, there is none like her in the Achaean land, not in sacred Pylos, not in Argos, not in Mycenae, not in Ithaca itself, not on the dark mainland. But you yourselves know this! Why do I have to praise my mother? Come then, do not drag things out with excuses! Don't turn away for too long from stringing the bow! Let's see it! And I myself will make trial of the bow. If I shall string the bow and shoot an arrow through the iron, my queenly mother will not leave this house to my sorrow and go with another, leaving me behind when I am able to wield the fine weapons of my father. (21.102–17)

Telemachus's self-designation as potential husband of his own mother contrasts sharply with his previous encouragement of Penelope to leave the house. But several new factors have emerged to alter the situation. First, he makes clear what is implicit in Penelope's announcement: namely, that the contest is open to anyone. By entering (and being allowed by the suitors to enter) the contest, he establishes the precedent for other newcomers to participate. Second, he knows that Odysseus is in the hall. If Telemachus should win the contest, it becomes his right to dispose of his winnings as he sees fit. He probably does not seriously intend to marry her himself if he wins, despite the strong tradition outside the *Odyssey* which has him marry another of Odysseus's sexual partners, Circe, and has his half brother, Telegonus, marry Penelope. If the Homeric audience, however, is aware of these other traditions, very few permutations are unimaginable, however "unthinkable" they may have been to Victorian scholars. There is little doubt that Telemachus wants to string the bow (21.126). Such success would establish his prowess, his manhood, in the eyes of his father, his mother, and the suitors. It would be a mark of his authority, his coming of age. Above all, he is acting to protect his father's interests. Telemachus would now be roughly the same age Odysseus was when he first acquired (and presumably first strung) the bow. Hence, when Odysseus, older, presumably, than the other competitors, strings the bow, he not only surpasses the abilities of the young studs; he matches the prowess he had when he was a youth himself. The suggestion that Telemachus would finally have been able to string the bow had it not been for a nod from his father warning him to desist from his attempts reminds us that for all his youth Telemachus too is more than a match for the suitors.

In a flash of vivid contrasts. Telemachus sheds his luxurious purple cloak, lays down his sword, then proceeds to dig a trench in the floor of the great hall and set up the axes.[1] He executes the task with skill, although, the Muse assures us, he has never done it previously. Before the suitors can enter the contest, Telemachus three times tries (and fails) to string the bow himself. On the fourth occasion, the Muse leads us to believe, he might well have succeeded had Odysseus not signaled him, with a Greek nod of the head, to stop. Penelope's reaction to Telemachus's words and his attempt to string the bow are not recorded. There isn't time.

The nod is the first indication Telemachus gets of his father's attitude toward the contest. A silent gesture, like Eurycleia's attempted silent glance to Penelope, tells him that Odysseus wants him to withdraw and the contest to proceed. Telemachus seems crestfallen, announcing that he is either worthless and weak or too young for the task. So Antinous takes over as master of ceremonies: they will proceed in order of their seating, from left to right, the way the butlers pour the wine.

Leiodes, son of Oenops (i.e., Smoothy, son of Wine-Face), who sits as close as possible to the wine bowl is, appropriately, the first suitor to try the bow. No less appropriately, he is a priest who presides over sacrifices, a kind of augur (we remember the Greek proverb "Wine is also truth"). Needless to say, his slender, uncalloused hands fail. He is dismayed and speaks allegorically of all the suitors whose hopes will be ruined by the bow. He suggests that they give up on the bow and try a competition of presents instead: Penelope should wed whoever offers most (21.161–62).

Although Antinous rejects the suggestion and mocks Leiodes' weakness

(21.168–74), he notes the stiffness of the bow and orders Melantheus to warm and grease it to make it suppler. But matters are not improved. They all try and, except for Eurymachus and Antinous himself, give up. They probably do not even notice Eumaeus and Philoetius leaving the hall with the beggar, who is about to disclose his identity to them. "Would they help the suitors or Odysseus if Odysseus returned?" Odysseus asks. Philoetius responds excitedly in the same vein as before, with utter committment to Odysseus: "Father Zeus, if only you would fulfill this wish that the man would come back. May some god guide him! Then you'd know what kind of strength I have, and how my hands would follow" (21.200–202). Eumaeus's reply is reported in indirect speech and simply echoes Philoetius: "And in the same manner Eumaeus prayed to all the gods that the wise Odysseus might return to his own home" (21.203–4). The order of reaction and the directness of their statements make Eumaeus seem less enthusiastic.

Once Odysseus discloses himself, he offers rewards to Eumaeus and Philoetius for their commitment to him in the event that they overpower the suitors. He will give each of them possessions, a house built near his own, and in his eyes they will be friends and brothers of Telemachus. With the revelation, of course, Eumaeus's relationship to the former Odysseus as well as Odysseus the beggar becomes completely inverted. He was, in childhood, virtually Odysseus's brother. He was the beggar's patron and protector. Now he is client not patron, son not brother. What he will gain, however, is his freedom and a place of his own. Odysseus had not missed the veiled requests Eumaeus was making earlier in their negotiating process.

Back in the palace the contest is itself taking a bizarre turn. Eurymachus, on trying and failing to string the bow, laments:

> Oh dear! I really grieve for myself and for all of us. It is not so much the marriage I grieve. For, although I am upset, there are many other Achaean women, some in sea-girt Ithaca and some in other cities; but I grieve that we fall so short of godlike Odysseus, for we are unable to string the bow: that is our shame, to be learned by men as yet unborn. (21.249–55)

What comes as a surprise to Eurymachus is not a surprise to Antinous, who has known all along that he and the others are inferior to Odysseus. What surprises the audience is the realization that this contest with the bow is not about Penelope at all. It is a contest with the absent Odysseus; and the suitors cannot measure up. Penelope is, in fact, irrelevant, as she is also, in a rather curious way, to Odysseus himself. He will resume his journey shortly after reestablishing his claim to his home in Ithaca. Ironically, her only real importance to most of the suitors, and perhaps to Odysseus himself, is probably the same as what Menelaus found in Helen. Helen is Menelaus's passport to Elysium, and Penelope is the suitors' and Odysseus's means of acquiring prestige. They want her precisely because she is the "chaste woman, married to Odysseus, son of Laertes," not because she is a beauty for whom they burn with passion.

These words uttered by the suitor Telemachus thought was his mother's favorite can hardly have been music to Penelope's ears. But they probably are to Odysseus's, for he now proposes to try the bow himself to see whether he still possesses the strength he had in his limbs before his wanderings (21.281–84). There could be no broader hint as to his identity. Yet Antinous (who knew Odysseus before his departure) misses it as the result of the perversity that is implicit in his very name—"opposite-minded." He assumes that the beggar is (like Leiodes, perhaps) under the influence of wine and recalls the centaur Eurytion's drunken intrusion into the Lapith Pirithous's palace, *domon*, which resulted in Eurytion's expulsion and disfigurement. The allusion to the Lapiths and Centaurs shows how close Antinous comes to appreciating the nature of the situation without actually recognizing it. He has probably either edited for his own rhetorical purposes a famous incident between Lapiths and Centaurs which left Pirithous's halls and the banqueters awash in a sea of blood or, as Petronius's Trimalchio does, misunderstood it. Eurytion is usually represented in the act of abducting Pirithous's bride at his wedding feast, an action which much more closely parallels the immediate situation. The problem is, of course, that the suitors are, under the circumstances, more like the Centaurs than is the disguised Odysseus. Eustathius, ever alert, noticed Antinous's omission and remedied it by reading *gamon*, "marriage," instead of *domon*, "palace" or "home." The Muse's point, however, is better seen if we keep the traditional text. Antinous either does not see how ironically apt his mythic reference is or is suppressing his recognition of that realization. Nagler may well be right to suggest that Antinous is "having one of those uncanny half-intuitions people get when they sense something is wrong but can't pin it down."[2] What is most on Antinous's mind is the fear he will be shamed by a beggar. He therefore tries to deter this potential competitor with abuse and threats, including shipment to Echetus, "Crippler of Men"—the same threat he had tried on Irus when he feared the latter would not fight strongly. If Echetus is, as Nagler suggests, an epithet for Hades, then the irony of Antinous's reference to Eurytion and Pirithous is further enhanced, for Pirithous's chief claim to mythic fame is also as the potential ravisher of brides. His quest was for the wife of Death himself, and its consequences were disastrous for himself: eternal, living death.

Antinous's outburst provides Penelope with a fleeting opportunity to avenge the slight Eurymachus has given her. If she is no better or no worse than any other Achaean woman as a wife, the suitors are no better (or more likely) candidates to be her husband than a wandering beggar is. Antinous, she declares, has no right to rob Telemachus's guest of his privileges. "Do you think that if this stranger strings the great bow of Odysseus, trusting in his strength and might, he will lead me to his home, and make me his wife?" asks Penelope (21.314–16). Penelope has shown her rhetorical shrewdness again. To humiliate the suitors, she allows the beggar to compete, but is not ready to grant the arrogant beggar who so resembles her missing husband the opportunity to win her in this way. Her unspoken pretext for this rider she attaches needs little explanation, from the suitors' point of view. The lady of the manor would not want to marry a beggar. But by dissociating the competition from its original purpose—to determine who will be her husband—she follows up on what Eurymachus has already done. If the beggar succeeds, as the assembled suitors fear he will, then anyone else who competes can do no better than come in second to a tramp, which is no passport to great status as Odysseus's successor in Penelope's chamber.

The point is not lost on Eurymachus, as his reaction shows (21.321–29). And when he has voiced it, Penelope crushes him rhetorically. Men who have so far ruined their reputations need not fear such reproaches. She insists that the beggar be allowed to try: "But come, give him the well-polished bow, so we can see" (21.336). If the beggar strings the bow, she will clothe him in a cloak, a tunic, and give him sandals. She will also provide him with a sharp javelin and a two-edged sword.

Penelope's authoritative stance irritates not only the suitors but Telemachus. None of the Achaeans has more right to give or deny the bow than I, he tells her, then orders her off to her chamber to busy herself with her own tasks: the loom and the distaff: "The bow shall be for men, for all, but most of all for me, since the authority in the house is mine" (21.352–53). Telemachus shows the same rudeness to his mother that he displayed at the opening of the *Odyssey*. Considering that the idea for the contest was hers and that she has some stake in the outcome, Telemachus's behavior is even more insulting than Eurymachus's. What seems to annoy Telemachus most is that Penelope has taken charge again. Perhaps he is also annoyed that she has taken a step which aggravates the situation, for he knows that the beggar is Odysseus, and that she has just created a situation where Odysseus can win the contest but be denied the right to reclaim his wife. Most important of all, however, Penelope has now contributed her part to making the slaughter of the suitors inevitable. It might well be that the Muse is here reusing a thread found in a different version, where Penelope and Odysseus have already agreed upon a plan of revenge, and Penelope's comment about not marrying the beggar is designed to overcome any resistance on the part of the suitors.[3] In the Homeric version, however, the Muse omits any previous acknowledgment of the beggar as Odysseus by Penelope. In short, the Muse creates a situation in which simple self-identification by Odysseus would not necessarily win instant acceptance of him by either his wife or her suitors. Penelope, on the one hand, keeps the disguised Odysseus at a distance and, on the other hand, ensures that the suitors will be eliminated. Had she consented to marry the beggar, who won the contest fair and square on terms she set and which were agreed to by the suitors, there would have been no need for the subsequent butchery.

As Penelope leaves to continue weeping in her chamber, Eumaeus takes the bow which he intends to deliver to Odysseus. His nerve fails him as he runs the gauntlet of the suitors' threats and insults, and he completes his mission only when Telemachus threatens to punish and expel him too. The ambivalence we have noted in his behavior and resolution is rarely more graphically illustrated. The bow is, however, finally set in its place, and Eumaeus orders Eurycleia to bar the doors. Philoetius secures the outer portico. Meanwhile Odysseus looks the horn bow over to see whether it has been damaged by bugs during his absence. Penelope's dream will prove not to have come from the ivory gates.

Odysseus, the singer of tales, strings the bow as easily as a skilled minstrel strings his lyre, as easily as the Muse narrates it. But the sound the string makes when he tests it is that of the swallow: the song of a Philomela rather than of the nightingale Procne to which the now-sleeping Penelope has compared herself. The detail, again, is significant, for it is still daylight, as Odysseus comments. The nightingale, unlike the swallow, is nocturnal. But the song the bow sings on this day of the festival of Apollo the Archer will be a song of death in the banqueting hall that eclipses any slaughter in Zethus's Thrace.

With as little difficulty as he strings the bow, Odysseus fires the arrow through the ax heads. He has accomplished the task Penelope had set for her successful suitor, even though she has evaded the consequences by ruling him out as a competitor for her hand. By the end of the next book there will be no one left to compete, for the slaughter is about to begin. Of those who collaborated with the suitors, only Phemius and Medon, a minstrel and a herald, will be allowed to live. Unless, of course, one counts among the collaborators Eumaeus, who has the saving sense to be kind to strangers, and Penelope, whom Odysseus could no more kill than Menelaus could kill Helen for reasons that are at once exactly the opposite and exactly the same. How Penelope will react to the death of her geese, on the other hand, is not altogether clear.

The Restful Sleep

By the end of *Odyssey* 22 Odysseus's victory seems complete. As Odysseus contemplates his victory and searches for signs of lingering life among the corpses, the Muse compares the heap of bodies to fish, netted by a fisherman, lying on the beach, yearning for the waters, their lives taken away by blazing Sun (22.381–88). It is a grisly image with numerous resonances. Most striking is the totally remorseless attitude Odysseus shows toward the slaughter he has perpetrated. The suitors lying before him (some still struggling vainly for life) appear to be creatures of a different order, not fellow humans. But even to say this is not to say enough. Fishermen catch fish for food, not simply to destroy them. Further, the simile unfairly blames Helios, the Sun, rather than the fisherman and his nets, for the death of the fish. This is the traditional reasoning which enabled men to justify the taking of life for the purpose of obtaining food in days when such niceties still bothered Europeans. The Roman priest invariably and ritually blamed the gods for commanding and the knife for accomplishing the death of the sacrificial victim. Odysseus, when addressing Eurycleia a few lines later, displaces blame from himself by attributing responsibility for the suitors' deaths to their own wantonness and the action of divine vengeance (22.411–18).

The implicit comparison between Odysseus and Helios would nicely complement that between Odysseus and Apollo the Archer if scholars were less intransigent in their determination to keep Helios and Apollo separate until the fifth century B.C.E. In the simile, the fish perish, as did Odysseus's crew, under the relentless glare of Helios. And the suitors, like Odysseus's crew, have brought doom upon themselves by eating forbidden food.

The reminder of the sea, however, is a reminder of Odysseus's past and of his future, if Teiresias's words have any significance separate from the rhetorical context in which Odysseus "reports" them. There is, we should recall, a strong mythic tradition that Odysseus's own death comes not only from the sea, but as the result of an injury inflicted by his son, Telegonus, child of Circe, with a fish bone. The instrument of his own death, then, lies hidden within the simile of the fish.

By the time Eurycleia arrives on the scene, Odysseus's own appearance is metamorphosed in simile to that of a lion fresh from feeding. He is a hideous sight to look upon, but, presumably, no longer menacing because he is satiated with blood. Eurycleia greets him, nonetheless, with joy and is about to shout her exultation aloud when Odysseus tells her, as he does each time he talks to her, to hold her tongue. She does, however, remind him and list for him those handmaids who slept with the suitors: twelve out of the total of fifty, a rather smaller percentage than might be expected, given the number of suitors.

Odysseus, concerned now with housekeeping, subdelegates to Telemachus, Eumaeus, and Philoetius the task of getting the women to clean up before taking them outside and putting them to the sword. Now we witness a crescendo of cruelty, culminating in the mutilation of Melantheus, which rivals any torments Antinous contemplated for Irus or Odysseus at the hands of his friend Echetus, "Crippler of Men." Odysseus's companions have leisure to plan more lingering and brutal deaths. Telemachus decides death by the sword is too noble for the maids and hangs them instead from a ship's cable. Again, there is a nautical, perhaps a piscatory touch, to their fates. But the Muse goes on to compare them, as they dangle, to snared thrushes and doves, birds symbolic of love and also used for food, whose attempt to reach their habitual resting places becomes the means of their entrapment.

Once the executions are over and the hall is cleaned and fumigated, Odysseus, still unwashed and changed, is greeted and kissed by the surviving maids with much (understandable) joy. Curiously, he himself is brought close to tears in emotional response to their effusive display and is described as coming to recognize all of them. Not even Odysseus is perfect. There are people in his household he himself did not remember clearly and recognize after twenty years, among them thirty-eight maids who knew him before he left.

The surviving maids are thus the older members of the staff whose loyalty may be as much attributable to their age as to personal regard for the master. That they acknowledge Odysseus now, in rags and covered with blood, may be as much a matter of prudence as of recognition. But it also shows that Eurycleia and Eurynome were not the only female servants who might have recognized Odysseus, and therefore that Eurycleia was by no means the only choice available to Penelope, earlier, when she wanted someone to bathe Odysseus.

There remain only two people connected with Odysseus's household who have not acknowledged him (whether or not they have recognized him): Laertes and Penelope. Odysseus, in fact, had instructed Eurycleia to bring Penelope to him along with the maids and other women in the house, while he was conducting the purification:

> Bring sulphur, old woman, remedy for pollution, and bring me fire, so that I can purge the great hall; and you order Penelope to come over here with her handmaidens, and urge all the women in the house to come. (22.481–84)

It is worth noting that here, as in all comments addressed to Eurycleia from the moment he has slaughtered the suitors, Odysseus drops the more intimate *maia*, "mother" (19.482 and 500), which he used when he needed her to keep quiet after she had recognized him, and reverts to the less courteous but more imperious *grēu,* "old woman" (22.481; compare 22.411), which he had used when dismissing her first observation that he, though a beggar, resembled Odysseus (19.383). *Maia,* we should add, is also the term of endearment Telemachus uses when addressing Eurycleia (20.129). Telemachus also stops using it and resorts to *grēu* after the slaughter (22.395). Penelope, by contrast, though she describes Eurycleia to Odysseus as an old woman never calls her *grēu* to her face.

Significantly, Odysseus also reiterates, in his indirect summons to Penelope, the outright word of command *anōchthi,* which he gave Eumaeus in book 19 when demanding that the queen meet him in the hall after sunset. The starkness of his order is more noticeable in the present context because it contrasts with the much milder instruction he sends on to the other women of the household derived from *otrynō,* "stir up," rouse," "urge." There is irony, as well as harshness, in his order. Penelope is probably the only person who has actually slept through the massacre of over a hundred suitors, the lynching of a dozen maids, the mutilation of Melantheus, and the general housecleaning. If anyone needs the verb *otrynō,* it is she. But we cannot blame Penelope alone for coming down so slowly. Eurycleia has obviously ignored Odysseus's instructions, as Eumaeus did earlier, though he had better justification. Eumaeus could claim that the orders came from what appeared to be a beggar. The question therefore arises as to why Eurycleia delays this part of her instructions. Must the wife always be the last to know?

There are some clues. As Eurycleia leaves to fulfill her task she suggests that Odysseus change his clothes: a cloak and a tunic to replace the tattered garments covering his shoulders. Since he is still covered with rags, she says, he might cause a very severe upset (22.489). To whom? Surely to Penelope. Wisely, Eurycleia does not go so far as to suggest a(nother) bath. Possibly she takes it for granted that one would bathe to remove the gore before putting on clean clothes if one wanted to cut a reasonably civilized appearance. Eurycleia is aware of how important clothes and appearances are to Penelope. The queen usually took care to look her best when appearing before the suitors, and Eumaeus, as we recall, was convinced that Odysseus could not appear before her in rags and without a cloak. No less noticeably, Penelope herself had not only outfitted Odysseus with the most elegant (and unwarlike) clothes before his departure for Troy but tried to persuade the disguised beggar, who so resembled Odysseus, to put on decent clothes as well as to have a bath. Odysseus, however, insists on being seen in his blood-soaked rags, as if determined that Penelope must acknowledge him in terms of the role he had assumed as the beggar, now bloodied by his eagle slaughter.

Eurycleia tries to rush nimbly to Penelope's side and awaken her. While there is a touch of pathos in the old servant's attempt at speedy movement, there is also some calculation. She has obviously told the handmaidens before she tells the mistress, in contravention of Odysseus's instructions. Further, as she delivers Odysseus's message, she softens the harshness of his command, as Eumaeus has done on an earlier occasion. Bringing a monarch orders is usually a tricky task. Eurycleia recasts the imperious summons as an announcement of good news, the fulfillment of her years of mournful dreaming:

> Wake up, Penelope, dear child, so you can see with your own eyes what you desired all these days. Odysseus is here, he has come home, though late, but he has come. He has killed the proud suitors, who troubled his house, devoured his possessions, and oppressed his son. (23.5–9)

Eurycleia does not even say that Penelope ought to come down and see her husband. She simply assumes that now her mistress's dream is fulfilled, she will come down of her own free will. Her approach is so tactful, that she even avoids alluding to Penelope's relationship with the suitors.

Penelope's reaction probably startles Eurycleia as much as it does the reader who opens *Odyssey* 23 for the first time. It is not simply that she disbelieves the old nurse and even claims Eurycleia must be mad. She says she is angry at being awakened from her nap because she has not slept so well since before Odysseus left for Troy. While she gives, that is, the impression that she still refuses to believe Odysseus has returned, she is also intent on conveying the notion that she has not really relaxed at all since his departure. She is also as silent about the subject of the suitors as Eurycleia has been about her mistress's relationship to them. Even when stirring from sleep, Penelope earns her epithet *periphrōn.*

Eurycleia responds by insisting that Odysseus is at home, that he is the stranger that everyone insulted, and that Telemachus knew all along who he was. Here again, what is not said is almost as interesting as what is said. Eurycleia doesn't mention that she herself has known Odysseus's identity from the time she bathed him. Nor does she make it clear how she knew that Telemachus has *palai,* "long since," recognized his father.

Penelope leaps from her bed, embraces her nurse, and weeps. Her questions now pertain not to Odysseus's identity, but to how, even granted that the stranger is Odysseus, as Eurycleia claims, he accomplished the slaughter of those awful suitors. We should not be misled by her sudden movement and tearful reaction. She has stirred from her bed, but not her room. And she wants a verbal description of how the slaughter was managed, not evidence that the slaughter has actually taken place, which a glance at the heaps of bodies outside the palace and the maids hanging in the yard would provide. Perhaps, of course, this is precisely the point: to ask for an account of what happened is not only an attempt to prompt the answer that she can come and see it all for herself but a strategy of delay. To ask the messenger how the massacre was achieved is to prompt a messenger speech and to defer any confrontation of the evidence.

"I didn't see it and I didn't ask about it," Eurycleia answers truthfully but resolutely. She must, by this point, be aware that prying Penelope out of her room is not going to be easy. She therefore mentions the evidence that is visible and tangible, adds that Odysseus sent her to summon her mistress, and suggests that she accompany her into Odysseus's presence. It's a sight that would delight her. There is no mention of the troubling aspects of the sight (such as the hanging maids).

Penelope's response is again interesting. She accepts, without further question, that the suitors are in fact dead, thereby reemphasizing that there is no need for her to see the evidence. In fact, she takes matters a stage further by protesting (and exaggerating) the nurse's joy at their doom: "Do not exult over them with loud laughter!" (23.59). Eurycleia has done nothing of the sort. But she dismisses the idea that the agent of vengeance was Odysseus as a *mythos*, a "tale," that is not genuine. She not only ignores Eurycleia's mention of Odysseus's summons but declares that her husband must be lost and far away. It must, rather, have been one of the immortals who killed the suitors. Odysseus is as dead as the suitors are.

While we can, by resorting to the Muse's comments about Athena's interposition of herself between Penelope and reality, account for her failure to see or overhear Eurycleia's earlier identification of Odysseus in the bath, the Muse denies us (and Penelope) any help from Athena at this point. However reluctantly, we must now concede that there are things Penelope does not wish to know or to see and which she therefore refuses to acknowledge. By accepting, on the basis of Eurycleia's word, without the supporting testimony of her own eyes, that the suitors are dead while rejecting what her own eyes have told her, that the stranger-beggar is Odysseus, Penelope reveals that she can adjust most readily to a world without suitors if it is also a world without Odysseus. That is where the gods are useful. It must have been they who destroyed her pet geese.

Eurycleia will have to try again. At this point, the nurse plays (with obvious reluctance) her final card: she admits that she recognized Odysseus while bathing him and mentions, though she reduces it to a genteel rebuke uttered in the wisdom of his heart, that Odysseus restrained her from communicating her recognition. To affirm the truth of what she declares, she tells Penelope to kill her most cruelly if her words prove false. There is not much the queen can do now but agree to go to her son, see the dead suitors, and the man who killed them:

> Dear mother, it is hard for you to tell the plans of the everlasting gods, although you are very clever. Nevertheless, let us go to my son, so that I may see the men who courted me dead, and him who killed them. (23.81–84)

Her comment, while it relegates Odysseus to anonymity, at least concedes, albeit quietly, that it was a single human hand that was responsible for their deaths. And she knows whose hand it was. As Penelope descends into the hall, the Muse describes her thoughts much as she describes those of Menelaus when he recognizes Telemachus in Sparta. She wonders whether she should hold aloof, question, or simply embrace her husband:

> So saying, she came down from her upper chamber. And her heart pondered much whether she should stay aloof and question her dear husband, or go up to him and kiss his head, taking his hands. (23.86–87)

There is no question at all that Penelope knows that her husband killed the suitors. She does not have to see him again to know it. She has known it, as we have suggested, from the very beginning. The questions are as they have been all along: why does she not want to know what she knows, and why is she so reluctant to acknowledge him? And the answers, by this point, surely, must be clear: because she does not want him back as he now is; because she does not wish to cease being what she has become.

In the Great Hall

If Odysseus is expecting a joyful embrace and kisses, he must be disappointed. As Penelope descends into the hall, he simply waits as she sits down quietly opposite him. This time she is in the light of the fire, while he is sitting by a pillar, looking down. No words are spoken:

> She was sitting in silence for a long time, and amazement [*taphos*] crawled into her heart: now she would gaze fully at his face, and now she would ignore him, for he was wearing mean clothes. (23.93–95)

These lines are considered obscure, largely because, it is contended, there is no clear antithesis between the verbs "gaze," *esidesken,* and "ignore," *agnōsaske.*[4] The clue to the dilemma lies in the first line of the citation, in the curious internal tension in the word *taphos.* Most obviously, in this context, it means "amazement" or "astonishment." But that is not its most common meaning in Greek outside the Homeric poems.[5] It also means "funeral feast" or "tomb." And that other meaning has its place too in the total silence following a slaughter amid a banquet. The sense of tomblike silence is fitting. The Muse used *taphos* in the sense of funeral feast in *Odyssey* 3.309–12 to describe the banquet Orestes gave for the Argives after killing his mother and Aegisthus.

Again, we find the uncomfortable proximity of the tale of Orestes' vengeance to that of Odysseus and Telemachus encapsulated in the pun on *taphos.* Penelope has no certain means of knowing what Odysseus's response to her will be. Amid so much slaughter, and with the contemptuous dismissal by her son her last waking recollection before Eurycleia disturbed her slumber, there must be a certain fear in her heart as to what Odysseus intends. Just as she has not gone over to him, he has not risen from where he sits or made any move toward her. She finds herself, then, in the middle of a scene of brutal judgment about which she was the last in the palace to learn and to which she has been summoned by the judge.

Penelope sometimes looks Odysseus straight in the face, as if, presumably, acknowledging him. Women were generally very careful not to look men directly in the eyes, since to do so was a sign of inappropriate intimacy—hence the care with which Penelope veils herself when appearing before the suitors.[6] Sometimes she makes a point of not acknowledging him by, presumably, glancing down at his rags.

It is Telemachus who breaks the silence with an opening rebuke that would sit well upon the tongue of Orestes:

> My mother, harsh mother, you have an unyielding heart. Why do you keep your distance from my father, and not sit by his side and ask him questions? No other wife could hold apart like this with an obstinate heart from her husband, who, after suffering many evils, has returned to his native land in the twentieth year. But your heart is always harder than a stone. (23.97–103)

Telemachus's opening formula has an ominous ring to it given the parallel, of which he too is conscious, between himself and Orestes. Sophocles may well have had these words in mind when he depicted Electra holding the urn which contains what she believes are the ashes of Orestes and lamenting that he will not be able to exact vengeance on their "mother no-mother" who now exults in her son's death (*Electra* 1154).

The threatening undertones are muted to some extent by what Telemachus says next. While it becomes evident that Penelope is not in any immediate danger, there is little doubt that she will not be permitted to resist acknowledging Odysseus indefinitely. Telemachus makes it clear that he accepts the stranger as his father and expects her, at the very least, to test the stranger's identity by questioning him. His point is well taken.

Penelope's reluctance to explore the stranger's identity is not what one would expect of a wife who wants her long-lost husband back.

Penelope, realizing she is not being brought to summary trial, adjusts her demeanor to the new conditions and adopts new tactics:

> My child, the heart in my breast is bewildered with awe, nor can I utter a word, ask a question, or look in his face. Yet, if he really is Odysseus, and he has come back home, surely we two will know each other easily, for we have tokens, which only we know. They are hidden from others. (23.105–10)

She explains her terrified, tomblike silence as bewildered awe, and in tones reminiscent of Sappho's description of her own reactions as she watches the man sitting across from her beloved. She cannot speak in Odysseus's presence because she is overcome by it. Nor can she look him in the face, she declares, although the Muse, just seconds ago, told us she was doing just this. There is something curiously detached about it all, as if she were watching her own reaction to her own responses.

Penelope's rhetoric is very cunning. Her contentions have, as all good rhetoric does, a basis in what the particular listener or listeners will take to be truth. She addresses her words to Telemachus as *her* child: in terms, that is, of a relationship both unquestioned and unquestionable. Paternity, Telemachus knows, is always more problematic. He himself comments at the opening of the *Odyssey* that no one really knows who his own father is. It is a matter of trust rather than of knowledge, especially in Telemachus's own case. He did not recognize Odysseus, even though he acknowledges him as his father.

Penelope marks out the boundaries with skill, attempting to distance her own act of acknowledgment from the prevailing mass acceptance, which is not necessarily based on recognition but on expediency and prudence. While expropriating Telemachus, Penelope maintains a certain distance from Odysseus by excluding him from second-person interchanges. She speaks of him in the third person and as if he also had problems recognizing her (which she knows he does not). She also tries to create a framework for her recognition which excludes all remoter third-person outsiders, by alluding to the need for personal recognition and acknowledgment: tokens by which she and Odysseus can test each other, if the man is Odysseus and if he has returned home.

Odysseus responds by granting Penelope her distance and moving on, with disdainful unconcern, to other, more pressing business. He smiles. "Let your mother [*ē toi mētēr*] test me," he tells Telemachus:

> Now she denies me my due [*atimazei*] and says I'm not Odysseus because I am filthy and wear rags. (23.115–16)

For the first time since his arrival at the palace, he refers to Penelope in terms other than "wife" or "wife of Odysseus, son of Laertes." She is now "your mother," as wives often are in the process of family disputes. It is a delightfully tit-for-tat reaction to her proprietary claim to Telemachus and to her distancing of herself from him. He continues: "As for us, let us figure out how everything will turn out best" (23.117). The real problem is that killing just one person with not many relatives forces a man into exile, a more menacing denial of rights. *Atimia,* denial of honor or rights, in a political sense often involved exile. So what if Penelope denies me household rights as husband? The very best you and I can expect in the larger scheme of things is to have to leave Ithaca altogether—in which case household rights are utterly irrelevant.

This said to Telemachus, Odysseus totally ignores Penelope for the next forty lines or so. There is both cold insult and calculated persuasion in his words. He has, in effect, reassured Penelope that he is not likely to be staying long in Ithaca. At the same time, Odysseus himself is not really riding the crest of a wave of rhetorical success. His advice to Telemachus, which he offers with a flourish at the end of his relegation of Penelope to the last item on his list of problems, is to figure out how to deal with the angry relatives. Telemachus, never impressive in managing situations or in taking the initiative, responds: "You keep your eyes open for that, dear father . . . we'll follow" (23.124–27). Odysseus has acquired arms, but not intellects, to help him in his dilemma. He is still, essentially, on his own.

Given his own emphasis on the need for immediate planning and action, Odysseus's own first order shows either that he was engaging in a little rhetorical bravado to gain ground in his battle with Penelope or that he is really at a loss. He instructs everyone to bathe and change and gives orders that the minstrel (presumably Phemius, whose continued existence, we must concede, was due to Telemachus's intercession) strike up a song so the casual passerby will think that a wedding feast is in progress. The idea, he claims, is that no one will then realize that there has been a massacre in his palace.

But if Odysseus's concern is only with passersby who remain outside the building, the music and noise would suffice. Anyone who actually entered the grounds could hardly miss the piles of dead suitors and hanging maids. The Muse gives us a clearer sense of what he achieves by providing us with the comments not of a real passerby but of a hypothetical one. He would, she says, draw the following conclusion: that someone had married the cruel queen, who lacked the heart and the stamina to wait for her husband. One of the advantages of the ruse, then, is that Penelope's image would suffer. The other is that it affords Odysseus a pretext for cleaning himself up without appearing to give rhetorical ground to Penelope, who has implied, as he has understood, that she cannot accept him because of his unworthy appearance. He has Eurynome bathe him, not, ostensibly, to make him more attractive to Penelope, but for external strategic reasons. But since external strategy does not require that he bathe and put on fresh clothes, that strategy is itself merely a mask for his real purpose, which is to win acknowledgment from his wife. "Eurynome bathed the greathearted Odysseus in his house and anointed him with oil, and cast about him a fair cloak and a tunic," the Muse notes (23.153–55). Athena does her part too, if we accept the authenticity of 23.157–62, as we probably should. Although most scholars who reject the lines worry about weaknesses in syntactical continuity, the most disturbing feature of the lines is surely their emphasis on the extent to which Odysseus needs to be "made over." Perhaps the most significant modification Athena makes is to his hair. When disguised as a beggar, he may have appeared to be at least partially bald, if there is any truth underlying Eurymachus's insult. Now the goddess makes his hair as curly as a hyacinth in blossom—one of the symbols of early springtime, of transient youth with its melancholy myths associated with Hyacinth and Ajax. So much for natural imagery. But the Muse adds the suggestions of technological wizardry too. Athena brings back color, as well as curl, to his hair as a skilled craftsman overlays silver with gold. She recreates an image, a phantasm, of the Odysseus Penelope loved. This should ease the pain of acknowledgment, bringing the "real" Odysseus closer to the idealized Odysseus of the queen's ivoried dreams.

While everyone else bathes and puts on fresh clothes, while Phemius sings whatever he sings, Penelope (still unchanged and unbathed since her nap) sits in silence, next to the wall in the light of the fire. Katz notes that "even when Penelope speaks her mind, it is hard to know what it is on."[7] We might go a little farther. When she speaks it is hard to know if what she says is what is really on her mind. And when she is silent, she is inscrutable. Perhaps her reaction (or nonaction) here is governed by the realization that she is, suddenly, the odd one out. Odysseus, bathed and nicely clad, sits down again on his chair across from his wife and finally addresses her directly:

> Strange woman [*daimoniē*], to you above all womankind the dwellers of Olympus really gave an unsoftened heart. No other wife would stand apart from her husband like this with an unyielding heart, when he, after suffering much, has returned in the twentieth year to his native land. But come, nurse, strew me a bed, so that I may lie down, for indeed the heart in her breast is of iron. (23.166–72)

Again, Odysseus fails to address Penelope as his wife. The vocative *daimoniē,* almost always used as a term of reprimand or reproach, underscores his annoyance. See how wrong you were, the hyacinthine vision seems to be saying. And to complete the temporal retrogression, Odysseus now provides Penelope and himself an opportunity to respond to words uttered and decisions made before his transfiguration.

First, he carefully phrases his rebuke indirectly in words lifted, en bloc, from what Telemachus has just said to Penelope and to which she has not adequately replied. He appropriates, then, his son's words instead of using his own, a rhetorical gesture which both gives Penelope a chance to reconsider her answer and, essentially, compels her to answer, since the words are not his formulation but Telemachus's.

The second phase of Odysseus's approach also involves the appropriation of words from another speaker, in this instance Penelope herself. When he tells Eurycleia to prepare him a straw bed, he is repeating the instruction Penelope had issued the night before (19.317). In doing so, he turns the clock back again and belatedly accepts her offer of hospitality. She cannot very well now countermand what she herself had ordered without appearing to reject him even as a guest. And, since he issues the order to Eurycleia, Penelope is placed in a hopeless impasse if she were so imprudent as to try to countermand it. There is no question as to whose order Eurycleia would obey at this juncture, if forced to choose between Odysseus and Penelope. If Penelope persists in her refusal to acknowledge Odysseus, she will lose control of her household completely.

In addition to opportunity mixed with coercion, however, he offers her encouragement. As a good diplomat offers an enemy some face-saving escape, so Odysseus makes it clear that he is not forcing Penelope to share the bed with him. The detail is important, for in declining to make claims to conjugal rights, he at one and the same time reminds her of those rights and eliminates some of the fears Penelope may have in this regard. Many a mythic maiden justifiably worries that some god might disguise himself as her husband in order to seduce her. That was how the faithful Alcmena became, unwittingly, an adultress. Odysseus's wife is more prudent than Heracles' mother—and that, in itself, is no small claim to mythic fame.

At the same time, however, Odysseus's mention of the bed is also a trap for Penelope. If she allows Eurycleia to set up a separate bed for this man who claims to be her husband, she will appear to everyone to be denying not that he is Odysseus, but that she is ready to be his wife again. She will no longer be able to claim either her role as the faithful, patiently waiting bride of Odysseus, son of Laertes, or her position as queen.

Even as she appears to be losing the battle of wills, Penelope has a few good punches left. She responds but begins by hurling the same reproachful vocative at him:

> Strange man, I do not behave haughtily, nor take you lightly, nor yet am too impressed. I do remember what sort of man you were when you

> went forth from Ithaca on a long-oared ship. But come Eurycleia, set up for him the well-made bed, outside of the well-built bridal chamber, which he made himself. Once you have brought the bed there, throw on bedding, fleeces, and cloaks, and shiny coverlets. (23.174–80)

The first part of Penelope's answer, like Odysseus's questions, is in response not to the immediate issues raised by Odysseus, but to his earlier, insulting comment about her to Telemachus: that she refuses to acknowledge him because she despises him for wearing mean clothes. It is not in response to the implications of Odysseus's immediate suggestion that she is depriving him of his rights. Perhaps that is why Penelope does not use the same verb. Her comment that she remembers what kind of man he was when he left for Troy may imply, among other things, that she does not need the "make-over" to convince her. In other words, she had, in fact, recognized him. She is finally acknowledging him as Odysseus, but not without a barbed hint at the changes in his appearance over twenty years.

Having clipped the eagle's wings a little, she now reiterates Odysseus's command to Eurycleia to prepare his bed. She makes the command her own again not only by restating it, but by amending it. And the amendment is significant. Odysseus's order was for the provision of a generic bed. Penelope instructs Eurycleia to take the bridal bed out of the chamber and make it up for him. It is a puzzling order and, as we soon realize, one that is impossible to execute. The Muse recognizes the problem by pointing out that this was the way Penelope made trial of her husband (23.181).

The trial is usually understood as simply her verification of the fact that the man before her knows the bed cannot be moved. The only man who knows this detail is Odysseus, who constructed the bed himself. But this is neither the beginning nor the end of the puzzle. Penelope has just seconds ago acknowledged his identity. She knows who he is. What we tend to forget is that her emended order to Eurycleia follows Odysseus's instruction to make him a fresh bed in the hall, like the one he was offered the previous night. That order, we and she have noted, was his concession to the possibility that she did not want to recognize him as her husband, her conjugal partner, not that she did not recognize him as (the changed) Odysseus—hence his failure to address her as "wife" in the speech during which he issues the instruction for the bed to be made.

Had Penelope simply acquiesced in Odysseus's order to Eurycleia, she would have been, in effect, renouncing further claim to be Odysseus's wife. So what she appears to be suggesting (to one unfamiliar with the nature of the bed) is that he can take the bridal bed outside the chamber and have it for himself, if that is how he feels about the matter. In short, she offers him his marriage bed outside and apart from her marriage chamber. Odysseus's angry response reveals the nature and the success (or, perhaps, the total failure) of Penelope's last strategem. To begin with, he addresses her immediately, if wrathfully, as "wife." Then, in this rare moment in the *Odyssey*, he tries to reason *as* he speaks rather than before he speaks: "Who has moved the bed?" "No one could have moved the bed." "Except for a god." "I built the chamber around the bed." "I don't know whether the bed is still in place or whether some man [*andrōn*] has moved it." *Anēr*, which designates man as "husband" rather than man as human rather than divine, suggests that Odysseus is perhaps not as confident as he declared in his statement that no human could have moved it.

The bed and the bedchamber, the bed and his marriage to Penelope, are indissociable. He could not have moved it out himself. The conundrum is that he really cannot have the bed without the bedchamber, without Penelope. Penelope knows this, and he knows it. At this moment, unless, of course, his dissimulation is so masterful that his outburst is actually contrived to produce this impression, Odysseus's powers of reasoning break down, for it never occurs to this master of lies and modified truth that his wife is lying to him, as she is. What Penelope gathers from her rhetorical exercise in mendacity is not just confirmation of Odysseus's identity, but, ironically, a sense that he trusts her. This achieved, she acknowledges and accepts both Odysseus and her husband as one and the same and calls him by name for the first time.

Despite the kisses and the tears with which she greets him, her lengthy speech does not reveal unalloyed joy:

> Do not be angry with me, Odysseus, since among men you are most in command of your senses. The gods granted us sorrow, those who begrudged that we remain with each other in our youth and come to the threshold of old age. But now do not be furious with me nor resentful, because I did not at first, when I saw you, greet you affectionately in this way. For the heart in my breast was always afraid that some man would come and beguile me with words—for there are many who contrive evil. (23.209–17)

Penelope responds to Odysseus's anger with acknowledgment and fear. Demonstrating one's trustworthiness and testing that of someone else through lies is, after all, a perilous procedure. She asks him no less than three times, in three different phrases, not to be angry with her. But what does she think he is angry about? And what is she asking forgiveness for? Ostensibly because she did not acknowledge him when she first saw him: because she did not move instantly from recognition to acknowledgment. She tries to define and circumscribe his anger by linking it to her failure to acknowledge him earlier rather than to any new irritation he may feel as it begins to occur to him that she has just tricked him into making this outburst with a lie.[8]

Yet there is indignation in her call for forgiveness. When she says she suspected he might have been one of those who beguile with words, since there are many who devise evil schemes, she points out obliquely, yet firmly, that he was hardly candid with her either. The detailed fictions of "his" activities and Odysseus's clearly fall into the category of deception and evil resourcefulness. And they are characteristics of which Odysseus boasts. To acknowledge him even though his physical disguise, constantly accompanied by verbal deception, seemed designed to discourage acknowledgment might have been imprudent and unwelcome.

We should remind ourselves, however, that until he massacres the suitors, Odysseus shows more approval of than irritation at Penelope's obliquity. He only becomes angry and contemptuous when she continues to withhold acknowledgment after the need for dissimulation has passed and after his identity is a matter of general knowledge in the palace. Here, we suspect, is the nub of the matter: he disclosed his identity to everyone else in the palace before he disclosed it to her. He must therefore have trusted her least.[9]

Penelope moves on now to an analogy between herself and the famous Helen. Its resonances are so complex that the passage in which it is made, along with the lines immediately following (23.218–24), were rejected as spurious by Aristarchus and many subsequent critics. Objections center on supposed literary and psychological "inconsistencies" and on the grounds that Helen's conduct, so sympathetically represented in these lines, is so different from Penelope's as to make the analogy inappropriate. What scholars call inconsistencies, however, are better described as psychological conflicts, common to all humans. Poets are not necessarily committed to presenting unidimensional characters who function with saintly single-mindedness. And even Saint Anthony had dreams that most people would be embarrassed to admit to.

> Nor would the Argive Helen, daughter of Zeus, have made love to a foreigner, had she known that the warlike Achaeans would bring her home again. (23.218–21)

Penelope's overt point is, in essence, quite simple. Even the notoriously unfaithful Helen, who, unlike Penelope, was not at all cautious around strangers, would have remained faithful if she had realized she would be brought back to Sparta (as she would have, if she had been married to someone like Odysseus). The ambivalent energy of the comparison, of course, also leaves open the innuendo that Penelope might have behaved as Helen did had she been married to someone like Menelaus. What makes her analogy so rhetorically satisfactory, of course, is not just the overt contrast it suggests between her own conduct and Helen's, but the unmentioned fact that Helen is not the slightest bit worse off for having been unfaithful. Menelaus has accepted her back.

The most glaring weakness in any analogy between Penelope and Helen is that Helen was never in the situation of being a wife left to her own devices for years while her husband was away. The only candidate of any mythic significance for contrasting conduct as the waiting wife is Clytemnestra, who would not be a prudent choice. Clytemnestra was suspected by Agamemnon from the outset—which is, presumably, why he left, perhaps stupidly, a poet to guard her while he was away. And in most traditions, she is not only aware Agamemnon will return, but well notified about (and well prepared for) his arrival. Since the potential analogy between the *nostoi* of Agamemnon and Odysseus looms ominously over most of the *Odyssey,* Penelope's comparison of herself with Helen serves, among other things, to block off comparison with Clytemnestra. What makes Helen rhetorically attractive is that she is so unthreatening to her husband on his return. Besides, if Helen's story of the disguised Odysseus's visit to Troy in the guise of a beggar had achieved any currency (after all, it was told by Helen in Telemachus's presence), she provides a wonderful precedent for recognizing Odysseus beneath the beggar without acknowledging that recognition.

Penelope concludes with two rhetorical masterstrokes:

> For now once you have explained the clear signs of our bed, which no other mortal has seen, just we alone and one single handmaid, the daughter of Actor, whom my father gave me when I came here. She looked after the doors of our stout bridal chamber. You have convinced my heart, cruel (unyielding) as it is. (23.225–30)

The first is this: she accepts the stranger as Odysseus her husband on the grounds that only three humans have ever seen (and could therefore describe) the bed: herself, Odysseus, and "the daughter of Actor." In short, her test of Odysseus's identity is also designed as a rhetorical demonstration of her fidelity to him. It is an ingenious, if not altogether watertight, enthymeme. Whoever the daughter of Actor is or was (and Penelope thinks it necessary to provide a brief résumé to jog Odysseus's memory), she certainly was not Eurycleia, whom Penelope has just asked to move the (immovable) bed.[10] Therefore, if Penelope is telling the truth, she must have been sleeping somewhere other than in her bridal chamber while the suitors were massacred and, in fact, throughout the narration of the *Odyssey,* for several of her maids have been present in her chamber.

And if she was sleeping elsewhere, then the integrity of her bridal bed is, except in the most symbolic and technical sense, irrelevant.

Penelope's second rhetorical masterstroke is reserved for the final line. Odysseus's description of the bed has convinced her heart, "cruel (unyielding) as it is." Penelope's attitude toward the word "cruel" has undergone something of an evolution. When she talks to Odysseus as the beggar in 19.329–31 she uses the expression "cruel (unyielding) heart" to describe a characteristic she deplores and which deservedly brings curses, during their lives, upon those who display it and mockery when they die. That is why it is so savage of Telemachus to turn that same censure on her. He accuses her of having a "cruel (unyielding) heart" when she does not greet her husband right away in the great hall. Penelope now turns that insult to rhetorical advantage. She has maintained the pose of the cruel beloved who will not yield to the entreaties of suitors and strangers and now apologizes to her husband for having subjected him to the same, heartless treatment. She has converted Telemachus's insult into a testimony to her own virtue.

As husband and wife embrace, the Muse offers a simile:

> So land is a delightful sight to men who are swimming because Poseidon has weighed down with wind and swollen waves and smashed their well-built ship upon the high seas. Only a few have escaped from the grey sea to the land by swimming, and their skin is encrusted with thick brine. They are delighted to have escaped evil and to step onto the seashore. (23.233–38)

The shipwreck, the escape to shore, the body encrusted in brine, are all reminiscent of the storm, stirred up by Poseidon, that brought Odysseus to Phaeacia. The allusion to Poseidon, whose enmity pursues Odysseus, heightens the sense that this simile points to Odysseus.

But it does not, as the next two lines show clearly:

> That was how welcome her husband was to her as she looked upon him, and she would not release her white arms from his neck. (23.239–40)

We separate the simile from the lines which establish its point of reference to recapture the effect the Muse seems to have had in mind: a simile that is obviously appropriate to the husband is being applied, rather, to his wife, who has hardly set foot outside the palace in twenty years. At least one detail, on retrospection, does fit Penelope better than Odysseus: a few other figurative "sailors" have escaped along with the survivor of the storm. Odysseus is the only survivor of his shipwreck. Of Penelope's crew, Eurycleia, Eurynome, three-quarters of her maids, some herdsmen, a herald, a poet, and a son have weathered the storm with her.

Since the Muse leads us to suspect that the storm simile pertains to Odysseus, she invites us to compare not only husband with wife but heroic endurance upon the sea with the upheavals in a domestic environment. The Muse thus sets Penelope on a par with Odysseus: a storm leaves you at the mercy of forces beyond your control. You cannot defeat it, you can only use your wits and skill to weather it, to survive it. The more unsettling aspect of this equation between Penelope and Odysseus is that it leaves Odysseus as, if not the sum total of the storm that has battered Penelope's life, at least the most recent and most violent phase of it. In this sense, her heroism is more complex and subtler than her husband's. The shipwrecked sailor of the simile can always resolve never to go near the sea again. Penelope, however, must remain a sailor, continuing to have her existence defined by a husband over whom she has little power and control. And she will soon be left again to fend for herself but without the freedom to be independent of her wandering husband.

They would have spent the remainder of the night in tears, the Muse adds, if Athena had not extended it beyond its normal length, after the fashion of Zeus's night with Alcmena. Once again, we sense an implicit, but, on this occasion, negative comparison with traditions of Heracles. In this instance, the extension of the night is to allow two exhausted mortals an opportunity for joy as well as tears, not to permit a disguised and amorous god to spend twice as much time working on the conception of the most powerful of all heroic sons. Indeed, there is no tradition that another child was born to Odysseus and Penelope after his return. It is also worth noting that, even when the weeping is over, Penelope is not quite ready to retire to her long-unused bridal couch with her long-absent husband, which is, eventually, made up for them by Eurycleia and Eurynome. At least four people have now seen the famous bed.

The battle of wills between Odysseus and Penelope does not cease upon the acknowledgment and reconciliation. The first words Odysseus utters to his wife after her tearful acceptance of his return is that they have not reached the end of their hardships. He alludes to another labor he has to fulfill, in Heraclean manner, according to what Teiresias's ghost has told him, then suggests they go to bed and rest.

There can be few moments in any epic or novel so charged with bitter irony enhanced by the casual and callous manner in which that irony is introduced. Twenty years of waiting, more than a hundred young suitors kept at bay: then the long-awaited husband, middle-aged and hardened in suffering, returns, wipes out everyone who has infringed upon his territory, only to hint that he will not be staying around long. Among a people involved in ships and sailing, Odysseus's casual reference to his next voyage would evoke memories of bitter thoughts and bitter complaints in many a sailor's wife who is married yet unmarried, not daring to stray for fear of reprisals on her husband's return. The husband's return, in fact, is more intolerable in many ways than is his absence, since the brief resumption of marriage interrupts the rhythm of life established during the years of waiting.

Penelope does not complain or protest. Again, she merits her epithet *periphrōn*. To complain would be both futile and, given Odysseus's temperament, downright dangerous. She does, however, insist on being told immediately:

> Your wedding bed will be ready for you whenever you wish it in your heart, for the gods have made you come back to your strongly built house and your native land; but since you have given thought to it and god put it in your heart, come, tell me this trial, since I shall hear of it later, I think. It will be none the worse if I hear about it right now. (23.257–62)

Her first word is *eunē*, which implies not just the bed but the sexual activity that occurs there, since this, she discerns, is what is foremost in Odysseus's mind now that the killing is over. She will comply whenever he is ready. But there is surely at least a touch of sarcasm in her statement that she will go along with what he wants since the gods have made him return, and that he might as well tell her what is going to happen, since a god put the thought in his mind. Learning it now won't make things worse.

Odysseus, though irritated by her request, nonetheless complies. He tells her about his future wanderings, his return home, and the gentle death that awaits him from the sea when he is an old man. He implies that all this is part of his destiny, but carefully avoids stating in so many words that the gods have forced him to undertake these new travels. As to what Penelope is to do in the meantime, he has no suggestions or comments, though he acknowledges that it will be tough on her. It certainly will. The massacre in the palace will surely not improve her relationship with the surrounding community, and she will need all her wits to manage on her own when Odysseus sets out again.

Penelope's reply to Odysseus's speech of twenty lines is short and again, understandably, touched with sarcasm: "If indeed the gods are to give you a prosperous old age, there is hope that you will escape evil" (23.286–87). She offers no observation about herself and how she can stay clear of misfortune, perceiving that such matters would be of no interest to him. Critics, especially those who like pretty, happy endings, are disappointed. Some, like Stanford, try to discern in them the light of hope at the end of the tunnel.[11] Perhaps, from her own point of view, there are consolations, for if Odysseus's return has set her back in the world of time, his impending departure will return her to the timeless and mythical existence she celebrated in tears for twenty years.

CONCLUSION

The bed is made. Odysseus and Penelope retire for the remainder of their long night. On this note, at 23.296, Alexandrian scholars wanted the epic to end. Some sections of what follows certainly seem like the product of a surrogate muse, notably the storytelling, in indirect speech, between husband and wife that occurs as soon as they have had enough of lovemaking. But since the received text does not end at 23.296, even scholars who think it should would never dare omit the remaining book and a third from a printed edition. It is therefore pointless to argue that the real *Odyssey* ends at 23.296, however pleasant it would be to view the epic without its extended and rather battered engrafted tail.

The Muse (or her surrogate) begins by giving a synopsis of Penelope's life during her husband's absence but keeps it to a minimum. In Odysseus's case, however, she gives a résumé of *Odyssey* 5–12 which many scholars find tedious and repetitive and therefore dismiss as inauthentic. They may be right. But some points are of interest, notably the absence of details about Odysseus's activities during the Trojan War. His Iliadic achievements are omitted. On balance, the résumé saps the rhetorical energy of the narrative. We are interested to know what kind of account of himself Odysseus will give Penelope but disappointed to find that he not only breaks a long-standing habit of changing his narrative to suit each listener but does not even speak it in his own voice.

Defenders of the authenticity of the passage note, with satisfaction, that Odysseus is honest and "up-front" about his relationships with Circe and Calypso. But an Odysseus who tells the truth ceases to be Odysseus. Perhaps that is the Muse's point: Odysseus's apparent candor and failure to reshape his narrative are not so much a measure of his newfound sincerity as of his indifference to Penelope's reaction, his indifference to narrating himself further. For him to stay with her would be rhetorical, mythic death—the end of his self-narration.

No reaction on Penelope's part is mentioned.

Justification for an account of the aftermath of the massacre in the hall is only a little stronger than the case for newfound sincerity. The Muse, through Odysseus's own voice, has made it clear that the recent slaughter will have an immediate backlash. Yet Odysseus takes no practical steps to anticipate it. Despite his reputation for cleverness and forethought, such strategic improvidence is not, in itself, a valid argument for the spuriousness of the text. Odysseus's art is more that of the tactician, whose success lies in finding his way out of tight corners into which he has painted himself by lack of strategic planning. His planning has not extended far beyond regaining his home and his wife.

When Odysseus awakens after his divinely extended night, his first thoughts are not of how to protect his palace against reprisals but of how to restock his farm with animals seized from the suitors' estates and of when to visit his father Laertes, who has been even more marginalized than Penelope. The only instructions he leaves as he walks out the door with Telemachus are for Penelope; and they are superfluous. She should go back to her chamber with the maids and not converse with any man. But there are virtually no men left for her to talk with. And many of her slaves have been hanged. Penelope is relegated to an isolation greater than that of her years of separation from Odysseus.

It has been argued that the *Odyssey* would not be complete without the reuniting of Odysseus with his father, Laertes. This contention strikes us as circular reasoning. It is in the text, it gives a pietistic sense of wholeness to the *nostos*, therefore it is needed. Once the need is accepted, the frequent allusions to Laertes elsewhere in the *Odyssey* are seen as pointing inexorably toward a scene bringing father and son together. A contrast with Teiresias's prophecies of further adventures for Odysseus illustrates the dilemma. These adventures are not in the text but are much more pointedly emphasized by Odysseus, who seems determined to move toward their fulfillment. To interpolate a narrative of them, however, the inventor would have to compose *Odyssey II: The Sequel.* Splicing in a reunion with Laertes involves far less work, even though it is less urgently anticipated in the text. Until Odysseus wakes up the morning after the massacre, in fact, he manifests not the slightest interest in the continued existence of his father, much less in visiting him. Odysseus, unlike Telemachus, does not need his father. He is pragmatic enough to pay attention only to those who can either assist or harm him. The need for the reunion is stronger in the reader than in the hero until we move into *Odyssey* 24 for the showdown with the suitors' relatives, when all hands are needed for the fight.

Odysseus's treatment of Laertes involves one of the most purposeless and baffling pieces of deception in the epic.[1] Odysseus arrives, in full armor, at the old man's farm, where he finds Laertes at work gardening. He wonders if Laertes will recognize him after so many years and debates whether to confess his identity immediately or to test his father with taunting words. He pursues the latter course. Even as a practical joke, there is little that can be said in favor of his decision, especially when he asks whose slave Laertes is—an insulting question Laertes never answers (or denies) directly. Although, in the course of his reply, Laertes adds, as an aside, that a guest about whom his visitor asks, the son of Laertes, is, in fact, his own son, he shows no sign of recognizing the visitor as his son.

Odysseus then generates a wholly and transparently fictional identity for himself and announces that he has not seen Odysseus for over four years, although the latter departed from him under good omens. This statement is taken by Laertes not necessarily as an announcement of Odysseus's death, but as news that, perhaps, minimizes any hopes he may have of seeing his son again before he himself dies. At this point Odysseus embraces the old man and proclaims who he is, but he is received with cool skepticism. Laertes demands and receives proof that his visitor really is his son: individualizing details ranging from his scar to his knowledge of the planting of the vines in Laertes' fields.

The whole mise-en-scène is very strange. If it is a wise man who knows his own father, what kind of a man does not recognize the man he has accepted as his own son and who was at least on the threshold of adulthood when he last saw him? Odysseus is not disguised as he stands before Laertes. He looks exactly as one might expect a returning warrior to look. Laertes is neither senile nor blind, and his failure to recognize Odysseus should not be attributed to the frailties of age. He is working in the fields and sufficiently in control of his language and thought to take in stride the suggestion that he is a slave and to avoid, with courtesy, censuring his visitor for assuming that he is. There is no clear way out of the dilemma. If the passage is genuine, perhaps the best way of coping with it is to reassert what we have been implying about all the recognitions in the epic: namely, that recognition, in the Muse's mind, is a complex process which cannot be predicted or readily generalized.

The *Odyssey* is a paradoxical work best understood, insofar as it can be understood in anything approaching clear-cut terms, as maintained by a constant tension between mutually opposed, contradictory truths. Athena, for example, is both an Olympian goddess who exists separately from and externally to Odysseus and his family and, at the same time, a kind of projection of each individual's internal thought processes.[2] Yet it is never possible entirely to separate these aspects of her presence. Athena never makes Telemachus, Odysseus, or Penelope do or think anything alien to what we perceive as their own "independent" emotional or intellectual predisposition, even when the Muse indicates that the thought or decision is incorrect. For example, Athena, disguised as Mentor, tells Telemachus that Odysseus is "among savage men" (1.197–98), even though he is, as she speaks, living safely, if sadly, in the nymph Calypso's land as the only male resident, civilized or savage. In fact, Athena's determination to get Odysseus released from Calypso's clutches sets the *Odyssey* in motion. There is no reason to assume Telemachus lacks the capacity to handle such knowledge: when Menelaus tells Telemachus that Odysseus is held captive by Calypso, the son does not give up on his father in disgust. The more likely explanation for Athena's "lie," which places Odysseus among the savages, is that it accords with what Telemachus probably imagines is Odysseus's plight. More travelers fall into the clutches of hostile tribes than are held captive by beguiling goddesses.

Athena's address to Telemachus in his sleep in *Odyssey* 15 when she wants to bring him home is similarly perplexing.[3] First, she rekindles his deeply ingrained suspicion that his mother is about to remarry and dispossess him, since now her interest rests with increasing the house of the man who marries her (15.10–26). Second, she warns Telemachus about the suitors' ambush (15.27–42). Scholars see here "concrete information beyond Telemachus's power to know, for a purpose of which he cannot be aware."[4] He cannot know where the ambush is set, but he has reason to fear trouble. He knew the suitors' hostility prior to his journey. He knows the geography of his island, knows where one is likely to set an ambush, and is thus able to circumvent it. Athena does not detail the route he should take. Once he arrives in Ithaca, it is natural for him not to return to his palace, where he suspects the suitors are trying to dispose of him. Eumaeus's hut is an obvious choice.

Similarly, when Telemachus surmises that Eurymachus is Penelope's favorite among the suitors, Athena confirms this supposition, even though the Muse's expressed opinion is that Amphinomus is the front-runner. Telemachus's assumption that his mother prefers Eurymachus is probably based on his own, rather negative opinion of Penelope and on his observation of Eurymachus's notable largesse and aggression as a suitor.

If we concede that Athena's words to Telemachus generally mirror his own inner debates, the paradoxical nature of Telemachus's thoughts about his father become more evident. We should not try to create an unrealistic and oversimplified partition of his personality in the interests of some artificial consistency, arguing that he, at heart, believes Odysseus dead and that it is only because of Athena's occasional, external reassurances that he entertains the idea that Odysseus may be alive. At the root of Telemachus's vacillation is the paradox that he both believes and does not believe that Odysseus is dead. When he acts on the assumption that Odysseus is alive, it is not simply in response to the promptings of external agencies, including the disguised Athena, but in response to the oscillation of his thoughts and the rhetorical needs of a given situation. It is important, at times, that he convey to the suitors his acceptance of Odysseus's death so that they cannot blame Penelope's indecision (or his own) on hopes either may hold that Odysseus will one day return. When Telemachus both believes and does not believe his father is dead, he is doing much the same as Sophocles' Oedipus, who believes and does not believe he is the son of Polybus of Corinth.

The Odyssean muse and the characters she depicts take it for granted that we live in a world of gods–of forces within and outside—that control the nature of existence, forces in constant conflict with one another and placing conflicting demands upon human beings. Any attempt to demarcate clearly the "internal" Athena from the "external" Athena is misleading, since the barrier between self and other is not so distinct in Homeric epic as in our thinking. In the *Odyssey*, thought is not just a function of the god but, in many instances, the god itself. In short, however much we may conceptualize Athena and other gods in human form, they are forces not bounded by form. They are simultaneously larger and smaller than humans. Externally, they manifest themselves in a variety of guises and with a variety of omens. Divine (or any other) power is enhanced by disguise. That is why Odysseus pays such careful attention to disguising both his person and his words. Internally the gods are, like Socrates' *daimon*, perhaps, the impulses that make or prevent decision. They rarely (except, Alcinous claims, among the Phaeacians) appear openly among a people, though they occasionally grant visions of themselves to individuals. That is why the public appearance of Athena to stop the fighting at the end of book 24 is so anomalous and startling until it is qualified in the final line of the epic by the addendum that she spoke the words which terrified the warring factions into a truce while in the assumed appearance of Mentor. At the same time, the notion that Mentor (even Athena disguised as Mentor) could produce such terror is hard to accept. It takes a more menacing manifestation of divine power, namely, a thunderbolt, to convince Odysseus that the fighting should stop.

The characters in the *Odyssey* are less inclined than we to assume the accuracy, stability, and reliability of the explicit. As we noted earlier, the word we translate as "safety" is for them "that which does not trip you up," *asphaleia*; the word we translate as "truth" is "that which does not elude you," *alētheia*. Most dilemmas in the narrative give graphic illustration of how difficult it is to know what kind of ground you are on and what is true. While the reader is informed by the Muse from the beginning of the epic that Odysseus is alive, Telemachus and Penelope have no means of knowing whether he is or is not. Nor does Odysseus, at any stage, have irrefutable proof that Penelope has been faithful to him. Each character, therefore, operates on the assumption that both major premises are true. Such behavior is not rhetorical sophistry. It reflects the reality of everyday life, as we can see best of all in Penelope's case.

Penelope lives in a social and mental limbo. She is both waiting wife and eligible widow, released, by her husband's prior consent from marriage obligations in the event of his prolonged absence. Her situation is that of many a woman throughout human history whose husband is "missing in action." If she is allowed by law to remarry, the shadow of her lost husband looms threateningly over her future. If she does not (or cannot) make the break, her youth and life slip away as she waits. Many wives of those missing in action do what Penelope does: they flirt while they wait but refuse to commit themselves to remarriage. Penelope, in her private anxiety and public statements, presents herself as though Odysseus were dead. Naturally enough. If she maintained publicly that Odysseus was still alive, she could not justify the presence of suitors in her house. They are there because she is, to all appearances, a widow eligible for remarriage. And she gives them little justification for thinking otherwise. Her excuse for delaying marriage is that she has not completed her final obligation to Odysseus's household: weaving Laertes' shroud. That Penelope devises a delay shows that it is also, if not equally, true that she assumes Odysseus is alive. It should not be surprising that while Penelope wants Odysseus back she does not want him back and that while she recognizes him when he arrives she does not recognize him. The Odysseus that returns is not the same man as the Odysseus that left.

Penelope is trapped in the sort of world Beckett describes in *Waiting for Godot.* But the Homeric muse adds a crueler irony. Her Godot actually arrives, destroys most of her world, then announces his almost immediate departure. She will be left waiting again.

The pluralistic, paradoxical texture of the *Odyssey*, like that of a great symphony, retains some of its allure even if we strip away the complex orchestration and try to isolate a single melody or theme. But what energizes the whole and endows it with its amazingly durable appeal, which survives the ages and even translation as few other works do, is that its complexity is such as to defy total reduction. What we have attempted to illuminate in this study amounts to no more than one or two aspects of its intricate composition and psychological depth: its anatomy of recognition and identity, its rhetoric of self-disclosure.

We hope we have shown that recognition and acknowledgment are two often separable phases of the same process. Their distinctness and separation tend to become vaster in proportion to the effects of that recognition anticipated by the individuals concerned. Helen, for example, has something to gain and virtually nothing to lose by acknowledging that she recognizes Telemachus as Odysseus's son, on the basis of his appearance, the moment she sets eyes on him. What she gains is the appearance of astuteness and keen observation. Indeed, her subsequent story of recognizing Odysseus when he visited her in Troy, disguised as a beggar, seems designed to expand on her remarkable powers of observation. She is pleased with herself for breaking through his disguise by bathing him. The person who unmasks the masked man is, in a sense, his superior, his vanquisher. Yet Helen's reflex acknowledgment of Telemachus's identity may leave doubts as to whether she could really have kept her recognition of Odysseus secret. Here we see, in fact, how the Homeric muse generates the kind of complex dialectic with the reader that constantly challenges us and, at the same time, shows how dangerous, as well as alert, a character may be.

Several modern critics conclude on the basis of Helen's instant acknowledgment of Telemachus's identity that she is more intelligent than her husband Menelaus, who is much slower to acknowledge what he has observed. Most ancient Greek readers, however, would have drawn the opposite conclusion. Menelaus also deduces that his visitor is Telemachus but has good reasons of his own to proceed more carefully. He is, in fact, frustrated by Helen's unguarded acknowledgment of her recognition, since he is not sure this is the most advantageous moment for declaring it.

If the critics who laud Helen's intellect and mock Menelaus's are right, Penelope is among the least intelligent characters in the *Odyssey*. Since the resemblance between Odysseus and Telemachus is so compelling, Penelope ought to be able to reverse the procedure and deduce that her visitor is Odysseus. Her contacts with Odysseus were, presumably, more intimate, if not more recent, than Helen's. Once this comparison arises in our minds—and Penelope's specific comparison of herself with Helen serves as a prompt to anyone who has remained oblivious to it before—we discern the Muse's longer-range narrative strategy in introducing Helen's recognitions of Telemachus and Odysseus in *Odyssey* 4. She shows *us* how compelling the resemblance is between father and son, how predictable Odysseus's beggar disguise is, and how it may be penetrated, and thus provides a basis for judging the responses of others.

Penelope probably suspects Odysseus is arriving on the basis of her conversation with Theoclymenus and probably recognizes him quickly. What complicates and delays her acknowledgment to herself, much less to anyone else, is that Odysseus is not the young prince he was. He is some ten years older than when Helen saw him in Troy. Further, he also pretends not to be who he is, giving the strong impression that he wants to be recognized but not acknowledged. While Telemachus would probably not have refused to tell Menelaus who he was if asked outright, Odysseus clearly dodges Penelope's direct questions about his identity.

For her part, Penelope has something to gain, a great deal to lose, and much sorrow to face once she acknowledges Odysseus. It is not just a matter of coquettish pride and minor self-vindication, as it is with Helen when she tells of Odysseus (who in some traditions was one of her many suitors) visiting her in Troy. Odysseus's reluctance to admit his identity provides Penelope with a possibly welcome pretext for withholding acknowledgment. Like Menelaus, she wants first to establish what is on her visitor's mind; unlike Menelaus, she is not necessarily relieved (or entirely happy) when she learns what it is. She too is aware that the beggar's disguise may be penetrated by stripping off his clothes and bathing him. Unlike Helen, however, she does not bathe him herself but delegates the task, adopting a strategy that enables his identity to be recognized but does not force her to admit that recognition. It is an odd procedure which shows, in our opinion, her paradoxical desire and reluctance to accept that Odysseus is home. And her disguised reaction is masked by the intervention of the ambiguously internal/external Athena who "prevents" her, if not from hearing the wash basin drop, at least from meeting Eurycleia's eyes to catch her significant look.

How one handles recognition, acknowledgment, and profession of identity is a key to survival in the Odyssean world, where safety lies in the avoidance of stumbling and truth resides in the ability to grasp the elusive. Survival depends on one's ability to "read" what is not self-evident. Most fail. Odysseus shows Polyphemus underestimating him, despite knowing the prophecy that he will be blinded by a stranger with that name. As Odysseus represents him, the Cyclops suffers not only because Odysseus fools him with simple wordplay, but also because his sense of self-importance will not allow him to conceive of defeat by such a puny mortal. Similarly the suitors, despite the beggar's prowess, do not seriously imagine that he might be Odysseus. Odysseus himself is even more symbolic of the catastrophic destruction awaiting the unwary than are the monsters he encounters in his travels. He rarely fails to annihilate, wittingly or unwittingly, what he touches, in the manner of Poe's Red Death. In that respect he is totally consistent throughout the epic. That is why Penelope's survival of Odysseus's return merits comparison, in simile, with the buffeting Odysseus has taken from the sea.

Other characters with good reason to recognize Odysseus respond differently to him because of their different circumstances and social positions. Eumaeus probably recognizes Odysseus at their first meeting but fears the suitors and stands to lose his status and perhaps his life if he acknowledges his recognition. He acknowledges Odysseus only when the danger of refusing to do so outweighs any threat from the suitors and when the prospect of tangible benefits helps him get over his timidity.

Eurycleia's case is somewhat different. She recognizes Odysseus almost instantly and states her recognition to his face when she bathes him, as Helen claims she did, and is satisfied by the tangible proof of the hunting scar. She does not, however, proceed to public acknowledgment, because Odysseus threatens to kill her. To all intents and purposes, then, she does not actually acknowledge him at all until after the suitors are killed. She even disguises her discovery from Penelope, on Odysseus's instructions. But her withheld acknowledgment changes her relationship with her mistress. She is trapped between divided loyalties and forced to give primary allegiance to her disguised master, even though she has no clear idea what he intends to do with Penelope.

The mise-en-scène of Odysseus in a hostile environment, disguised as a beggar, and recognized but not betrayed by the woman who bathes him is a model that can be, and is, used twice in the *Odyssey* in different ways. The first, Helen's, is the most rudimentary and apparently explicit. The second, Eurycleia's, is part of a more complex dramatic environment. The genius of the Homeric muse is not just in the redeployment of such model scenes but in using the audience's recollection of the simpler model to enhance its appreciation of the more complex. There is a crescendo of complexity in the processes of recognition described in the epic as the consequences for the recognizer (if not for the recognized) become more personal and all-encompassing. Once we have grasped the sophistication of the later, more complex Eurycleian model, we may return to the earlier and appreciate that its simplicity is not intrinsic but arguably the result of Helen's narrative pruning.

Although, in general, the recognition scenes become more complex as the epic proceeds, the Muse takes particular delight in defying our expectations at almost every turn, sometimes leading us to expect an outcome totally different from what occurs or reminding us that as recognition does not always culminate in acknowledgment, so, in some cases, acknowledgment occurs without recognition. The most obvious instance is that of Telemachus, who has no real basis for recognizing Odysseus but needs a father capable of recapturing control of the family estate. At the opposite end of the spectrum, we have Laertes, if we accept the authenticity of book 24. Odysseus's father, who ought to be able to recognize his son, does not recognize Odysseus at all. His failure to do so until the most mechanical presentation of verbal evidence assures him that his visitor must be Odysseus turns the scene in his garden into something of a dark comedy. Odysseus approaches, dressed as a warrior and certainly not disguised, with a playful but cruel "Guess who's here?" and a thin verbal blindfold. Yet when he declares his identity to the uncomprehending Laertes, his father neither recognizes nor acknowledges him. He demands proof. And the physical proof and recollection of things past ultimately satisfy Laertes that Odysseus has come home. Laertes is marginal to Odysseus's thoughts and plans. This father and son hardly know each other. We may, perhaps, reverse Telemachus's cynicism: it is a wise father who knows his own son. Perhaps indeed, the Muse suspects we may be aware of the tradition found later in Euripides, Plutarch, and Hyginus that Odysseus was really the child of the notorious liar Sisyphus, not of Laertes.[5]

A no less dramatic variant on the theme of failure to recognize the recognizable occurs when Odysseus, newly arrived in Ithaca from Scheria, does not recognize his homeland until informed by Athena (whom he also does not recognize) disguised as a shepherd. While Odysseus's difficulties are not quite so profound as, say, Hannibal's when he returns, after over fifteen years in Italy, to Carthage, which he last saw when he was nine years old, there is a certain amount of similar pathos and irony which sets the scene for the difficult recognitions that follow. Odysseus has spent half his life away from Ithaca. It is not surprising that it seems unfamiliar, even though he knows that the Phaeacians were supposed to convey him there and that his treasure chest is tangible reassurance that Alcinous has not broken his promise.

Odysseus's inability to recognize his homeland is a reminder that Ithaca has changed just as he has changed. Indeed, it would be hard for anyone who has ever been to Ithaca to recognize the island on the basis of Athena's description. Most people he will meet he has never seen before or has not seen since they were children. Nothing is static. And the tactics needed to regain control of his domain are very different from those he had to employ in Phaeacia. To be recognized in Ithaca he must establish not simply that he is Odysseus, but that he is the Odysseus that was, the Odysseus from before the Trojan War.

There are, in fact, no fewer than five Odysseuses in the *Odyssey*, corresponding to five aspects or phases of his life. Of the first Odysseus—the one remembered by Penelope, Eurycleia, even Antinous—we get occasional glimpses in the *Odyssey*, mostly in terms of his youthful prowess as a hunter. The Muse does not incorporate into her narrative stories of his resistance to enrollment in the Trojan expedition. We see him departing clothed as if he were going to a party rather than to a battle. This is the Odysseus whom Eurycleia recognizes, for whom Penelope waits: an Odysseus expert in hunting, who knows the number of trees in Laertes' garden. He is a local prince with local interests, a hunter with a faithful wife and a newborn son.

The second Odysseus is also rather sketchily represented in the *Odyssey*. This is the Iliadic, warrior Odysseus, veteran schemer of the Trojan War, the companion of Menelaus and Agamemnon. He emerges mostly in the poetic retrospective of Demodocus, in the accounts of Menelaus and Helen, and in the narrative of the Otherworld in *Odyssey* 11.

The Odysseus who returns to Ithaca is neither the first nor the second outlined above, but a third. Unlike Agamemnon and Menelaus, he is not, essentially, defined and shaped by the Trojan War, since he has spent almost as long returning from it as he spent fighting in it. His return to his homeland is thus, inevitably, different. Menelaus, who fought to recover his faithless wife, has clearly rooted himself in Sparta for the remainder of his life as a rich, married, family man. Agamemnon is killed immediately upon his return by his faithless wife's lover. What future there is belongs to Clytemnestra and his children. The returning Odysseus is more the product of his return journey than of the Trojan War. Even his treasure chest contains valuables from Phaeacia, not from Troy.

The third Odysseus is, however, quite different from the *Argo*'s Jason, who brings back not only his original ship and the object of his quest, the Golden Fleece, but a foreign princess, Medea, who is, in some traditions, Circe's niece. Aside from the treasure Alcinous gives him, Odysseus brings home, in the *Odyssey*, no tangible relics of this third Odysseus. In fact, he conceals the chest until after he has reestablished control of his house. In the process of that concealment, he patches and translates bits and pieces of his Argonautic experiences into a fourth and wholly fictional identity: that of the Cretan Odysseus.

The third Odysseus, while not completely born in Phaeacia, is finalized there because the second, Iliadic, Odysseus is meaningless in the distanced environment of Alcinous's court, and because the first has no notably heroic dimensions. Although Odysseus strives, at first, to be recognized and acknowledged as the famous, Iliadic, second Odysseus who contrived the stratagem of the wooden horse at Troy, the Phaeacians are, on the whole, as indifferent to the heroics and heroes of Troy as Americans would be to the career of, and tales of prowess uttered by, a successful cricketer from Australia.

Odysseus does his best to entice the Phaeacians into recognizing and acknowledging him as the Iliadic hero by deliberately deploying the tears and cloak technique that Telemachus had successfully, if unintentionally, deployed at Menelaus's court and which Menelaus had read perfectly. The contrast between the two incidents is illuminating. In the first, Menelaus, alert for clues, "reads" Telemachus's anxiety. In the second, Odysseus stages the clues which Alcinous notices but does not "read."

Thus Odysseus generates a new persona in Scheria. This third Odysseus is based on a folkloric representation of his adventures subsequent to the Trojan War: Odysseus the wanderer, the pirate, living on plunder in a Sinbad-like world of exaggerated extremes, of monstrous and threatening male figures and alluring, if dangerous, females. It is a fantasy with marked sexual overtones. Yet through the twists, turns, and disguises of his narrative one element emerges with increasing clarity and demonstrates that no matter how much of what he says is pure invention there lurks beneath it a marked change in his underlying character. He has become reluctant to stay in one place and in one environment, no matter how seductive that environment may be. This change in his character is illustrated by both the Muse and himself, chiefly in the descriptions of his relationships with various female figures. Whether their initial impulse is to harm him (as in Circe's case), to possess him as a permanent, even immortal, lover (Calypso), or to take him as a husband (Nausicaa), all attempt to root him in a particular place.

If we set Odysseus's relationships in sequence, we will note that he has to be prompted by his crew to leave Circe after a year. After seven years with Calypso, however, he is depressed and ready to leave. Yet, while he stays, he is on the most intimate personal terms with both Circe and Calypso. With Nausicaa, however, he is cautious from the beginning. He politely yet firmly declines her very thinly veiled overtures. It is at least partially for her benefit that he incorporates into his account to the seagoing Phaeacians his encounter with the dead Teiresias and the prophecy which condemns him to continue wandering until he reaches a people who do not know what an oar is. Nor is it surprising that he reiterates precisely this prophecy to Penelope within seconds of being acknowledged by her in Ithaca. The third Odysseus is, then, the incurable wanderer, whose focus is, at least intermittently, on getting home.

Of all the disguises Odysseus employs when he returns to Ithaca, none is more vital than his veiling of his third, now dominant identity, with a fourth, Cretan persona which is a fusion of the second (Iliadic) Odysseus with the metamorphosed fragments of the third. We might compare him to the historical English king, Richard the Lionheart, who betrays those who wait for and serve him loyally during his absence by leaving them again, shortly after his return, exposed by virtue of their loyalty to the not particularly tender mercies of his brother and treacherous rival, John. How willingly anyone in Odysseus's household would have aided him in his massacre of the suitors if they had known he was intending to leave again soon is debatable. In the massacre, Odysseus destroys others who want to possess things he does not want to have. Penelope's caution, then, is based on her increasing awareness that the Odysseus who has returned is not the same as the Odysseus who left twenty years ago. It is not just that he is older or that his status is, apparently, lower.

The first Odysseus dies, symbolically, with his old hunting dog Argus when the master recrosses the threshold of his palace. The wandering but powerful beggar in the halls is but a disguised reduction of the third Odysseus, the wandering pirate. The fourth persona, the Cretan identity Odysseus claims on arrival in Ithaca, masks but does not entirely conceal the instability of the third. The Cretan, who has no interest in farm and home, does not plan to stay long in Ithaca, the home which the second Odysseus sought.

Cretans are famous not only for their prowess in lying but for their skill with the bow.[6] Hence we may discern yet another motive for Penelope's decision to set up the contest of the bow, prompted perhaps by Odysseus's assumed identity. Since the bow is a characteristically Cretan weapon, it serves as a means of testing Odysseus's Cretan identity, his new persona, not only as a means of discovering whether he or anyone else can rival the first and now lost Odysseus Penelope married. It may even be a means of reconciling the two Odyssean personae with which Penelope is confronted, for Penelope does not make the naive error Eurycleia makes. Eurycleia assumes that an old hunting scar confirms the return of the first, hunting Odysseus she loved. Penelope, by contrast, understands that recognition involves noting what a person is or has become, not simply putting a name to a face. Thus her choice of the old bow as the means of establishing the identity of her new husband marks, in a way, her realization that whatever happens, she will be acquiring a different husband. The bow, we recall, was deliberately left behind by Odysseus when he went to Troy, and was never, so far as we know, used by him as a weapon to kill other humans, much less essentially defenseless humans. But the returning eagle-Odysseus of Penelope's nightmare fantasy is a predatory creature who will prey on her greedy but imbellicose geese. And he will trap them, as a hunter traps his quarry or a fisherman his catch, in the snare of his own palace. Penelope not only serves as the lure; she equips him with the formerly innocent hunting bow as a weapon of human massacre.

Penelope declines to marry the still disguised Odysseus when he wins the contest and declines to acknowledge him even when he and his victory are evident to everyone else. She accepts him only when there is no alternative but to do so. Ultimately the paradox is that she both recognizes and does not recognize the man she married. When he leaves for a second time, her recollections will be less affectionate. She has seen, as Heracles' relatives see, the darker side of the heroic nature, the side which modern critics often try to avoid acknowledging. The heroes' more-than-human powers endow them with demonic capabilities for destruction as well as for helping the human condition. But few leave such a trail of total desolation as Odysseus. He is not, like Wilfred Owen, just the warrior-poet as survivor, but the warrior-poet as the agent, if not the only cause, of the desolation which he survives in solitude. The fourth Odysseus, in fact, seeks his own isolation. The futility of further waiting by Penelope for this hero emerges in other tales of Odysseus's house which Homer's audiences probably knew well: tales which leave Odysseus dead, Telemachus married to Circe, and Penelope to the (very) youthful Telegonus—tales involving a fifth Odysseus.

The Homeric muse acknowledges that Odysseus, unlike Agamemnon and Menelaus, comes home twice. On that second homecoming, he will die not tragically but accidentally and quite unheroically. This fifth Odysseus, whose presence is discernible in faint echoes of other traditions here and there in the *Odyssey*, is the ultimately displaced hero who survives now mostly in the fragmentary testimony of lost tragedies and mythographers, but whose shadowy presence informs and shapes, in curious ways, the various faces the hero presents in the Homeric epic. The genius of the Homeric muse is surely in contriving an earlier, albeit temporary, return for Odysseus which has, in the course of centuries and millennia, become canonical and displaced his other, later return from modern literary memory to all intents and purposes. The *Odyssey*, far from being a codification of prior oral tradition, is more probably a new synthesis which took its audiences by storm and became, with remarkable speed, the canonical version. Yet, paradoxically, our awareness of the fainter and, we would suggest, *older*, more mythically typical Odysseus makes the listener and reader more sympathetic to the tales of Penelope's treachery and infidelity which are such an integral part of these other traditions. She cannot be expected to wait loyally for the bloodied lion to return again.

NOTES

Introduction

1 For Charles Perrault, see G. Finsler, *Homer in der Neuzeit von Dante bis Goethe* (Leipzig and Berlin: Teubner, 1912) 189ff.; F. d'Aubignac, *Conjectures académiques ou dissertation sur "l'Iliade"* (Paris: François Fournier, 1715); F. A. Wolf, *Prolegomena ad Homerum* (Berlin: Calvary, 1871; original publication, 1795). For a summary of scholarship on the orality of the epic genre in early Greece and other cultures and the question of the poeticity of oral poetry, see P. Zumthor, *Oral Poetry: An Introduction*, trans. K. Murphy-Judy (Minneapolis: University of Minnesota Press, 1990) esp. 79–96.

2 H. J. Rose, *A Handbook of Greek Literature* (New York: E. P. Dutton, 1960) 34–46; Rose's objection that the same sort of inconsistencies could be used to prove the multiple authorship of Molière's *Les femmes savantes* and Shakespeare's *Othello* has gone largely unheeded: "No one supposes Shakespere [*sic*] or Molière to have written these plays in conjunction with any one else; but when it comes to Homer, such arguments as the following have been offered, and taken seriously" (43).

3 M. Parry, "L' épithète traditionelle dans Homère: Essai sur un problème de style homérique" (Diss., Paris, 1928; published by Société éditrice, Les belles lettres).

4 See the recent, and cautiously conservative, study by H. D. Rankin, *Celts and the Classical World* (London: Croom Helm, 1987); for discussion of bards, see pp. 272–76. Julius Caesar himself describes the druids as guardians of Celtic lore and tradition, which were not permitted to be written down but were passed on orally from one generation to the next (*Gallic Wars* 6.13–14). The bards—called *bardoi* by Diodorus (5.31.2–5)—are poets who sing to the lyre, elevate their fellow men with praise, and are feared for their terrible powers of rebuke. They even intervene, along with the druids, to charm combatants into peace when they are in mid-battle. The privileged position of the bards, the *beirdd* among the Brythonic Celts and *filid* among the Goedelic, was maintained well into the sixteenth century and even longer in the remoter areas of Ireland. As Celtic war-

riors attracted the attention of the Greeks and Romans on account of their curious attire and savage ferocity, their bards and poetically trained druids drew attention for their special powers and influence in Celtic society. Tomas O Criomhthain in his now classic Gaelic autobiography, *An t-Oileneach* (The islandman), records at the beginning of this century his childhood fear of the village poet who might satirize him. See S. O Tuama, *An Duanaire, 1600–1900: Poems of the Dispossessed* (Dublin: Dolmen Press, 1981) xvii–xxii, esp. xix: "During the bardic period, from 1200 to 1600 approximately, noble Irish families, of whom there were many hundreds, had maintained hereditary poets with great honour and ceremony."

5 B. L. Ullman, "The Origin and Development of the Alphabet," *AJA* 31 (1927) 311–28; id., "How Old Is the Greek Alphabet?" *AJA* 38 (1934) 359–81; R. Carpenter, "The Antiquity of the Greek Alphabet," *AJA* 37 (1933) 8–29; id., "The Greek Alphabet Again," *AJA* 42 (1938) 58–69.

6 M. Ventris and J. Chadwick, *Documents in Mycenaean Greek* (Cambridge: Cambridge University Press, 1956), esp. chaps. 1 and 2; J. Chadwick, *The Decipherment of Linear B* (Cambridge: Cambridge University Press, 1958).

7 But when that literacy did break down, the very next Greek epic, *Digenis Akritas,* the product of the dark years of failing literacy and the struggles against Arabs and Turks, emerged in a very rustic Byzantine Greek, and, in those areas of the Balkans where Greek had lost ground among the people, in a Bulgarian version.

8 G. S. Kirk, "The Poet and the Oral Tradition," in *The Cambridge History of Classical Literature,* ed. P. E. Easterling and B. M. W. Knox (Cambridge: Cambridge University Press, 1985) 1: 45–46.

9 C. R. Beye, *Ancient Greek Literature and Society,* 2d ed. (Ithaca, N.Y.: Cornell University Press, 1987) 12.

10 Carpenter, "The Greek Alphabet Again," 69.

11 For a survey of the arguments, see M. Bernal, *Cadmean Letters: The Transmission of the Alphabet to the Aegean and Further West before 1400 B.C.* (Winona Lake, Ind.: Eisenbrauns, 1990) esp. 1–26.

12 P. James, *Centuries of Darkness* (New Brunswick, N.J.: Rutgers University Press, 1993) xxi–xxii; cf. C. Torr, *Memphis and Mycenae* (Cambridge: Cambridge University Press, 1896); J. Lieblein, *Recherches sur la chronologie égyptienne d' après les listes généalogiques* (Christiana: A. W. Brogger, 1873); I. Velikovsky, *Ages in Chaos* (London: Sidgwick and Jackson, 1953).

13 A. Parry, "Language and Characterization in Homer," *HSCP* 76 (1972) 1.

14 G. Nagy, *The Best of the Achaeans: Concepts of the Hero in Archaic Greek Poetry* (Baltimore: Johns Hopkins University Press, 1979); B. B. Powell, *Homer and the Origin of the Greek Alphabet* (Cambridge: Cambridge University Press, 1991). Nagy, it should be added, maintains that the *Iliad* and the *Odyssey* did not take fixed form until as late as the age of tyrants (seventh century B.C.E.) ("Ancient Greek Epic and Praise Poetry: Some Typological Considerations," in *Oral Tradition in Literature,* ed. J. M. Foley [Columbia: University of Missouri Press, 1986] 96). For the possibility of later, Athenian insertion into the corpus of the *Odyssey* in the sixth century, see W. S. Barrett, *Euripides, Hippolytos* (Oxford: Oxford University Press, 1964) 9, who contends that the mention of Phaedra in *Odyssey* 11.321–25 must be such an instance.

15 Kirk, "The Poet and the Oral Tradition," 1: 42–51; quotation from p. 43.

16 Nagy, *Best of the Achaeans*, 15.
17 R. Finnegan, *Oral Poetry* (Cambridge: Cambridge University Press, 1977) 2.
18 R. D. Dawe, *The "Odyssey": Translation and Analysis* (Sussex, England: Book Guild, 1993) 16, 27; cf. pp. 21, 873.
19 R. Lamberton, *Homer the Theologian: Neoplatonist Allegorical Reading and the Growth of the Epic Tradition* (Berkeley: University of California Press, 1986) 300.
20 M. C. Stokes, *Plato's Socratic Conversations: Drama and Dialectic in Three Dialogues* (London: Athlone Press, 1986) 318–19. Cf. Lamberton, *Homer the Theologian*, 13: "It seems to have been generally true in antiquity that exegesis was the province of the educator, and specifically of the philosophical educator. Only infrequently was such exegesis given an importance that implied a pretense to permanence, and so only infrequently has it entered the preserved literature, beyond the scholia." See also G. Nagy, "Homeric Questions," *TAPA* 122 (1992) 17–60.
21 M. Lynn-George, *Word, Narrative, and the "Iliad"* (Atlantic Highlands, N.J.: Humanities Press International, 1988) 58.
22 R. Palmer, "Allegorical, Philological, and Philosophical Hermeneutics: Three Modes in a Complex Heritage," in *Contemporary Literary Hermeneutics and Interpretation of Classical Texts*, ed. S. Kresic (Ottawa: Éd. de l' Université d' Ottawa, 1981) 24; M. Väisänen, *La musa dalle molte voci: Studio sulle dimensioni storiche dell' arte di Catullo* (Helsinki: Societas historica Finlandiae, 1988) 9–28.
23 P. Assouline, *An Artful Life: A Biography of D. H. Kahnweiler, 1884–1979*, trans. Charles Ruas (New York: Grove Weidenfield, 1990) 99.
24 M. N. Nagler, *Spontaneity and Tradition: A Study in the Oral Art of Homer* (Berkeley: University of California Press, 1974); N. Austin, *Archery at the Dark of the Moon: Poetic Problems in Homer's "Odyssey"* (Berkeley: University of California Press, 1975); S. L. Schein, *The Mortal Hero: An Introduction to Homer's "Iliad"* (Berkeley: University of California Press, 1984) 3: "The fact that the *Iliad* is composed in formulaic language and meter and according to strict narrative conventions does not mean that it is therefore unoriginal or inartistic"; R. P. Martin, "Telemachus and the Last Hero Song," *Colby Quarterly* 29 (1993) 222–40, esp. 227–28.
25 P. Vivante, *Homer* (New Haven: Yale University Press, 1985) 12.
26 M. M. Willcock, "The Search for the Poet Homer," *G&R* 37, no. 1 (1990) 1–13.
27 Lamberton, *Homer the Theologian*, 21.
28 P. Pucci, *Odysseus Polutropos: Intertextual Readings in the "Odyssey" and the "Iliad"* (Ithaca, N.Y.: Cornell University Press, 1987) 27, 30.
29 A. Ford, *Homer: The Poetry of the Past* (Ithaca, N.Y.: Cornell University Press, 1992).
30 J. S. Clay, *The Wrath of Athena: Gods and Men in the "Odyssey"* (Princeton: Princeton University Press, 1983) 3; see also p. 6.
31 B. C. Fenik, *Homer, Tradition and Invention* (Leiden: Brill, 1978) 90.
32 J. Griffin, *Homer on Life and Death* (Oxford: Clarendon Press, 1983) xiii–xvi; quotation from p. xiv.
33 Lamberton, *Homer the Theologian*, viii–ix; cf. F. Buffière, *Les mythes d'Homère et la pensée grecque* (Paris: Les belles lettres, 1956); and G. M. A. Grube, "How Did the Greeks Look at Literature?" in *Lectures in Memory of Louise Taft Semple*, 2d ser., 1966–70, ed. C. G. Boulter et al. (Norman: University of Oklahoma Press, 1973)

99; for the question of explicit and implicit reading of the Homeric epics, see L. Slatkin, *The Power of Thetis: Allusion and Interpretation in the "Iliad"* (Berkeley: University of California Press, 1991).

34 See Hermogenes *On Invention* 204ff. (Rabe).

35 For a full discussion, see F. Ahl, "The Art of Safe Criticism in Greece and Rome," *AJP* 105 (1984) 174–208.

36 G. E. Lessing, *Laocoön: An Essay on the Limits of Painting and Poetry*, trans. E. A. McCormick (Baltimore: Johns Hopkins University Press, 1984) 71–73.

37 Slatkin, *Power of Thetis*, 2–3; see pp. 2–9 passim.

38 A. Heubeck, S. West, and J. B. Hainsworth, *A Commentary on Homer's "Odyssey" (Oxford: Clarendon Press,* 1988) 340: "The story appears to be an invention, for it is otherwise quite unknown to mythology."

39 M. M. Willcock, "Mythological Paradeigma in the *Iliad*," *CQ* 14 (1964) 141–54; quotation from p. 141.

40 M. L. West, trans., *Hesiod, Theogony and Works and Days* (New York: Oxford University Press, 1988) viii–ix. For the *Odyssey* especially, see also M. L. West, *Hesiod, Works and Days* (Oxford: Clarendon Press, 1978) 60–61.

41 West, *Hesiod, Theogony and Works and Days*, 74 (on *Theogony* 1011–12); cf. M. L. West, *Hesiod, Theogony* (Oxford: Clarendon Press, 1966).

42 L. di Gregorio, ed., *Scholia vetera in Hesiodi Theogoniam* (Vita e pensiero, Universit' Cattolica, Scienze filologiche e letteratura 6: Milan, 1975) 123.

43 J. G. Frazer, *Apollodorus, The Library* (London: Heinemann, 1921) 2: 288 n. 2.

44 Sophocles treated the story of Odysseus's pretended madness in his now lost *Odysseus Mainomenos.* Cf. Apollodorus 3.7. See D. Sutton, *The Lost Sophocles* (Lanham, Md.: University Press of America, 1984) 94 and the sources cited.

45 Parry, "Language and Characterization in Homer," 22.

46 Ibid.

47 L. Ghali-Kahil, *Les enlèvements et le retour d'Hélène dans les textes et les documents figurés* (Paris: E. de Boccard, 1955); J. D. Beazley, *Attic Red-Figure Vase Painters*, 2d ed. (Oxford: Clarendon Press, 1963) 458, no. 1; G. K. Galinsky, *Aeneas, Sicily, and Rome,* Princeton Monographs in Art and Archaeology 40 (Princeton: Princeton University Press, 1969) 40–41.

48 Galinsky, *Aeneas, Sicily, and Rome,* 40 and the sources cited. See also V. Ussani's important article "Enea traditore," *SIFC,* n.s. 22 (1947) 108–23; F. Ahl, "Homer, Vergil, and Complex Narrative Structures in Latin Epic: An Essay," *ICS* 14 (1989) 22–31.

49 N. Horsfall, "The Aeneas Legend and the *Aeneid,*" *Vergilius* 32 (1986) 8–17; quotation from pp. 16–17.

50 For a recent discussion of the problem of the crew members' *atasthlaliai* (acts of "reckless disregard" or "heedless recklessness"), see V. Pedric, "The Muse Corrects: The Opening of the *Odyssey,*" *YCS* 29 (1992) 48–49, who perceives Odysseus's account of the crew devouring the cattle of the Sun as an attempt to exculpate them on grounds of necessity due to the god's arbitrariness.

51 E.g., Clay, *Wrath of Athena,* 34–38.

52 For this reason art is always an ambiguous tool for the moralist and other propagandists. That is why Plato saw Homer as a very threatening figure in his ideal state. In Plato's mind, Homer's moral polyvalence and pluralism threatened public morals and therefore had to be censored or banned. In fact, Socra-

tes talks of "thoroughly cleansing [*diakathairontes*] again [*palin*] the city [*polin*]" (*Republic* 3.399E) by banning the use of complex musical forms and the instruments used to express them (*Republic* 3.398C–399E; see also 2.377D–3. 403C; 10.606C–608B). The phrase is curiously resonant of Sophocles *Oedipus Tyrannus* 100–101, where Creon, recently returned from Delphi, announces the gist of the oracle's response as to how the plague afflicting Thebes can be removed from the city: "By banishing or paying out again [*palin*] killing for killing, since this bloodshed makes stormy going for our city-state [*polin*]."

1. Rival Homecomings

1 That is why it seems to us that the supposed tension and rivalry between poet and muse which has much preoccupied scholars is rather beside the point. See Pedric, "The Muse Corrects," and references cited by Pedric (especially on p. 39).

2 A. Rees and B. Rees, *The Celtic Heritage* (London: Thames and Hudson, 1961) 316.

3 Apollodorus *Epitome* 7.17. Telegonus was recognized by Hagias in his epic, *The Returns*, and by another Cyclic poet, Eugammon of Cyrene, who composed an epic about the adventures of Telegonus called the *Telegony*. According to Eugammon, Telegonus was a son of Odysseus by Calypso, not by Circe. See G. Kinkel, *Epicorum Graecorum Fragmenta* (Göttingen: Vandenhoek and Ruprecht, 1988) 56, 57ff.; Eustathius on Homer *Odyssey* 16.118, op. 1796 adds Telademus. Hyginus (*Fabulae* [Myths] 125) gives him two sons, Nausithous and Telegonus, by Circe. As to Telegonus, see Apollodorus *Epitome* 7.36ff.

4 For *odynē*, see W. B. Stanford, *The "Odyssey" of Homer*, 2d ed., 2 vols. (New York: St. Martin's Press, 1965) on 1.62. For the Odysseus/Zeus wordplay, see M. Steinrück, *Leise Laute: Arbeiten über das Verhältnis von Rhytmus und Lautresponsion bei Archilochos* (Lausanne and Basel: Petra Tergum, 1991) 5. For the connection of the name Odysseus with *odyssaomai*, see the extensive discussion of Clay, *Wrath of Athena*, 59–65, 70 n. 31. Clay does not, however, connect the name Odysseus with Zeus; see p. 63.

5 For a discussion of Athena's dominance over the action of the *Odyssey*, whether through her presence or absence, wrath or support of Odysseus, see Clay, *Wrath of Athena*, 40–53, 182–83, and passim.

6 Pindar frag. 100 (Snell); Apollodorus *Epitome* 2.38; Servius on *Aeneid* 2.44.

7 D. Frame, *The Myth of Return in Early Greek Epic* (New Haven: Yale University Press, 1978) 33.

8 Frame, *Myth of Return*, 37.

9 For last words of first books, see F. Ahl, *Metaformations: Soundplay and Wordplay in Ovid and Other Classical Poets* (Ithaca, N.Y.: Cornell University Press, 1985) 167–68.

10 See Sutton, *Lost Sophocles*, 46, 88–94, and the sources cited. These references will be discussed in more detail below.

11 See Pucci, *Odysseus Polutropos*, 198–99; J. Svenbro, *La parole et le marbre: Aux origines de la poétique grecque* (Lund: Studentlitteratur, 1976) 20–21; against this, see Ford, *Homer*, 108–9.

12 The suggestion by K. Atchity and E. J. W. Barber, "Greek Princes and Ae-

gean Princesses: The Role of Women in the Homeric Poems," in *Critical Essays on Homer*, ed. K. Atchity with R. Hogart and D. Price (Boston: G. K. Hall, 1987) 29, that the kind of garment Penelope was weaving takes three years to produce is interesting—though a competent modern Turkish or Iranian weaver could produce several large and spectacular carpets in three years.

13 About Mycena we know very little (unless, as daughter of Inachus, she is identical with Io, beloved of Zeus); but as the eponymous heroine of Mycenae, it is not unlikely that she too was involved in some relationship with a god.

14 Apollodorus 7.38; Pausanias 8.12.5ff.; Cicero *On the Nature of the Gods* 3.22.56; Tzetzes, scholia on Lycophron 772; Servius on *Aeneid* 2.44.

15 *Odyssey* 12. 50–51 and 161–62 (he ties himself to the base of the mast [*histopedē*]); 12.421–25 and 438 (the mast saves him from Scylla and Charybdis); 14.310–12 (riding on the mast, he drifts for nine days till he reaches the land of the Thesprotians); 5.315–16 (the mast is broken during a storm after he leaves Calypso's island).

16 5.62 (Calypso's idyllic tranquillity as Hermes arrives); 7.104–10 (the Phaeacian women at work); 10.221–26 and 253–54 (Circe and the illusory tranquillity of her residence); 13.107–8 (the nymphs in the bay of Phorcys).

17 A. Kirchhoff, *Die homerische "Odyssee" und ihre Entstehung* (Berlin: Wilhelm Hertz, 1859) esp. viii, also 136ff.; cf. id., *Die Composition der "Odyssee": Gesammelte Aufsätze* (Berlin: Wilhelm Hertz, 1869). The results of Kirchoff's analysis were accepted later by Wolf, Wilamowitz, and Jebb. See H. Fränkel, *Early Greek Poetry and Philosophy*, trans. M. Hadas and J. Willis (New York and London: Harcourt Brace Jovanovich, 1975) 23. E. R. Dodds, *The Greeks and the Irrational* (Berkeley: University of California Press, 1951) 10, takes the separateness of the "Telemachy" for granted. Doubts whether the Telemacheia at one time was an independent poem still creep into a number of more recent scholarly works; see D. Page, for example, the last of the old-time Analysts, in *The Homeric "Odyssey"* (Oxford: Clarendon Press, 1955) 52–73.

18 See Ahl, "Complex Narrative Structures," 8–10.

19 1.432–33.

20 For the marginal place of a *nothos* (illegitimate, bastard) in the Greek family, see C. B. Patterson, "Those Athenian Bastards," *ClAnt* 9 (1990) 40–73; on Megapenthes specifically, see pp. 47–48 n. 40.

21 Apollodorus *Epitome* 6.13 and 14; Euripides *Andromache* 967–81; *Orestes* 1653–57; scholia on Euripides *Andromache* 32; Hyginus *Fabulae* (Myths) 123; Eustathius on *Odyssey* 4.3; scholia on Homer *Odyssey* 4.4; Ovid *Heroides* 8.31ff.; Servius on *Aeneid* 3.297 and 330; Vergil *Aeneid* 3.330.

22 P. L. Fermor, *Roumeli: Travels in Northern Greece* (New York: Harper and Row, 1966) 46.

23 For a discussion of the scene and the social implications of Eteoneus's suggestion, see J. Roisman, "Some Social Conventions and Deviations in Homeric Society," *Acta Classica* 25 (1982) 35–41. For a list of servants' suggestions in the epic, see S. D. Olson, "Servants' Suggestions in Homer's *Odyssey*," *CJ* 87 (1992) 219–27.

24 The difficulty is that most of our picture of Homeric customs is extrapolated from the epics and not from independent evidence. It is not clear how common it was in any real-life social situation for a guest to be received and not to identify himself.

25 For further discussion, see Chapter 7.
26 The encounter between Odysseus and Penelope is one of the most intriguing scenes in the epic and has justifiably attracted endless scholarly attention. For the possibility of an early recognition and its actual postponement, whether for psychological or structural reasons, or for the sake of characterization, see, for example, P. W. Harsh, "Penelope and Odysseus in *Odyssey* XIX," *AJP* 71 (1950) 1–21; J. Russo, "Interview and Aftermath: Dream, Fantasy, and Intuition in *Odyssey* 19 and 20," *AJP* 103 (1982) 4–18; C. Emlyn-Jones, "The Reunion of Penelope and Odysseus," *G&R* 31 (1984) 1–18; and earlier treatments of the episode cited in these discussions.
27 2.113–120. Herodotus suggests that Homer knew the story but rejected it. The potion would certainly have been more useful to her at Troy than on the journey back with Menelaus, which, in Menelaus's account in *Odyssey* 4.351–586, took them through Egypt. On Helen's drug, see Ann Bergren, "Helen's 'Good Drug': *Odyssey* IV 1–305," in *Contemporary Literary Hermeneutics and the Interpretation of Classical Texts*, ed. S. Kresic (Ottawa: Éd. de l'Université d'Ottawa, 1981) 201–14.
28 Indeed, we should recall that Eurycleia herself is found later in book 4, in dialogue with Penelope when the narrative returns to Ithaca (4.741–58).
29 Again, see Bergren, "Helen's 'Good Drug' "; id., "Language and the Female in Early Greek Thought," *Arethusa* 16 (1983) 63–95, and esp. 79–80.
30 And at a time made special not only by Telemachus's visit but by the double marriage of Menelaus's two children (only one of whom is by Helen).
31 For a discussion of competition between bards, and a possible rivalry between a bard and the Muses, see Ford, *Homer*, 93–120. One can claim that to some extent any narrator in the epic becomes a pseudocompetitor with the Muse. See also Claude Calame, *The Craft of Poetic Speech in Ancient Greece*, tr. J. Orion (Ithaca, N.Y.: Cornell University Press, 1995) 27–44.

2. Arrival at Scheria

1 See F. Bömer, *P. Ovidius Naso, Metamorphosen, Buch 14–15* (Heidelberg: Carl Winter Universitätsverlag, 1986) 65–66.
2 For Odysseus's ship, see L. Casson, *Ships and Seamanship in the Ancient World* (Princeton: Princeton University Press, 1971) 217–19.
3 See Aratus *Phaenomena* 918; Theophrastus *De signis tempestatum* (On indications of storms) 2.28; Aelian *De natura animalium* (On the nature of animals) 7.7; cf. Callimachus *Epigrams* 59; *Hymn to Delos* 12; also the following allusions in the *Greek Anthology*: 7.285 (Glaucus); 7.295 (Leonidas of Tarentum); 7.374 (Marcus Argentarius).
4 *mergus quod mergendo in aquam captat escam.*
5 Aristophanes of Byzantium *Historia animalium* (History of animals) Ep. 1.141; Dionysius *De avibus* (On birds) 2.6. See D'Arcy W. Thompson, *A Glossary of Greek Birds* (Hildesheim: Georg Olms, 1936) 28–29.
6 Pausanias 1.5.3, 1.41.6; Lycophron *Cassandra* 359. See the discussion in M. Détienne and J.-P. Vernant, *Les ruses de l'intelligence: La métis des Grecs* (Paris: Flammarion, 1974) 201–41 (esp. 204–5).

7 The identification of Athena with the shearwater is sufficiently common that it led Thompson(*Greek Birds,* 29, on *Odyssey* 5.337, 353) to make the same assumption Odysseus probably makes, since he adduces this very passage from the *Odyssey* as further evidence of the identification of Athena and the shearwater. The word *aithyia* occurs nowhere else in Homer.

8 See above, p. 30.

9 *Odyssey* 5.454–57; 6.137. See also above, note 2.

10 Rees and Rees, *Celtic Heritage,* 48. Travelers are often marooned in mysterious enchanted places for periods of seven (or multiples of seven) years in Celtic myth. Rees and Rees note that such places, with their Otherworldy quality, "transcend mundane time. . . . A very short time in the Other World corresponds with a very long time in this world. Many . . . stories . . . tell of a man who returns after a seemingly brief sojourn in that enchanted world and finds that his contemporaries are dead" (343).

11 When the sanctuary (and with it the olive tree) was destroyed by fire, the Athenians, ordered by Xerxes to make a sacrifice in the area the next day, discovered that the olive had grown a new branch about a half meter long.

12 For the view that the reference to Athena's going to the house of Erechtheus is a reference to the primitive Mycenean idea that the goddess resides in Erechtheus's house rather than vice versa, see Stanford, *"Odyssey" of Homer,* on 6.80.

13 See Apollonius *Argonautica* 4.537–51 and 986–92, with notes ad loc. of E. Livrea, *Apollonii Rhodii Argonautica, Liber Quartus* (Florence: La nuova Italia, 1973), and G. Paduano and M. Fusillo, *Apollonio Rodio, Le Argonautiche* (Milan: Biblioteca universale Rizzoli, 1986). Identification with Crete or Thera seems more plausible, though still unnecessary; see J. V. Luce, *Lost Atlantis: New Light on an Old Legend* (New York: McGraw-Hill, 1969) 171–72. On the Phaeacians and the Cyclopes, see E. Dolin, "Odysseus in Phaeacia," *GräzBeitr* 1 (1973) 273–82; R. Mondi, "The Homeric Cyclopes: Folktale, Tradition, and Theme," *TAPA* 113 (1983) 17–38.

14 J. S. Clay, "Goat Island: *Od.* 9.116–141," *CQ* 30 (1980) 261–64, for instance, suggests that the original home of the Phaeacians was the delightful island, full of goats, off the coast of the Cyclopes' land mentioned in *Odyssey* 9.

15 If Laestrygonia actually existed, it could hardly have been much farther south than Denmark if it had days long enough for the running of two flocks by an enterprising shepherd. Such extended periods of daylight do not occur in Sardinia, where some scholars situate the Laestrygonians.

16 It is possible for information to flow among the characters without an explicit statement: consider the example of Arete and Odysseus in book 7, where Arete's enquiry rests on the assumption that Odysseus said before that he had come to the Phaeacians after wandering over the sea (7.239), although this information was given to Nausicaa but not to the royal couple (6.170–72). Cf. B. Fenik, *Studies in the "Odyssey,"* Hermes Einzelschrift 30 (Wiesbaden: Franz Steiner, 1974) 129. In 12.374–90, Odysseus tells the Phaeacians how Hyperion's daughter told him what had befallen to his cattle, and how Hyperion threatened to shine among the dead and Zeus prevented him from doing so. Odysseus says he heard the story from Calypso, who in turn had learned about it from Hermes. The outer audience, however, was not privy to this exchange of information.

17 See G. P. Rose, "The Unfriendly Phaeacians," *TAPA* 100 (1969) 387–406.

18 We should add that there is nothing to suggest that Odysseus is aware of the divinity of the disguised Athena until much later in the epic, when the goddess identifies herself to him on the seashore in Ithaca.

19 See, for example, G. E. Dimock, *The Unity of the "Odyssey" (Amherst: University of Massachusetts Press,* 1989) 78.

20 E.g., D. J. N. Lee, *The Similes of the "Iliad" and the "Odyssey" Compared* (Cambridge: Cambridge University Press, 1964) 22–23; H. Fränkel, *Die homerischen Gleichnisse* (Göttingen: Vandenhoeck and Ruprecht, 1921) 69–70. For an analysis of the lion similes in the epic, see W. T. Magrath, "Progression of the Lion Simile in the *Odyssey*," *CJ* 77 (1982) 205–12. For the mock-heroic touch, see also R. Lattimore, "Nausikaa's Suitors," *Illinois Studies in Language and Literature* 58 (1969) 90–91.

21 Fränkel, *Die homerischen Gleichnisse,* 70, remarks, for example, that a nude man bears at least some resemblance to a nude lion, since lions never wear clothes anyway.

22 Such encounters are shown in vase paintings. See, for instance, the lower part of the kalyx krater of the Pan Painter, Geneva MF 238, *ARV* 615.1, where a young man pursues a woman while her attendants flee.

23 For the awakening sexuality of Nausicaa and the analysis of the episode as a typical allurement scene, see Nagler, *Spontaneity and Tradition,* 81–85; N. Forsyth, "The Allurement Scene: A Typical Pattern in Greek Oral Epic," *CSCA* 12 (1979) 107–20. Forsyth points to patterns of resemblance between the Nausicaa episode in Scheria and Penelope scenes following Odysseus's return to Ithaca. He regards the episodes as type scenes of allurement, which contain similar patterns of beautification of the woman with reference to Aphrodite or the Graces and removal of the veil as a mark of chastity.

24 There is some resonance in both texts in the color of the ball, which in both cases is referred to as *porphyreē* (*Odyssey* 8.372–73; Anacreon 13.1). For further discussion of what are taken as Homeric echoes in Anacreon's poem, see A. E. Harvey, "Homeric Epithets in Greek Lyric Poetry," *CQ* 51 (1957) 213.

25 H. T. Wade-Gery, *The Poet of the "Iliad"* (Cambridge: Cambridge University Press, 1952) 3, suggests that the audience must have known the exact shoot of the palm tree Odysseus is referring to, since they visited Delos during the festivals. This seems a little farfetched to us. Unless we locate the composition of this part of the *Odyssey* fairly precisely within a given time period, it is unlikely that the particular palm would still have been alive, much less that it would have a still recognizable shoot. For Apollo's Delian palm, see Pausanias 8.48.3; Cicero *Laws* 1.1; Theophrastus *Enquiry into Plants* 4.13.2; Pliny *Natural History* 16.99. For Leto's tree as the olive, see Callimachus frag. 194; *Hymn* 4.262. Leto's usual symbol is the *phoinix,* the palm tree which gave her support and rest during her labor. See F. Ahl, "Amber, Avallon, and Apollo's Singing Swan," *AJP* 103 (1982) 373–411.

26 See Apollodorus 1.2.2; Hesiod *Theogony* 136, 404, 409 (with M. L. West ad loc. in *Hesiod, Theogony* [Oxford: Clarendon Press, 1966]); cf. Pliny *Natural History* 4.66.

27 Pliny *Natural History* 13.26–28; cf. Theophrastus *Enquiry into Plants* 2.2.10, 3.3.5. Cf. C. H. Kahn, *The Art and Thought of Heraclitus* (Cambridge: Cambridge University Press, 1979) 109. Syrie, island of the solstices in *Odyssey* 15.403–6, is

often identified with Delos. Cf. P. Walz, "'Ἠλίου Τροπαί: Notes sur l'Odyssée, XV, 404," *REHom* 1 (1931) 3–15; Stanford, *"Odyssey" of Homer,* on 15.403–4. So Leto is linked with the *phoinix,* symbolic of the moon and the lunar calendar. But the *phoinix* is not the only hieroglyphic symbol for the year. The primary symbol is "Isis, that is to say, 'woman'" (Horapollo 1.3). If Leto's name itself means "woman," her *phoinix* and "woman" would be interchangeable anyway. Curiously too, the island of Delos and its palm seem associated with a great deal of solar (Apollonian) and lunar (Artemisian) imagery in Greek writers: with the solstices of the "wandering" sun (going daily east and west, seasonally north and south) and with the passing of the lunar year. Delos (or an island often taken to be Delos) is connected in *Odyssey* 15.403–6 with the northern and southern boundaries of the sun's seasonal movements. The palm, the *phoinix,* in Pythagorean symbolic interpretations of Egyptian hieroglyphs, represents the year: "It is the only tree producing a branch at each rising of the moon; it completes the year in twelve branches. . . . To represent a month, the Egyptians show either a palm tree or a moon inverted" (Horapollo 1.3; 1.4). See Ahl, "Amber, Avallon, and Apollo's Singing Swan," for fuller discussion.

28 See Thompson, *Greek Birds,* 306–9.

29 In 34 C.E., the *phoinix* itself was reported to have returned: Tacitus *Annals* 6.28. Plutarch (*Isis and Osiris* 354E–F and 363F) compares Pythagorean symbolism with Egyptian hieroglyphs. J. G. Griffiths, *Plutarch, De Iside et Osiride* (Cambridge: Cambridge University Press, 1970), 287, denies hieroglyphs are used symbolically. But see Porphyry *Life of Pythagoras* 8; Clement of Alexandria *Stromateis* (Miscellanies) 5.555. To a large extent, however, it is irrelevant whether or not the orginal writers of hieroglyphs used them symbolically. Almost all Greek writers (and Egyptians writing in Greek) took them to be symbolical at least from the fifth century B.C.E.

30 The outer audience would appreciate the use of the verb *gymnousthai,* which in the *Iliad* designates a part of the body stripped of the shield and vulnerable to the strike of a spear or arrow: 12.388–89, 427–28; 16.311–12, 399–400.

31 As Stanford, *"Odyssey" of Homer,* notes on 7.8, the name Apeire is usually "connected by philologists" with *ēpeiros,* "mainland." He feels it could as well mean "boundless" or "the impassable lands." We favor the latter explanation, since so many names mentioned in the Phaeacian narratives are vague geographically. It would be appropriate that a people who had migrated from "High Beyondland" might acquire their domestic help from the rather Anaximandrian "Boundlessland."

32 W. Donlan, "Glaucus and Diomedes," *Phoenix* 43 (1989) 5, sees special significance in the fact that Euryalus's gift is the only military item among all the Phaecacian gifts given to Odysseus. Euryalus's gift comes to complement his apology for insulting Odysseus and thus reinstates the social harmony between the host and the guest. Since the insult revolved around Odysseus's appearance as a merchant and not an athlete, the gift confers on the guest his proper status as a warrior.

33 Plutarch (*Themistocles* 24) tells us that the Molossians regarded sitting down at the hearth as the most sacred form of supplication, and as almost the only method that could not be refused. It is also of interest that Plutarch suggested that there is a possibility that Themistocles was instructed to adopt that form of supplication by Phthia, the wife of Admetus, the ruler whom Themistocles was supplicating, in which case it is clear that he had dealings with the lady of the

house before approaching her husband. For suppliants sitting at the hearth, see also Pindar frag. 81; Thucydides 1.136.

34 Frame, *Myth of Return,* 79 n. 73.

35 Rose, "The Unfriendly Phaeacians," 390–91, 397, attempts to make a distinction between the royal family, who offer proper hospitality, and the Phaeacian commoners, who dislike strangers.

36 "Him [Alcinous] pass by, and throw your hands around my mother's knees, so that you may quickly see with joy the day of your return, even if you are far away. For if she likes you, then there is hope that you will see your dear ones, and return to your well-built house and to your native land" (6.310–15).

37 See N. Austin, "The Wedding Text in Homer's Odyssey," *Arion* 1, no. 2 (Spring 1991) 238–39.

38 But cf. Hainsworth on 6.26, in Heubeck, West, and Hainsworth, *Commentary on Homer's "Odyssey,"* "Always as here, a decorative epithet."

39 Compare Alcinous's instruction to Arete at a later juncture, to prepare a good chest for Odysseus's treasures, to give him a newly washed cloak and tunic, and to prepare a bath (8.424–32).

40 C. R. Beye, *The "Iliad," the "Odyssey," and the Epic Tradition* (New York: Doubleday, 1966) 198.

41 See also S. D. Olson, "Women's Names and the Reception of Odysseus on Scheria," *EchCl* 36, n.s. 11 (1992) 1–6.

42 Cf. M. I. Finley, *The World of Odysseus* (New York: Viking, 1972) 103–4: "That a repressed memory of ancient matriarchy is reflected in some of the verses [of the Phaeacian episode] seems a fragile argument." For the myth of matriarchy, see J. Bamberger, "The Myth of Matriarchy: Why Men Rule in Primitive Society," in *Woman, Culture, and Society,* ed. M. Z. Rosaldo and L. Lamphere (Stanford: Stanford University Press, 1974) 263–80. See also L. E. Doherty, "Tyro in *Odyssey* 11: Closed and Open Readings," *Helios* 20 (1993) 3–15, who observes: "A story such as Tyro's can thus be read as a potent fantasy—even a fantasy of power—for the women of patriarchal culture such as that portrayed in the *Odyssey*" (6).

43 Echeneus: "Friends, our queen, who knows her way around situations, did not miss the mark in her words or go contrary to our own thought" (11.344–45); Alcinous: "This word will indeed hold, as long as I am alive and rule the Phaeacians, lovers of the oar" (11.348–49).

44 Alcinous's conciliatory words, which suggest that Odysseus must wait until the next day to be sent on his way (11.348–52), refer to Alcinous's inability to honor his former pledge to send Odysseus on his way. Thus, although he appears to echo what his wife has said earlier, Alcinous places his own imprint on the dispatch of the foreigner whom he insists is his *xenos.*

45 The more common understanding of Alcinous's response is well represented by Heubeck on 11.347–53, in Heubeck, West, and Hainsworth, *Commentary on Homer's "Odyssey"*: "Alcinous will translate the suggestion made by Arete and supported by Echeneus (*epos*) into action (347). He points to his position as king as assurance that his word may be relied on, with good reason: his decision involves altering the promise made the day before, and delays the sailing, which had been firmly fixed (*tekmairomai* 7.317) for the following day (*aurion es* [7.318]), until the next day (*es aurion* 351)." Heubeck seems to have made a mistake here, since the first promised "morrow" has already passed at the time Alcinous is speaking. There has been no further promise about Odysseus's de-

parture until this speech of Alcinous, which postpones departure again until another "morrow" (which could be just as vague as the first). Alcinous clearly answers the points made by Arete and Odysseus: he agrees to the suggestion of further gifts; he responds to Arete's call not to proceed too hastily in sending their guest on his way with the commitment "tomorrow" (*es aurion*), and he reassures Odysseus, referring back to Odysseus's concern about his return expressed in 332. Alcinous declares that he will take care of the voyage home. For the time being he avoids the question as to when Odysseus should continue his story.

46 His *eiskomen*, "we think of you as" (11.363), like Arete's *phainetai* "he appears" (11.336), shows how both their judgments are based on hunches.

3. Friction in Phaeacia

1 On the importance of not revealing one's name as a measure against an unforeseen danger, see C. S. Brown, "Odysseus and Polyphemus: The Name and the Curse," *CompLit* 18 (1966) 193–202.

2 Frame, *Myth of Return*, 79–80.

3 "Indeed I could tell of still more troubles I suffered by the will of the gods. But allow me now for all my sorrow to eat my dinner, for there is nothing more shameless than a hateful belly, which orders one to remember it" (7.213–17).

4 "So he said, and godlike Odysseus was glad, and he spoke in a prayer, and he said and named him: Father Zeus, may Alcinous accomplish everything that he spoke. And may he have unquenchable glory over the fruitful earth, and may I come home to my native land" (7.329–33).

5 If anything, Menelaus may be happy about his brother's death, since the leading position in the Peloponnese now passes to him. If the *Odyssey* took final form in the sixth century, such a transfer of power might have resonances of contemporary politics. It was in this period that Sparta became the principal power in the Peloponnese, taking over the position from Argos. We should also note that a brother seems to gain priority by being married to Helen. She was passed on, after Paris's death, to Paris's brother Deïphobus.

6 See 16.226–28; 19.278–82; 23.338–41.

7 Aristotle comments in the *Poetics* that the third type of recognition is the one that is due to memory. As an example he gives the "tale of Alcinous": when Odysseus hears the minstrel "he remembered and burst into tears, and thus they were recognized" (1465A). There must have been a version of the story in which Odysseus's tears prompted his instantaneous recognition—unless Aristotle's memory of Homer is as faulty as his memory of Sophocles sometimes is. See F. Ahl, *Sophocles' "Oedipus": Evidence and Self-Conviction* (Ithaca, N.Y.: Cornell University Press, 1991) 16–18.

8 See also, for example, Hainsworth on 8.86, in Heubeck, West, and Hainsworth, *Commentary on Homer's "Odyssey."*

9 Odysseus's offer to compete even in a footrace—though he eventually refuses to participate (8.230–33)—might be a strategy to keep Arete and Nausicaa on his side (despite his rejection of a royal marriage) and thus head off the possibility that he will end up angering everybody. As F. M. Cornford points out in "The Origin of the Olympic Games," in *Themis*, 2d ed., ed. J. E. Harrison

(Cambridge: Cambridge University Press, 1927) 231–35, a footrace is traditionally a contest for the bride. Thus it is possible that Odysseus is hinting that he might be interested, after all, in the young princess. Lattimore, "Nausikaa's Suitors," 91–97, suggests that the participation of Nausicaa's three brothers in the contest implies that brother-sister marriage was customary among the Phaeacians. But after the remarkable victory of Clytoneus in the previous footrace in which Laodamas participated (8.115–25), it should be clear that Laodamas does not stand a chance of winning his sister's hand no matter how much his father loves him beyond the others.

10 Dimock, *Unity of the "Odyssey,"* 98.

11 Pausanias 3.12.1.

12 For the different approaches of the Phaeacians and Odysseus regarding competition, see also Dimock, *Unity of the "Odyssey,"* 99–100.

13 It is interesting that Alcinous mentions Zeus, not Poseidon, as the god who lavished exceptional powers on the Phaeacians (8.245). After all, Poseidon is Alcinous's grandfather, and the Phaeacians see him as their ancestor. Alcinous must be remembering that Odysseus blames Poseidon for the shipwreck and the sufferings he endured at sea as he tried to swim to Phaeacia (7.250–79). Thus, although it would seem natural for Alcinous to affiliate himself with Poseidon, he carefully mentions Zeus instead, since in this context he needs Odysseus's cooperation at least to some degree. Later on, once Odysseus commits himself to spread word of Phaeacian *aretē*, and Alcinous prepares his departure and his gifts in return, he gives him a golden cup so that Odysseus will remember him all his days as he pours libations in his home to Zeus (8.431–32). Once again the king is ever careful not to mention Poseidon when speaking to Odysseus.

14 For Alcinous's speech and its "rambling" character, see Hainsworth on 8.241–49, in Heubeck, West, and Hainsworth, *Commentary on Homer's "Odyssey."* We disagree, however, with Hainsworth's contention that "the passage requires little attention from poet or audience, being no more than a transition to the dancing scene that follows." It seems, rather, that the idea of the dance comes to Alcinous as he tries to sort out in his mind the proper answer to Odysseus's challenge.

15 For the view that Alcinous's insistence that Odysseus should declare his name amounts to an invitation to sing his own *kleos*, or praise song, see A. Webber, "The Hero Tells His Name," *TAPA* 119 (1989) 11–13.

16 And there is a subtle irony in having the claim for compensation attributed to Poseidon of all gods. But Odysseus does not seem to be bothered by the idea. There may also be some reason to suspect that the song's implications for the guest are evident to the inner audience of Phaeacians as well as to the bard. Euryalus, coerced into apologizing to Odysseus, may well be alluding to these resonances when he prays: "May the gods grant you to see your wife and your native land" (410–11). Odysseus's children, usually mentioned by Alcinous, are omitted.

17 For further discussion, see H. M. Roisman, "Like Father Like Son: Telemachus's *kerdea*," *RhM* 136 (1993) 1–22. Austin, *Archery at the Dark of the Moon*, 74–80, maintains, on the other hand, that the epithet denotes quite the opposite of forthrightness: tact and diplomacy.

18 See Ahl, "The Art of Safe Criticism in Greece and Rome," 174–208.

19 In fact, as Demodocus compares Odysseus to Ares, a protagonist in Demodocus's earlier narrative of Aphrodite's infidelity, a listener aware of Odys-

seus's own courtship of Helen in his youth may wonder whether Demodocus, or the Muse, is alluding to that tradition here. We may also recall Helen's own story in *Odyssey* 4 of Odysseus's visit to her. As Austin points out, the Phaeacian episode surpasses even the preceding narrative of the *Odyssey* in its perfection of insinuation and innuendo within the constituent narratives (*Archery at the Dark of the Moon,* 191–200).

20 E.g., Stanford, *"Odyssey" of Homer,* ad loc.; C. P. Segal, "The Phaeacians and the Symbolism of Odysseus' Return," *Arion* 1, no. 4 (1962) 27–29; Fenik, *Studies in the "Odyssey,"* 43–44; Austin, *Archery at the Dark of the Moon,* 197; W. G. Thalmann, *Convention of Form and Thought in Early Greek Epic* (Baltimore: Johns Hopkins University Press, 1984) 165; H. Foley, "Reverse Similes and Sex Roles in the *Odyssey,*" *Arethusa* 11 (1978) 7–26.

21 For a discussion of the validity of assuming hidden motives on the part of the character, especially in the Phaeacian episode, see Griffin, *Homer on Life and Death,* 62–64.

22 "And tell me your land, your people and your city, so that our ships focusing their thoughts may take you there. For the Phaeacians have no pilots, nor steering oars, such as other ships have, but their ships understand by themselves the thoughts and minds of men, and they know the cities and rich fields of all peoples, and with the greatest speed cross the gulf of the salt sea, hidden in mist and cloud, nor ever have fear of harm and ruin" (8.555–63).

23 *Iliad* 17.670; 23.65, 105.

24 Stanford, *"Odyssey" of Homer,* on 9. 86; P. Cauer, *Grundfragen der Homerkritik,* 3d ed., 2 vols. (Leipzig: Hirzel, 1921–23) 638.

4. Cyclopes Reinvented

1 As has already been observed by scholars no less than by Alcinous, Odysseus assumes the role of a poet. For the relationship between the epic and its presentation of the past, and Odysseus and the truth, see also Ford, *Homer,* esp. 57–89, 118–25. For a detailed study of the problem of lying and truth in early Greek poetry, see L. Pratt, *Lying and Poetry from Homer to Pindar* (Ann Arbor: University of Michigan Press, 1993) 17–22.

2 For a recent study of *mythos* and *epos* in the context of speech performance, see R. P. Martin, *The Language of Heroes: Speech and Performance in the "Iliad"* (Ithaca, N.Y.: Cornell University Press, 1989) 12–16 (extracts): "Muthos is, in Homer, a speech-act indicating authority, performed at length, usually in public with a focus on full attention to every detail"; "A muthos focuses on what the speaker says and how he or she says it, but epos consistently applies to what the addressee hears"; "Muthos is associated with the speaker's action in giving a message, whereas epos refers to the transmission of the message, the end-product of the speech process."

3 This point actually brings up the issue of amateur and professional bard, which translates in the scene into an opposition between the bard who allegedly sings about his own experience and the one who sings about the experiences of others. See C. P. Segal, "Bard and Audience in Homer," in *Homer's Ancient Readers: The Hermeneutics of Greek Epic's Earliest Exegetes,* ed. R. Lamberton and J. J. Keaney (Princeton: Princeton University Press, 1992) 5–11 and passim.

4 For a recent discussion of *alētheia,* see Pratt, *Lying and Poetry,* 11–24.
5 Plato *Cratylus* 411D; *Republic* 621A–D; see Pratt, *Lying and Poetry,* 17–20; M. Détienne, "La notion mythique d' ALETHEIA," *REG* 73 (1960) 27–35; Ahl, *Metaformations,* 47, 322; id., "Ars Est Caelare Artem (Art in Puns and Anagrams Engraved)," in *On Puns: The Foundation of Letters,* ed. Jonathan Culler (Oxford: Basil Blackwell, 1988) 27–28 and sources cited.
6 For a concise and general overview of the idea of truth in Greek literature, see C. G. Starr, "Ideas of Truth in Early Greece," *PP* 23 (1968) 348–59.
7 Part of the fun of seafaring, one would think, is the navigation, not just the rowing. Even though there will surely be critics who see nothing weird about the Phaeacians having automatic ships (whose day is yet to come), setting forth in such automatic ships seems at odds with what Nausicaa had earlier told Odysseus of Phaeacian love not for bow or quiver, "but for masts and oars of ships, and for shapely ships, rejoicing in which they cross over the grey sea" (6.270–71). They must be "oar lovers," as they are described at the very beginning of the episode, in the most literal of senses. Indeed, this epithet is used for the Phaeacians when the Muse describes Athena's intent to "intermingle" (*migeiē* 5.386) her hero among them; and the epithet recurs five more times in description of the Phaeacians (8.96, 386, 535; 11.349; 13.36).
8 It is curious that the only other people of whom this epithet is used in the *Odyssey* are the Taphians (an obscure, but real people). And the context, again, is defined by Athena. In *Odyssey* 1.180–81, she disguises herself and announces to Telemachus that she is Mentes, king of the "oar-loving" Taphians. In the only other non-Phaeacian use of the word, Telemachus is simply reiterating the claim of the pseudo-Mentes as he introduces the still-disguised Athena to the suitors in 1.418–19.
9 See C. S. Byre, "Narration, Description, and Theme in the Shield of Achilles," *CJ* 88 (1992) 33–42.
10 For the impropriety of a head of a household not greeting a guest upon the guest's arrival, the ramification of this kind of ineptitude on Alcinous's part toward Odysseus, and Odysseus's anticipation of imminent danger because of Alcinous's conduct, see Rose, "The Unfriendly Phaeacians," 394–96.
11 We have given line 9.112 a slightly different meaning from that usually understood: "Neither assemblies to take counsel nor appointed laws." It seems that the lines that follow elaborate further on 112 and focus on the place and type of government.
12 W. Suerbaum, "Die Ich-Erzählungen des Odysseus: Überlegungen zur epischen Technik der Odyssee," *Poetica* 2 (1968) 156ff. For the problems of the description of the cave from the sea and a discussion of the mixture of the hero's and poet's voices in the description, see also F. Müller, "Darstellung und poetische Funktion der Gegenstände in der Odyssee" (Diss., Marburg, 1968) 109–15.
13 The traditional epithet of a man "who feeds on bread" makes a particularly splendid contrast between Polyphemus and other humans, since the Cyclopes do not even grow grain, much less make bread, but live on a diet of animal protein.
14 There is no mention of a promontory or a cliff overhang which might obscure the view from the cave. In Euripides *Cyclops* 85–88 the ship is in full view from the cave, and Silenus sees the mounting company before they arrive at the cave.

15 Apollodorus 3.10.3ff.: Zeus struck Asclepius with a thunderbolt. Apollo slew the Cyclopes who fashioned the thunderbolt for Zeus. According to Pherecydes, quoted by the scholiast on Euripides *Alcestis* 1, it was not the Cyclopes, but their sons whom Apollo slew. The passage of Pherecydes quoted by the scholiast runs as follows: "To him [that is, to Admetus] came Apollo, to serve him as a slave for a year, at the command of Zeus, because Apollo had killed the sons of Brontes, of Steropes, and of Arges. He killed them to get back at Zeus, because Zeus had killed his son Asclepius with the thunderbolt at Pytho; for Asclepius raised the dead by his medicines."

16 He and his men are not Argives or Cretans (much less Cephallenians), but generalized "Achaeans." They have lost their way on the seas while sailing home from Troy, he says; but he does not say where "home" is. Compare the introduction of Odysseus's party in Euripides' *Cyclops,* where Odysseus not only identifies himself by name but specifies that he is Odysseus of Ithaca, the lord of the Cephallenians (103). In Euripides, Odysseus's Trojan exploits are mentioned second (107).

17 *Krios* occurs only twice in Homer, and both instances occur in this narrative. That the first recorded use of *krios* as "battering ram" is in Xenophon does not mean that the word did not carry this sense earlier. There are battering rams (with heads of rams) portrayed in early Mesopotamian art, and anyone who ever hoped to take a citadel of the Mycenaean age would have had to know what one was and needed a word for it. We face the same problem here as we do in other versions of the Odysseus myth: there will be those who contend that what is not attested in Homer must be post-Homeric and cannot be adduced to illuminate a Homeric text.

18 Apollodorus 1.1.1.

19 Apollodorus 2.2.1. For the duality in their depiction in Greek literature, see G. S. Kirk, *The Nature of Greek Myths* (London: Penguin Books, 1974) 85–86, 207, who sees Polyphemus as an outsider to their kind.

20 For a much simpler but more "popular" version of the courtyard, we can look at the court that Eumaeus built for himself. The Muse tells us he built it "with huge stones and surrounded it with a coping of shrubbery" (14.10).

21 West, *Hesiod, Theogony,* on *Theogony* 505.

22 For Mycenae, see Pindar frag. 169; Euripides *Heracles* 15, 944; *Iphigeneia at Aulis* 152, 265, 845, 1500; Sophocles *Heracles* frag. 207 N.2; Pausanias 2.16.5, 7.25.6; Eustathius on *Iliad* 2.559; scholia on Euripides *Orestes* 965; Nonnus *Dionysiaca* 41.269; Seneca *Thyestes* 406; *Hercules Furens* 1002; scholia on Vergil *Aeneid* 6.636; scholia on Statius *Thebaid* 1.630; cf. 252. For Tiryns, see Bacchylides 10.77; Apollodorus 2.2.1; Strabo 8.372; Pausanias 2.25.8, 7.25.6. For Nauplia, see Strabo 8.373.

23 Later ancient scholars tend to see three rather than two types of Cyclopes. The scholiast to Aristides 52.10 (3: 408 Dindorf) comments: "They say there are three kinds of Cyclopes, those of Odysseus, being Sicilians, the Wall Builders, and those called Uranian" (on the "Wall Builders," see *RE* 22 [1922] 2328–47 [2332]; cf. scholia on Hesiod *Theogony* 139 and 144). According to this description the Wall Builders are not associated in any way with the more savage breeds, but, as Hellanicus (according to the scholia on Hesiod *Theogony* 139; cf. 144) observes, they are "gods themselves" (*autoi hoi theoi*). It might be that this distinction is made to enable their literary existence in spite of the legend according to which Apollo killed the Cyclopes in retaliation for Zeus's killing of Asclepius.

24 In some mythical traditions the fire-god equals the smith and metal forger; see *RE* 22 (1922) 2440.
25 If we are right in this matter, Athena's appearance in the episode is not extraneous and "mechanical," as Hainsworth suggests in his comments on 8.7 and 192–93 in Heubeck, West, and Hainsworth, *Commentary on Homer's "Odyssey."*

5. The Ironic Lord of Death

1 It is perhaps worth noting that in a work which is so pungent a satire of epic, Petronius's *Satyricon*, the hero, Encolpius, is rendered impotent after being unable to consummate his relationship with Circe—who is much offended by this insult to her charms (*Satyricon* 127–30). It is also worth mention that Encolpius, when in Croton, adopts the name Polyaenus—the epithet given to Odysseus by the Sirens in *Odyssey* 12.184.
2 Dimock, *Unity of the "Odyssey,"* 141.
3 11.57–58: "Elpenor, how did you come under the murky darkness? Coming on foot, you outstripped me in the black ship." We tend to accept Stanford's understanding of these lines, according to which Odysseus thinks Elpenor was left behind alive, rather than Heubeck's: "Odysseus' question as to how Elpenor on foot had reached Hades before them does not imply that Odysseus has failed to recognize his companion is dead: the question is not so much an expression of surprise as an attempt to elicit information" (in A. Heubeck and A. Hoekstra, *A Commentary on Homer's "Odyssey"* [Oxford: Clarendon Press, 1989] ad loc.). It is unlikely that once Odysseus has found his way to Hades by ship with Circe's help he would want information about how to make the journey on foot.
4 1.55; 4.182; 5.436; 6.206; 10.281; 11.93; 13.331; 17.10, 483, 501; 19.354; 20.224; 24.289.
5 See also Dawe, *"Odyssey,"* 435–36 (note on 11.116–37) and sources cited.
6 Since they know of no salt, they would have been unable to conserve any meat, and since they do not recognize an oar, it is unlikely they would trade for salt with merchants coming from the seashore. For trade in salt with saltless people of the hinterland, see A. Zimmern, *The Greek Commonwealth: Politics and Economics in Fifth-Century Athens* (New York: Oxford University Press, 1961) 24–25.
7 Aristarchus rejected lines 11.157–59 as spurious. Many others followed him; for references, see Heubeck on 11.156–59, in Heubeck and Hoekstra, *Commentary on Homer's "Odyssey."*
8 H. Roisman, *Loyalty in Early Greek Epic and Tragedy* (Kōnigstein/Ts: Anton Hain, 1984) 70–72.
9 For various explanations of the inconsistency, see Heubeck on 11.181–203, and references, in Heubeck and Hoekstra, *Commentary on Homer's "Odyssey"*; M. A. Katz, *Penelope's Renown: Meaning and Indeterminancy in the "Odyssey"* (Princeton: Princeton University Press, 1991) 58, and references.
10 In his account Demodocus makes no mention of any children born as a result of the affair between the destructive Ares and the alluring Aphrodite. The omission of Harmonia, their mythic child, is probably wise, rhetorically. Demodocus's point seems to mock Hephaestus's jealous deployment of his art and his consequent ridiculousness, to avoid focusing on the less humorous matter of

the resulting illegitimate child. An audience familiar with the myth of Harmonia would realize the grim consequences for mortals in this divine amour. The narrator may suppress details of a story in full awareness that the listener will supply them. This is the essence of ancient *emphasis.* Hephaestus's gift to Harmonia of an evil necklace crafted for her wedding is instrumental in triggering one of the great wars of Greek tradition: the civil war between Oedipus's sons, Eteocles and Polyneices.

11 H. M. Roisman, "Penelope's Indignation," *TAPA* 117 (1987) 59–68.

12 Plutarch, *Greek Questions* 43 (301D); Hyginus, *Fabulae* 201. Cf. H. M. Roisman, "Eumaeus and Odysseus—A Covert Self-Revelation?" *ICS* 15, no. 2 (1990) 215–38.

13 The phrase *sos pothos* is ambiguous in its structure. Does Anticleia mean "yearning for you," with *sos* taken for the objective genitive *sou*? The commentaries usually offer *Iliad* 19.336–37 as a parallel construction: *emēn* . . . / . . . *angeliēn,* "news of me." While such an interpretation makes sense, helping to explain the cause of her premature death, the sentence structure allows another interpretation. Anticleia couples *sos pothos* with *sa mēdea* and with *sē aganophrosynē* in a parallel structure, although in both cases of Odysseus's *mēdea* and his alleged *aganophrosynē,* the possessive adjectives if converted to a genitive would perform the function of a subjective, not an objective, genitive. If the phrase *sos pothos* is taken along with the other two possessive adjectives, one can construe Anticleia's words as "your longing, and your counsels, glorious Odysseus, and your gentleness, took my honey-sweet life." In this case Anticleia would be referring to Odysseus's own longing for his home and family, which would go along with her formerly expressed wonder that he has not even yet come home from Troy or seen his wife (11.160–62). It is, then, not her longing for him, but her sorrowful sense of his longing for his family that burdened her life—a sensitive and sophisticated concern of a mother. Or, if one chooses to adopt a meaning founded upon other uses of the base *poth-* in both epics, that meaning might simply imply a lack, an absence of any given people or objects. It is then Anticleia's worry about the bereavement Odysseus must have been experiencing that brought her to grave. We prefer the meaning "yearning for you."

14 *Mēdea* can carry the meaning of "care." It is the sole occurrence of the word with this meaning in the epics; it takes an objective genitive, which further supports the sense "yearning for you." See note 13 above.

15 Penelope, wishing to establish a familiarity between Eurycleia and Odysseus so he will allow the old servant to wash his feet, describes Eurycleia in terms that will make Odysseus look upon her favorably; she says that Eurycleia *pykina phresi mēde' echousa* ("has prudent counsels in her heart," 19.353).

16 R. Fitzgerald, trans., *Homer, The Odyssey* (New York: Anchor Books, 1963): "Only my loneliness for you, Odysseus, for your kind heart and counsel, gentle Odysseus, took my own life away"; E. V. Rieu, trans., *Homer, The Odyssey,* rev. D. C. H. Rieu (Baltimore: Penguin Books, 1991): "It was my heartache for you, my glorious Odysseus, and for your wise and gentle ways, that brought my life with all its sweetness to an end"; R. Lattimore, trans., *The "Odyssey" of Homer* (New York: Harper, 1967): "Shining Odysseus, it was my longing for you, your cleverness and your gentle ways, that took the sweet spirit of life from me"; Dawe, *"Odyssey"*: "No, it was longing for you, it was your counsels and your gentle ways, glorious Odysseus, that took from me my life, sweet as honey."

17 E.g., *Iliad* 3.202, 208, 212; *Odyssey* 13.89. For the generally negative overtones of *mēdea* in epic, see, for example, *Iliad.* 23.24, 176.
18 The only other occurrence of *aganos*, "kind, gentle," in connection with Odysseus is in his description of his prayers to the Naiad Nymphs on the seashore of Ithaca. He claims he addresses them with *euchōlai aganai* ("kind prayers," 13.357).
19 See also Semonides 34 for the imagery of a bitch guarding puppies.
20 The name of the Lydian king Candaules, according to the poet Hipponax (frag. 1), means "Dog Choker" and is the Lydian equivalent for Hermes. Greenewalt may therefore be correct in associating the name with *kandaulos*, a kind of Lydian stew; see C. H. Greenewalt, Jr., *Ritual Dinners in Early Historic Sardis*, Classical Studies 17 (Berkeley: University of California Publications, 1976) esp. 45–54; and M. Détienne and J.-P. Vernant, *La cuisine du sacrifice en pays grec* (Paris: Gallimard, 1979) 215–37.
21 For *schetlios* used of Odysseus, see *Odyssey* 9.494, 11.474, 12.279, and 20.45. For *schetlios* used of Achilles, who otherwise is referred to as *nēleēs*, see *Iliad* 9.630; 16.203; 22.41, 86. In one occurrence in the *Odyssey* the epithet *schetlios* is substituted for *nēleēs*, in the phrase "ruthless sleep": *hypnos / schetlios* (10.68–69) for *nēlei hypnōi* (12.372).
22 *Schetliē* in 23.150. Throughout the epic the Muse connects husband and wife through an intricate fabric of phrases and words. Thus we find that the only characters who are said to have a *pacheia cheir* ("broad hand") are Penelope and Odysseus. Both are compared to a lion, the knowledge of *kerdea* is almost exclusive to them, and the word *histos* in its two different meanings (ship's mast and web beam of a loom) links the two characters throughout the epic.
23 *Odyssey* 3.46; 6.90; 9.94, 208; 14.78; 18.426; 21.293; *Iliad* 4.346; 6.258; 10.569, 579; 12.320; 18.545, 568. Teiresias uses it also to refer to Odysseus's journey home at *Odyssey* 14.78, and Penelope to her dream about the geese at *Odyssey* 19.551.
24 G. Radke, "Tyro," *RE* 7.A.2 (1848) 1869–75; H. W. Roscher, *Ausführliches Lexikon der griechischen und römischen Mythologie* (Hildesheim: Georg Olms, 1992) 5: 1458–66. A. Nawrath, "Salmoneus," *RE* n.s. 1.A.ii (1920) 1989–90; K. Latte, "Kretheus," *RE* 11.ii (1922) 1822–23.
25 It was not until Lucian that the mythic tradition took up this point in the story, making Enipeus protest Poseidon's impersonation; see Lucian *Dialogues* 13. Even Lucian in his *Dialogues* is unable to save Tyro from her rejection by Enipeus. And the only excuse the lecherous Poseidon can offer Enipeus is that he took her because Enipeus did not want her: "Yes, Enipeus, but only because you didn't want her."
26 Cf. Propertius 1.13.21f.; 3.19.13f.
27 Apollodorus *Library* 1.9.8.

6. Alcinous Strikes Back

1 *Iliad* 2.636–37.
2 Heubeck on 11.371–72, in Heubeck and Hoekstra, *Commentary on Homer's "Odyssey."*
3 *Iliad* 1.424; 2.524, 534, 542, 545, 556, 568, 578, 619, 630, 637, 644, 652,

710, 737, 747, 749, 759, 762; 3.143; 10.194; 12.87, 124, 251; 13.690, 717, 801, 833; 16.551, 753; 18.525; 24.327, 573; *Odyssey* 1.331; 2.11, 413; 8.46, 104; 10.231, 257; 15.431, 541; 17.214; 18.207; 19.196; 20.145, 175.

4 Some see the "evil woman" mentioned as Helen. We agree with Dawe, *"Odyssey,"* 451 (note on 11.384), that the more likely candidate is Clytemnestra.

5 An ironic touch of the Muse, considering the fact that a good part of the poem is concerned with the disguise of Odysseus's true *eidos*, "appearance." For the theme of disguise and recognition of Odysseus, see S. Murnaghan, *Disguise and Recognition in the "Odyssey"* (Princeton: Princeton University Press, 1987) 3–55. For the juxtaposition of *eidos* and the true nature of a hero, see Martin, "Telemachus and the Last Hero Song," 232–34.

6 For Agamemnon's prompt return, see Proteus's tale at *Odyssey* 4.512–22.

7 Dawe, *"Odyssey,"* 455 (note on 11.457–64).

8 He says nothing, for example, of his return from Tenedos to Agamemnon, who decided not to set out for home before offering hecatombs in an attempt to appease Athena (3.143–65). This is the last time Menelaus saw Odysseus, and Odysseus was the last hero to see Agamemnon before he was murdered, we are told. But Odysseus fails to mention this detail. Rather, he transfers the tale of his last encounter with Agamemnon to the Otherworld.

9 See also Nagy, *Best of the Achaeans*, 22–25, 34–35.

10 No one assumes, however, that Heracles is mourning his death. In fact, he seems more upset about his fate while alive in the service of Eurystheus than about his death (11.620–22). Similarly, Agamemnon's soul, when portrayed as *achnumenē*, is not necessarily upset at being dead, but upset at the events in the world of living which led to his death (11.388).

11 *Iliad* 18.72; 24.328; *Odyssey* 16.22; 19.522, 543; 22.447; 24.59.

12 Apollodorus *Epitome* 5.11.

13 M. Edwards, *Homer: Poet of the Iliad* (Baltimore: Johns Hopkins University Press, 1987) 221. See also Beye, *Epic Tradition*, 136.

14 Ovid *Metamorphoses* 14.25–74.

15 For the variety of relationships between the *aoidos*, singer, and his craft, see Ford, *Homer*, passim.

16 For a pre-Homeric *Argonautica* as a source and model for Odysseus's adventures in books 9–12, see Heubeck on 12.55–72, and references, in Heubeck and Hoekstra, *Commentary on Homer's "Odyssey."*

17 On Circe, see Dawe, *"Odyssey," on* 12.273–74.

18 Heubeck on 12.269, in Heubeck and Hoekstra, *Commentary on Homer's "Odyssey."*

19 Dawe, *"Odyssey,"* on line 294.

20 Ibid., on line 333.

7. Recognizing Discrete Identities

1 For a brief overview, see T. Cave, *Recognitions: A Study in Poetics* (Oxford: Clarendon Press, 1988) 10–54.

2 U. Hölscher, *Untersuchungen zur Form der "Odyssee": Szenenwechsel und gleichzeitige Handlungen* (Berlin: Weidmann, 1939) 65.

3 Dawe, *"Odyssey,"* 713 (note on 19.479). Russo, in J. Russo, M. Fernández-Galiano, and A. Heubeck, *Homer's "Odyssey,"* vol. 3, *Books XVII–XXIV* (Oxford: Oxford University Press, 1992) 99, argues that 19.478–79 are, in fact, "the biggest obstacle to the theory that Homer has tried to describe in this book a subtle and veiled awareness on Penelope's part of the identity of the stranger." Penelope, however, is no less reluctant to acknowledge Odysseus when he stands in the hall with dead suitors all around him and after she has been told explicitly by Eurycleia and Odysseus himself that her husband is before her eyes.

4 Fenik, *Studies in the "Odyssey,"* 45.

5 Ibid., 46.

6 One obvious instance from outside Homer is Dido's remark in *Aeneid* 4 to Anna (to the reader's surprise, since Anna's existence has not previously been alluded to) that Anna should try to persuade Aeneas to stay in Carthage (4.6–30, 416–24). Dido contends that Aeneas regularly visits Anna and entrusts to her all his hidden secrets. What these hidden secrets are and why Aeneas entrusts them to Anna is never revealed either by the characters of the *Aeneid* or by Vergil in his narrative capacity. If we look for an answer, we are forced to look outside the *Aeneid* itself, perhaps to the tradition mentioned by Varro in which Anna was Aeneas's lover.

7 For *nōnymos,* see 1.221–22, referring to Telemachus, and 14.181–82, referring to the clan of Arcisius, Odysseus's family. *Anōnymos* is equally rare.

8 "Yet he did not speak the truth" (13.254).

9 Orsilochus, according to E. Müller-Graupa, *RE* 18.2 (1942) 1420, is a Cretan, a fabricated son of Idomeneus, whom Odysseus mentions in his conversation with Athena (13.260). But is the story of killing Orsilochus so preposterous? The assumption that Orsilochus is a "fabricated son" of Idomeneus, rather than an allusion to another mythic tradition, is based on an earlier assumption that Homer's muse was working with a unified tradition rather than patching together a narrative from varied sources and traditions.

10 See Pratt, *Lying and Poetry,* 17–24, 90–92.

11 *Homeric Hymn* 7.6–10. For Phoenicians, see Odysseus's story at 14.285–98; for Thesprotian sailors, see his story at 14.334–46.

12 The device of the Trojan horse is rendered at times by *mēchanē.* Compare 12.392, where Odysseus uses *mēchos.*

13 Aristotle *Rhetoric* 1365b; see Ahl, "The Art of Safe Criticism in Greece and Rome," 198. For the Odyssean technique of describing emotions by inference from the characters' words rather than by stating them explicitly, see Harsh, "Penelope and Odysseus in *Odyssey* XIX," 10. For Eumaeus's careful and pointed use of words, see also his prayer in 14.424, where he does not merely pray for Odysseus's return but would like to see him return to his own house: *honde domonde,* that is to say, to have him regain the authority and power he once had.

14 Sutton, *Lost Sophocles,* 46, 88–94, and sources cited. There is no particular reason to suppose that the Sophoclean myths are merely developments based on the Thesprotian subnarrative within the Cretan lie, since the Thesprotian king's name is different (Pheidon in the *Odyssey,* Tyrimmas in Sophocles).

15 C. Trahmann, "Odysseus' Lies" (*Odyssey,* Books 13–19)," *Phoenix* 6 (1952) 31–43.

8. First Encounters with Eumaeus

1 Other such clues occur, for instance, in the passage beginning at 14.31. There, Odysseus sits down, frightened by the dogs, and, the Muse notes, "the staff fell out of his hand" (14.31). The language and metrical structure are re-echoed when Eumaeus, hearing the dogs barking, hurries out to the yard, "and the piece of leather fell out of his hand" (14.34). The counterpointing of the statements suggests the accord between two characters who meet after a long separation. One is reminded of a similar rapport between Odysseus and Penelope, in the incident in which Penelope thinks to herself that Odysseus's clothes are dirty but says nothing of it, and Odysseus expresses her thought (23.115–16). See also Roisman, "Eumaeus and Odysseus—A Covert Self-Revelation?"

2 For a similar uncertainty, see 14.192–95. Up to the late protasis, one may think that Odysseus, by suggesting that he and Eumaeus be left alone while others work, will reveal himself.

3 The emphasis in the Muse's comment in 16.457–59 that Athena renewed Odysseus's disguise so that the swineherd would not know him by appearance and reveal the secret to Penelope is, in our view, on the threat to his "cover." Just as Athena prevented Eurycleia from drawing Penelope's attention to the identity of the beggar, so she prevents acknowledgment in this case. The need for disguise says nothing of any covert recognition by Eumaeus or Eurycleia. The lack of disguise might have been understood by Eumaeus as an indication that a formal revelation was forthcoming, and that there was no need for secrecy anymore. This would be an unwelcome development at the moment.

4 The only other similar instance is the tale Menelaus tells Telemachus and Peisistratus about Agamemnon (4.78–112), but there again Menelaus had recognized Telemachus and did not need to ask his identity (4.141–50), or he suspected the youngster to be Orestes and found it more politic to voice his version of the past events. See Ahl, "Complex Narrative Structures," 8–10. For additional anomalies in the convention of *xenia* in the scene, see Fenik, *Studies in the "Odyssey,"* 30–31.

5 See J. du Boulay, "Strangers and Gifts: Hostility and Hospitality in Rural Greece," *Journal of Mediterranean Studies* 1 (1991) 38–42.

6 On the use of the base *kerd-*, see Roisman, "Penelope's Indignation," esp. 66; id., "*Kerdion* in the *Iliad*: Skill and Trickiness," *TAPA* 120 (1990) 23–35. See also F. Bamberger, "*Kerdos* et sa famille (emplois homérique): Contribution au recherches sur le vocabulaire de la 'richesse' en grec," *CLMA* 3 (1976) 1–32; I. J. F. de Jong, "Homeric *kerdos* and *ophelos*," *MusHelv* 44 (1987) 79–81; A. Cozzo, *Kerdos: Semantica, ideologie e societ' nella Grecia antika,* Filologia e critica 56 (Rome: Edizioni dell' Ateneo, 1988).

7 See Roisman, "Like Father Like Son: Telemachus's *kerdea*." It is only toward the end of the epic, when Telemachus has acquired experience and indicated that he too can use situations to his own advantage, that the Muse accords him the trait of *kerdea* (20.257).

8 For Odysseus's habit of distrust, see, for example, J. Griffin, *Homer, The Odyssey* (Cambridge: Cambridge University Press 1987) 83–84.

9 By subconscious recognition we mean a recognition which at first is not plain and clear to Eumaeus but which motivates him to act in a certain way. For the Homeric ways of dealing with characters' levels of awareness, especially that of

Penelope, see Russo,"Interview and Aftermath: Dream, Fantasy, and Intuition in *Odyssey* 19 and 20," 4–18. While in Penelope's case, the subconscious comes out through her fears, hopes, and dreams, in Eumaeus's case we note it in the sequence of increasingly positive interactions with Odysseus which cannot be explained in terms of any specific statement of acknowledgment.

10 C. H. Whitman, *Homer and the Heroic Tradition* (Cambridge, Mass.: Harvard University Press, 1958) 301. For the importance of the swineherd and his close association with kingship in Irish and Welsh tradition, see Rees and Rees, *Celtic Heritage,* 178–79.

11 Cf. Stanford, *"Odyssey" of Homer,* on 14.147.

12 Stanford, *"Odyssey" of Homer,* on 14.152, does not prove his claim that *neitai,* "is in the very process of returning," regularly has a quasi-future sense. The tense emerges from the semantics of the verb. Here Odysseus does not use a clear future statement.

13 Odysseus hints time and again as to his identity, but in a contrived and covert manner, relying, among other things, on his craft and mastery of language. In telling Eumaeus of his escape from the Thesprotians' ship, he alters the formulaic phrase *hoi moi phroneonti doassato kerdion einai* to *sphin ephaineto kerdion einai* (14.355; in both cases: "seemed to me more profitable"), thereby hinting at who he is, but at the same time avoiding a possible formal acknowledgment. For relevant discussion, see Roisman, "Eumaeus and Odysseus—A Covert Self-Revelation?" 225–26.

14 The only Odyssean occurrence of a word with the *thelg-* base which is not connected with Odysseus describes how Aegisthus seduced the virtuous Clytemnestra into betraying her husband: he "beguiled her with words," *thelgesk' epeessin.* The fact that she has been the victim of seduction and beguilement, however, does not diminish her responsibility for succumbing. Her subsequent action is described as *ergon aeikes,* "a shameful deed" (3.264–65).

15 *Odyssey* 5.46–47; cf. *Iliad* 24.342–43; cf. also the derivative *thelktēria.*

16 For Telemachus's ardent wish to witness his father's return, see 1.113–18.

17 See Ahl, "The Art of Safe Criticism in Greece and Rome," 197–200.

18 Odysseus expresses keen interest in the way Eumaeus watches over the flocks and in Eumaeus's awareness that Odysseus would want to know how his herdsmen tend the flocks (14.526–27; 17.246); Petronius *Satyricon* 31.2: *vinum dominicum ministratoris gratia est,* "The master's wine is the servant's way of thanking."

19 A subconscious recognition implicit in the cloak scene was suggested by Murnaghan, *Disguise and Recognition in the "Odyssey,"* 108, who accepts that the loan of the cloak can be a covert expression of recognition. Murnaghan sees the loan as a part of the social institution of hospitality, which, in turn, serves as a substitute or alternative for a recognition of identity (91–117). She believes, however, that Odysseus reveals himself to Eumaeus and is recognized by him only in book 21 (see 13 n. 19, 20–21, 38–39, 74, 107, 151–52).

20 As Suetonius observes of Domitian, "He never set forth a particularly cruel proposal without a preamble about clemency" (*Domitian* 11).

21 Murnaghan's suggestion (*Disguise and Recognition in the "Odyssey,"* 167) that Eumaeus is *moved* by (rather than able to decode) the account of how Odysseus cleverly arranged the loan of a cloak to the beggar attributes too much sentimentality and too little astuteness to the swineherd. Eumaeus's hospitality seems designed to impress his guest with his graciousness and competence.

9. Turning Points and Returns

1 Athena's further advice to Telemachus to entrust his property to a female household slave until he himself marries is puzzling and quite rightly ignored by the young man. When Telemachus returns, he entrusts his interests to his friend Peiraeus, who has no obligations to the family in a larger sense. How a female slave (who would fall under Penelope's authority) would be able to conceal his possessions from Penelope is not at all clear. Curiously, neither Athena nor Telemachus thinks Eumaeus a suitable guardian of his interests, even though Athena tells Telemachus to go directly to him upon his return to Ithaca, and even though he himself regards Eumaeus as a valuable source of inside information about what is happening in the house.

2 See Thompson, *Greek Birds,* s.vv. *pēnelops, chēn.*

3 For the significance of a positive sentiment in the compound social value of loyalty, see Roisman, *Loyalty in Early Greek Epic and Tragedy,* passim.

4 We doubt whether one should see lines 388 and 429 as interpolation. The lines are meant to be ambiguous. But see Stanford, *"Odyssey" of Homer,* ad loc.

10. Telemachus

1 Eurycleia makes a similar offer of information when she recognizes Odysseus; she volunteers to name all the treacherous maids (19.495–98).

2 The following provision is included in the event that a dog urinates or defecates on someone else's property, according to A. W. De Quoy, *The Irish Wolfhound in Irish Literature and Law* (Roanoke: McLean, 1971) 63–64: "The excrement must be removed as well as the soil under it until there is no evidence of any liquid. Sod is put down and *covered with cow dung* for one month. The ground is then tamped down with the heel and fine clay of the same quality as that in the adjacent soil is added. Compensation must be paid to the landowner: butter, dough, and curds, each in the same bulk as that of the excrement. Moreover, if the offense occurred in the presence of the dog's owner, the latter is liable for trespass."

3 See F. Ahl, "Uilix Mac Leirtis: The Classical Hero in Irish Metamorphosis," in *The Art of Translation: Voices from the Field,* ed. R. Warren (Boston: Northeastern University Press, 1989) esp. 190–94.

4 There is also, however, an intimation of Achilles' respect for dogs in *Iliad* 23.161–77, where he slaughters numerous humans and animals on the pyre of his beloved Patroclus but kills only two of his friend's nine lapdogs.

5 A. B. Lord, *The Singer of Tales* (Cambridge, Mass.: Harvard University Press, 1960) Appendix III, 252–55, gives examples of recurrent accounts of recognition of heroes by animals, especially horses, in Yugoslavian songs of returning heroes.

6 See discussion by Ahl, "Uilix Mac Leirtis: The Classical Hero in Irish Metamorphosis," 173–98.

11. Penelope's Intervention

1 Katz, *Penelope's Renown,* 77–113.

2 See J. Winkler, *The Constraints of Desire: The Anthropology of Sex and Gender in Ancient Greece* (New York: Routledge, 1990) 129–61.

3 See Dawe, *"Odyssey,"* 646 (note on 17.492).
4 Ahl, *Sophocles' "Oedipus,"* 71–72.
5 On Penelope's chambers and their location, see Russo on 17.492–506, in Russo, Fernández-Galiano, and Heubeck, *Homer's "Odyssey."*
6 Most instances are in narrative passages, where the term is used as a general description of the Greek men feasting at Odysseus's house, and their courtship is not emphasized. In speeches it occurs in addresses of a suitor to his companion and creates an elevated and respectable tone: 2.90, 105–6, 203–4; 18.285–86; 20.270–71; 22.45–46; 24.140–41; for a similar attempt at deference and respect (ironical?) in Odysseus's and Telemachus's words, see 17.415, 18.61–62, and 21.427–28. Otherwise it is used as an ethnic and geographic signifier or in reference to Ithacans who participate in the assembly. In fact, in many cases the text makes clear that the term *Achaioi* includes other Ithacans than the suitors, and the latter are mentioned separately (e.g., 2.86–87, 111–12, 115, 264–65; 3.216–17, 220; 4.343–44; 16.75–76).
7 See M. M. Winkler, "Classical Mythology and the Western Film," *Comparative Literature Studies* 22 (1985) 514–40.
8 Athena, disguised as Mentor, uses it to prompt Telemachus to disperse the suitors (1.274); cf. Antinous to Telemachus (2.113); Penelope to Eumaeus (17.508); Eurynome to her two attendants (18.182). In the *Iliad* the imperative is used by Agamemnon to Menelaus (10.67); Iris to Hector (11.204); Zeus to Iris (15.160); Odysseus to Achilles (19.160, 171), and Achilles to Agamemnon (23.158).

12. Comely Thighs and Broad Shoulders

1 E.g., Dimock, *Unity of the "Odyssey,"* 232–33.
2 The mention of pigs is puzzling, since there is no suggestion of free-range swine anywhere else in the *Odyssey*, even in Circe's domain. In Ithaca, they are confined to the partially newly built sties of Eumaeus. Perhaps Odysseus is here working out on Irus some residual annoyance with the condescending treatment he has received from Eumaeus, who freely consumes and serves his master's pigs and whose dogs almost tore him to pieces.
3 D. B. Levine, "Penelope's Laugh: *Odyssey* 18.163," *AJP* 104 (1983) 172–80. He supports his thesis with many instances in Greek literature where laughter accompanies deception.
4 J. S. Clay, "Homeric *achreion*," *AJP* 105 (1984) 73–76.
5 Nagler, *Spontaneity and Tradition*, 64–111, discusses at length the motif of Homeric women who appear to other characters with a veil and accompanied by two attendants. The presence of the attendants and the veil suggest sexual chastity.
6 Telemachus assumes she knows about the fight between the two beggars, since he assures her that the outcome was not what the suitors expected (18.233–34). Eustathius comments on 18.234 that Telemachus misunderstands Penelope's concern. She is referring to Antinous hitting Odysseus with a stool, but Telemachus thinks she is referring to the fight with Irus. The point is that Telemachus thinks his mother witnessed the fight with Irus or at least is aware of it.
7 This is the meaning of *eirethizō*. The attempt to soften the meaning to "prod" so it will be synonymous with *peiraomai* (so Russo on 19.45, in Russo, Fer-

nández-Galiano, and Heubeck, *Homer's "Odyssey"*) suppresses Odysseus's provocation of Penelope and the maids. The claim of A. Thornton, *People and Themes in Homer's "Odyssey"* (Dunedin, New Zealand: University of Otago Press, 1970) 84–87, that the meaning of the verb here is the common "provoke to anger," which anticipates Odysseus's provocation of Melantho, explains Odysseus's provocation of Melantho, but not his intent to provoke Penelope.

8 "Or Odysseus may come back, there is still room for hope. But even if he has perished and is never more to return, here is Telemachus his son, by grace of Apollo grown to be such a man. No sinful woman in the palace escapes him, since he is no longer a child" (19.84–88).

9 See Roisman, *Loyalty in Early Greek Epic and Tragedy,* 67–68.

10 This observation sheds a new light on Antenor's address to Helen regarding the identification of Odysseus below the Trojan walls (*Iliad* 3.204), and the story of his visit with Menelaus to Troy to negotiate Helen's return. Antenor, we soon learn, favors returning Helen and all the treasures she has brought and thus putting an end to the war (7.348–53). His address to Helen as *gynai* is condescending and reflects his displeasure with her and the troubles she has brought upon Troy.

11 This is how Paris addresses Helen: *Iliad* 3.438; Hector, Hecuba: *Iliad* 6.441; Priam, Andromache: *Iliad* 24.300; Menelaus, Helen: *Odyssey* 4.148, 266; Alcinous, Arete: *Odyssey* 8.424; and Poseidon, Tyro, after he has seduced her: *Odyssey* 11.248.

12 23.183, 203, 248, 254, 350, 361.

13 Aristarchus thought lines 19.130–33 (describing the islands of the suitors and the damage the suitors bring to Odysseus's house) an interpolation. On the contrary, they are appropriate here within the subcontext of Penelope's rhetorical purpose: she may not be as beautiful as she was twenty years ago, but she is still admired by many young men.

14 For different interpretations of the phrase, see W. J. Verdenius, "Hesiod, *Theogony* 35," *Mnemosyne* 11 (1958) 22–24; West, *Theogony,* on 35; M. M. Willcock, *The "Iliad" of Homer, Books XIII-XXIV* (New York: St. Martin's Press, 1984) on 22.126; N. Richardson, *The "Iliad": A Commentary,* vol. 6, *Books 21–24* (Cambridge: Cambridge University Press, 1993) on 22.126–28.

15 See Roscher, *Lexikon,* 1: 994–98; 3: 3352–56; cf. Russo on 19.163, in Russo, Fernández-Galiano, and Heubeck, *Homer's "Odyssey"*; West, *Theogony,* on 35. The best-known version is that in Ovid *Metamorphoses* 1.299ff.; cf. Ahl, *Metaformations,* 101–2.

13. Courting One's Own Wife

1 "Tell me what sort of clothing he was wearing on his body, what sort of a man he himself was, and the comrades that followed him" (19.218–19).

2 *Aitizōn ana dēmon,* 19.272–73; 19.298–99: "how he might return to his dear native land after such a long absence, whether openly or in secret."

3 Cf. Russo on 19.404, in Russo, Fernández-Galiano, and Heubeck, *Homer's "Odyssey."* There may perhaps be an allusion here to doubts that Laertes was his father.

4 Sutton, *Lost Sophocles,* 46.

14. Prelude to the Massacre

1 The verb *syntithēmi* usually indicates a diagnostic process rather than the sense of hearing. The occurrence of *ops,* "voice," with *syntithēmi* is unusual, however. *Ops* more frequently occurs with *akouein* and *klyein: Iliad* 4.435; 16.76; 20.380; 22.451; *Odyssey* 10.221; 11.421.

2 For the hapax *antēstin* and the possible position of Penelope, see Fernández-Galiano on 20.387, in Russo, Fernández-Galiano, and Heubeck, *Homer's "Odyssey."*

15. Penelope and the Bow

1 The absence of paving on the palace floor has excited much scholarly commentary which we do not propose to enter. It is, however, worth noting that if the contest of the bow is, as we have suggested, a conflation of two traditions, one set inside the palace and one outside, this scene may reflect its origins in the "external" tradition, with its hecatomb at the shrine of Apollo the Archer. As it is, the beautifully polished doors and elegant furnishings seem at odds with the dirt floor. For different views of the palace floor and where the contest was held, see Fernández-Galiano's introduction to *Odyssey* 21, in Russo, Fernández-Galiano, and Heubeck, *Homer's "Odyssey,"* esp. 133–37.

2 M. Nagler, "Penelope's Male Hand: Gender and Violence in the *Odyssey,*" *Colby Quarterly* 29 (1993) 241–57; quotation from p. 243.

3 For such a possibility, see Dawe, *"Odyssey,"* 769 (on 21.314–19).

4 See, for example, Stanford (*"Odyssey" of Homer*) and Heubeck (in Russo, Fernández-Galiano, and Heubeck, *Homer's "Odyssey"*) on lines 23.94–95.

5 See also P. Chantraine, *Dictionnaire étymologique de la langue grecque* (Paris: Klincksieck, 1970) 423, s.v. *thaptō.*

6 "Eye-to-eye engagement is universally a first step in a train of action that further defines the interaction of gazer and gazee. On eye contact, predator and prey or rival and rival, or lover and loved, are alerted, tensed for what may come next, and a move follows" (V. Garrison and C. Arensberg, "The Evil Eye: Envy or Risk of Seizure? Paranoia or Patronal Dependency," in *The Evil Eye,* ed. C. Maloney [New York: Columbia University Press, 1972] 291–92).

7 Katz, *Penelope's Renown,* 191.

8 Her statement, *houneka s' ou to prōton, epei idon, hōd' agapēsa* (23.214), can be read in two ways: *hōde* may be construed as an extension of *epei idon,* as suggested by Stanford—that is to say, "right from the moment I saw you"—or we can understand the adverb in the meaning of "in the way," in which case Penelope is apologizing for not having embraced and kissed her husband "in the way I am doing now" right when she saw him. The way she is doing it now is the conventional way of greeting, and Odysseus was greeted in this way by everyone to whom he disclosed himself. Penelope, however, was prevented from greeting him, since he never formally disclosed his identity to her. See Roisman, "Penelope's Indignation," 64–65.

9 For a full discussion of the subject, see Roisman, "Penelope's Indignation," 59–68, and references.

10 For the likelihood that the daughter of Actor is Eurynome, see Hayman,

cited in Stanford, *"Odyssey" of Homer*, J. A. Scott, "Eurynome and Eurycleia in the *Odyssey*," *CQ* 12 (1918) 75–79; Fenik, *Studies in the "Odyssey,"* 191 n. 98. For the claim that the daughter of Actor died and was replaced by Eurynome, in which case no one knows about the bed but Penelope and Odysseus, see Stanford on 23.228. One has to wonder then whether the bridal chamber received any care whatsoever for twenty years, since no servant was allowed to enter it.

11 Stanford, *"Odyssey" of Homer*, on 23.286–87; for a summary of other views, see Katz, *Penelope's Renown*, 190–91.

Conclusion

1 It is difficult to accept the claim that the revelation of his name to Polyphemus after blinding him and his subsequent persecution by Poseidon are the causes of Odysseus's attempt to hide his identity from the helpless Laertes. Odysseus must have, after all, some judgment as to who are his friends and who are his enemies. But see C. R. Beye, *Ancient Epic Poetry: Homer, Apollonius, Virgil* (Ithaca, N.Y.: Cornell University Press, 1993) 149.

2 See Dodds, *Greeks and the Irrational*, 1–18; Edwards, *Homer: Poet of the "Iliad,"* 129. See also M. Nilsson, "Götter und Psychologie bei Homer," *ArchRW* 22 (1924) 374ff.

3 Cf. W. F. Otto, *The Homeric Gods: The Spiritual Significance of Greek Religion*, trans. M. Hadas (London: Thames and Hudson, 1979) 182–84.

4 Clay, *Wrath of Athena*, 137.

5 Euripides, *Cyclops* 104; Plutarch, *Greek Questions* 43 (301D); Hyginus, *Fabulae* 201. See above, p. 130. Odysseus mentions seeing him among the dead (*Od.* 11.593–600), but gives no hint that he thought Sisyphus might be his father.

6 W. McLeod, "The Range of the Ancient Bow," *Phoenix* 19 (1965) 1–14 (esp. 2).

BIBLIOGRAPHY

Ahl, F. "Amber, Avallon, and Apollo's Singing Swan." *American Journal of Philology* 103 (1982) 373–411.

———. "The Art of Safe Criticism in Greece and Rome." *American Journal of Philology* 105 (1984) 174–208.

———. *Metaformations: Soundplay and Wordplay in Ovid and Other Classical Poets.* Ithaca, N.Y.: Cornell University Press, 1985.

———. "Ars Est Caelare Artem (Art in Puns and Anagrams Engraved)." In *On Puns: The Foundation of Letters,* edited by Jonathan Culler, 17–43. Oxford: Basil Blackwell, 1988.

———. "Homer, Vergil, and Complex Narrative Structures in Latin Epic: An Essay." *Illinois Classical Studies* 14 (1989) 1–31.

———. "Uilix Mac Leirtis: The Classical Hero in Irish Metamorphosis." In *The Art of Translation: Voices from the Field,* edited by R. Warren, 173–98. Boston: Northeastern University Press, 1989.

———. *Sophocles' "Oedipus": Evidence and Self-Conviction.* Ithaca, N.Y.: Cornell University Press, 1991.

Assouline, P. *An Artful Life: A Biography of D. H. Kahnweiler, 1884–1979.* Translated by Charles Ruas. New York: Grove Weidenfield, 1990.

Atchity, K., and E. J. W. Barber. "Greek Princes and Aegean Princesses: The Role of Women in the Homeric Poems." In *Critical Essays on Homer,* edited by K. Atchity with R. Hogart and D. Price, 15–37. Boston: G. K. Hall, 1987.

Aubignac, F. H. *Conjectures académiques ou dissertation sur "l'Iliade."* Paris: François Fournier, 1715.

Austin, N. *Archery at the Dark of the Moon: Poetic Problems in Homer's "Odyssey."* Berkeley: University of California Press, 1975.

———. "The Wedding Text in Homer's *Odyssey.*" *Arion* 1, no. 2 (Spring 1991) 227–43.

Bamberger, F. "*Kerdos* et sa famille (emplois homérique): Contribution au recherches sur le vocabulaire de la 'richesse' en grec." *Centres de recherches comparatives sur les langues de la Méditerranée ancienne* 3 (1976) 1–32.

Bamberger, J. "The Myth of Matriarchy: Why Men Rule in Primitive Society." In

Woman, Culture, and Society, edited by M. Z. Rosaldo and L. Lamphere, 263–80. Stanford: Stanford University Press, 1974.

Barrett, W. S. *Euripides, Hippolytos.* Oxford: Oxford University Press, 1964.

Beazley, J. D. *Attic Red-Figure Vase Painters.* 2d ed. Oxford: Clarendon Press, 1963.

Bergren, A. "Helen's 'Good Drug': *Odyssey* IV 1–305." In *Contemporary Literary Hermeneutics and the Interpretation of Classical Texts,* edited by S. Kresic, 201–14. Ottawa: Éd. de l'Université d'Ottawa, 1981.

———. "Language and the Female in Early Greek Thought." *Arethusa* 16 (1983) 63–95.

Bernal, M. *Cadmean Letters: The Transmission of the Alphabet to the Aegean and Further West before 1400 B.C.* Winona Lake, Ind.: Eisenbrauns, 1990.

Beye, C. R. *The "Iliad," the "Odyssey," and the Epic Tradition.* New York: Doubleday, 1966.

———. *Ancient Greek Literature and Society.* 2d ed. Ithaca, N.Y.: Cornell University Press, 1987.

———. *Ancient Epic Poetry: Homer, Apollonius, Virgil.* Ithaca, N.Y.: Cornell University Press, 1993. Revision of *The "Iliad," the "Odyssey," and the Epic Tradition.*

Bömer, F. *P. Ovidius Naso, Metamorphosen, Buch* 14–15. Heidelberg: Carl Winter Universitätsverlag, 1986.

Boulay, J. du. "Strangers and Gifts: Hostility and Hospitality in Rural Greece." *Journal of Mediterranean Studies* 1 (1991) 37–53.

Branham, R. B. *Unruly Eloquence.* Cambridge, Mass.: Harvard University Press, 1989.

Bremmer, J. "Plutarch and the Naming of Greek Women." *American Journal of Philology* 102 (1981) 425–26.

Brommer, F. *Odysseus: Die Taten und Leiden des Helden in antiker Kunst und Literatur.* Darmstadt: Wissenschaftliche Buchgesellschaft, 1983.

Brown, C. S. "Odysseus and Polyphemus: The Name and the Curse." *Comparative Literature* 18 (1966) 193–202.

Buffière, F. *Les mythes d' Homère et la pensée grecque.* Paris: Les belles lettres, 1956.

Byre, C. S. "Narration, Description, and Theme in the Shield of Achilles." *Classical Journal* 88 (1992) 33–42.

Calame, C. *The Craft of Poetic Speech in Ancient Greece.* Translated by J. Orion, with a preface by J.-C. Cloquet. Ithaca, N.Y.: Cornell University Press, 1995.

Carpenter, R. "The Antiquity of the Greek Alphabet." *American Journal of Archaeology* 37 (1933) 8–29.

———. "The Greek Alphabet Again." *American Journal of Archaeology* 42 (1938) 58–69.

Carpenter, T. H. *Art and Myth in Ancient Greece.* New York: Thames and Hudson, 1990.

Casson, L. *Ships and Seamanship in the Ancient World.* Princeton: Princeton University Press, 1971.

Cauer, P. *Grundfragen der Homerkritik.* 3d ed. 2 vols. Leipzig: Hirzel, 1921–23.

Cave, T. *Recognitions: A Study in Poetics.* Oxford: Clarendon Press, 1988.

Chantraine, P. *Dictionnaire étymologique de la langue grecque.* Paris: Klincksieck, 1970.

Clay, J. S. "Goat Island: *Od.* 9.116–141." *Classical Quarterly* 30 (1980) 261–64.

———. *The Wrath of Athena: Gods and Men in the "Odyssey."* Princeton: Princeton University Press, 1983.

———. "Homeric *achreion.*" *American Journal of Philology* 105 (1984) 73–76.

Cornford, F. M. "The Origin of the Olympic Games." In *Themis,* 2d ed., edited by J. E. Harrison, 212–59. Cambridge: Cambridge University Press, 1927.

Cozzo, A. *Kerdos: Semantica, ideologie e società nella Grecia antika.* Filologia e critica 56. Rome: Edizioni dell' Ateneo, 1988.

Dawe, R. D. *The "Odyssey": Translation and Analysis.* Sussex, England: Book Guild, 1993.

De Quoy, A. W. *The Irish Wolfhound in Irish Literature and Law.* Roanoke: McLean, 1971.

Détienne, M. "La notion mythique d' ALETHEIA." *Revue des études grecques* 73 (1960) 27–35.

Détienne, M., and J.-P. Vernant. *Les ruses de l'intelligence: La métis des Grecs.* Paris: Flammarion, 1974.

———. *La cuisine du sacrifice en pays grec.* Paris: Gallimard, 1979.

Dimock, G. E. *The Unity of the "Odyssey."* Amherst: University of Massachusetts Press, 1989.

Dodds, E. R. *The Greeks and the Irrational.* Berkeley: University of California Press, 1951.

Doherty, L. E. "Tyro in *Odyssey* 11: Closed and Open Readings." *Helios* 20 (1993) 3–15.

Dolin, E. "Odysseus in Phaeacia." *Gräzer Beiträge* 1 (1973) 273–82.

Donlan, W. "Glaucus and Diomedes." *Phoenix* 43 (1989) 1–15.

Easterling, P. E., and B. M. W. Knox, eds. *The Cambridge History of Classical Literature.* Vol. 1, *Greek Literature.* Cambridge: Cambridge University Press, 1985.

Edwards, M. *Homer: Poet of the "Iliad."* Baltimore: Johns Hopkins University Press, 1987.

Emlyn-Jones, C. "The Reunion of Penelope and Odysseus." *Greece & Rome* 31 (1984) 1–18.

Fenik, B. C. *Studies in the "Odyssey."* Hermes Einzelschrift 30. Wiesbaden: Franz Steiner, 1974.

———, ed. *Homer, Tradition and Invention.* Leiden: Brill, 1978.

Fermor, P. L. *Roumeli: Travels in Northern Greece.* New York: Harper and Row, 1966.

Finley, M. I. *The World of Odysseus.* New York: Viking, 1972.

Finnegan, R. *Oral Poetry.* Cambridge: Cambridge University Press, 1977.

Finsler, G. *Homer in der Neuzeit von Dante bis Goethe.* Leipzig and Berlin: Teubner, 1912.

Fitzgerald, R., trans. *Homer, The Odyssey.* New York: Anchor Books, 1963.

Foley, H. "Reverse Similes and Sex Roles in the *Odyssey.*" *Arethusa* 11 (1978) 7–26.

Ford, A. *Homer: The Poetry of the Past.* Ithaca, N.Y.: Cornell University Press, 1992.

Forsyth, N. "The Allurement Scene: A Typical Pattern in Greek Oral Epic." *California Studies in Classical Antiquity* 12 (1979) 107–20.

Frame, D. *The Myth of Return in Early Greek Epic.* New Haven: Yale University Press, 1978.

Fränkel, H. *Die homerischen Gleichnisse.* Göttingen: Vandenhoek and Ruprecht, 1921.

———. *Early Greek Poetry and Philosophy.* Translated by M. Hadas and J. Willis. New York and London: Harcourt Brace Jovanovich, 1975.

Galinsky, G. K. *Aeneas, Sicily, and Rome.* Princeton Monographs in Art and Archaeology 40. Princeton: Princeton University Press, 1969.

Garrison, V., and C. Arensberg. "The Evil Eye: Envy or Risk of Seizure? Paranoia or Patronal Dependency." In *The Evil Eye*, edited by C. Maloney, 286–328. New York: Columbia University Press, 1972.

Ghali-Kahil, L. *Les enlèvements et le retour d' Hélène dans les textes et les documents figurés.* Paris: E. de Boccard, 1955.

Greenewalt, C. H., Jr. *Ritual Dinners in Early Historic Sardis.* Classical Studies 17. Berkeley: University of California Publications, 1976.

di Gregorio, L., ed. *Scholia vetera in Hesiodi Theogoniam.* Vita e pensiero, Universita Cattolica, Scienze filologiche e letteratura 6. Milan, 1975.

Griffin, J. *Homer on Life and Death.* Oxford: Clarendon Press, 1983.

———. "Homeric Words and Speeches." *Journal of Hellenic Studies* 106 (1986) 36–57.

———. *Homer, The Odyssey.* Cambridge: Cambridge University Press, 1987.

Griffiths, J. G. *Plutarch, De Iside et Osiride.* Cambridge: Cambridge University Press, 1970.

Grimm, W. "Die Sage von Polyphem." In *Kleinere Schriften*, edited by W. Grimm, 4: 428–62. Guetersloh: E. Bertelsmann, 1887.

Gross, N. P. "Nausicaa: A Feminine Threat." *Classical World* 69 (1976) 311–17.

Grube, G. M. A. "How Did the Greeks Look at Literature." In *Lectures in Memory of Louise Taft Semple*, 2d ser., 1966–70, edited by C. G. Boulter et al., 87–129. Norman: University of Oklahoma Press, 1973.

Harsh, P. W. "Penelope and Odysseus in *Odyssey* XIX." *American Journal of Philology* 71 (1950) 1–21.

Harvey, A. E. "Homeric Epithets in Greek Lyric Poetry." *Classical Quarterly* 51 (1957) 206–23.

Heubeck, A., and A. Hoekstra. *A Commentary on Homer's "Odyssey."* Vol. 2. Oxford: Clarendon Press, 1989.

Heubeck, A., S. West, and J. B. Hainsworth. *A Commentary on Homer's "Odyssey."* Vol. 1. Oxford: Clarendon Press, 1988.

Hölscher, U. *Untersuchungen zur Form der "Odyssee": Szenenwechsel und gleichzeitige Handlungen.* Berlin: Wiedmann, 1939.

Horsfall, N. "The Aeneas Legend and the *Aeneid.*" *Vergilius* 32 (1986) 8–17.

James, P. *Centuries of Darkness.* New Brunswick, N.J.: Rutgers University Press, 1993.

Jong, I. J. F. de. "Homeric *kerdos* and *ophelos.*" *Museum Helveticum* 44 (1987) 79–81.

Kahn, C. H. *The Art and Thought of Heraclitus.* Cambridge: Cambridge University Press, 1979.

Katz, M. A. *Penelope's Renown: Meaning and Indeterminancy in the "Odyssey."* Princeton: Princeton University Press, 1991.

Kinkel. G., ed. *Epicorum Graecorum Fragmenta.* Leipzig: Teubner, 1877.

Kirchhoff, A. *Die homerische "Odyssee" und ihre Entstehung.* Berlin: Wilhelm Hertz, 1859.

———. *Die Composition der "Odyssee": Gesammelte Aufsätze.* Berlin: Wilhelm Hertz, 1869.

Kirk, G. S. *The Nature of Greek Myths.* Baltimore: Penguin Books, 1974.

———. "The Poet and the Oral Tradition." In *The Cambridge History of Classical Literature*, edited by P. E. Easterling and B. M. W. Knox, 1: 42–51. Cambridge: Cambridge University Press, 1985.

Lamberton, R. *Homer the Theologian: Neoplatonist Allegorical Reading and the Growth of the Epic Tradition.* Berkeley: University of California Press, 1986.

Lattimore, R., trans. *The "Odyssey" of Homer.* New York: Harper, 1967.

———. "Nausikaa's Suitors." *Illinois Studies in Language and Literature* 58 (1969) 88–102.

Lee, D. J. N. *The Similes of the "Iliad" and the "Odyssey" Compared.* Cambridge: Cambridge University Press, 1964.

Lessing, G. E. *Laocoön: An Essay on the Limits of Painting and Poetry.* Translated by E. A. McCormick. Baltimore: Johns Hopkins University Press, 1984.

Levine, D. B. "Penelope's Laugh: *Odyssey* 18.163." *American Journal of Philology* 104 (1983) 172–80.

Lieblein, J. *Recherches sur la chronologie égyptienne d' après les listes généalogiques.* Christiana: A. W. Brogger, 1873.

Livrea, E. *Apollonii Rhodii Argonautica, Liber Quartus.* Florence: La nuova Italia, 1973.

Lord, A. B. *The Singer of Tales.* Cambridge, Mass.: Harvard University Press, 1960.

Luce, J. V. *Lost Atlantis: New Light on an Old Legend.* New York: McGraw-Hill, 1969.

Lynn-George, M. *Word, Narrative, and the "Iliad."* Atlantic Highlands, N.J.: Humanities Press International, 1988.

Magrath, W. T. "Progression of the Lion Simile in the *Odyssey.*" *Classical Journal* 77 (1982) 205–12.

Martin, R. P. *The Language of Heroes: Speech and Performance in the "Iliad."* Ithaca, N.Y.: Cornell University Press, 1989.

———. "Telemachus and the Last Hero Song." *Colby Quarterly* 29 (1993) 222–40.

McLeod, W. "The Range of the Ancient Bow." *Phoenix* 19 (1965) 1–14.

Mondi, R. "The Homeric Cyclopes: Folktale, Tradition, and Theme." *Transactions of the American Philological Association* 113 (1983) 17–38.

Moulton, C. "The End of the *Odyssey.*" *Greek, Roman and Byzantine Studies* 15 (1974) 153–69.

Müller, F. "Darstellung und poetische Funktion der Gegenstände in der Odyssee." Diss., Marburg, 1968.

Müller-Graupa, E. *RE* 18.2 (1942) 1420.

Murnaghan, S. *Disguise and Recognition in the "Odyssey."* Princeton: Princeton University Press, 1987.

Nagler, M. N. *Spontaneity and Tradition: A Study in the Oral Art of Homer.* Berkeley: University of California Press, 1974.

———. "Penelope's Male Hand: Gender and Violence in the *Odyssey.*" *Colby Quarterly* 29 (1993) 241–57.

Nagy, G. *The Best of the Achaeans: Concepts of the Hero in Archaic Greek Poetry.* Baltimore: Johns Hopkins University Press, 1979.

———. "Ancient Greek Epic and Praise Poetry: Some Typological Considerations." In *Oral Tradition in Literature,* edited by J. M. Foley, 89–102. Columbia: University of Missouri Press, 1986.

———. *Pindar's Homer: The Lyric Possession of an Epic Past.* Baltimore: Johns Hopkins University Press, 1990.

———. "Homeric Questions." *Transactions of the American Philological Association* 122 (1992) 17–60.

Nawrath, A. "Salmoneus." *RE* n.s. 1.A.ii (1920) 1989–90.

Nilsson, M. "Götter und Psychologie bei Homer." *Archiv für Religionswissenschaft* 22 (1924) 363–90.

Nortwick, T. van. "Penelope and Nausicaa." *Transactions of the American Philological Association* 109 (1979) 269–76.

Olson, S. D. "The Stories of Agamemnon in Homer's *Odyssey*." *Transactions of the American Philological Association* 120 (1990) 57–71.

———. "Servants' Suggestions in Homer's *Odyssey*." *Classical Journal* 87 (1992) 219–27.

———. "Women's Names and the Reception of Odysseus in Scheria." *Echos du monde classique/Classical Views* 36, n.s. 11 (1992) 1–6.

Otto, W. F. *The Homeric Gods: The Spiritual Significance of Greek Religion.* Translated by M. Hadas. London: Thames and Hudson, 1979.

O Tuama, S. *An Duanaire, 1600–1900: Poems of the Dispossessed.* Dublin: Dolmen Press, 1981.

Paduano, G., and M. Fusillo. *Apollonio Rodio, Le Argonautiche.* Milan: Biblioteca universale Rizzoli, 1986.

Page, D. *The Homeric "Odyssey."* Oxford: Clarendon Press, 1955.

Palmer, R. "Allegorical, Philological, and Philosophical Hermeneutics: Three Modes in a Complex Heritage." In *Contemporary Literary Hermeneutics and Interpretation of Classical Texts,* edited by S. Kresic, 15–37. Ottawa: Éd. de l'Université d' Ottawa, 1981.

Parry, A. "Language and Characterization in Homer." *Harvard Studies in Classical Philology* 76 (1972) 1–22.

———, ed. *The Making of Homeric Verse: The Collected Papers of Milman Parry.* Oxford: Oxford University Press, 1971.

Parry, M. "L' épithète traditionelle dans Homère: Essai sur un problème de style homérique." Diss., Paris, 1928. Published by Société éditrice, Les belles lettres.

Patterson, C. B. "Those Athenian Bastards." *Classical Antiquity* 9 (1990) 40–73.

Pedric, V. "The Muse Corrects: The Opening of the *Odyssey*." *Yale Classical Studies* 29 (1992) 39–92.

Peradotto, J. *Man in the Middle Voice: Name and Narration in the "Odyssey."* Princeton: Princeton University Press, 1990.

Podlecki, A. J. "Guest-Gifts and Nobodies in *Odyssey* 9." *Phoenix* 15 (1961) 125–33.

Powell, B. B. *Homer and the Origin of the Greek Alphabet.* Cambridge: Cambridge University Press, 1991.

Pratt, L. *Lying and Poetry from Homer to Pindar.* Ann Arbor: University of Michigan Press, 1993.

Pucci, P. *Odysseus Polutropos: Intertextual Readings in the "Odyssey" and the "Iliad."* Ithaca, N.Y.: Cornell University Press, 1987.

Radke, G. "Tyro." *RE* 7.A.2 (1948) 1870–75.

Rankin, H. D. *Celts and the Classical World.* London; Croom Helm, 1987.

Rees, A., and B. Rees. *Celtic Heritage.* London: Thames and Hudson, 1961.

Richardson, N. *The "Iliad": A Commentary.* Vol. 6, *Books* 21–24. Cambridge: Cambridge University Press, 1993.

Rieu, E. V., trans. *Homer, The Odyssey.* Revised by D. C. H. Rieu. Baltimore: Penguin Books, 1991.

Risch, E. "Namensdeutungen und Wortklärungen bei den ältesten griechischen Dichtern." In *Eumusia: Festgabe fur E. Howald*, 72–91. Zurich: Erlenbach, 1947.

Roisman, H. M. *Loyalty in Early Greek Epic and Tragedy*. Königstein/Ts: Anton Hain, 1984.

———. "Penelope's Indignation." *Transactions of the American Philological Association* 117 (1987) 59–68.

———. "Eumaeus and Odysseus—A Covert Self-Revelation?" *Illinois Classical Studies* 15, no. 2 (1990) 215–38.

———. "*Kerdion* in the *Iliad:* Skill and Trickiness." *Transactions of the American Philological Association* 120 (1990) 23–35.

———. "Like Father Like Son: Telemachus's *kerdea*." *Rheinisches Museum für Philologie* 136 (1993) 1–22.

Roisman, J. "Some Social Conventions and Deviations in Homeric Society." *Acta Classica* 25 (1982) 35–41.

Roscher, W. H. *Ausführliches Lexikon der griechischen und römischen Mythologie*. Vols. 1, 3, and 5. Hildesheim: Georg Olms, 1884–86, 1902–9, 1992.

Rose, G. P. "The Unfriendly Phaeacians." *Transactions of the American Philological Association* 100 (1969) 387–406.

———. "Odysseus' Barking Heart." *Transactions of the American Philological Association* 109 (1979) 215–30.

Rose, H. J. *A Handbook of Greek Literature*. New York: E. P. Dutton, 1960.

Russo, J. "Interview and Aftermath: Dream, Fantasy, and Intuition in *Odyssey* 19 and 20." *American Journal of Philology* 103 (1982) 4–18.

Russo, J., M. Fernández-Galiano, and A. Heubeck. *Homer's "Odyssey."* Vol. 3, *Books XVII–XXIV*. Oxford: Oxford University Press, 1992.

Schaps, D. "The Woman Least Mentioned: Etiquette and Women's Names." *Classical Quarterly* 27 (1977) 323–30.

Schein, S. L. "Odysseus and Polyphemus in the *Odyssey*." *Greek, Roman and Byzantine Studies* 11 (1970) 73–83.

———. *The Mortal Hero: An Introduction to Homer's "Iliad."* Berkeley: University of California Press, 1984.

Scott, J. A. "Eurynome and Eurycleia in the *Odyssey*." *Classical Quarterly* 12 (1918) 75–79.

Segal, C. P. "The Phaeacians and the Symbolism of Odysseus' Return." *Arion* 1, no. 4 (1962) 27–29.

———. "Bard and Audience in Homer." In *Homer's Ancient Readers: The Hermeneutics of Greek Epic's Earliest Exegetes*, edited by R. Lamberton and John J. Keaney, 3–29. Princeton: Princeton University Press, 1992.

Slatkin, L. *The Power of Thetis: Allusion and Interpretation in the "Iliad."* Berkeley: University of California Press, 1991.

Snodgrass, A. *Archaic Greece: The Age of Experiment*. Berkeley: University of California Press, 1980.

Stanford, W. B. *The "Odyssey" of Homer*. 2d ed. 2 vols. New York: St. Martin's Press, 1965.

Starr, C. G. "Ideas of Truth in Early Greece." *La parola del passato* 23 (1968) 348–59.

Steinrück, M. *Leise Laute: Arbeiten über das Verhältnis von Rhytmus und Lautresponsion bei Archilochos*. Lausanne and Basel: Petra Tergum, 1991.

Stokes, M. C. *Plato's Socratic Conversations: Drama and Dialectic in Three Dialogues.* London: Athlone Press, 1986.

Suerbaum, W. "Die Ich-Erzählungen des Odysseus: Überlegungen zur epischen Technik der Odyssee." *Poetica* 2 (1968) 150–77.

Sutton, D. *The Lost Sophocles.* Lanham, Md.: University Press of America, 1984.

Svenbro, J. *La parole et le marbre: Aux origines de la poétique grecque.* Lund: Studentlitteratur, 1976.

Thalmann, W. G. *Conventions of Form and Thought in Early Greek Epic.* Baltimore: Johns Hopkins University Press, 1984.

Thomas, C. G. "Matriarchy in Early Greece: The Bronze and Dark Ages." *Arethusa* 6 (1973) 173–95.

———. "Penelope's Worth: Looming Larger in Early Greece." *Hermes* 116 (1988) 257–64.

Thompson, D'Arcy W. *A Glossary of Greek Birds.* Hildesheim: Georg Olms, 1936.

Thornton, A. *People and Themes in Homer's "Odyssey."* Dunedin, New Zealand: University of Otago Press, 1970.

Torr, C. *Memphis and Mycenae.* Cambridge: Cambridge University Press, 1896.

Trahmann, C. "Odysseus' Lies" (*Odyssey,* Books 13–19)." *Phoenix* 6 (1952) 31–43.

Ullman, B. L. "The Origin and Development of the Alphabet." *American Journal of Archaeology* 31 (1927) 311–28.

———. "How Old Is the Greek Alphabet?" *American Journal of Archaeology* 38 (1934) 359–81.

Ussani, V. "Enea traditore." *Studi italiani di filologia classica,* n.s. 22 (1947) 108–23.

Väisänen, M. *La musa dalle molte voci: Studio sulle dimensioni storiche dell' arte di Catullo.* Helsinki: Societas historica Finlandiae, 1988.

Velikovsky, I. *Ages in Chaos.* London: Sidgwick and Jackson, 1953.

Verdenius, W. J. "Hesiod, *Theogony* 35." *Mnemosyne* 11 (1958) 20–24.

Vivante, P. *Homer.* New Haven: Yale University Press, 1985. Wade-Gery, H. T. *The Poet of the "Iliad."* Cambridge: Cambridge University Press, 1952.

Walz, P. "Ἡλίου Τροπαί: Notes sur l'Odyssée, XV, 404." *Revue des études homériques* 1 (1931) 3–15.

Webber, A. "The Hero Tells His Name." *Transactions of the American Philological Association* 119 (1989) 1–13.

West, M. L. *Hesiod, Theogony.* Oxford: Clarendon Press, 1966.

———. *Hesiod, Works and Days.* Oxford: Clarendon Press, 1978.

———, trans. *Hesiod, Theogony and Works and Days.* New York: Oxford University Press, 1988.

West, S. "Laertes Revisited." *Proceedings of the Cambridge Philological Society* 215, n.s. 35 (1989) 113–43.

Whitman, C. H. *Homer and the Heroic Tradition.* Cambridge, Mass.: Harvard University Press, 1958.

Wilamowitz-Moellendorff, U. von. *Die Heimkehr des Odysseus.* Berlin: Weidmann, 1927.

Willcock, M. M. "Mythological Paradeigma in the *Iliad.*" *Classical Quarterly* 14 (1964) 141–54.

———. *The "Iliad" of Homer, Books XIII-XXIV.* New York: St. Martin's Press, 1984.

———. "The Search for the Poet Homer." *Greece & Rome* 37, no. 1 (1990) 1–13.

Winkler, J. *The Constraints of Desire: The Anthropology of Sex and Gender in Ancient Greece,* 129–61. New York: Routledge, 1990.

Winkler, M. M. "Classical Mythology and the Western Film." *Comparative Literature Studies* 22 (1985) 514–40.

Wolf, F. A. *Prolegomena ad Homerum.* Berlin: Calvary, 1871. Originally published in 1795.

Woodbury, L. "Gold Hair and Grey, or The Game of Love: Anacreon Fr. 13:358 PMG, 13 Gentili." *Transactions of the American Philological Association* 109 (1979) 277–87.

Zimmern, A. *The Greek Commonwealth: Politics and Economics in Fifth-Century Athens.* New York: Oxford University Press, 1961.

Zumthor, P. *Oral Poetry: An Introduction.* Translated by K. Murphy-Judy. Minneapolis: University of Minnesota Press, 1990.

INDEX